Case Studies in Human Ecology

Case Studies in Human Ecology

Edited by

Daniel G. Bates

and

Susan H. Lees

Hunter College
City University of New York
New York, New York

PLENUM PRESS • NEW YORK AND LONDON

Library of Congress Cataloging-in-Publication Data

On file

ISBN 0-306-45245-6 (Hardbound)
ISBN 0-306-45246-4 (Paperback)

© 1996 Plenum Press, New York
A Division of Plenum Publishing Corporation
233 Spring Street, New York, N. Y. 10013

Printed in the United States of America

Contributors

William S. Abruzzi, Department of Anthropology, Pennsylvania State University, Ogontz Campus, Abington, Pennsylvania 19002

Thomas Amorosi, NABO, Department of Anthropology, Hunter College, City University of New York, New York, New York 10021

Gerald F. Bigelow, Peary-MacMillan Arctic Museum and Arctic Studies Center, Bowdoin College, Brunswick, Maine 04011

Naomi H. Bishop, Department of Anthropology, California State University, Northridge, California 91330

Scott Cane, Culture and Heritage, P.O. Box 1773, Port Lincoln, South Australia 5606, Australia

Daniel C. Clay, Department of Sociology, Michigan State University, East Lansing, Michigan 48824

W. Thomas Conelly, Department of Anthropology, Indiana University of Pennsylvania, Indiana, Pennsylvania 15705

Wen Dazhong, Institute of Applied Ecology, Chinese Academy of Sciences, P.O. Box 4176, Shenyang, China

James F. Eder, Department of Anthropology, Arizona State University, Tempe, Arizona 85287

Steven Folmar, Section on Internal Medicine and Gerontology, Bowman Gray School of Medicine, Wake Forest University, Winston-Salem, North Carolina 27157

Elliot Fratkin, Department of Anthropology, Smith College, Northhampton, Massachusetts 01063

John Hart, Division of International Conservation, Wildlife Conservation Society, Bronx, New York 10460

Terese B. Hart, Division of International Conservation, Wildlife Conservation Society, Bronx, New York 10460

Patricia Lyons Johnson, Department of Anthropology and Women's Studies Program, Pennsylvania State University, University Park, Pennsylvania 16802

Louise D. Lennihan, Department of Anthropology, Hunter College, City University of New York, New York, New York 10021

Laurence A. Lewis, Graduate School of Geography, Clark University, Worcester, Massachusetts 01610

Thomas H. McGovern, NABO, Department of Anthropology, Hunter College, City University of New York, New York, New York 10021

Robert McC. Netting, Late of the Department of Anthropology, University of Arizona, Tucson, Arizona 85721

David Pimentel, New York State College of Agriculture and Life Sciences, Cornell University, Ithaca, New York 14853

Eric Abella Roth, Department of Anthropology, University of Victoria, Victoria, British Columbia V8W 2Y2 Canada

Daniel Russell, NABO, Department of Anthropology, Hunter College, City University of New York, New York, New York 10021

Ian Scoones, Drylands and Sustainable Agriculture Programmes, 3 Endsleigh Street, London WC1H 0DD, England

Glenn Davis Stone, Department of Anthropology, Washington University, St. Louis, Missouri 63130

M. Priscilla Stone, Department of Anthropology, Washington University, St. Louis, Missouri 63130

Preface

This volume was developed to meet a much noted need for accessible case study material for courses in human ecology, cultural ecology, cultural geography, and other subjects increasingly offered to fulfill renewed student and faculty interest in environmental issues. The case studies, all taken from the journal *Human Ecology: An Interdisciplinary Journal*, represent a broad cross-section of contemporary research. It is tempting but inaccurate to suggest that these represent the "Best of *Human Ecology.*" They were selected from among many outstanding possibilities because they worked well with the organization of the book which, in turn, reflects the way in which courses in human ecology are often organized.

This book provides a useful sample of case studies in the application of the perspective of human ecology to a wide variety of problems in different regions of the world. University courses in human ecology typically begin with basic concepts pertaining to energy flow, feeding relations, material cycles, population dynamics, and ecosystem properties, and then take up illustrative case studies of human-environmental interactions. These are usually discussed either along the lines of distinctive strategies of food procurement (such as foraging or pastoralism) or as adaptations to specific habitat types or biomes (such as the circumpolar regions or arid lands). The articles collected here work well with either approach, but are presented in terms of their direct relevance to broadly defined subsistence activities and transformations within them. Thus they are arranged in three sections reflecting foraging or hunting and gathering, pastoralism, and agriculture. This arrangement is simply a means of emphasizing some shared problems and environmental challenges faced by the populations under discussion. All the studies illustrate points of general significance using original data; most, too, offer interesting methodological implications.

In addition to the cooperation of the authors of these case studies, without whose enthusiasm and assistance this volume would not have been possible, the editors wish to thank a number of individuals. Foremost, we owe a great debt to Andrew P. Vayda, who established *Human Ecology* 24 years ago. We are also very grateful to Eliot Werner at Plenum for his long-standing support for environmental research and, in particular, for his support for the journal; his efforts have helped to make the journal an important venue for communicating research results on environmental problems by social scientists. Alan Duben, Nancy Flowers, David Gilmore, Greg Johnson, and Judith Tucker offered useful suggestions regarding the introduction. Pauline Herrmann was tireless in her efforts to communicate with the scholars involved. Murphy Halliburton organized the manuscripts as they came in and made recommendations as to the organization of the volume; further, he carried out a voluminous correspondence with authors as they revised their papers. Kee Howe Young, currently editorial assistant for the journal *Human Ecology,* took responsibility for final manuscript preparation.

Contents

Introduction

At no time in human history is understanding the environmental implications of human activities as vital to as many people as it is today. The world's population, still growing rapidly, stands in excess of 5.6 billion and is not expected to level off until the mid 21st century, when it may reach 12 billion. The environmental impacts of this phenomenon are still unknown, but efforts to address this overriding ecological question are central to human ecological research. Those in the growing field of human ecology have joined naturalists, environmentalists, and social scientists in an effort to understand human environmental interactions and to ameliorate, if possible, such negative impacts as may affect long-term human well-being. As natural scientists, ecologists are interested in three very broad questions. One, how does the environment affect the organism? Two, how does the organism affect its environment? Three, how does an organism affect other organisms in the environments in which it lives? The quest for answers to these questions encompasses almost everything ecologists do. Human ecology links the subject matter of anthropology, biology, geography, demography, economics, and other disciplines in an attempt to understand relationships between people and their environments in terms of these three areas of inquiry.

This volume reflects recent and important contributions to human ecology by scholars who approach the field from differing specializations and interests. What ties them together is a concern with the characteristics and consequences of human environmental interactions. Each case study in this collection describes original research on how people make use of available resources, shape their environments, and respond to specific challenges or threats to their livelihood.

For more than two decades, the pages of *Human Ecology: An Interdisciplinary Journal* have documented the development of the field. As researchers utilize new approaches and tools, they also implicitly critique the strengths and weaknesses of older models and assumptions. Contemporary studies reflect an increase in historical awareness, a concern about both national and international policy, interest in extra-local human interactions (particularly but not exclusively market-oriented interactions), and a focus on the environmental consequences for populations that display inequality or divergent interests along lines of gender, class, ethnicity, or other distinctions.

Even so, many of the characteristics of contemporary human ecological research resemble those of earlier studies. Thus, while there have been important ecological studies of urban populations, by and large, human ecology remains focused on rural populations. Much of the work in the field has been in Third World regions, and considerable attention continues to be paid to indigenous or traditional practices and how they have been affected by changing technology and market interactions.

In contemporary human ecology there is never an assumption of timelessness or total isolation. While historical change and external influence might once have been regarded as annoying distractions or distortions of indigenous systems, they are now the focus of attention. Whereas earlier ecological anthropologists tended to ask how traditional practices and beliefs enabled a population to maintain itself in a specific environment, today we are more likely to ask: What are the problems confronting the people of this place? How do they deal with them? And we are more likely today to be aware of the fact that not all members of the group may share the same problems to the same degree, or regard them in the same light. Human ecologists have drawn on demographic and evolutionary theory as well as upon biological models derived from field ecology. Today, in addition, emphasis is also placed on the role of decision-making at the individual or household level, individual strategizing, and optimization of risk, costs, and benefits.

CHANGING APPROACHES TO HUMAN ECOLOGY

It is useful to review briefly some of the ways in which human ecological research has developed in recent years. Humans, along with every other form of life, can be seen as part of a single biosphere—the global cycle of matter and energy that includes all organic things and links them to the inorganic. All organisms depend on energy, information, and matter. Unlike plants, most of the energy and matter that animals use are not taken directly from the sun and the earth; rather, they are produced by other organisms and cycled among species through feeding relationships. Humans breathe the oxygen emitted by plants, and plants take in carbon dioxide emitted by humans and millions of other species of animals. Such relationships, taken together, constitute a vast network of individuals exchanging the energy, nutrients, and chemicals necessary to life; humans and bacteria are involved in the same type of process.

However, while the utility of global models is obvious in the investigation and description of such postulated phenomena as "global warming" and the "greenhouse effect," or the worldwide impact of habitat destruction, such as that due to the clearing of rain forests in Borneo and the Amazon, such a scale is of limited use in the study of localized or regionally specific problems. It is at the local level, for reasons both of theory and practicality, that researchers concerned with humans come to employ a variety of distinctive approaches. These include lines of investigation as diverse as the ecosystems approach (see Moran, 1990, for good reviews), evolutionary ecology (see Winterhalter and Smith, 1981; Durham, 1990; Cronk, 1991; Golly, 1993), cultural materialism (see Harris, 1979), political ecology (see Peet and Watts, 1994), the political economy approach (O'Conner, 1988), population ecology (see Pianka, 1974; Ellison, 1994; Campbell, 1995), "progressive contextualization" (Vayda, 1983), and the "ecology of cumulative change" (see Lees and Bates, 1990). The intellectual roots are diverse although, ultimately, most draw on the works of Darwin, Marx, and the formal models of game theory and economics.

The Ecosystems Approach to Ecology

The most commonly employed general model of localized interactions among organisms and their environments is the so-called "ecosystem" approach (Golley, 1993). The ecosystem model provides a way of positioning each component of a network of interacting individuals, populations, and communities (groups of locally interacting populations) so that one can see the effects of each on the other. Such a model, whether employed explicitly with its parameters stipulated and key values stated or, as is often the case, used implicitly in discussions of environmental stability, underlies much ecological thinking. This model is enshrined in U.S. public policy as the model for habitat management—of rangelands, national parks, and marine resources.

The usefulness of the ecosystem concept is, first, that it can be applied to virtually any environment where the constituent components are found. Second, and more important, the ecosystem concept allows us to describe organisms in dynamic interaction with one another, with other species, and with the physical environment. We can chart and quantify the flow of energy and nutrients and specify the interactions critical for the maintenance of any local population. Thus the ecosystem concept gives us a way of describing how any population influences and is influenced by its surroundings. It was a unifying model in much human ecological study in the 1960s and 1970s. An early and influential instance of such an approach is Roy Rappaport's *Pigs for the Ancestors* (1968), which showed how components of a dynamic system were mutually limited and how changes in variables were restored through homeostatic or self-regulating mechanisms. A more recent example is the multidisciplinary Turkana Ecosystem Project directed by Michael Little and Neville Dyson Hudson (Little et al., 1988). A shared emphasis is on linkages within a human-dominated ecosystem that maintain a dynamic equilibrium, hence allowing the system to persist.

THE DISTINCTIVENESS OF HUMAN ECOLOGY

The ecosystem approach has contributed to understanding systemic change as well as the seeming persistence in equilibrium of some populations over long periods in their habitats. But as many have noted, there are limitations to this approach (see, for example, Lees and Bates 1990). Some of the limitations have to do with theory; the ecosystem model has little to offer most evolutionary and economic studies where the focus is on the outcome of individual actions. An equally important set of limitations concerns the treatment of species within ecosystems, in terms of the functional roles they play in system processes, such as "food chains." The special attributes of the human species pose problems for modeling local interactions as discrete or bounded systems.

Human distinctiveness becomes strikingly evident when we look at the habitats and niches that our species occupies. The *habitat* of a species is the area where it lives, its surroundings. Its *niche* is its "way of making a living," as defined by what it eats, what eats it, how it defends itself, and how it reproduces and rears its young. Most species are limited to a few habitats and a relatively narrow niche. By contrast, humans occupy an exceptionally broad niche and live in an extremely wide range of habitats. Indeed, there are very few habitats, from deserts to Arctic ice sheets to tropical rain forests, where human beings have not found a way to thrive.

Once humans enter a habitat, they tend to strongly affect the life chances and reproductive rates of the other populations through the use of human technology. Although other species use tools, no other species has developed them to the extent humans have, and no other species depends to such a great extent on tools for its survival. Human technological expertise has allowed humans to transform a vast variety of materials—including some rather unlikely ones—into sources of usable energy. The use of tools has enabled the species to create artificial environments such as farms and cities, which maintain very high human population densities by greatly increasing the inflow and outflow of energy, materials, and information. The use of technology has allowed local populations to engage in very different lifestyles, which vary by cultural tradition as well as in basic economic or productive organization.

Much, if not most, technology has been developed explicitly to facilitate energy transfer, capture, and storage in ways unique to humans. A persistent focus in human ecology has been upon energy flows; the Turkana Project, for example, carefully documented intra- and interspecific energy transfers (Little et al., 1988). Economists deal with energy indirectly, as when they define human labor productivity as the monetary value of what is produced (dollar value added per hour of work) by a unit of human labor. Energy is an alternative and more generalized measure of productivity, one that offers new insights into the changing role of human labor in relation to technological developments. Ultimately, of course, all human societies are energy dependent; most, if not all, are power limited in some way. However, the nature of energy limits or power "bottlenecks" in the ecological system or economy vary greatly according to how the flow of energy is organized as well as to the technology employed. Leslie White (1949) was an early proponent of the idea that the nature of human society was structured by its ability to utilize extrasomantic sources of energy; Howard Odum (1971) developed a more ecologically directed model of societal energy flows.

A recent analysis of labor productivity as bioenergetics is an interesting and revealing case in point (see Giampietro, Bukkens, and Pimentel, 1993: 229–260). As European economies developed, they moved from being limited by power shortages in the form of human labor to being constrained by limits on extrasomatic energy sources, mainly the availability of wood in the 18th century, coal in the 19th century, and oil today (pp. 238–239). Mechanized use of extrasomatic (exosomatic) energy sources, fossil fuel, or hydroelectric power, for example, distinguish the technologically advanced societies. In the United States, about 230,000 kilocalories of energy are expended per capita; in Burundi, central Africa, 24,000 are expended (p. 244). Moreover, in the United States, only 10% of the country's "total time" (the population × 24 × 365) is allocated to work; in Burundi, 25% of the nation's "total time" is needed; in short, Burundians must work twice as hard to extract a fraction of the usable energy that the U.S. worker does. Where human labor constitutes the main "power supply," and energy to support it comes largely from standing biomass (crops, trees, etc.), as it does in at least 18 countries, there is little "spare" energy to devote to anything other than maintaining current infrastructure, reproduction, and food procurement (p. 244).

The implications for societal development and ecological relations in general, as noted by earlier scholars, can be measured in many ways at levels ranging from the individual worker to the individuals and his or her dependents, groups of co-workers, and the like. Giampietro and his colleagues chose to look at production and energy utilization at the societal level—that is, the bioenergetics of defined populations. Any system can be seen as having energy *sources* and energy *converters* which generate power or useful work. In preindustrial or partially industrialized societies, energy sources are largely in standing biomass—the trees, plants, and animals available to support humans—which is converted into useful work via human labor, to support the population and its material culture. This may be supplemented by animal traction, but even so, the available power is limited. In the United States in the 1850s, 91% of energy expended came from standing biomass; today only 4% does, with the balance being fossil fuels (as we saw earlier), converted into useful work by machinery. Industrial societies are more limited by energy sources; nonindustrial societies by the low rate at which energy can be converted with human labor only partially amplified by animals and machinery (pp. 241ff).

The ecological implications are serious; adding the use of even one bullock for every ten villagers in India would have had the effect of doubling the power level per capita in that country, but it would still remain more than a thousand times less than the per capita power level in the United States. Preindustrial societies respond to the energy bottleneck by scheduling agricultural activities to be as constant as possible throughout the year in order to avoid periods of peak demand. Thus traditional farmers often make use of a mix of crops and livestock, each with different labor demands (p. 254). In industrial agriculture this is not necessary as labor is not the main means of converting energy—machines are. However romantic the notion may be of humans living directly from the fruits of their own labor, assisted by the family's horses or oxen, mechanical conversion of energy is vastly more productive and is necessary to raise standards of living. Should such a preindustrial system discover a means of converting its standing biomass into energy at a faster rate, thus facilitating more useful work, it would be doing so with a fearful impact on its environment. In the Sahel and the Sudan, the World Bank forecasts that by the year 2000, in a rural population of 40 million, 19 million will run out of wood, while 3.7 million will be severely short of food (Giampietro et al., 1993: 252). On the other hand, should a region undergo rapid industrialization of agriculture, people will be displaced as their labor is less needed on the farm, contributing to rural–urban migration and subsequent poverty in the cities.

Another continuing concern in human ecology has to do with how humans perceive themselves, other people, and their environments. We rely upon and are dramatically affected by our symbolic interpretations and representations of ourselves and other things (White, 1949). Symbols guide the ways we interact with the organic and nonorganic elements of our environments by making the environment intelligible in ways specific to our cultures—say, by representing what is "good to eat" and what is not or who may eat what and when and how.[1] Of major importance to humans is the way we distinguish group differences symbolically, thereby creating and maintaining cultural diversity. This cultural diversity is often an important element of our social environment, affecting the ways in which individuals or groups interact with one another and other elements of their environments. As a result of uniquely human communicative abilities, humans respond to environmental and other problems with greater rapidity than other species. This is because language greatly enhances learning and the transmission of ideas. Language, even without writing, allows learning to be a cumulative process. As Daniel Dennett puts it, language allows humans to design adaptive arrangements that for other species would require vast periods of evolutionary time and space, if possible at all (1995).

Intraspecific exchange is another hallmark of the human species. Our propensity to engage in exchange of goods, services, and information among widely separated individuals and groups has the effect of vastly extending the range of our resources and of our impacts upon them. It is rare today for a local population to rely entirely on local resources. For example, the fact that people who live in U.S. northern cities may get necessary vitamin C from oranges produced on southern farms means that whatever determines incomes of people in New York and their grocery-buying habits can have an effect on land use in citrus-growing areas of Florida. With reference to what was often regarded as a self-sufficient foraging society, Edwin Wilmsen (1989), using archaeological evidence associated with the San-speaking regions of Southwestern Africa, finds that, far from being isolated, trade goods indicate that they have been integrated to a considerable degree into distant markets long before the present century.[2]

---

[1] Roy Rappaport (1979: 97–144) lays out the problem of interpretation of the environment in terms of a cognized environment which consists of a cultural construction or model upon which people base their decisions and actions. Marvin Harris (1979) shares this notion, in his distinction between *emic* and *etic* behavior, the former reflecting meaning conferred by culture, the latter, not. Harris applies his notion of cultural materialism directly to understanding people's food habits in his book *Good to Eat* (1985).

[2] This is a controversial issue among Africanists. Richard Lee and others, while not disputing the fact that there has been mercantile activity in some parts of the Kalahari, argue that it was highly regionalized and episodic, and that any possible impacts on local people such as in the Dobe area have yet to be empirically established (Lee and Guenther 1993: 226).

Human populations are socially differentiated in ways which are significant for ecological research. Humans not only engage in division of labor beyond that associated with age and role in gender, but also create systems of perpetuated subordination and inequality, such as caste, class, and other forms of differentiated economic and political statuses. Such inequality has major environmental ramifications. The fact that there are no physical limits on the accumulation of wealth in a market economy, for example, has important consequences for the way that natural resources are exploited. And the fact that the nominal owners of resources control the means of exploiting them, but do not necessarily live and work near them, has important consequences for other people who do. Thus, local people may be powerless to prevent their central government from granting rights to foreign companies to exploit local resources with little regard for indigenous peoples or long-term impacts. The Penan of Sarawak are a case in point; foreign timber companies working with national government officials are rapidly clearing the forest in which Penan people live (Davis, 1993).

There are other ramifications of group differentiation. A population might deliberately destroy the resource base of a group they perceive as enemies and wish to dislodge—a classic stratagem of warfare. A local population might knowingly over-exploit its own resources in the expectation of moving on to new ones, often at the expense of neighboring groups. While there may be analogous examples from non-human populations, humans are clearly distinctive in the extent to which intergroup competition and subjugation takes place.

The impact of cultural diversity, exchange, and perpetuated inequality on the ways that humans interact with environments has grown with time and with changes in human social organization since the earliest hominids developed tool technology. Throughout time, the pace of change has accelerated as well. Most human ecologists require conceptual tools beyond those of general ecology in order to address the factors that affect changing human relationships with their environments because of the influence of the complex relationships humans have with one another.

RECENT DIRECTIONS IN HUMAN ECOLOGY

Human ecologists, concerned with a species which is culturally diverse, whose local populations display considerable internal behavioral diversity and great behavioral plasticity, have come to rely on new approaches and methods of study. This has not meant that the earlier approaches were entirely abandoned; rather their strongest points have been built and expanded upon. The most useful legacy of the first generations of modern ecological studies is the awareness of both interconnections, and the obligation to attempt to quantify or measure interactions and interrelationships. Thus, recent studies in human ecology continue to be very explicit about interactions and present detailed quantitative data, as illustrated by the chapters in this volume.

Human ecologists, of necessity, tend to be eclectic in their use of basic concepts, since their objectives are rarely to describe ecosystems, but are rather to focus on specific aspects of interactions between humans and selected environmental features. Not all the concepts of ecosystems ecology are useful in this endeavor, and some in fact may obscure important particulars of human behavior. It makes little sense, for example, in studies of hunter–gatherer subsistence practices, to simply view humans as another "top predator" or a local population as occupying a trophic level in an ecosystem. At the very least it must be recognized that the number of humans in the environment is not necessarily dependent upon the local prey population. Should the prey population decrease or disappear, humans may obtain their meat by other means—for example, by trading with another population. Thus the notion of local carrying capacity at any level of technological complexity has to be employed very cautiously where humans are concerned.

Changes in the field of human ecology over the past twenty years or so reflect and are a the product of an awareness of historical and political factors in shaping human–environment interactions. Practical politics and people's ideas about human–environment relationships have always influenced one another, but perhaps never so intensely and explicitly as now. Environmentalist movements attempt to exert pressure on political bodies to regulate human use (and abuse) of our environments, while their opponents resist them, both making use of scientific ecological studies. Ecologists now recognize the potential use of their work in influencing policy, and many, by now, have had experience in working with groups whose task is the formulation of environmental policy.

Consequently, human ecologists have become very much aware of the role of power relations in determining human uses of the environment, and of the history of changes in these relations which result in changing human-environment interactions. It is perhaps this awareness that most clearly distinguishes human ecology as a discipline from the ecologies focused on other species. We see human behavior as a product of specific historic interactions; its persistence or its change requires explanation in specific terms as well, and cannot be assumed.

FOOD PROCUREMENT STRATEGIES AND HUMAN ECOLOGY

In the mid-19th century, social evolutionists such as Lewis Henry Morgan (1877) and Edward B. Tylor (1878) laid out evolutionary schemes which placed human societies on an ascending scale of development from simple to complex. Many of these schemes related types of subsistence practices (which most closely link humans with our environments) to types of social organization. Thus, the earlier, simplest types of subsistence practices, presumably those which relied on non-domesticated plants and animals, characterized as "hunting and gathering," were linked with egalitarian bands, which had little social structure beyond kinship. As societies became dependent upon domesticated plants and animals, they developed more restrictive access to resources and concomitant social structures to enforce such regulation. Karl Marx and Friedrich Engels, relying heavily on Lewis Henry Morgan, similarly related modes of production to social systems.

While 20th-century social scientists repudiated the simplistic, ethnocentric, sometimes racist notions of the 19th-century social evolutionists, the idea of evolutionists' identification of subsistence practices as means of discovering and analyzing important similarities and differences among human groups continued to be productive. Julian Steward, who coined the term "cultural ecology" (1955: 30–42) and initiated the development of ecological study within cultural anthropology, formulated the concepts of "multilineal evolution" (1955: 11–29) and "cultural core" (1955: 6–8) to highlight the importance of both subsistence practices and environmental variables. Elman Service (1958) and Morton Fried (1967), adhering more closely to Leslie White's (1959) "unilineal" position, resurrected earlier schema associating hunting–gathering with bands, horticulture and pastoralism with tribes and chiefdoms, and intensive agriculture with states.

In the 1960s and 1970s, former students of Steward, most notably Eric Wolf (1982), turned the attention of those interested in the material aspects of human society more towards history, and particularly the history of trade and of unequal relationships, an orientation that came to be known as the "political economy" approach in anthropology. Subsequently others, such as A. P. Vayda (1983, 1988), emphasized the specificity of problems experienced by local groups and individuals, and advocated a more actor-oriented approach. Both orientations have had an impact on approaches taken in human ecology (Orlove, 1980).

Today, we still regard it as useful to examine different types of subsistence practices such as foraging, pastoralism, and extensive and intensive agriculture, but we do so with a different perception of what these are and how they operate than that of even a half century ago. We recognize, for example, that the contemporary foragers we study today are a product not only of their own immediate history but also a long history of interaction with other, nonforaging populations. We recognize the importance of trade and of unequal social, political, and economic relationships in all subsistence practices. We are particularly mindful of the destructive impact many of the interactions have had on the local groups we study, and of the role of unequal power relationships in this destructiveness. Cultural differences, as well as power differences, are of central importance in most contemporary analyses of environmental crisis and degradation.

Ecological studies, whether subscribing to an ecosystems approach or not, have long been concerned with stability on the one hand and change on the other. Concern about the role that humans play in changing the face of the earth derives, in part, from anxiety about the future of our own habitats, as well as an interest in improving the lot of the poor and vulnerable. Human ecologists are increasingly interested in documenting change and its sources, both in environmental events (Lees and Bates, 1990) and in the historical processes of population growth, technological development, economic expansion, and political change.

The case studies in this volume examine different modes of livelihood with a view to understanding external influences and processes of change. The time frames utilized for describing change range, according to the problem addressed, from a season, to decades, to centuries. While in most cases the human–environment relationship is the subject of study as an end in itself, in many cases it is also a critical component of explaining major historical processes such as shifting relations of subordination or dependence between populations (as in Lennihan, Chapter 15), or the decline and extinction of a colonial population (as in McGovern et al., Chapter 4), or alternatively, the flourishing of a colony in an unfamiliar and to them, unpredictable habitat (as in Abruzzi, Chapter 16). It is hoped that this collection of diverse case studies will demonstrate the explanatory power and richness of an ecological approach.

REFERENCES

Campbell, B. (1995). *Human Ecology*, Second Edition. Aldine de Gruyter, Hawthorne.

Cronk, L. (1991). Human behavioral ecology. *Annual Review of Anthropology* 20: 25–54.

Davis, W. (1993). Death of a people: logging in the Penan homeland. *Cultural Survival Quarterly* (Fall) 17(3): 15–20.

Dennett, D. C. (1995). *Darwin's Dangerous Idea: Evolution and the Meanings of Life*. Simon & Schuster, New York.

Durham, W. (1990). Advances in evolutionary culture theory. *Annual Review of Anthropology* 19: 187–242.

Ellison, P. T. (1994). Advances in human reproductive ecology. *Annual Review of Anthropology* 23: 255–275.

Fried, M. (1967). *The Evolution of Political Society.* Random House, New York.

Giampietro, M., Bukkens, S.G.F., and Pimentel, D. (1993). Labor Productivity: A Biosocial Definition and Assessment. *Human Ecology* 21(3): 229–260.

Golley, F. B. (1993). *A History of the Ecosystem Concept in Ecology: More than the Sum of Its Parts.* Yale University Press, New Haven and London.

Harris, M. (1979). *Cultural Materialism.* Random House, New York.

Harris, M. (1985). *Good to Eat.* Simon and Schuster, New York.

Lee, R. B. and Guenther, M. (1993). Problems in Kalahari historical ethnography and the tolerance of error. *History in Africa* 20: 185–235.

Lees, S. and Bates, D. (1990). The Ecology of Cumulative Change. In Moran, E. (ed). *The Ecosystem Approach in Anthropology.* University of Michigan Press, Ann Arbor, pp. 247–277.

Little, M. A., Galvin, K., and Leslie, P. W. (1988). Health and Energy Requirements of Nomadic Turkana Pastoralists. In de Garine, I. and Harrison, G. A. (eds). *Coping with Uncertainty in Food Supply.* Oxford University Press, Oxford, pp. 288–315.

Moran, E. (1990). Ecosystem Ecology in Biology and Anthropology: A Critical Assessment. In Moran, E. (ed). *The Ecosystem Approach in Anthropology.* University of Michigan Press, Ann Arbor, pp. 3–40.

Morgan, L. H. (1877). *Ancient Society.* Meridian Books, Cleveland.

O'Connor, J. (1988). Capitalism, nature, and socialism: A theoretical introduction. *Capitalism, Nature, and Socialism* 1: 11–38.

Odum, H. (1971). *Environment, Power, and Society.* Wiley-Interscience, New York.

Orlove, B. (1980). Ecological anthropology. *Annual Reviews in Anthropology* 9: 235–273.

Peet, R. and Watts, M. (1994). Introduction: Development theory and environmentalism in an age of market triumphalism. *Economic Geography* 69(3): 227–253.

Pianka, E. R. (1973). *Evolutionary Ecology.* Harper & Row, New York.

Rappaport, R. A. (1968). *Pigs for the Ancestors.* Yale University Press, New Haven.

Rappaport, R. A. (1979). On Cognized Models. In *Ecology, Meaning and Religion.* North Atlantic Books, Richmond, pp. 97–144.

Service, E. (1958). *Profiles in Ethnology.* Harper and Row, New York.

Steward, J. (1955). *Theory of Culture Change.* University of Illinois Press, Urbana.

Tylor, E. B. (1878). *Early History of Mankind.* John Murray, London.

Vayda, A. P. (1983). Progressive contextualization: Methods for research in human ecology. *Human Ecology* 11(3): 265–281.

Vayda, A. P. (1988). Actions and Consequences as Objects of Explanation in Human Ecology. In *Environment, Technology and Society.* No. 51, pp. 2–7.

White, L. (1949). The Symbol: The Origin and Basis of Human Behavior. In *The Science of Culture.* Farrar, Straus and Giroux, New York.

White, L. (1959). *The Evolution of Culture.* McGraw-Hill, New York.

Wilmsen, E. (1989). *Land Filled with Flies: A Political Economy of the Kalahari.* Chicago University Press, Chicago.

Winterhalter, B. and Smith, E. R. (1981). *Hunter–Gatherer Foraging Strategies: Ethnographic and Archeological Analyses.* The University of Chicago Press, Chicago.

Wolf, E. (1982). *Europe and the People Without History.* University of California Press, Berkeley.

I

Foraging

Securing a livelihood based on plants and animals that grow "wild" rather than being cultivated or herded by humans is generally subsumed under the general category "foraging," used here interchangeably with "hunting and gathering." Few groups today, however, rely exclusively or primarily on such resources, but clearly, before the development of plant and animal domestication, all humans were foragers, and this form of livelihood characterized humanity for most of its existence. As humans spread across the world in the Upper Paleolithic period, they brought with them highly sophisticated hunting and gathering techniques that they modified for the many different habitats they entered. Long after the domestication of plants and animals was initiated, and humans began to depend increasingly on cultivated plants and domesticated animals, foraging continued to be important to the subsistence of many groups, sometimes on a seasonal basis.

Complete dependence upon foraging has usually required a nomadic or seminomadic way of life, in that people usually need to move about from place to place as they exploit seasonally available nondomesticated resources. Of course, contemporary foragers generally live in resource-poor areas, richer areas having been taken over by more powerful groups, and hence they exemplify, perhaps, a greater need for extreme mobility. A nomadic existence has a number of social and cultural repercussions. Non-pastoral nomadic groups can afford to acquire very little in the way of material culture—possessions that have to be carried about. They are unlikely to invest much in permanent features, like substantial shelter or public construction, or even wells, dams on rivers, fences, and so forth. Depending on the habitat, their numbers are likely to be relatively small and, at least during most of the year, widely dispersed.

Because their numbers are small, population densities low, and because they are unlikely to harvest more resources than they can consume themselves (because they are unable to store or carry much), the impact of nonpastoral nomadic groups on their environments is likely to be somewhat less compared with other groups, as long as their interaction with other groups is at a relatively low level. This is not to say that they do not

13

have any impact at all. Because they are the most versatile predators in their habitats, they obviously affect the populations of the species on which they feed. Further, they may actively shape their habitats through such practices as regular burning (see, for example, Gottesfeld, 1994). Hunters are believed by some to have caused the extinction of Pleistocene megafauna in the New World (Martin and Wright, 1967), and, after Europeans created a market for skins and meat, hunters nearly caused the extinction of the North American bison and other modern animals in recent times. Gatherers have carried wild seeds with them into new habitats: this is how, many believe, plant domestication was started.

Today's foragers cannot be understood out of the context of the groups with whom they interact, and which themselves are involved in agriculture, pastoralism, and sometimes industrial production. Many foraging groups cultivate crops and keep livestock themselves, using foraging as a supplement to their domesticated resources either directly or through trade with other groups. The implications of each of these situations for the impact of their foraging activities are varied but potentially substantial. Hunters who supply meat, fur, and hides for other populations, for example, are not limited by their own needs for these products; hence, they may engage in more intensive exploitation than otherwise. Gatherers who can depend on cultivated plants for most of their calories may chose different sorts of plants to collect than those who have no access to domesticates.

The question of exactly how foragers make a living on scarce resources is one which has absorbed human ecologists for decades. Julian Steward's classic work, *Basin-Plateau Sociopolitical Aboriginal Groups* (1938), about the Paiute of western North America, documented the annual cycle of a seminomadic group dependent upon resources that alternated concentration and dispersal; Steward's observation of the interdependence between sociopolitical institutions and the ecology of human subsistence in this instance became the basis for his formulation of the "cultural ecology" approach to the study of human behavior. More detailed observations of forager subsistence strategies were revived in part as a consequence of a landmark study by Richard B. Lee of the !Kung Bushmen of the Kalahari Desert in Southern Africa, and his cross-cultural comparison of these foragers with others around the world (1968). Lee pointed out that some foragers rely more on plant foods gathered by women than on animal foods hunted by men. The traditional appellation used to describe early humans, "Man the Hunter," would be a misrepresentation not only because it ignored at least half the population but also because it ignored what were likely to have been the more important sources of food.

Substantial advances in understanding the subsistence strategies of foragers were made as a consequence of borrowing from general ecological models, most particularly the models derived from optimal foraging theory, which assumes that people will attempt to maximize energy returns for energy expended. Scott Cane's chapter in this volume examines the issues of food storability and seasonality in accounting for what foragers do, and when. Excellent reviews of ecological and economic issues in forager research are provided by Elizabeth Cashdan (1989) and Ernest Burch and Linda Ellanna (1994). Jon Erlandson (1994) offers a fine-grained archaeological analysis of the long-term ecological history of a coastal North American hunter–gatherer population, from 7,000 to 11,000 BP.

Perhaps the most contentious issues in forager research today concern the tendency of some researchers to project idealized conceptions of "pristine" or "prehistoric" peoples onto living groups. The most notorious of such debates arose in the context of the identity of the Tasaday, who were put forward as an isolated relic of prehistoric antiquity, then thought to be instead a refugee group or perhaps even the product of calculated fraud (Yengoyan, 1991; Headland, 1993). Somewhat less colorful but equally heated and scientifically more interesting is the debate about the social and economic history of the Kalahari peoples known as the Bushmen or the Dobe !Kung (Schrire, 1980; Wilmsen, 1989; Solway and Lee, 1990; Gordon, 1992; Lee, 1993). These debates have brought to the forefront the need to acknowledge and understand the nature of interactions between foragers and other groups. The chapters in this part by Hart and Hart and Eder both focus upon the impacts of such interactions on the foragers' ways of life, the former with a view to understanding better the strategies of foraging that result from a trade relationship, the latter in order to document the specific history of change over a century.

To close this section on foraging we include a chapter on a mixed economy that incorporates fishing, the hunting of large sea mammals, agriculture, and domesticated livestock (McGovern et al.). While the chapter illustrates the struggle of a population to survive under increasingly hostile environmental conditions and unfavorable interactions with other populations, it also shows the complexity of human subsistence practices in any one society. Human ecologists often focus on one resource extraction practice, or aspect of a practice, at a time, even while they are mindful of the influence of a whole array of other simultaneous practices. Foraging plays a significant role in many societies that do not depend on foraging alone.

These studies illustrate the importance to human ecology of the issues of time and space. In each of these studies, seasonality is an important factor, and to an increasing degree, cumulative change arising from interactions with other groups. Foragers move; interactions with others affect patterns of movement, but in ways that are specific to not only the character of the resources exploited but also to the character of the interactions. An understanding of the objectives of the people involved, as well as their knowledge and perception of their world, is critical to an explanation of their patterns of life.

BIBLIOGRAPHY

Burch, E. S. Jr., and Ellanna, L. J. (1994). *Key Issues in Hunter-Gatherer Research.* Berg, Oxford and Providence.

Cashdan, E. (1989). Hunters and gatherers: Economic behavior in bands. In Plattner, S. (ed). *Economic Anthropology.* Stanford University Press, Stanford, pp. 21–48.

Erlandson, J. M. (1994). *Early Hunter-Gatherers of the California Coast.* Plenum, New York.

Gordon, R. (1992). *The Bushmen Myth.* Westview Press, Boulder, CO.

Gottesfeld, L. M. J. (1994). Conservation, territory, and traditional beliefs: An analysis of Gitksan and Wet'suwet'en subsistence, Northwest British Columbia, Canada. *Human Ecology* 22(4): 443–465.

Hart, T. D. and Hart, J.A. (1986). The ecological basis of hunter–gatherer subsistence in African rainforests: The Mbuti of Eastern Zaire. *Human Ecology* 14: 29-57.

Headland, T. N. (1993). *The Tasaday Controversy: Assessing the Evidence.* Thomas N. Headland, ed. Special Publication No. 28. Scholarly Series. American Anthropological Association, Washington, DC.

Lee, R. B. (1968). What hunters do for a living, or how to make out on scarce resources. In Lee, R.B. and Devore, I. (eds). *Man the Hunter.* Aldine, Chicago.

Lee, R. B. (1993). *The Dobe Ju'hoansi,* 2nd edition. Harcourt Brace, Orlando.

Martin, P. S. and Wright, H.E., Jr., eds. (1967). *Pleistocene Extinctions: The Search for a Cause.* Yale University Press, New Haven.

Schrire, C. (1980). An enquiry into the evolutionary status and apparent identity of the San hunter–gatherers. *Human Ecology* 8: 9–32.

Solway, J. S., and Lee, R. B. (1990). Foragers, genuine or spurious? *Current Anthropology* 31(2): 109–146.

Steward, J. (1938). *Basin-Plateau Aboriginal Sociopolitical Groups.* Smithsonian Institute, Bulletin 120, Washington, DC.

Wilmsen, E. M. (1989). *Land Filled with Flies: A Political Economy of the Kalahari.* University of Chicago Press, Chicago.

Yengoyan, A. (1991). Shaping and reshaping the Tasaday: A question of cultural identity— a review article. *The Journal of Asian Studies* 50: 265–273.

1

Australian Aboriginal Subsistence in the Western Desert

Scott Cane

If anyone were tempted to characterize hunter–gather subsistence as "simple," Scott Cane's study of the traditional seasonal round of the inhabitants of the Great Sandy Desert would disabuse them of the notion. His study, conducted over six years with the Gugadja people, meticulously documents the resources utilized and the methods of their procurement and processing. He assesses the relative nutritional contribution and importance of key foods, providing quantified data on seed collection and processing — a key element in Aboriginal diet and one which allows them to exploit a habitat characterized by seasonally extreme aridity. Seeds are stored for the aptly named "hungry season." It has long been known that seeds were important to Australian hunter–gatherers; Cane, however, shows that this is not true in terms of caloric intake. Seeds require much effort in collection, winnowing, and particularly in preparation for final cooking and consumption. It is because of their storability that they are vital. By documenting dietary shifts from season to season, Cane demonstrates that it is inaccurate to characterize such economies as primarily based on "hunting" or "gathering"; what people eat and how much effort they expend depends on the season.

Originally published in *Human Ecology: An Interdisciplinary Journal,* 15(4)(1987): 391–434.

Scott Cane, Culture and Heritage, P.O. Box 1773, Port Lincoln, South Australia 5606, Australia.

Case Studies in Human Ecology, edited by Daniel G. Bates and Susan H. Lees. Plenum Press, New York, 1996.

INTRODUCTION

This paper presents recent information regarding traditional Aboriginal subsistence in the Great Sandy Desert, north Western Australia (Figure 1). Aboriginal people belonging to the Pintubi and Gugadja linguistic units lived a full hunter–gatherer existence in this part of Australia until the mid-1950s and early 1960s, when they moved from the desert onto cattle stations, missions, and government settlements scattered around the desert fringe.

For this research, many months over a period of six years were spent with Gugadja people, visiting old campsites and documenting subsistence activities. The first section presents a generalized picture of the traditional seasonal found to provide the reader with a broad view of Aboriginal subsistence in the region, and to act as a backdrop against which more

Figure 1. Location of study area.

detailed, quantitative data relating to specific subsistence activities can be presented. The paper presents this data by identifying the resources used by desert Aboriginal people and describing the various methods of procurement and processing. An assessment is made of the nutritional contribution and importance of various key foodstuffs.

ENVIRONMENTAL SETTING

The Great Sandy Desert is a vast expanse of undulating sand on which the dominant landforms are seemingly endless longitudinal dunes. These run east–west over 1000 km across the Canning Basin (Fletcher, 1965; Brown, 1960).

From a botanical point of view, the landscape has been described as "desert in its more limited sense" (Gardiner, 1944, p. 56), and is generally described as mixed shrub steppe (Beard and Webb, 1974). By and large, the botanical landscape has remained much as it was prior to the arrival of Europeans. The only real changes have been a decrease in fire frequency (related to decreased Aboriginal land use in the region) and the introduction of feral cats and camels. No rabbits, foxes, donkeys, or pigs have colonized the area.

Animals life is relatively scarce. Small birds congregate around waterholes and occasionally bustards (*Eupodotis australis*) are found on the plains. Populations of large animals such as dingos, emus, and kangaroos are small, and the number of small marsupials has declined over the recent past, partly because of changes in fire frequency (Bolton and Latz, 1978) and the introduction of feral cats mentioned above.

The stark and desolate landscape of the study area is matched by the harshness of its climate. According to the Climatic Atlas of Australia (1975), the study area falls within a region which experiences the highest average summer (39°C) and winter (24°C) temperature range in Australia. This corresponds to an equally high evaporation rate of between 4000–4500 mm a year. The average rainfall at Balgo, a small mission 100 km north of the study area, is only 268 mm (Beard and Webb, 1974, p. 26). This rainfall is unpredictable, and over the last 40 years has varied from as little as 91 mm to over 900 mm per year (Bureau of Meteorology).

SEASONAL ROUND

Most researchers working in the Western Desert of Australia have noted the flexibility and mobility of desert life (Long, 1971; Thomson, 1975;

Myers 1976; Could, 1969; Tonkinson, 1978). This is certainly a characteristic of life in the study region, were the availability of food and water
each year has an impact on the distance people travel, the camps they travel
to, and the amount of time they stay in one place. This pattern is also
complicated by other factors such as the need to obtain raw materials, fulfill
social obligations, and attend ceremonies. Nevertheless, there is a system
which may be described as starting with the wet season, to which the desert
inhabitants generally adhere.

During the wet season (December–February), family groups spread
out across the desert plains. Fresh rains usually come in huge thunder-
storms at this time of year, leaving drinkable water in the ephemeral stream
beds, claypans, numerous little rock pools in the hills, as well as in all the
major catchments. The relative abundance of water at this time of year
means that people can disperse in search of fresh food, and men travel
great distances to get stone for making stone tools or to collect resilient
wood for making spears. People congregate and travel great distances to
attend ceremonies, but, most importantly, families travel to areas that have
not been foraged over since the previous wet season.

However, the wet season is not a particularly fertile season. No new
supplies of food have yet begun to grow and there are only limited supplies
of edible fruits, seeds, and tubers left from the previous year. Game is also
spread across the landscape and rarely encountered. This time of the year
is characterized by a relative scarcity of food so that people have to move
constantly from camp to camp to collect enough food for their survival,
and everyone is involved in the food quest.

Once the wet season rains fall, plants begin to grow. After several
months the spinifex changes from a dry straw yellow color to a bright green,
and seeds and fruit begin to appear. This growing season is called the
"green grass time" by the Aborigines and lasts from about March until
May. At this time of year, as temperatures begin to moderate, Aboriginal
families move to large surface waterholes around fertile standplains and
begin to harvest *Ipomoea* tubers. Migrating birds come into the desert, but
local game is still widely dispersed.

The "green grass time" merges into the "cold time." Cold easterly
winds make the first few months of this season quite chilly, although frosts
are rare. Temperatures drop to 6–8°C at night and rise to about 25°C during the day. The cold winds often prevent sleep, and people sit naked
around fires in the late hours of the night and then rest and rise about
mid-morning. Occasionally, the cold time is plagued by weeks of miserable
winter drizzle.

However, this is a time of economic prosperity, and plant foods such
as *Ipomoea* and *Vigna* tubers, *Acacia* and grass seeds, and *Solanum* fruits

are abundant. People live semipermanently around soaks and large water-holes and focus their economic attention on abundant, easily gathered tubers. Women are the principal food gatherers and the men have ample leisure to pursue ceremonial interests. Compared to the rest of the year, this is a time of affluence, characterized by feasting, leisure, ceremonies, and social interaction.

The end of the cold season is heralded by the sudden appearance of warm westerly winds and the movement of reptiles from hibernation. The Aborigines call this spring season the "goanna get up time," and it lasts from about August until October. The relatively affluent lifestyle of the previous few months fades away and family groups slowly return to the serious business of survival in a desert environment. Temperatures steadily rise to a nightly average of 22°C and a daily average of 36°C. People fall back to large rockholes in the rocky country, escarpments, and ranges. The landscape begins to dry out and the plains are burned to attract game and stimulate the growth of new grass seeds and tubers the following year. The subsistence base becomes more generalized. Lizards and kangaroos are hunted, and fruits, *Cyperus* bulbs, *Vigna* tubers, and grass seeds are gathered. Acacia and eucalyptus seeds are collected and stored for the hot season. Both men and women spend most of the day in the pursuit of food. This time of year is thus characterized by economic diversity.

As the "goanna get up time" melts into the "hot time," temperatures rise (reaching occasional maximums of over 50°C), waterholes dry up, and supplies of food dwindle. This is the harshest time of year and family groups travel to the largest rockholes in their territory. These rockholes are usually not visited until the end of the year, and if reserved until then have the capacity to carry people through harsh dry seasons. People remember such rockholes deteriorating to no more than muddy soaks, and it is likely that they occasionally run dry. Permanent springs are rare. There are, for example, only two in an area of about 18,000 sq. km surrounding the study area.

As the hot time progresses, the supplies of food available to the Aborigines camped at these rockholes decreases. The accessible supplies of stored Acacia and eucalyptus seeds run out, and the drought tubers (*Cassia notabalis* and *Clerodendrum floribundum*) are used up. If rain has not come by December, economic activity comes to a virtual standstill. People try to take it easy during the hot time to conserve food and water. The responsibility of providing food falls to the men, and women stay at camp and look after children and elderly people. People wear bark sandals to protect their feet from the hot sand and, when possible, cover their heads and shoulders with layers of wet mud to reduce heat stress. After a time, the only food left to collect within the foraging radius of the rockhole is the goannas which have been missed earlier in the year. The men leave camp before dawn and return at dusk, foraging as far as 15 km from the main camp in search of food. The average calorific daily intake under these conditions is only about 800 kcal per person.

The size and number of the major waterholes control foraging movement. Water shortages and heat stress prevent people from traveling to areas where food is still available and, in a sense, people become trapped on foraging "islands" around large waterholes. If rains fail to come, tension runs high and fights are common. Sometimes, people begin to starve and are fed blood drained from the arms of healthier individuals to get them through the last harsh few weeks of the year. The Aborigines aptly call this the "hard time" or "hungry time."

The availability of water keeps a lid on population levels. While other seasons are relatively affluent, the severity of the hard time means that population can never rise beyond a level that can be supported by local supplies of food and water. In this sense, the hard time proves to be a natural limit on population; Western Desert Aboriginal society consists of small, isolated family groups with a population density of as low as one person to 150–200 sq. km.

The Aborigines survive through the hard times, waiting anxiously for the summer rains. Throughout December and January, thunderclouds gather on the horizon, slowly building in intensity. Humidity rises until, eventually, large earth-shaking rainstorms come. As soon as these rains fall, the Aborigines escape from the permanent waterholes and spread out widely over the sandplains in search of food.

FOOD RESOURCES

The general picture of the environment and Aboriginal seasonal subsistence activities described provides a backdrop for more detailed information about the distribution, use, significance, and nutritional value of the different resources in the desert environment.

Plant

Within the study area, 126 plants were recorded which were recognized and named by the Aborigines. One hundred and two of these plants provide materials suitable for 138 different economic, social, and medicinal functions. Various parts of 70 plants produce edible seeds, tubers, fruits, nectars, excretions, and an additional seven plants contain edible insects or larvae.

Cleland and Tindale (1959, p. 120) claim that there are probably more than 1200 vascular plants in Central Australia, and O'Connell et al. (1983, p. 83) provide an estimate of approximately 5000 species for the Alyawara territory. Clearly, ethno-botanical investigations in arid Australia account for only a limited range of the available flora, but nevertheless appear to identify the major economically useful species found in the region. The data illustrated in this paper are representative of the economically important plant foods used within the northern parts of the Western Desert.

SEEDS

Data relating to seeds in the diet of Aboriginal people have been presented in Cane (1987). Rather than reproduce this data, some of the key points will be summarized. The data presented are some of the first quantified data of seed collection and processing methods by hunting and gathering peoples, and raises some interesting questions about the processing methods and the significance of wild seeds in traditional diets.

Edible seeds are collected from 42 different plants by Aborigines. These include 11 species of Acacia, 18 species of grass, four species of eucalyptus, three succulents, two herbs, and four other miscellaneous shrubs.

Distribution and Availability

The vast majority of seeds grow on the sandplains and nearby creeks, waterholes, and alluvial flats adjacent to rocky ground. The major species (*Panicum cymbiforme, Panicum australiense,* and *Fimbristylis oxystachya*) grow in large patches extending over many hectares on the sandplains. They respond well to fire and in the past were maintained by regular burning.

Acacias and eucalyptus trees also grow extensively on the sandplains and along the sides of sand dunes. The major seed-bearing Acacias (*A. coriacea, A. stipuligera,* and *A. holosericea*) grow on deep well-drained sand and around waterholes. Edible herbs and succulents grow on flood plains and shallow pockets of sand in the hills.

Most of the edible seeds ripen during the winter months (Figure 2), although some of the Acacias and eucalyptus seeds also ripen during the hotter months. The Aborigines describe the seasonal availability of the key species as follows:

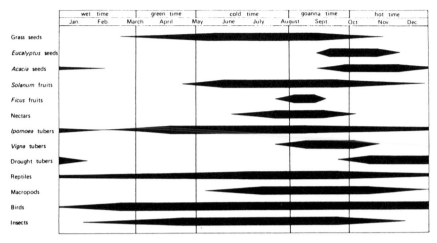

Figure 2. Seasonal availability of major foodstuffs.

Summer. This is the hot time and few plants produce edible seeds. Two acacias (*Acacia holosericea, A. Stipuligera*) and one succulent are said to be consumed. The succulent usually ripens toward the end of the dry season and can also be eaten then.

Autumn. Four plants produce seeds quickly after rain (*Eragrostis tenellula, Brachiaria muliiformis, Echinochloa colunum, Daspalidium rarium*). Two succulents (*Portulaca filifolia,* followed by *P. oleracea*) ripen toward the end of autumn and may be consumed then or in early winter. Spinifex (*Triodia pungens* and *T. basedowii*) also begins to ripen. These seeds are said to be eaten, although the seeds are very small and usually are only consumed if other food is scarce.

Winter. The cold time is the best time for seed harvesting. Tasty, large, and easily collected seeds are relatively abundant. The most economically important grass seeds ripen at this time of year. These include *Eragrostis eriopoda, Panicum cymbiforme, Fimbristylis oxystachya, Panicum australiense,* and *Echinochloa colunum.*

Spring–Summer. Seed consumption in the spring is dominated by the acacias. One notable exception is a large, hard seed of a small shrub (*Scirpus dissachanthus*), which requires soaking and longer baking. The acacias become increasingly important through the later spring but tend to run out in the vicinity of waterholes as summer approaches. Then resident populations rely heavily on meat — usually lizards. The women complain that the processing of acacia seed is very tiring. The most important are *A. tenuissima, A. adsurgens, A. aneura, A. ciracea, A. tumida,* and *A. holosericea.*

It is apparent that a few species, including the acacia and herbs, ripen during the wet seasons. They are followed by the succulents (*Portulaca*) during the autumn. Most of the grasses ripen during the winter. During the spring and early summer, the bulk of the acacia and eucalyptus seeds ripen.

Some of the acacia seed are stored at this time for use later during the hot or hungry season (*A. holosericea, A. stipuligera, A. coriacea* and possibly *A. tumida*). Apparently, the seeds are collected for storage by stripping seed-laden branches straight from trees just prior to ripening, or when they have ripened. These branches are piled into heaps on the hard, flat surface of subterranean termites' nests and beaten with sticks to dislodge the seeds. The seeds are then scraped up. The same technique is used when the Aborigines want to store the seeds. In this case, the piles of seed pods and branches are covered with spinifex, which protects them from birds and reptiles until the Aborigines return to use them.

Seeds storage appears to be a very important aspect of the economic strategy in this part of arid Australia. Without it, survival during the last few months of each year would be more difficult than it already is. Even with the benefit of seed storage, supplies of vegetable food within the vicinity of the major waterholes often run out. When this occurs the Aborigines have to rely heavily on lizards or stray catches of game.

PREPARATION

The preparation of seeds is clearly a very strenuous and time-consuming operation. It involves four stages: Collection, winnowing, grinding, and backing. The method of processing is similar for all seeds, whether they are from grasses, eucalyptus trees, or herbaceous shrubs. Some of the methods of processing acacia seeds may be different, but there is little reliable data.

The collection of grass seed is relatively easy, and it is possible to collect roughly 1000 g of seed in a half an hour. Most grass seeds are stripped straight from the grass into a wooden dish by running/rubbing the heads of seeds through a loosely clenched fist. Some of the grasses (particularly *F. oxystachya* and *P. australiense*) could also be collected from the ground or from the surface of ants' nests. Ants collect these seeds to eat the nodules (eliaosome, Berg, 1975; O'Connell et al., 1983) and leave the seeds scattered around their nests. Once collected, the outer husks of most seeds have to be removed. This is done by rubbing handfuls of seeds between the heel of one hand and the palm of the other. As this is done, the seeds are dropped onto wooden dishes so the wind can blow some of the unwanted vegetable matter away (see also Tindale, 1974, p. 99, 1977, and O'Connell et al., 1983 for different techniques).

When seeds have been husked, they are placed into a large softwood dish (*luandja*) to be separated from contaminating sticks, sand, and stones. Women are very efficient at separating seeds and can separate about 1.5 kg of rubbish from 500 g of seeds in about 40 minutes. However, this time varies according to the kind of litter mixed with the seeds. Each different material has to be winnowed out separately, and this often necessitates between three and five different winnowing operations.

When the seeds begin to separate, the winnowing dish is tilted slightly and balanced between the last fingers and the ball of the thumb of the lower hand. The rocking motion is continued with the other hand, and the ball of the thumb on the lower hand is used to jar the lower end of the dish and spill the clean seeds into another dish (ivirra), where they are collected for grinding. After the seeds have been cleaned, they are either ground directly or soaked for several hours beforehand. Seeds are only soaked to soften them, but this is not done if the Aborigines are hungry.

When the women are ready to start grinding they set the grinding slab into the ground and place a wooden dish under the lip of the slab. A small quantity of seeds is placed on the grinding slab and a steady trickle of water is dribbled onto them to facilitate grinding and to help the flow of seeds down the grinding groove and onto the wooden dish. Seed grinding is the most arduous part of the preparation process and takes about 50% of the total time required to make seed cakes. An average time of about 1 hour to grind approximately 200 g of seeds provides a reasonable indication of the effort required.

When the seeds are ground, the paste is either eaten raw or several small dampers are baked in a campfire. In the latter case, the raw paste is placed in a shallow depression dug into hot ashes. A small fire of spinifex or dry twigs is lit over the paste to dry the crust of the damper. The paste is then covered with hot ashes and baked for 10–20 minutes.

We prepared four dampers from different grass seeds. Briefly, the preparation time for each meal means a handling time of about 5 hours per kg of damper and gives a return of about 350 kcal per hour.

Less is known about the processing techniques of acacia seed. Some of the acacias can be eaten without grinding after being roasted in the fire (particularly *A. coriacea;* see also O'Connell et al. 1983). Returns for such seeds are very high, in the order of 4000–5000 kcal an hour (O'Connel et al., 1983, p. 92).

A limited amount of information was recorded regarding the processing of acacia seeds in this project. According to Aborigines in this area, acacia seeds are first soaked in water and squashed. This produces a milky liquid which can be drunk. The remaining squashy mixture is spread onto the surface of flat termites' nests, and dried in the sun. When this mixture is dry, it is collected and roasted in hot sand, then winnowed to get rid of any contaminating sand. When cleaned, it is ground up and winnowed again in order to separate the edible seeds from the inedible black seed cases contained within the mixture. The clean seeds are then reground with water. The ground watery paste is eaten raw and never cooked. Aboriginal women describe this process as follows:

> We can eat like milk, soak him in water. Hot time. Squash him, eat him up like shhhh (mimic slurping). Put him on ant bed now, start again, cook him. When you dry, juice, juice we can eat. Finish, leave him ant bed, flat one. Burn him now, hot sand. Start again, shake him, shake him, clean him up, finish. Alright we can start now. Rock now, grinding put him in grindstone now. We can shake him again, black one, on top one, shake him, shake him, finish now. Take him wooden dish. For man that one, for husband and wife. We can eat anything, not really damper, not really damper, gurrunba. Can't cook him. We got no fire, no law, no law, no law. Just eating.

> We two fellow; gunandru (*A. coriacea*), gilgidi (*A. holosericea*), guarrba (*A. tumida*), mirrinda (unidentified), minyingurra (*A. tenuissiuma*), ngadurrdi (*A. tumida*) mandja (*A. aneura*). That the different one, he got no law. We can't cooking damper, nothing. No. He can burn you, finish you. You'll drop. Only that first time we can cook him, that's all. Hard work that. women. Husband gone for hunting.

The Aborigines describe the raw paste as *gurrunba,* and Hansen (1977, p. 35) interprets the term this way:

> Kurrunpa, spirit. A person's spirit, located near the stomach, leaves the body after death and returns to the birth site. The spirit is responsible for involuntary actions, vomiting, hiccoughs, etc. The spirit is personalised and said to leave one's body and go on walkabouts. One's dreams while sleeping are activities of the kurrunpa. Entrance and exit from the body is through the navel.

It is apparent from these descriptions that several species of acacia seeds utilized in this region are toxic. There are no other references to the use of toxic seed foods in Australia. In fact, very little is known about the processing techniques for acacia seeds at all. The only other published account is in O'Connell et al. (1983), but this is based on incomplete observations and does not mention anything about toxicity. Clearly, this is an area of desert subsistence that requires more research. Toxic plants are

Table 1. Nutritional Analysis of Bush Foods[a]

Scientific name	Aboriginal name	Moisture (g/100 g)	Protein (g/100 g)	Fat (g/100 g)	Ash (g/100 g)	Carbohydrate (g/100 g)	Minerals (g/100 g)			Ascorbic acid (mg/100 g)	Kilo Calorie (per/100 g)
							Ca	K	Na		
Seeds											
Panicum australiense and *Fimbristylis oxystachya*	Yidagadji Lugara										
(Cooked damper)		53.30	5.28	1.83	11.16	28.43	12.01	91.52	34.89	—	158.57
Chenopodium rhadinostachyum	Galbarri										
(Cooked damper)		3.67	12.32	6.29	11.30	66.42	21.23	172.02	50.37	—	373.86
(Raw seed)		51.09	14.30	1.31	11.86	21.44	127.39	282.38	39.84	—	161.69
Panicum australiense	Yidayadji										
(Cooked damper)		—	15.37	—	—	—	—	—	—	—	365.01
(Raw seed)		25.71	13.32	1.83	21.84	37.30	25.25	175.41	45.58	—	241.76
Fimbristylis oxystachya	Lugarra										
(Cooked damper)		—	13.82	4.78	9.80	—	—	50.73	22.55	—	380.99
(Raw seed)		32.60	7.10	11.96	22.57	25.77	16.90	182.70	43.96	—	244.70
Panicum cymbiforme	Gumbulyu										
(Cooked damper)		6.54	10.72	19.03	22.93	40.78	10.97	78.96	12.06	—	404.57
(Raw seed)		47.54	8.47	4.33	7.51	32.15	25.25	216.98	54.81	—	196.01
Stylobasium spathulatum	Nirdu										
(Raw nut)		10.88	.31	.11	1.51	87.19	321.00	290.43	55.79	—	300.04

Tubers											
Ipomoea costata											
(Cooked)	Garndi	64.30	1.23	.54	.94	32.99	89.26	299.21	32.66	—	134.96
(Raw)		78.76	.81	.13	1.19	19.11	72.28	286.17	56.82	3.62	83.01
Cyper rotondus	Djunda	31.24	1.73	.43	3.06	63.54	57.22	470.12	195.18	—	277.03
Elderia sp.	Mulbu	52.22	2.53	3.80	20.43[b]	21.02	24.46	277.81	53.88	—	150.25
Fruits											
Solanum chippendalei	Wilgarrba	55.95	4.40	.55	2.33	36.77	121.73	830.65	51.56	45.25	201.64
Solanum centrale	Gawarrba	77.99	3.84	1.52	2.12	14.33	59.66	782.23	35.13	26.55	—
Ficus platypoda	Widjirgi	55.47	1.79	1.21	2.08	39.45	163.22	200.32	54.04	—	193.88
Mukia sp.	Ngalbuwandji	84.13	5.20	.19	1.60	8.88	33.52	456.55	82.20	—	70.09
Meat											
Varanus acanthurus (cooked)	Djaran	44.47	32.52	14.96	6.85	1.20	173.77	174.25	480.64	—	327.14
Varanus gouldii (cooked)	Banggabari	51.54	25.90	13.87	8.02	.67	185.08	242.11	407.93	—	245.28
Eupodatis australis (cooked)	Barrulga	60.41	29.12	6.58	2.35	1.54	33.51	247.58	355.26	—	164.03
Miscellaneous											
Sap: *Acacia acradenia*	Mawida	10.88	.31	.11	1.51	87.19	321.00	290.43	55.79	—	300.03
Wasp galls											
(*Eucalyptus aff. terminalis*)	Malagudu	45.01	9.66	16.12	3.61	25.60	132.07	155.40	60.96	—	—

[a] Nutritional analysis done by J. Gedeon, W.A.I.T. Dept. Home and Consumer Studies, Perth.
[b] Sample contaminated in sand.

Table 2. Collection Times and Calorific Returns Recorded
for *Vigna lanceolata*

Collector	Weight (gm)	Total (kcal)	Time (min)[a]	Kcal/hr
Bye Bye	120	104	15	414
Budja Budja	570	497	120	248
Bye Bye	120	104	120	52
Budja Budja	260	224	120	112
Budja Budja	260	224	30	448

[a] Does not include travel.

consumed elsewhere in Australia (Beaton, 1977), and the Tonga of Zambia also apparently utilize the toxic seeds of *Acacia albida* (Lee, 1979, p. 181).

Preparing seed cakes from the two herbs (*Chenopodium inflatum* and *C. rhadinostachyum*) utilized in the region is also relatively complicated. The Aborigines have to remove the aromatic flavor of the plant and the herbaceous material surrounding the seeds before they can be consumed. This is achieved by rubbing the herbaceous mixture of seeds with spinifex ash. This is rubbed together until the seeds start to separate from their herbaceous cover. They are then winnowed clean and soaked several times until the water they were washed in tastes clean.

We prepared one seed cake from *C. rhadinostachyum*. Briefly, the energy value of the damper converts to a handling rate of 5.3 hours for every kilogram of damper produced and gives a return of 300 kcal per hour.

ROOTS AND TUBERS

Six species of underground plant fookd are utilized in the study area. Three of these (*Ipomoea costata*, *Vigna lanceolata*, and *Cyperus rotondus*) are very important food items whereas another two (*Clerodendrum floribundum* and *Cassia notabilis*) are fibrous, difficult to prepare, and are generally used in times of drought. One truffle (Elderia sp.) is consumed in the region but this is a luxury item only encountered occasionally (see Table 2).

Distribution

Ipomoea tubers are collected from the sandplains, the best tubers being located on deeper, better-drained sandplains. *Vigna* tubers are found in varying quantities on virtually all creek lines, and sometimes on sandplains adjacent to alluvial plains and seepages from higher ground. *Cyperus rotondus* is a sedge-like grass that produces a small cluster of onion-shaped tubers close to the surface of the ground. This resource is found in places that are seasonally inundated with water.

Most of the edible roots are available for consumption all year round although their relative abundance varies throughout the year. *Cyperus rotondus* bulbs are available a few months after wet season rains and are then ready for harvesting for the rest of the year; "he is ready when you dry, this time now (June), he can stop through the hot time too."

Ipomeoa tubers are also available throughout the year, although their relative importance varies considerably. The Aborigines consciously stimulate the production of new tubers from surface runners by burning, "when the cold time finish" (about August). Sweeney (1947, p. 295) records that these runners are also produced after a good rain.

New tubers are harvested toward the end of the green grass time (May–July). When these are exhausted, the Aborigines turn to the deeper tubers on the roots of the "mother" or main plant. The older tubers are often quite large and are usually located between 50–75 cm below the surface of the ground. They swell sufficiently to crack the ground around the middle of the cold season (June–July), and with the help of this marker are most efficiently gathered at this time of year.

As the cold season finishes *Vigna* tubers begin to swell. These can be harvested for a few months around September. *Vigna* tubers are a staple food of the goanna get up time (August–October), but are said to dry up by the extreme end of the hot season (November–December).

Both *Vigna* and *Ipomoea* tubers are very important food items in the traditional diet. If they fail to produce, the local population has to move away and forage in other areas. The women say:

> We been looking anytime. Alright we got to go another place now, nothing. Can't find him djirilbadja (*Vigna*) or garndi (*Ipomoea*). No stopping this one, this place. No stopping. Keep going, keep going. We've been having wirrgal (*Solanum centrade*) and different one djirilbadja (*Vigna*), long one, skinny one, yunala (unidentified species).

Cassia notabilis and *Clerodendrum floribundum* are both consumed during the hot time. *C. notabilis* is considered to be "a rubbish one" and apparently produces a fibrous tuber which makes a "crack like garndi" (*Ipomoea*) during the latter part of the year.

Table 3. Collection Times and Calorific Returns
Recorded for *Cyperus rotondus*

Collector	Weight (gm)	Total (kcal)	Time (min)[a]	Kcal/hr
Budja Budja	950	2631	240	657
Nyami	1500	4155	240	1039

[a] Does not include travel.

Processing Techniques

Most of the edible roots are relatively easy to process. For example, the bulbs of *Cyprus rotondus* are simply dug by hand, roasted quickly in hot sand next to a campfire, and then rubbled between two hands to remove the outer skin. When in good supply, this is a very easy resource to gather, and, on one occasion, 12 adults collected enough bulbs to feed themselves (and had approximately 300 grams left over) in just 20 minutes. On two other occasions, the returns were substantially lower, but still yielded between 600–1000 kcal per hour (Table 3).

The edible roots used during the hard time are more difficult to process. The techniques used to process either species was not observed, but it is said that before *C. notabilis* could be eaten, they had to "cook him, throw him in the fire, clean him, rub him, cook him again and then eat him." Peile (1980, p. 60) describes how *Clerodendrum Floribundum* was also roasted in a fire and then the "cooked endoderm is peeled off and the cooked phloem is eaten, but not the pith."

Ipomoea tubers yield the highest returns of all the edible roots collected by the Aborigines. The young shallow tubers are the easiest to collect. Often, the Aborigines could collect up to a dozen tubers from one root. The larger tubers growing on the older roots are more difficult to gather, and the Aborigines often have to dig up to 1 m below the surface to get them. The total quantities gathered on 24 different occasions show that the amounts vary from as low as 250 g an hour to over 4700 g an hour (Table 3). The average gathering rate is 1254 g an hour and, using the calorific value of cooked *Ipomoea* tubers (135 kcal per 100 g; Table 1), gives an average calorific return of 1690 kcal an hour. The best figure recorded was 6345 kcal an hour. This is virtually the same as the estimate given by O'Connell et al. (1983, p. 85).

Ipomoea tubers are rarely eaten until cooked. Before tubers are eaten, they are grilled for a few minutes on top of hot coals and then baked in shallow earth ovens for about 20 minutes. When cooked, the tubers are eaten by hand without the aid of wooden or stone scoops as done in Central Australia (O'Connell, 1974).

Vigna tubers grow within 20 cm of the ground surface and are very easy to collect. The tubers are simply exposed with a digging stick and snapped off the root. Often, women collect tubers along the full length of a root, in which case they dig shallow trenches several meters along the surface of the ground. When sufficient quantities of tubers have been collected, they are taken back to camp and backed by the handfuls for 5–10 minutes.

EDIBLE FRUITS

Distribution and Availability

Edible fruits are collected from 12 plants. These are widely distributed throughout the region, occurring both on the rocky ground and on the sandplains. The bush plum (*Santalum lanceolatum*) is found consistently on deep sand and adjacent water bodies. The wild fig (*Ficus platypoda*) is confined to sheltered rocks and gorges in the hills. Two wild species of orange (*Capparis lasiantha* and *C. loranthifolia*) and a wild cucumber (*Mukia* sp.) are located on the small flood plains among the hills.

Solanum plants produce great quantities of fruit. These ripen gradually over a long period of time and can be harvested consistently between June and August. Several of these species are stored, and this extends the time these fruits are available into the hot season (December). *Ficus* fruits and wild cucumbers (*Mukia* sp.) ripen quickly and are only available for a short period at the end of the cold season. *Capparis* fruits ripen around December and provide a limited supply of food in the early part of the wet season.

Processing Techniques

With the exception of two species of bush tomato (*S. diversiflorum* and *S. chippendalei*), all the fruits can be picked and eaten directly. They are usually consumed while people are foraging. Two species of *Solanum* cannot be eaten until the astringent liquid and black seeds contained within the plant are cleaned from the inside of the fruit. This is done by biting or twisting the fruit open, shaking out the inedible black seeds, and cleaning the internal flesh by rubbing it with a thumbnail or with sand. *Solanum*

Table 4. Collection Times and Calorific Returns
Recorded for *Solanum chippendalei*

Collector	Weight (gm)	Total (kcal)	Time (min)[a]	Kcal/hr
Peter	450	907	30	1815
Nyami	2200	4436	30	8872
Sunfly	3600	4546	30	9092
Jimi	4400	8872	20	17742

[a] Does not include travel.

are very easy to gather and are either collected in wooden dishes or skewered onto a length of *Sida virgata*. For example, on one occasion, *S. chippendalei* was collected from an unharvested crop of shrubs at an average rate of 5325 g an hour. This gave a calorific return of 9380 kcal an hour, or enough to feed four people for a day (Table 4). This is similar to the return recorded for *S. centrale* by O'Connell et al. (1983) among the Alyawara in Central Australia and Gould (1969, p. 262) in the southern portion of the Western Desert.

The Aborigines store two species of bush tomato (*S. chippendalei* and *S. diversiflorum*), which can be kept for several years if necessary (see also Thomson, 1975; Gould, 1969, 1980; Peterson, 1977). When these species are stored, they have to be carefully cleaned and cooked. This is done by turning them continuously in hot ashes so that they do not burn. When cooked, the flesh is removed from the fire and winnowed free of sand and foreign matter. The cooked flesh is then mashed with water and rolled into a ball, covered with grass, and wound up with twine. Sometimes the Aborigines mix cooked *Ipomea* tubers with the fruit. These balls of food are kept for consumption during the hot time, given to young men when they go into ritual isolation, or are traded with visiting people for meat.

NECTARS AND EDIBLE GUMS

A variety of nectares and edible gums are consumed in the study area. The most important of these is the nectar of *Grevillea eriostachya, Hakea macrocarpa, H. suberea,* and the sap of *Acacia acradenia*. These species are commonly found on the sand plains and produce edible substances between July and September. These sweet foods are a luxurious addition to the diet.

Table 5. Collection Times and Calorific Returns Recorded for Witchetty Grubs

Collector	Weight (gm)	Total (kcal)	Time (min)[a]	Kcal/hr
Five people	385	1001	10	6006
Nyami and Budja Budja	490	1274	60	1274
Bye Bye	470	1222	60	1222

[a] Does not include travel.

INSECTS

Six plant species are hosts for a variety of edible insects. The most important of these is the witchetty grub (*Cossidae* sp.; see Tindale, 1935) which can be found in great quantities in coolibah trees (*Eucalyptus microtheca*) along creeks and waterholes. Witchetty grubs can be found in these trees by the appearance of a red spot on the white bark of the tree, and are removed by simply opening the bark with an axe or rock and pulling the grub out with a hooked twig (*yanggu*) or the fingers. They are eaten raw or roasted quickly on hot coals. Witchetty grubs gathered in this way are easy to collect. They are collected at a rate of about 30–40 grubs (400 g) an hour, giving an average calorific return of about 1000 kcal per hour (Table 5; see also O'Connell et al., 1983; Tindale, 193).

Another insect food frequently sought is the wasp parasite and its larvae, inhabiting the coccid galls on the desert bloodwood (*Eucalyptus* aff. *terminalis*). These trees only grow on flanks of sanddunes, and the galls are collected during the cold season while still hosting the parasite (Sweeney, 1947; Peile, 1980).

WOODEN IMPLEMENTS

Two of the most important plants used to make wooden implements in the region are two species of acacias, mulga (*Acacia aneura*) and *A. pachycarpa*. Both species grow on laterite plains and flood plains, although the distribution of mulga is quite restricted. Mulga is used to make large ceremonial boards, parrying shields, spear throwers, women's clubs, boomerangs, and punishment spears. *A. pachycarpa* is primarily used to make boomerangs.

Seven plants growing on the sandplains are used to make wooden implements. Two species of acacia (*A. coriacea* and *A. pruinocarpa*) are quite commonly used to make boomerangs. The straight saplings of *A. adsurgens* are used to make digging sticks, clubs, and, occasionally, hunting spears, although the best woods for spear-making are *Acacia cowleana* and *A dictyophleba*. *A. cowleana* is not as resilient as *A. dictyophleba* and is only used when the latter is not available. *A. dictyophleba* is highly prized but is quite rare, growing in dense, isolated stands in remote sand dune country. People travel to these areas during the wet season to obtain the wood (also see Gould, 1969).

Eucalyptus is also used to make wooden artifacts. Hardwood digging bowls are made from the bloodwood (*E. terminalis*) and coolibah (*E. microtheca*). Bark dishes are made from the smooth white bark of *E. aspera* and *E. microtheca*.

One of the most important woods in the region is the bean tree (*Erythrina vespertilio*). This is a light, tough softwood and is used to make the large winnowing dishes and men's shields. Bean trees are found in greatest abundance along the numerous small creeks running from hills.

The only species found on the hills used for making implements is *Acacia rhodophloia*. This is used to make hooked fighting boomerangs (Table 6).

Miscellaneous

Apart from obtaining food and wooden implements from plants found in the study area, the Aborigines use various plants for other purposes. These include ceremonial decorations, twines, baskets, water filters, children's spears, head pads, shoes, adhesives, medicines, and ashes for mixing with tobacco. A brief description of these is provided in Tables 7 and 8.

ANIMALS

Within the literature, there is only a limited amount of information available on the animal foods eaten by Aboriginal people in the Western Desert (Could, 1969, 1980; Tonkinson, 1978; Meggitt, 1962; Lawrence, 1969; Long, 1971).

Throughout this project, it has been difficult to assess the wildlife resources likely to have existed in pre-contact times because the marsupial fauna is largely nocturnal and has changed somewhat during the last 50 years (Frith, 1978). The most important influences on the local fauna appear to be the introduction of cats and the decrease in fire frequency. Bolton and Latz (1978) suggest that the decreased fire frequency in the desert

Table 6. Major Plants Used for Wooden Implements

Scientific name	Aboriginal name	Habitat	Relative importance	Use
Acacia adsurgens	Ngardja	Sandplains	Minor	Spears, fighting sticks, digging sticks
Acacia coriacea	Mandja	Laterits plains	Major	Spear throwers, fighting sticks, shields, punishment spears, ceremonial boards
Acacia coriacea	Gundandru	Sandplains	Major	Boomerangs and punishment spears
Acacia cowleana	Garna garns	Sandplains	Moderate	Hunting spears
Acacia dictyophleba	Gulada	Sandplains	Major	Hunting spears
Acacia pachycarpa	Badieri	Flood plains	Major	Boomerangs
Acacia pruinocarpa	Mandila	Sandplains	Minor	Boomerangs
Acacia rhodophloia	Djarrgadjiri	Rocky ground	Moderate	Hooked boomerangs
Erythrina vespertilio	Gumbubanu	Creek lines	Major	Shields, dishes, fire sticks
Eucalyptus aspera	Gilgilba	Sandplains	Moderate	Hardwood and bark dishes
Eucalyptus microtheca	Dindjil	Near water	Moderate	Hardwood and bark dishes
Eucalyptus terminalis	Waldji	Sanddunes	Moderate	Hardwood dishes
Triodia pungens	Djinalba	Sandplains	Major	Resin

Table 7. Some Plants with Medicinal Functions

Scientific name	Aboriginal name	Habitat	Relative importance	Use
Acacia ancistocarpa	Wadayurru	Sandplains	Major	Leaves chewed and saliva rubbed in open wounds
Acacia pachycarpa	Badieri	Flood plants	Moderate	Walwadjeri and Djaru people use as medicine
Carissa lanceolata	Managudji	Near water	Moderate	Leaves used as antiseptic
Cleome viscosa	Djilbirrngarning	Sandplains	Moderate	Twine wound around aching part of body
Eucalyptus brevidolia	Mangaburru	Rocky ground	Minor	Juice from bark rubbed onto wound
Euphorbia coghlaniis	Yibi Yibi	Sandplains	Moderate	Sap rubbed into skin to stimulate lactation
Halogaris aspera	Bandingunmaunma	Flood plains	Major	Smoke inhaled for cold
Ipomoea costata	Garndi	Sandplains	Minor	Twine wound around aching part of body
Sacristenna australe	Ngarmalu	Rocky ground	Moderate	Sap rubbed into skin to stimulate lactation
Streptoglossa bubakii	Manyanii	Laterite plains	Moderate	Smoke inhaled against colds
Streptoglossa macrocephala	Ngunungunu	Laterite plains	Moderate	Smoke inhaled against colds
Tribulopis angustifolia	Yibi Yibi	Sandplains	Moderate	Sap rubbed into skin to stimulate lactation

Table 8. Plants Used as Tobacco or Ash Mixed with Tobacco

Scientific name	Aboriginal name	Habitat	Relative importance	Use
Acacia cuthbertsonii	Wilbiiya	Laterite plains	Minor	Dry twigs burned for ash
Acacia ligulata	Wadarrga	Sandplains	Minor	Dry twigs burned for ash
Acacia pruinocarpa	Djawil	Sandplains	Minor	Dry twigs burned for ash
Eucalyptus camaldulensis	Yabulin	Creeks	Minor	Bark burned for ash
Eucalyptus microtheca	Dindjil	Waterholes	Major	Bark burned for ash
Grevillea stenobotrya	Yanandi	Deep sand	Major	Leaves burned for ash
Nicotania bethamiana	Ngandju	Rock shelters	Major	Tobacco: leaves dried and mixd with saliva and ash
Templetonia incarna	Ngdjeri	Sandplains	Minor	Leaves used as tobacco

since the Aborigines left the region has destroyed the habitats and populations of some of the small marsupials. Feral cats also appear to be responsible for the decrease in the population of small marsupials, and are recorded as preying on small birds and reptiles as well (Frith, 1978, p. 91). Carnegie (1898, p. 214) recorded that feral cats were in the desert before the turn of the century, they are part of the subsistence base of people in the region today. Rabbits, cattle, and camels are rare and seem to have had little influence on the local environment.

MAMMALS

Distribution

Large mammals are relatively scare and restricted in their distribution. Red kangaroos (*Megaleia rufa*) are usually located on alluvial plains and flood plains. During the wet season, they tend to spread widely over the country but move back to the vicinity of major waterholes as surface water contracts. The aborigines feel that this particular field area is good kangaroo country and said there were, in fact, "too many kangaroos." This seems to be a fairly relative observation because the combined population must be less than 40 individuals. The population of euros (*Macropus robustus*) in the region is equally small. These macropods live in the hills.

Wallabies, bandicoots, rats, mice, and dasyurids used to live on the sandplains, but their numbers seem to have decreased considerably in the recent past. The Aborigines say a number of species are "finished" in the region and only five burrows of the rabbit-eared bandicoot have been recorded (*macrotis lagatis*; Bolton and Latz, 1978; Could, 1969). Carnegie (1898) makes frequent references to the collection of bandicoots by Aborigines before the turn of the century. The Aborigines say the population of echidnas (*Tachyglossus aculeatus*) living in the hills has also been reduced, but that the dingo population is about the same.

Hunting Techniques

Large animals are hunted by men. The hunting spears used are only accurate up to a distance of about 20 m (Horne and Aiston, 1924, p. 79; Love, 1936, p. 81) and, as a result, the men stalk the animals very carefully, from downwind. Often they cover themselves with a disguise of spinifex and branches. Sometimes the men work in groups and use fire to drive

Table 9. Disposable Articles Used by Aborigines

Scientific name	Aboriginal name	Habitat	Relative importance	Economic use
Amphigogon caricinus	Binbiri (grass)	Sandplains	Moderate	Heat pad
Crotalaria cunninghamii	Nyalibi	Sanddunes	Major	Sandals and twine
Gonocarpus eremophilus	Yulgurru yulgurru	Sandplains	Minor	Tuft used as basket
Ipomoea muelleri	Wandidjarra	Near water	Minor	Twine and basket
Rhyncharrhena linearis	Gulibi	Sandplains	Moderate	Twine
Sida cardiophylla	Yurrungudu	Sandplains	Moderate	Basket
Sida virgata	Dadji dadji	Sandplains	Moderate	Skewer for *solanum* fruits
Stackhousia intermedia	Bimbirri (grass)	Sandplains	Moderate	Heat pad
Tinospora similacina	Waragi	Sandplains	Moderate	Twine

Table 10. Plants Used in Decoration

Scientific name	Aboriginal name	Habitat	Relative importance	Use
Acacia ancistocarpa	Wadayurru	Sandplains	Major	Used by oung men during ceremonies
Didymotheca tepperi	Nilbi nilbi	Sandplains	Major	Used by old men during ceremonies
Erythrina vespertilio	Gumbubanu	Creeks	Major	Seeds threaded on hair string, also fertility beads
Eucalyptus ondontocarpa	Warilu	Sandplains	Moderate	Seeds capsules threaded on hair strong with *Erythrina* beads
Euphorbia coghlarii	Yibi Yibi	Sandplains	Minor	White sap used as paint
Euphorbia wheeleri	Yibi Yibi	Sandplains	Minor	White sap used as paint
Macregoria racemigera	Gigl Gigl	Sandplains near water	Minor	Placed in childrens' hair
Mirbelia viminalis	Marrabii	Sand, laterite plains	Major	Lit during ceremonies
Mollugo molluginea	Madagurru	Rocky ground	Major	Flower beads colored with pigment and stuck on with blood
Styloblasium sparthulatum	Nirdu	Sandplains	Moderate	Seeds threaded on hair string

Table 11. Plants with Miscellaneous Values

Scientific name	Aboriginal name	Habitat	Relative importance	Economic use
Acacia acradenia	Wilbut	Sandplains	Minor	Sap eaten
Acacia cuthbertsonii	Wilbiiya	Laterite plains	Minor	Shade for kangaroos
Acacia holosericea	Gilgidi	Near water	Minor	Bark for sandals
Acacia pruinocarpa	Djawil	Gravelly sand	Minor	Sap eaten and shade
Aeschynomene indica	Manabulgu	Near water	Moderate	Childrens spears and spear throwers
Calytrix longiflora	Bugara	Sandplains	Minor	Bush tea
Cassia venusta	Galbirr galbirr	Laterite, sandy	Minor	Emus eat seen
Carissa lanceolata	Managudji	Swamp margin	Minor	Insect repellant
Chenopodium auricomum	Yiliyili	Swamp floors	Minor	Sign of water
Eremophila maculata	Darrdjanpa	Sandplains	Minor	Emu food
Eriachne mucronata	Birilba	Rocky ground	Moderate	Water filter
Eriachne flaccida	Galuburrudju	Claypans	Moderate	Water filter
Eucalyptus species		Vrious	Moderate	Branches and leaves used like plates
Grevillea wickhamii	Yidingga	Sandplains	Minor	Reptiles eat seed
Petalostylis cassioides	Djangulari	Sandplains	Moderate	Bush tea, water
Rhagodia spinescens?	Murrlu murrlu	Swamps	Minor	Sign of water
Sida virgata	Dadji dadji	Sandplains	Moderate	Children's spears
Triodia longiceps	Lanu lanu	Rocky ground	Minor	Sweet excretion from leaves

the animals into the range of other hunters lying in wait. The men spear the animals at about thigh level, hoping to prevent the animal from hopping away when hit.

When first killed, the animals are gutted and taken to camp for cooking. When cooked, the hind legs are dislocated at the hip, the tail removed, and all the fur burned off. Hot coals are placed in a deep earth oven, and the animal is laid on top of these and covered with the remaining coals and hot sand. The tail is cooked separately and the stomach, intestinal fat, liver, and kidneys are grilled on top of the coals. If the people are not too hungry, the animal is left to cook for several hours. Otherwise, it is eaten partially raw. Blood which spills into the intestinal cavity is often drained and drunk as well.

Bandicoots are rather more difficult to get, and it requires a lot of digging to remove them from their deep underground nests. Carnegie (1898, p. 242) records that when caught, the fur is plucked off and grilled on the coals of a fire.

Dietary Importance

Carnegie's (1898) numerous references to Aborigines consuming bandicoots suggests that these are probably the most important marsupials in the traditional diet. The Aborigines value kangaroo meat, but probably do not manage to kill them very often. Only eight were shot in the 10 month period of this study. Even with a vehicle and .22 rifle, many hunts were unsuccessful. Large marsupials are probably more important in the overall diet between August and December, when populations contract around available waterholes, and the heat causes them to rest more often during the day.

REPTILES

Distribution and Availability

Lizards are apparently a major source of food for feral cats (Frith, 1978, p. 91) but despite this, Aborigines claim they are more abundant today than in the past, possibly as a result of reduced predation by people. The major species hunted include the centralian blue tongue (*Tiliqua multifasciata*), the great desert skink (*Egernika kintorei*), and two monitors (*Varanus gouldii* and *V. acanthurus*), but there are many small dragon lizards (*Amphibolurus* sp.)

caught and eaten by children. The Aborigines seem to regard geckos (*Diplo-dactylus* sp.) with distaste. Lizards are found widely on the sandplains and dunes, and the ridge-tailed monitor (*V. acanthurus*) is found in rocky crevices in the hills.

Snakes are not common in this part of the desert and the most commonly caught are pythons (*Aspidites melanocephalus* and *Aspidites ramsayi*). One species of edible toad (*Notaden nichollsi*) is collected in the region.

Lizards and snakes are available all year round but hibernate during the winter. The centralian blue tongue and ridge-tailed monitor are the first to leave their nests after winter and herald the start of the goanna get up time (September–October). The desert spadefoot toad (*Notaden nichollsi*) is most commonly gathered when it leaves its nest to breed during the wet season. It is also collected after winter drizzle when it comes to the surface to feed.

Collection and Consumption

Both men and women gather reptiles. Once the tunnel of a lizard is found, its nest is located by beating the ground with the heel of the foot or a digging stick. The animal is then dug out and bashed on the head. Both snakes and lizards are baked in shallow earth mounds. Before lizards are cooked the intestines are pulled out through the anus or hooked through the side of the neck with a stick. When gutted, reptiles are grilled on hot coals until almost bursting and then baked for about 20 minutes. Before the desert skink (*E. kintorei*) is cooked, it is scaled with a stick.

Lizards are relatively easy to collect, and the average collection rate (including travel time) for the 167 lizards collected in 1982 was 733 g per hour. This gives a return of approximately 2000 kcal an hour based on the average calorific value of cooked specimens (Table 1).

Dietary Importance

Lizards are the main source of protein and fat for the Aborigines living in the desert. They are critically important during the last few weeks of the hot season. If rains come unusually late, lizards are virtually the only food the Aborigines have to survive on. At these times, life is quite difficult and often people starve. The men said that, under these conditions, they leave camp before sunrise in pursuit of food and return after dark. They said they would try to collect about three goannas for their families. The average weight of the goannas collected was 456 g. This converts to a calorific value of 1304 kcal per goanna. Therefore, three of these goannas only yield 3912 kcal of energy. If the number of people in an average family is five people (see Cane, 1984), then this daily ration is only enough to provide each person with 782 kcal of energy a day!

BIRDS

Both birds and their eggs form an important part of the traditional diet. Emus (*dromaius novaehollandiae*) and bustards (*Eupodotis australis*) are the most commonly sought species, but emus are rather rare. For example, during the study period, only eight emus were seen, and none shot. Bustards are common and are easily hunted. Flocks of from 20–30 birds were seen feeding on freshly burned ground, and smaller flocks were seen of between three and five birds on the flood plains.

DISCUSSION

The nature of the information presented in this paper raises certain questions about the traditional anthropological view of desert Aborigines' subsistence. It raises questions about the resource base, adaptive strategies, division of labor, settlement patterns, and a variety of other issues, which, in the absence of quantified data, have only been partially understood in the past. In the remainder of this paper, some of these issues are examined.

Regional Differences in Subsistence

It is apparent that there are regional differences in the nature of subsistence strategy practiced by Aboriginal people living in different parts of the Western Desert. These differences result largely from cultural and geographic factors. For example, in comparison with their southern neighbors from the Gibson Desert (Gould, 1969), the Aborigines of the Great Sandy Desert appear to have enjoyed greater economic diversity and greater seasonality in the availability of resources. The Ngatatjara to the south do not enjoy access to important resources such as *Ipomoea* or *Vigna* tubers and are not recorded to have stored and utilized Acacia and eucalyptus seeds. Conversely, *Chenopodium* and *Eragrostis* seeds and *Ficus* fruit are major resources in the Gibson Desert, but are comparatively unimportant to the Gugadja in the Great Sandy Desert, who also do not have access to *Canthium* or quandong fruits (*Santalum acuminatum*; Gould,

1969, 1982). Similarly, the annual subsistence round practiced by the Gugadja is not stimulated or governed by the location and size of erratic rain showers, unlike that of the Ngatatjara, who seem to be forever on the lookout for rain. In the Great Sandy Desert, the Aborigines spread out during the summer in search of unused supplies of food. They congregate around large waterholes during the winter, where abundant supplies of fruits, seeds, and roots allow participation in large ceremonies. Toward the end of the dry season, the Aborigines move back to major rockholes and practice a generalized hunter–gatherer subsistence strategy.

The Gugadja practice a very similar subsistence system to the Walpari and Alyawara to the east (Meggitt, 1962; O'Connell et al., 1982). Their resource base is almost identical, the processing methods are the same, and the seasonal round is similar.

Highlighting the regional diversity in the subsistence strategies practiced by desert Aborigines, however, is the difference between these groups and the Bagundji of the margin of the arid zone in eastern Australia (Allen, 1974). Here, the Aborigines congregate in large groups along river banks during the summer months. This is a time of high productivity and the Aborigines collect fish, shellfish, bulrushes, and migratory birds. By comparison, winter is a difficult time, and the Aborigines split up into small groups and focus their attention on mammals, seeds, fruits, and tubers. Both the Gugadja and Bagundji practice seed storage quite extensively.

The Nature of Subsistence

The information presented in this paper suggests that subsistence is not overly opportunistic. The seasonal availability of resources combined with the detailed environmental knowledge of Aboriginal peoples make hunting and gathering activities quite predictable and reliable. For example, the availability of vegetable tubers during the cold season is very predictable and allow relatively large groups of people to live semi-permanently around large waterholes. Furthermore, the Aborigines take conscious steps to store acacia, eucalyptus, *Stylobasium* seeds, and *Solanum* fruits for periods of food shortages. They also have a conscious policy of burning the land to stimulate new tubers, grass seeds, and *Solanum* fruits, and to attract game. Hunting and gathering behavior is most opportunistic and generalized between the goanna get up time and the wet season (August–March) when the Aborigines forage widely for a variety of different resources.

Desert subsistence cannot be characterized as either affluent or unduly harsh (Thomson, 1964; Sahlins, 1968; Lee, 1968; Gould, 1969; O'Connell and Hawkes, 1981). Rather it varies between these two extremes. The best time is the cold season when easily gathered resources such as tubers and fruits are abundant and women only have to spend a few hours gathering to provide sufficient food for an average family. This is a time of affluence, characterized by feasting, leisure, and social interaction. It is a time of ceremonial activity, when up to 300 people congregate for religious purposes. The goanna get up time (August–October) is more arduous and, at this time of year, both men and women spend most of the day foraging. The last part of the year, from October until the first wet season rains (January) sees a decline in economic activities. People congregate around major waterholes and collect whatever food (usually goannas) is available within a foraging radius of about 15 km from the waterhole. This is a harsh time of year, and food supplies often dwindle to the point of virtual starvation. When wet season rains fall, family groups spread out across the country gathering a variety of resources, left over from the previous year.

Sexual Division of Labor

Contrary to popular belief (Gould, 1969; Peterson, 1970; Hiatt, 1970; Maddock, 1970) women are not always the principal food gatherers in the desert. The role of the sexes in the collection of food appears to vary seasonally. Women are the principal food gatherers during the cold season (May–August), whereas both men and women make a substantial contribution to the diet during goanna get up (August–October). Men take over the role of food collecting during the hot season (October–December); both men and women collect food during the wet season and green grass time (January–April). Men and women shared many of the subsistence activities. Neither sex is adverse to collecting wild fruits, eggs, small marsupials, tubers, or witchetty grubs, although seeds are always processed by women and men always do the hunting.

Importance of Desert Resources

The main foods utilized in the northern part of the Western Desert are seeds, wild fruits, tubers, reptiles, marsupials, birds, and grubs.

Without doubt, edible roots are the most important and easily gathered food in the region. *Ipomoea* tubers are the most important of the five root crops and are usually the major resource used to support ceremonies whenever rainfall is heavy enough to allow sufficient people to gather. *Vigna* tubers are also very important, but are generally only available for a short time between August and September. The edible bulb of

C. rotondus can be harvested all year but is only available in relatively small amounts throughout the area.

Except for the *Solanum* fruits, the fruits eaten in the study area are treated as luxury items, additional to the daily fare, and are generally consumed as people traveled. Gould (1969, 1980) records that *Ficus* fruits are a desert staple, but their ripening period is so short that this is unlikely. The *Solanums* make a more substantial contribution to the diet and, with the exception of *S. centrale,* are consumed in great quantities when available. *S. centrale* is said to produce very bad headaches if too much is eaten.

Most foods are available in a broadly defined season, although some, such as *Ipomoea* and *Cyperus* tubers, reptiles, birds, and witchetty grubs, can be obtained all year. Most of the vegetable foods ripen during the cold season (May–August), and, as the year progresses, a greater diversity of less abundant foods are available. Supplies of food begin to run out and are often in short supply during the hot season and wet season (November–February).

Vegetable foods do not always constitute between 70–80% of the traditional diet (Meggitt, 1957; Gould, 1969. This figure may be true for some of the winter months, but it varies seasonally. Animal foods become increasingly important during the spring, and eventually dominate the diet, e.g., lizards during the early summer (December).

Importance of Seeds

It has always been assumed that seeds are an important part of the traditional diet in arid Australia (Gould, 1969, 1980; Allen, 1974; Meggitt, 1957; Tindale, 1974; O'Connell et al., 1983; Lawrence, 1969). The information presented in this paper suggests that this assumption is not entirely correct.

Grass seeds are difficult to process, and unless the major species are particularly abundant and close to campsites, they usually constitute a "bread and butter" kind of backstop to the subsistence system.

The processing times recorded in this paper convert to a handling rate of between 3–6 hours for each kilogram of damper processed from various seeds. This translates to an energy return of between 246–810 kcal per hour. The average handling time is therefore 5 hours to produce 1 kg of food and a return of only 340 kcal an hour. If, for example, grasses are "staple" foods and constitute between 30–50% of the traditional diet as suggested by Gould (1969, 1980, 1982), then one woman would have to work between 10–15 hours a day simply to provide an average family of five with less than half their daily calorific intake. These figures might be slightly exaggerated given that the women are relatively unfit and out of practice, but, nevertheless, they give some idea of the effort involved in processing seeds. Therefore, unless large supplies of relatively easily processed grass seeds are available, they probably constitute only about 20% of the daily diet. The Aborigines always prefer to get large game, lizards, tubers, and various fruits rather than grass seeds. The unique value of seeds, however, is both that (unlike many other food items which are only available seasonally, and can fail to ripen in abundance in any given year), they can be stored, and they can always be found somewhere. Seeds are most abundant and of greatest economic importance during the coldest seasons (between June–October), but become quite scarce during the hot and wet seasons (November–March). Grass seeds are notably more important during large ceremonies when other local resources are pushed to their limits.

With regard to the relative importance of individual species of seeds, it is apparent that, with the exception of the three species of spinifex, the grass seeds are the most desirable. Among the grasses, *Panicum australiense, P. cymbiforme,* and *Fimbristylis oxystachya* appear to be the most important. Most of the other grass seeds are of moderate importance and are used in a supplementary fashion in the diet. The edible shrubs, acacias, eucalyptus, spinifex, and the succulent *T. verrucosa* are generally at the bottom of the list, although their relative importance in the daily diet increases during the hot season (or in the case of spinifex, in the late wet season) when everything else is in short supply.

CONCLUSIONS

This paper presents data recorded during the final phases of hunter–gatherer activity in arid Australia. It is perhaps the last reliable data on hunter–gatherer subsistence economies from arid environments anywhere in the world. The paper has been written to provide a complete picture of Aboriginal economic life in the Western Desert. Several smaller, less detailed studies have been conducted in the Western Desert, but none have been able to fully explain the nature of desert subsistence. As such, some of these papers have presented limited interpretations of Aboriginal subsistence, which this paper supplements and develops. These new data suggest new interpretations and rectifys some past misconceptions about desert subsistence.

Most obvious perhaps is the predictability of both seasons and the availability of resources. In earlier studies, extreme opportunism was noted by ethnographers. This impression must now be questioned as it is apparent that, while generalized/opportunistic hunting and gathering did occur in specific seasons, Aboriginal people also live in semi-permanent camps for extended periods throughout the year. These camps are located at major waterholes, and people focus their economic activity on key resources. The locations of reliable food and water resources are well known. In this sense, Aboriginal life is quite secure and predictable.

Aboriginal people also have access to a much larger and more reliable resource base than previous studies have shown. Foods such as reptiles, *Ipomoea* and *Vigna* tubers, and *Solanum* fruits are staple resources. Other foods such as *Ficus* fruits and nectars are luxury items, and others (spinifex seeds and fibrous tubers) are used as drought foods.

Grass and acacia seeds appear less significant in the diet than previously thought. Processing these foods is such a difficult and time-consuming task, it is unlikely that seeds can contribute more than 20% of the daily diet at most sites. Seeds are stored, however, to help people through lean times of the year.

The availability of resources fit within a broad seasonal rhythm. Vegetable foods dominate the diet during the cold season, contributing up to 70% of the food consumed. The diet becomes more generalized, utilizing both meat and vegetable foods, during the spring, with reptiles being virtually the only food collected (contributing 80–90% of the foods eaten) during the late dry season (December). With these seasonal fluctuations there are changes in the resource base. Thus, the old notion of extreme desert hardship and the contemporary notion of hunter–gatherer affluence are inaccurate. Rather than either of these two extremes, there is an alternating rhythm of affluence, leisure, and social initiations in the winter, and economic hardship and stress during the spring and summer.

This broader, more complicated view of subsistence in the Western Desert points to the value of long-term, quantitative research into hunter–gatherer economies, and provides a reliable source from which human adaptation in marginal environments can be understood.

REFERENCES

Allen, H. (1974). The Bagundji of the Darling Basin: Cereal gatherers in an uncertain environment. *World Archaeology* 5: 309–322.

Beard, J. S., and Webb, J. (1974). *Vegetation Survey of Western Australia: Great Sandy Desert.* University of Western Australia Press, Perth.

Beaton, J. (1977). *Dangerous Harvest.* Unpublished Ph.D. thesis, Department of Prehistory, Australian National University, Canberra.

Berg, R. Y. (1975). Myrmecochorous plants in Australia and their dispersal by ants. *Australian Journal of Botany* 23: 475–508.

Bolton, B. L., and Latz, P. K. (1978). The western hare wallaby *Lagorchestes hirsutus* in the Tanami Desert. *Australian Wildlife Research* 5: 285–293.

Brown, G. A. (1960). *Desert dune sands of the Canning Basin*. Bureau of Mineral Resources Board.

Cane, S. B. (1987). Aboriginal seed grinding and its archaeological record: A case study. In Harris, D. R., and Hillman, G. C. (eds.), *Foraging and Farming: The evolution of plant exploitation. One World Archaeology* 13: 99–119.

Cane, S. B. (1984). *Desert camps: A Case Study of Stone Tools and Aboriginal Behavior in the Western Desert.* Ph.D. thesis, Department of Prehistory, The Australian National University.

Carnegie, D. W. (1898). *Spinifex and Sand.* Pearson, London.

Cleland, J. B., and Johnston, T. H., (1939). Aboriginal names and uses of plants at the Granites, Central Australia. *Transactions Royal Society of South Australia* 63: 22–26.

Cleland, J. B., and Tindale, N. B. (1959). The native names and uses of plants at Haast Bluff, Central Australia. *Transactions Royal Society of South Australia* 82: 123–140.

Climatic Atlas of Australia (1975). Map set 1. Government Printer, Canberra.

Fletcher, H. D. (1965). The desert areas of Australia. *Australian Natural History* 15: 98–102.

Frith, H. J. (1978). Wildlife resources in central Australia. In Hetzel, B. S., and Frith, H. J. (eds.), *The Nutrition of Aborigines in Relation to the Ecosystems in Central Australia.* CSIRO, Melbourne, pp. 87–96.

Gardiner, G. A. (1944). The vegetation of Western Australia. *Journal of the Royal Society of Western Australia* 28.

Gould, R. A. (1968). Living archaeology: The Ngatatiara of Western Australia. *Southwestern Journal of Anthropology* 24: 101-122.

Gould, R. A. (1969). Subsistence behavior among the Western Desert Aborigines of Australia. *Oceania* 39(4): 253–274.

Gould, R. A. (1977). Puntajarpa rockshelter and the Australian Desert culture: *Anthropological Papers of the American Museum of Natural History* 54(1).

Gould, R. A. (1980). *Living Archaeology.* Cambridge University Press, Cambridge.

Gould, R. A. (1982). To have and not to have: The ecology of sharing among hunter gatherers. In Williams, N. M., and Hunn, E. S. (eds.), *Resource Manager: North American and Australian Hunter–Gatherers.* AAAS Select Symposium 61.

Hansen, L. E. (1977). *Pintubi/Luritja Dictionary.* Summer Institute of Linguistics, Alice Springs.

Hiatt, B. (1970). Woman the gatherer. In Gale, F. (ed.), *Woman's Role in Aboriginal Society.* Australian Institute of Aboriginal Studies, Canberra, pp. 2–8.

Horne, G., and Aiston, G. (1924). *Savage Life in Central Australia.* Macmillan, London.

Lawrence, R. (1969). Aboriginal habitat and economy. Occasional paper No. 6, Department of Geography, Australian National University, Canberra.

Lee, R. B. (1968). What do hunters do for a living, or, how to make out on scarce resources. In Lee, R. B., and De Vore, I. (eds.), *Man the Hunter.* Aldine, Chicago, pp. 30–48.

Lee, R. B. (1979). *The Kung San.* Cambridge University Press, London.

Long, J. P. M. (1971). Arid region Aborigines; the Pintubi. In Mulvaney, D. J., and Golson, J. (eds.), *Aboriginal Man and Environment.* Australian National University Press, Canberra, pp. 263–270.

Love, J. R. B. (1963). *Stone Bushmen of Today.* Blackie & Son, London.

Maddock, K. (1970). *The Australian Aborigines: A Portrait of Their Society.* Allen Laine, London.

Meggitt, M. J. (1957). Notes on the vegetable foods of the Walbiri of Central Australia. *Oceania* 28: 143–745.

Meggitt, M. J. (1982). *Desert People.* Angus and Robertson, Sydney.

Myers, F. R. (1976). *To have and to Hold: A Study of Persistence and Change in Pintubi Social Life.* Unpublished Ph.D. thesis, Bryn Mawr University.

Newland, S. (1921). Annual address of the President. *Journal of the Royal Geographical Society of Australia.*

O'Connell, J. F. (1974). Spoons, knives and scrapers: The function of Yilugwa in Central Australia. *Mankind* 9: 189–194.

O'Connell, J. F., and Hawkes, J. (1981). Alyawarra plant use and optimal foraging theory. In Winterholder, B., and Smith, E. (eds.), *Hunter–Gatherer Foraging Strategies: Ethnographic and Archaeological Analyses.* University of Chicago Press, Chicago.

O'Connell, J. F., Latz, P. K., and Barnett, P. (1983). Traditional and modern plant use among the Alyawarra of Central Australia. *Economic Botany* 37(1): 80–109.

Peile, a. R. (1978). Gugadja Aborigines and frogs. *Herpetofauna* 10(1): 9–74.

Peile, A. R. (1980). Preliminary notes on the ethnobotary of the Gugadja Aborigines at Balgo, Western Australia. *Western Australia Herbarium Research Notes* 1(3): 59–64.

Peterson, N. (1970). The importance of women in determining the composition of residential groups in Aboriginal Australia. In Gale, F. (ed.), *Women's Role in Aboriginal Society.* Australian Institute of Aboriginal Studies, Canberra, pp. 9–16.

Peterson, N. (1977). Aboriginal uses of Australian solonaceae. In Hawkes, J. G., Lester, R. N., and Skedling, A. D. (eds.), *The Biology and Taxonomy of the Solonaceae.* Linnean Society Symposium Series No. 7, London, pp. 171–788.

Sahlins, M. D. (1968). Notes on the original affluent society . In Lee, R. B., and de Vore, I. (eds.), *Man the Hunter.* Aldine, Chicago, pp. 85–89.

Sweeney, G. (1947). Food supplies of a desert tribe. *Oceania* 17: 289–299.

Terry, M. (1928). *Untold Miles.* Selwyn and Blount, London.

Terry, M. (1931). *Hidden wealth and hiding people.* Putnam, London.

Terry, M. (1937). *Sand and Sun.* Joseph, London.

Thomason, D. F. (1964). Some wood and stone implements of the Bindiby Tribe of Central Western Australia. *Proceedings of the Prehistoric Society* (17): 400–422.

Thomson, D. F. (1975). *Bindubi Country.* Nelson, Melbourne

Tindale, N. B. (1935). Initiation among the Pitjantjarra Natives of the Mann and Tomkinson Ranges in South Australia. *Oceania* 6(2): 199–224.

Tindale, N. B. (1974). *Aboriginal Tribes of Australia.* Australian National University Press, Canberra.

Tindale, N. B. (1977). Adaptive Significance of the Panara or grass seed culture of Australia. In Wright, R. V. S. (ed.), *Stone Tools as Cultural Markers.* Australian Institute of Aboriginal Studies, Canberra, pp. 345–349.

Tonkinson, R. (1978). *The Mardjudjara Aborigines.* Holt, Rhinehart and Winston, New York.

Warburton, P. E. (1975). *Journey of the Western Australia.* Sampson and Low, Marson, Low and Searle, London.

2

The Ecological Basis of Hunter–Gatherer Subsistence in African Rain Forests: The Mbuti of Eastern Zaire

Terese B. Hart and John A. Hart

While it is well established that the Mbuti pygmies, hunter–gatherers of the Ituri Forest of Zaire, trade forest products and labor for agricultural foods, it has been assumed that this is a recent development, following contact with shifting cultivators. From field investigations over a five-year period, Hart and Hart found that, while the Mbuti can identify a large number of edible plant species, they actually gather very few of them. Instead, they trade meat, which is seasonally abundant, as well as their own labor for agricultural products rich in starch and carbohydrates. While game is available throughout the year, they cannot profitably utilize protein as a main caloric intake; lean meat requires more calories to digest than it supplies, a point illustrated by what the explorer Henry Stanley called in 1890 the "starvation camps" in the middle of the Ituri: People were dying while surrounded by game. Hart and Hart found that almost all of the oil-rich plant foods collected came from secondary forests rather than from that part of the Ituri hitherto unpenetrated by cultivators. Using historical data from early travellers, archaeological evidence, and linguistic connections linking various Mbuti groups to different cultivators, Hart and Hart make the

Originally published in *Human Ecology: An Interdisciplinary Journal,* 14(1)(1986): 29–55.

Terese B. Hart and John A. Hart, Division of International Conservation, Wildlife Conservation Society, Bronx, New York 10460.

Case Studies in Human Ecology, edited by Daniel G. Bates and Susan H. Lees. Plenum Press, New York, 1996.

case that the great evergreen primary forests of the Ituri were probably not capable of sustaining hunter–gatherers in significant numbers prior to the coming of cultivators, about 4000 years ago. This a good illustration of complex and interdependent ties that link what might appear to be distinct adaptations. Here agriculture has made the forest a more hospitable environment for specialized hunter–gatherers by providing a reliable source of energy-rich foods as well as by producing patches of secondary forest in which to forage.

INTRODUCTION

The Mbuti pygmies of the Ituri Forest in Zaire do not, for the most part, practice agriculture.[1] Their current economy is based on nomadic hunting and gathering activities in tropical evergreen forest, and trade relationships with forest-dwelling shifting cultivators. Trade between Mbuti and cultivators has been thought to be recent, with the Mbuti originally living independently as hunter–gatherers in the forest where they now occur. It is assumed that they developed a dependency on cultivated foods after agriculturalists migrated into the forest (Turnbull, 1965a,b; Cavalli-Sforza, 1972; Abruzzi, 1979; Tanno, 1981; Harako, 1976, 1981; Ichikawa, 1981). This historical interpretation, however, has recently been questioned (Hart, 1979; Bailey and Peacock, 1988), based on an examination of current subsistence patterns of Mbuti.

Until recently, the only evidence pertinent to an evaluation of Mbuti history has come from genetic and morphological studies (Cavalli-Sforza, 1972, 1977; Hiernaux, 1977). These studies, however, do not provide information on Mbuti independence as hunter–gatherers, or when they entered the areas they now occupy.

Another line of evidence, which has never been explored, is the capacity of the forest environment to support a hunter–gatherer economy. In this paper, we present a survey of food resources available to hunter–gatherers in forest occupied by Mbuti today. Our analysis concentrates on: (1) The distribution and seasonality of gathered foods and meat, and

[1]In this paper, for ease of reference, we refer to all pygmies of the Ituri Forest as Mbuti. This does not mean that the Mbuti constitute a single ethnic entity. Notably, the northern and eastern Efe differ in language, hunting style, and in other ways from the Mbuti of the central and southern forest. Where necessary, we will differentiate between different Mbuti groups in geographic terms.

(2) the potential of forest foods to serve as replacements for agricultural food in the Mbuti diet.

The time and labor involved in processing foods, and the technology available to hunter–gatherers prior to contact with agriculturalists are also important in determining diet (Colchester, 1984). These factors are considered, but are not fully analyzed here.

This analysis is possible because a major part of the Ituri Forest is unsettled by agriculturalists. Current population density is one or fewer persons per square kilometer over most areas used by the Mbuti (St. Moulin, 1976). Most of the Ituri Forest fits the description of climax evergreen forest for the region (Lebrun and Gilbert, 1954). Secondary forest, which has grown after an agricultural opening has been abandoned, can be distinguished from this undisturbed primary forest (T. Hart, 1985). Many of the Mbuti's important gathered food plants grow in secondary forest. Throughout this analysis we distinguish between gathered foods available in undisturbed forest and in agriculturally modified areas.

BACKGROUND

Archeological data establishing an ancient occupation of the closed evergreen forest of Central Africa by hunter–gatherers are still not available. Evidence from pollen cores, lake level changes, and plant and animal biogeography indicate that the a real extent of humid evergreen forest in Africa fluctuated during the Pleistocene (Hamilton, 1982), having undergone reductions of perhaps as much as 50% (Livingstone, 1980). Excavations at Matupi Cave, in the eastern Ituri Forest, revealed recurrent episodes of human occupation, the oldest dating between 32,000–40,700 years BP (Van Noten, 1977). None of these occupations, however, occurred during a forest phase. At all levels where microliths were found, they were associated with bones of savanna animals or other evidence of a savanna edge environment.

Historically, many pygmy groups in Central Africa are known to have had long contact with outside markets and intensive agriculture (Bahuchet and Guillaume, 1982). Until recently, the Mbuti have been more isolated (Turnbull, 1965b). Nevertheless, even the earliest accounts describe relations between Mbuti and subsistence-level shifting cultivators (Schweinfurth, 1874; Schebesta, 1933; Putnam, 1948; Turnbull, 1965a). These reports concur that the main products Mbuti received in exchange for labor and forest products were iron tools and agricultural foods, in particular cassava, plantains, cultivated yams, and sweet potatoes—all foods rich in starch.

Plant foods gathered from the forest contribute only a small proportion of the total calories in current Mbuti diets. Over 60% of their caloric intake is agricultural food (Ichikawa, 1983; Bailey and Peacock, 1988). There have been no direct observations, even under conditions of crop failure, of Mbuti camps that subsisted solely on gathered foods for more than a brief period.

Trade for cultivated, carbohydrate foods is prominent in the subsistence of many so-called forest hunter–gatherers throughout the tropical latitudes (Gardner, 1972; Sinha, 1972; Eder, 1978; Endicott, 1984; Milton, 1984; and see especially Peterson, 1978 for summary). The history of these exchange relationships and the former habitats of the hunter–gatherers remain obscure. Any attempted analysis, as Hayden (1981) has pointed out, must be based on greater knowledge of the limitations of rain forest habitat for hunting and gathering groups.

Meat is currently one of the Mbuti's most frequently acquired forest foods, and surplus quantities are regularly traded (Hart, 1978; Ichikawa, 1983). Our question is whether this meat could provide the Mbuti with a source of calories in the absence of agricultural starch. Lean meat diets require a greater caloric intake due to energetic costs of metabolizing protein (Speth and Spielman, 1983). It is noteworthy that in reports of meat as the major component of the diet, it is the animals with fat-rich bodies that are the dietary staples (Stefansson, 1956; Bose, 1964; Hill, Hawkes, Hurtado, and Kaplan, in press).

The immigration of shifting cultivators into the Central African forests brought not only agricultural foods but also new environments. The secondary communities which grow from abandoned gardens contain feral cultigens and pioneer plant species which are otherwise rare or absent in the forest. Although these plants become established through natural dispersal, their occurrence in the forest is dependent on environments of agricultural origin. These plants include a number of edible species which are freely gathered. It is important to differentiate between gathered foods from mature forest and those from secondary forest, as the problem examined here is whether resources from the mature forest, in the absence of agricultural activity, are likely to have supported hunter–gatherers.

METHODS

The data presented in this paper were collected on a 600 km^2 study area around Epulu in the central Ituri Forest between February, 1981–May, 1985. Current settlement is concentrated in the village of Epulu and surrounding clearings (about 500 people). One hundred twenty-five to 150

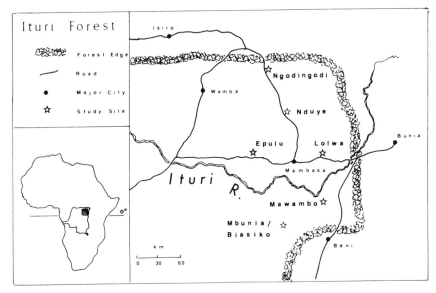

Figure 1. The Ituri Forest and location of study sites of recent Mbuti research.

nomadic Mbuti also use the area. From the accounts of Stanley (1890), the central Ituri Forest 100 years ago contained only small, widely scattered agricultural clearings. Much of the region was uninhabited (Stanley's "starvation camps" were located in this area). The area remains little changed today. Further details on the Epulu area may be found in Turnbull (1965a).

Comparative data collected in the Mbunia/Biasiko area in the southern Ituri Forest between March, 1973–May, 1975 (Hart, 1979) are also presented. Other recent field studies among the Mbuti of the Ituri Forest to which we compare our results include Bailey and Peacock (1988), at Ngodingodi; Terashima (1983) at Nduye; Tanno (1976, 1981) and Ichikawa (1981, 1983) at Mawambo-Teturi; and Harako (1976, 1981) at Lolwa (see Figure 1 for location of study sites).

In the study reported here, food-plant density and distribution were measured by recording all trees larger than 10 cm diameter at breast height (dbh) and all lianes larger than 2.5 cm in diameter on 25 m × 25 m plots. Twenty-four plots were sampled in each of two primary forest types; 32 plots were sampled in secondary forest. Plots were located at intervals of 175 m along three randomly chosen transects within each forest type.

Seasonality of important food plants was investigated by recording patches of fruits and seeds on the ground along transects four meters wide and 200–600 m in length that followed the net hunt. Transects were conducted during 15 one-week sampling periods over the 27-month field period, with 7–13 km of transect censused each period for a total of 136 km. Sampling periods covered the yearly seasonal cycle, with 3–4 sampling periods conducted during each season between 1981–1983. Transects were conducted primarily in mature forest types on the study area.

Observations on the seasonality of plant foods not recorded on the transects were made by locating individual trees and lianes and following their fruiting periods. Availability of edible dormant seed of one species, *Ricinodendron heudelotii,* was measured by recording seed availability on random plots under trees 6–9 months post-fruiting.

Hunting returns were assessed by accompanying Mbuti hunters on net hunts at eight camps of known size and composition. Hunting camps were located 6–30 km from Epulu. The data were collected during stays of 5–10 days during which time we accompanied all hunts. All animals caught were identified and weighed prior to butchering. The amount of meat captured per capita is calculated on a per adult unit (AU) basis, where individuals older than about 12 years are calculated as 1 AU and children less than 12 are calculated as 0.5 AU.

The body fat of the blue duiker, the most commonly caught species, was measured by the percentage of kidney covered by fat. This measure was taken year round on butchered animals to determine seasonal variation in fattiness.

Seasonal availability of certain highly sought gathered foods (honey and termites) was determined based on gathering patterns of the Mbuti. In the case of honey, additional observations were made of the phenology of several major bee-visited tree species.

General observations of Mbuti gathering activities were made during our visits to forest hunting camps and at base camps near the settlement of Epulu.

FOREST ENVIRONMENT

The Ituri Forest (Figure 1) covers about 70,000 km² of the upper water-shed of the Ituri River. It is bordered by savanna in the north and northeast, and the Western Rift highlands to the east and southeast. It is contiguous with sparsely inhabited forest to the south and west. Altitude varies from 600 m in the west to about 1200 m in the east.

Rainfall in the Ituri region is locally variable, as shown by records from three stations at the northern (Angbalare and Ngodingodi) and eastern (Beni) limits of the forest (Figure 2). Bultot (1971), summarizing

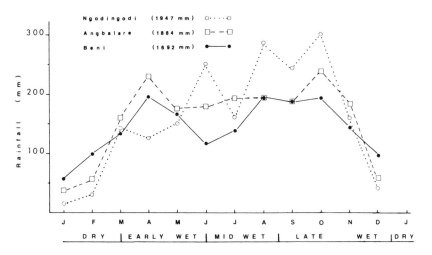

Figure 2. Monthly rainfall from three recording sites in the Ituri Forest region. Sources: Bailey and Peacock (in press) for Angbalare and Ngodingodi, Bourlière and Verschuren (1960) for Beni.

data collected between 1930–1959 at recording stations in eastern Zaire, reports mean annual precipitation between 170–180 cm in the Ituri Forest area, with an annual rainless period of no more than 40 days. The second half of December and the months of January and February are drier, and we shall refer to this period as the dry season. The rest of the year, despite irregular peaks in precipitation, is considerably wetter, and we have divided it into early wet season (March through May), mid-wet season (June to mid-August), and late wet season (mid-August to mid-December; Figure 2).

The forest occupied by the Mbuti today varies floristically. We distinguished two primary forest types based on the presence of one or more species of dominant Caesalpiniaceous trees. The "mbau forest" is recognized as particularly distinctive by Mbuti and botanists alike (Schnell, 1976; Gerard, 1960; Lebrun and Gilbert, 1954). Over 70% of the canopy is composed of a single species, *Gilbertiodendron dewevrei*. Because of the high, single-species dominance, this forest is floristically less rich than many other tropical evergreen forests, with an average of ten species larger than 20 cm dbh per hectare (T. Hart, 1985).

The remaining primary forest we classify as "mixed forest." It is considerably less uniform than mbau forest. No single species makes up more than 40% of the canopy, except in small local stands. The most important species include *Julbernardia seretii* and *Cynometra alexandri*. The higher diversity of this forest (mean 53 species larger than 20 cm dbh per hectare; T. Hart, 1985) is more typical of tropical evergreen forests worldwide.

Both mbau and mixed forest grow on a variety of soil types (T. Hart, 1985). Mbau forest occurs in the southern and western half of the Ituri region. Continuous stands of *G. dewevrei* may cover hundreds and perhaps even 1000 km^2 or more. Mixed forest occurs throughout the Ituri Forest region, and is the dominant forest in the northern and eastern Ituri. Riparian and swamp formations comprise a small percentage of the total area in both forest types. Our study site in the central Ituri Forest is located at a transition between mbau and mixed forest, with extensive stands of both in the area.

The only large areas of secondary forest in the Ituri Forest are all of agricultural origin. Small-scale shifting cultivation, as practiced in the Ituri region, entails abandonment of gardens after several years of successive cropping. If this land is not reclaimed for agriculture after a fallow of a decade or more, the vegetation will regain the structure and diversity, but not the floristic composition, of the mature forest. Secondary forest can be recognized botanically for at least 50 years, and, if the original clearing was large enough, for well over 100 years, by the high proportion of deciduous species and the low frequency of the Caesalpiniaceous dominants, characteristic of the mature forest (T. Hart, 1985). Today, most young secondary forest is concentrated along the road; however, past patterns of agricultural settlement are recorded in the vegetation as small patches of secondary forest of varying age throughout the forest.

PLANT RESOURCES

Important Wild Food Species

The Mbuti recognize many wild edible plants (see list of 38 species in Hart, 1979, and 55 species in Tanno, 1981). They do not, however, consider all these foods to be of equal value. The list of foods pertinent to our problems must include all gathered plant foods that could replace agricultural foods in the Mbuti diet. Because agricultural food is the major source of energy in Mbuti diet today, we are interested in examining wild plant foods of high caloric content. We identified 14–15 such species (Table 1). These species are known to contain important reserves of starch or oil (Wu Lueng, 1968), or are evaluated highly by the Mbuti for their ability to relieve hunger. Many of these species are gathered and eaten when available; however, this is not the only criterion for inclusion on the list. For instance,

Table 1. Major Gathered Plant Foods of the Mbuti in the Central Ituri Forest

Species	Family	Life form	Part eaten
Irvingia robur	Irvingiaceae	tree	seed
I. grandifolia	Irvingiaceae	tree	seed
I. excelsa	Irvingiaceae	tree	seed
Treculia africana	Moraceae	tree	seed
Ricinodendron heudelotii	Euphorbiaceae	tree	seed
Celtis adolphi-friderici	Ulmaceae	tree	seed
Gilbertiodendron dewevrei	Caesalpiniaceae	tree	seed
Tetracarpidium conophorum	Fuphorbiaceae	liane	seed
Tieghemella africana	Sapotaceae	tree	fruit and seed
Elaeis guineensis	Palmae	tree	fruit and seed
Canarium schweinfurthii	Burseraceae	tree	fruit
Dioscorea (3-4) *spp)*	Dioscoreaceae	vine	tuber and bulbil

the Mbuti recognize *R. heudelotii* and *C. adophi-friderici* as having high food value, but they are not frequently eaten today, presumably because they are labor intensive to gather and prepare.

Our list of major plant foods does not include species in which the calories are principally simple sugars (mainly ripe fruits). Such fruits may be eaten freely, but Mbuti do not consider these species important sources of energy, referring to them as children's foods. We have also found by experience that most of these species are not sustaining. The only fruits included in our list are oil-rich fruits of *C. schwienfurthii* and *E. guineensis* and the apparently starchy fruit of *Tieghemella africana*.

Our list of important gathered plant species includes most of the species identified by Tanno (1981) as evaluated highly by Mbuti of the Mawambo area. Species included by Tanno, but not considered here, are *Ipomea chisochaeta, Balanites wilsoniana,* and *Annonidium mannii. Ipomea* spp are found only in recently abandoned gardens and along the roadside in our study area. *B. wilsoniana* is generally found in higher altitude forests, e.g., Uganda (Hamilton, 1981). We did not record it on the central Ituri study area and it is rare in the southern Ituri Forest (J. Hart, unpublished data). *A. manni* occurs over the entire forest, and is gathered occasionally. It cannot be eaten in large quantities, and was not ranked highly by Mbuti of the central Ituri because of its astringency. *C. adolphi-friderici, Tieghemella africana,* and *E. guineensis* are included on our list, although not included by Tanno.

Table 2 provides composition data for important wild food species for which information is available (Wu Lueng, 1968). Also included are data for cultivated dietary staples: Cassava, *Manihot esculenta,* plantain, *Musa*

Table 2. Composition of Major Gathered Plant Foods and
Selected Cultivated Foods in Mbuti Diet

Species	Composition (100 g edible portion)			
	Energy (kcal)	Fat (g)	Carbohydrate (g)	Protein (g)
Gathered foods				
I. gabonensis	670	68.9	16.6	7.5
Threculia africana	377	5.6	70.4	12.6
R. heudelotii	530	43.1	23.4	21.2
G. dewevrei	353	0.6	82.3	4.8
T. conophorum	429	18.3	40.9	28.7
E. guineensis	540	58.4	12.5	1.9
C. schweinfurthii	239	13.5	33.5	11.5
Dioscorea spp	112	0.1	26.5	1.5
Cultivated foods				
Manihot esculenta	149	0.2	35.7	1.2
Musa paradisiaca	135	0.3	32.1	0.3
Arachis hypogaea	549	44.8	23.2	23.2

Source: Wu Lueng (1968), except G. dewevrei in Tanno (1981).

paradisiaca, and peanuts, Archis hypogaea. Overall, wild foods compare favorably with cultivated species on a caloric basis. Many edible wild seeds contain fat and protein levels comparable to those in ripe peanuts.

Distribution and Abundance

The plot inventories of primary and secondary forests show that important food species, with the exception of G. dewevrei, are rare (Table 3). Most species were recorded as fewer than three individuals in a total area of 3 ha encompassed by the primary forest plots (mixed and mbau). Individuals of two of the 12 major food species, Tieghemella africana and T. conphroum did not occur on any plots.

G. dewevrei is abundant in mbau forest, where it makes up 80% of all trees greater than 10 cm dbh. Omitting totals of G. dewevrei, we found that other food trees in mbau forest average less than 1 per hectare, and account for only 0.2% of all trees present. Secondary forest has a higher density of food trees than either of the two mature forest types (one-way ANOVA, $p < .05$). Food trees averaged 13 per hectare in secondary forest, and comprised 3.3% of total trees present (Table 3).

Table 3. Frequency of Important Gathereed Food Species (Trees and Lianes) on Sample Plots

Species[a]	Forest type[b]		
	Mixed	Mbau	Secondary
I. robur	2	0[c]	1
I. grandifolia	1	0	2
I. gabonensis	2	1	1
Treculia africana	1	0	2
R. heudelotii	2	0	11
C. aldophi-friderici	1	0	1
G. dewevrei	0	385	3
T. conophorum	0	0	0
Tieghemella africana	0	0	0
E. guineensis	0	0	2
C. schwemfurthii	0	0	3
Dioscorea spp[c]	absent	absent	present
Food trees	9	1[d]	26
Percent total trees	1.3	0.2	3.3
Food trees per hectare	6.00	0.67	13.00

[a] Numbers of trees larger than 10 cm dbh and lianes larger than 2.5 cm dbh.
[b] Twenty-four plots of 625 m² each in secondary forest.
[c] Presence absence data only recorded.
[d] Excluding G. dewevrei.

Differences in density of food plants in the three forest types may be related to growth requirements of these species. The botanical literature, as well as our personal observations, suggest that many of these species are light-demanding and unstable to persist in the shade of mature forest understory.

Habitat designations taken from the literature indicate that eight of the species listed in Table 1 are typically found in secondary forests, deciduous forests, river edges, and gallery forests on the savanna (Table 4). The only species reportedly restricted to closed evergreen forests was G. dewevrei. This was also the only important food tree that we found as seedlings and saplings in the shady understory.

Observations on some of the more widely ranging wild food species emphasize how agricultural activity favors the spread and local abundance of light-demanding species. For instance, Hamilton (1981) writes of C. schweinfurthii, in Uganda, as being most common in areas opened by intensive agriculture. Dalziel (1937) reports that in West Africa, seedlings of this species and Irvingia spp may be protected, and seeds planted in the vicinity of permanent villages. On our own study areas we saw seedlings and saplings of C. schweinfurthii most commonly associated with human-made openings, including old village sites and hunting camps.

Table 4. Habitat Requirements of Major Gathered Food Species

Species	Favored habitats	Source
Irvingia robur	Forests	Bamps (1948)
I. grandifolia	Forests	Bamps (1948)
I. excelsa	Evergreen and semi-deciduous forests	Bamps (1948), Hamilton (1981)
Treculia africana	Swamps, river banks, and gallery forest	Hamilton (1981), Lebrun and Gilbert (1954)
R. heudelotii	Secondary, deciduous, and gallery forests	T. Hart (unpublished data)
C. adolphi-friderici	Semi-deciduous forest	T. Hart (unpublished data)
G. dewevrei	Evergreen forest, forms extensive stands	Bamps (1948), T. Hart (unpublished data)
T. conophorum	Forests, old secondary forest?	Dalziel (1937), T. Hart (unpublished data), Dieterlan (1978)
Tieghemella africana	Forest	T. Hart (unpublished data)
E. guineensis	Secondary forest, farm bush, and cultigen	T. Hart (unpublished data)
C. schweinfurthii	Deciduous, gallery, and secondary forests	Dalziel (1937), Hamilton (1981), T. Hart (unpublished data), Lebrun and Gilbert (1954)
Dioscorea spp	Broken, secondary, and hill forests; also savanna edge	Burkill (1939), Coursey (1967, 1976), Schnell (1957)

The oil palm, *E. guineensis,* is even more strictly associated with human activity. This species was probably native to riparian habitats of forest fringe of the savanna (Moore, 1973). It does not grow in the primeval forest, although it is capable of persisting for many years in abandoned forest gardens and often forms groves around settlements (Hartley, 1977). Now prized by Mbuti, the oil palm could only have become available in the forest after the arrival of agriculture.

Wild yams have some of the same limitations as light-dependent food trees because of their habit of regularly renewing above-ground parts (Burkill, 1939). Most Zairean species of *Dioscorea* do not range into heavily forested areas. Those that do—for instance, *D. preussii, D. semperflorens, D. minutiflora, D. smilacifolia* and *D. baya*—are most frequent in fallow gardens and secondary forest (Burkill, 1939).

On our food plant surveys, yams were only found in secondary forest plots and not in mature forest plots (Table 3). Yams appear to be particularly rare in the region dominated by monospecific mbau forest. During our field work in the southern Ituri (Biasiko area) where large stands of mbau predominate, yams were only collected on drier, more open hilltops or in recent secondary forest. Even in these habitats, however, they were not abundant (Hart, 1979). On our central Ituri study area, Mbuti occasionally found and extracted yams from mixed forest. These tubers were often too small or woody to be edible.

Hladik, Bahuchet, Ducatillion, and Hladik (1984) undertook a survey of yams and other tuber-bearing plants in closed forest of northeastern Gabon and in semi-deciduous forests of the Lobaye region of Central African Republic. Many fewer yams were found on plots in the evergreen Gabon forest than in the Lobaye region, which is located near the savanna border and has a long history of agricultural settlement (Bahuchet, 1972). In one closed forest plot in Gabon, yams were completely absent; however, plants were found nearby in a more open setting along a road. The distribution of edible tubers found by Hladik *et al.* (1984) is in agreement with observation that yams require relatively open or disturbed environments.

However, there are other factors affecting yam availability as well. Hladik, et al. (1984) report that a number of species in the Lobaye forest produce large tubers (commonly up to 5 kg, and in one species, up to 200 kg). Although some of the same yam species occur in the Ituri region (Burkill, 1939), we never recorded tubers even as large as 5 kg excavated in the central Ituri Forest.

Major wild food species of primary forest are not only rare, but also occur as widely dispersed individuals. Thus, it is difficult for foragers to locate near concentrated food sources. This is an important difference between plant food resources available to Mbuti and those available to other hunting and gathering groups in more open environments. Pertinent comparisons include the tuberous food plants exploited by the Hadza which occur in large clumps (Vincent, in press), and *Ricinodendron rautanenii,* the mongongo nut, a staple in the diet of the Kalahari San, which forms extensive groves in edaphically well-defined areas (Lee, 1973). The only clumped food resources of the Mbuti include the oil palm (*E. quineensis*) and yams both gathered from secondary forest, and *G. dewevrei,* discussed more fully below.

Seasonality

Results of the fallen fruit transects show pronounced patterns of presence and absence for most major food species (Table 5). During the late wet season food availability is at a peak, with an average of 0.60 producing trees per kilometer of transect. Ripe fruit is scarce during the late dry and early wet season. This is consistent with observations that these are periods of peak flowering, whereas peak fruiting occurs during the wetter months (Janzen, 1967; Frankie, Baker, and Opler, 1974; and for Zaire forests, Dieterlen, 1978). During the dry and early wet seasons, individual trees of major food species bearing ripe crops of fruit or seed are especially rare, (0–0.151 trees/km). Mbuti describe most forest foods as unavailable during these months.

Observations from our earlier study in the southern Ituri, though less detailed, also reveal marked seasonality of gathered foods (Table 5). As in the central forest, there is a general peak in food availability and in gathering activity during the later wet season and an absence of the gathering of all but yams during the dry season (Hart, 1979).

Large areas of *G. dewevrei* flower and fruit gregariously. *G. dewevrei* seeds are large (mean 35 g wet weight), with a thin, easily removed seed coat covering soft, starchy cotyledons. During periods of peak seed fall, fresh seeds cover the forest floor for tens to hundreds of square kilometers at a density of three seeds/m² (T. Hart, 1985). The entire season of seed availability lasts only 2–3 months (October–December in the central and southern Ituri). If the seeds do not germinate quickly, they rot, are attacked by weevils, or are destroyed by rodents. By the beginning of the dry season, no edible *G. dewevrei* seed remains, even in mast years, and the mbau forest becomes empty from the perspective of human gatherers.

Irregularity from year to year is characteristic of many major food species. In the southern Ituri, all of the foods which were abundant in 1974 were scarce in 1973 (Table 5). Similarly, in the central Ituri during our

Table 5. Seasonality of Major Edible Food Species in the Ituri Forest

	Season			
	Dry	Early wet	Middle wet	Late wet
Central Ituri (1981-1983)				
Sampling periods	2	4	2	5
Transects (km)	23.4	30.5	37.2	44.8
Species:				
I. robur			x	x
I. grandifolia			x	x
I. excelsa			x	x
R. heudelotii			x	x
C. adolphi-friderici	x			x
G. dewevrei				x
Total food species	1	0	5	7
Fruit trees/1000 m[a]	0.151	0.000	0.137	0.643
	(0.082)	(0)	(0.117)	(0.262)
Southern Ituri (1973-1975)[b]				
Species[c]				
I. robur				S-A
I. gabonensis				S-A
Tetraculia sp.		S		S
G. dewevrei			S-A	S-A
T. conophorum		P	S-A	S-A
C. schweinfurthii				S-A
Dioscorea spp	P	P	P	P

[a] Number of trees bearing ripe fruit per 1000 m transect; mean and standard deviation (in parentheses) for sampleing periods.
[b] Source: Hart (1979).
[c] A = abundant, large quantities peresent or eaten once or more per week; S = scarce, eaten less than once per week and small quantities only present; S-A = scarce one year, abundant the next; and P = present, abundance not assessed.

1981–1983 study, most food plants produced well for only one year, and some, such as *T. conophorum,* appeared only during the third year.

The impact of seasonality may be allayed if food resources can be stored, or otherwise remain available between seasons. Several species, *R. heudelotti, C. adolfi-fredericii, Irvingia* spp, and *Tieghemella africana* have hard seed coats and exhibit delayed germination (T. Hart, 1985). These are among the characteristics of the mongongo nut (*R. rautanenii*), which allow it to be gathered by the !Kung San of the Kalahari as a year-round food staple (Lee, 1973).

We made a study of year-round availability of seeds of *R. heudelotti,* and congener of the Kalahari mongongo. For nine trees, sampled 6–9 months after fruit fall, seed density averaged 0.72 edible seeds/m^2 (*SE* =

0.296) immediately under the canopy. This compares with densities of 10–25 seeds at the end of fruiting season (J. Hart, unpublished data). Most seeds which remain under the trees at the end of the fruiting season are destroyed by rodents or rot over the succeeding months.

ANIMALS AND OTHER NONPLANT RESOURCES

Many modern Mbuti bands emphasize one of two hunting methods, archery or net-hunting. Spears are used in conjunction with both technologies. The distinction between net-hunters, occupying the western and southern forest, and archers, occurring in the east, was noted 20 years ago (Turnbull, 1965b). It has been less widely recognized that the geographical distribution of the two hunting technologies is not mutually exclusive. Archer and net-hunting bands co-occur in the eastern forest (Harako, 1976) and in the northern forest (J. Hart, unpublished data). Hunting bands in the western Ituri (Avakubi area) use both nets and bows extensively (J. Hart, unpublished data).

Hunting method is not associated with forest type. Net-hunting is practiced widely in the mixed forest of the central Ituri and in mbau-dominated district of the west and south. Similarly, archery is practiced in the mixed forests of the north and east and in the mbau district of the western Ituri by sedentary Mbuti associated with Bali agriculturalists. Hunting method appears to be better correlated with the ethnic identity of the agricultural associates of the Mbuti (Ichikawa, 1983). Bands that use nets are mostly associated with Bila, Ndaka, and Pere, all of whom are Bantu-speaking people, and who, according to the oral histories of at least some, introduced net hunting technology to the Mbuti (Harako, 1976; Hart, 1979; Putnam, 1948). Pygmy bands that do not use nets are generally associated with Sudanic-speaking Lese and related peoples. Net hunting may be currently advancing into the Lese areas under the impetus of commercial meat trade.

Both net and bow are suited for hunting a variety of small to medium-sized terrestrial animals. Only the bow, however, is effective against arboreal primates. The net hunt, nevertheless, may yield large quantities of meat (Harako, 1976; Tanno, 1976; Hart, 1978, 1979; Terashima, 1983; Ichikawa, 1983).

The net hunt is the principal hunting method practiced by Mbuti on our central Ituri study site. Our interest in hunting is specifically whether animals caught by Mbuti could provide a caloric substitute for scarce wild plant foods.

Seven species of antelope and the water chevrotain comprise over 90% of total net captures by weight (Hart, 1979). These ungulates range in size

Table 6. Small Ungulate Fauna of the Ituri Forest: Principal Wild
Meat Source of the Mbuti Net-Hunters

| | | Adult weight (kg) | | |
Species	Vernacular	Mean	SD	n
Small				
Neotragus batsei	Pygmy antelope	2.4	0.2	7
Cephalophu monticola	Blue duiker	4.8	0.7	60
Medium				
Hyemoschus aquaticus	Chevrotain	11.6	1.2	16
Cephalophus nigrifrons		13.6	1.3	7
Cephalophus leucogaster		16.7	1.1	16
Cephalophus weynsi	Red duikers	17.9	1.8	21
Cephalophus dorsalis		21.0	1.0	7
Large				
Cephalophus sylvicultor	Yellow-back duiker	68.0[a]		

[a] *Source:* Emmons, Gautier-Hion, and Dubost (1983).

from 2.5–68 kg (Table 6). The blue duiker *Cephalophus monticola* is the most frequently caught species (J. Hart, 1985).

Hunting Productivity

Table 7 shows hunting returns for eight Mbuti camps in the central Ituri study area. These camps are grouped by distance from permanent settlement. The final column reports kilograms of meat caught daily per kilogram human body weight, assuming each adult unit to be 40 kg, as calculated by Hill (1982). Days during which no hunt occurred are included in the calculation, as well as nonhunting members of the camp. The calculations were made as though all the meat was consumed, although this was never the case, as much of it was traded.

On a per human body weight basis, net hunting returns from the central Ituri are among the highest reported for any tropical hunting peoples studied to date (Hill, 1982). The average for all eight camps is 2.9×10^{-2} kg meat (daily) per kilogram human body weight. These returns are comparable to those reported from the Teturi-Mawambo area (Tanno, 1976), and more than twice the level reported from the southern Ituri (Hart, 1978). Factors that may account for lower catches in the southern Ituri forest are greater agricultural clearing and widespread market hunting

Table 7. Hunting Returns from Mbuti Camps in the Epulu Area

Distance[a]	Camp	Days	Hunts	Adult units (AU)[b]	Nets	Net meat (kg)	Total meat (kg)	Kg/AU/day total meat	Kg/BW/day × 10⁻² total meat[c]
Near	KK I	10	9	65.0	22	507	598	0.78	2.3
	KK II	7	6	34.5	16	253	253	1.05	2.6
	Eb	4	4	35.0	15	115	115	0.82	2.1
Intermediate	Ek	10	9	57.5	22	447	527	0.92	2.3
	T	9	8	52.5	20	535	535	1.13	2.8
	K III	5	5	39.0	9–21	222	222	1.14	2.9
Remote	I	5	5	33.0	12	283	283	1.72	4.3
	B I	6	6	63.0	24	555	640	1.69	4.2

[a] Distance from permanent settlement: near, less than 5 km; intermediate, 5–20 km; remote, greater than 20 km.
[b] Adult unit (AU): individuals 12 years or older = 1 AU; individuals less than 12 years = 0.5 AU.
[c] Kilograms total meat per kilogram body weight per day (1 AU = 40 kg).

(Hart, 1978). We also have evidence that extensive areas of mbau forest support lower ungulate populations than do mixed forest (J. Hart, 1985).

Meat as a Source of Energy

Fat content of animals caught determines whether they could serve as replacements for calories Mbuti now consume in the form of cultivated carbohydrate crops. If low in fat, meat protein must be metabolized for energy. This is an inefficient source of calories that puts a physiological strain on the body if carried on for prolonged periods (Speth and Spielman, 1983; Nelson, 1975; Stefansson, 1956).

We will concentrate on duikers as a source of meat calories. Mbuti kill other animals, but even among the archers, duikers are important game (Harako, 1976; R. Bailey, personal communication; D. Wilkie, personal communication). Several species, including pythons, pigs, leopards, and a number of viverrids are highly regarded for their fattiness. These species are either rare or otherwise infrequently caught.

We used the percentage of kidney covered by fat as an index of fattiness (KFI). The mesentery fat, including the kidney fat, was stripped and roasted if the KFI exceeded 40%. This corresponds to about 20 g of fat and tissue in blue duikers and up to 50 g or more in the largest duikers. Animals were likely to have high KFI only in the years of mast seed fall of forest dominants, especially *J. seretii* or *C. alexandri*. Even then animals remained fat only through the dry season. By early wet season, and over the rest of the year, KFI averaged less than 15%, with fewer than 10% of animals exceeding a KFI of 40% (Figure 3). Even if antelope carcasses had high KFI, low levels of lipids in the meat are evident. Mbuti do not consider duiker as fatty meat. Cooking produces no skimmable fat, and Mbuti prefer to cook their meat in generous quantities of palm oil when they have it.

It is interesting that contemporary Mbuti do not themselves consider meat an alternative to starch as a dietary staple, even when they have meat in abundance. Mbuti speaking KiBila and KiPakombe distinguish between protein hunger (*ekbelu*) and calorie hunger (*njala*). In the central Ituri, Mbuti often complained of *njala* in remote hunting camps. These camps had the highest per capita hunting returns, and large quantities surplus meat, dried for trade, but agricultural produce was scarce. Milton (1984), citing Silverwood Cope, reports the same phenomenon among the Maku hunters of the Amazon basin. When they ran out of cassava in the forest, no matter how much meat was in camp, "they have no food."

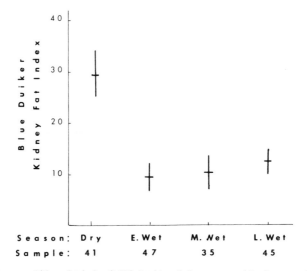

Figure 3. Average kidney fat index (±SE) for blue duiker captured in the central Ituri Forest, 1981-1983. Kidney fat index measured as percent of kidney covered by fat.

Honey and Other Insect Resources

Honey, alate termites, the grubs of palm beetles, and several species of caterpillars are highly sought wild foods. Both honey and termites are high in available calories (Wu Lueng, 1968). The seasonality of these foods, however, limits their importance in the diet to a few months of the year, as indicated by the studies of Hart (1979), Ichikawa (1981), and Bailey and Peacock (1988). These are not months of lowest wild plant food availability. Termite alate, for instance, emerge at the peak of the rainy season. In the southern Ituri, termites were eaten in November of 1973 and December of 1974 (Hart, 1979). During our 27-month study in the central Ituri, termites were gathered only in November 1981.

Honey becomes abundant only after mass flowering of nectar-providing, honeybee-pollinated trees. In the central Ituri, the most important flower species is *J. seretii*; in both 1981 and 1982, peak flowering was in June. *C. alexandri*, another important species, flowers earlier but still after the first rains. These flowering dates correspond with the honey season, which started in June 1973 and May 1974 in the southern Ituri (Hart, 1979; Ichikawa, 1981), and not until after May in the northern Ituri in 1981 (Bailey and Peacock, in press).

Honey, including that of stingless honey bees (*Meliponini*) may be found sporadically at other times of the year; but during some years, it never becomes abundant. Poor honey years are, in fact, common as the gregarious flowering of *B. laurentii* is supra-annual. *G. dewevrei,* significantly, is not a honey tree; the flowers are bird-pollinated and are not visited by *Apis mellifera,* the honeybee (T. Hart, 1985).

Palm grubs and caterpillars are apparently rare resources. The grubs are excavated from downed and rotting raphia palms whenever they are found. Downed palms are rare in the forest and are more frequent in abandoned gardens where they are owned by individual villagers who planted and then tapped them for wine. Mbuti may be thus constrained from exploiting many potential collecting sites. As for caterpillars, the Mbuti at Epulu claim they are highly prized food, but during the 27 months of our field work, we recorded no local outbreaks.

MBUTI GATHERING

Despite the general reference to the Mbuti as forest hunter–gatherers, the early literature contains no direct observations or evidence of Mbuti living in the closed equatorial forest for extended periods without agricultural food (Schebesta, 1933, 1936). Assertions that the Mbuti ". . . existed solely on forest foods for from three to six months, with ease" (Turnbull, 1965, p. 18, 1965b,c) were based on hearsay or assumptions and were not substantiated by direct observation.

Bailey (personal communication) and Bailey and Peacock (in press) report Mbuti in the northern Ituri spending 6 days without agricultural food and complaining of hunger in the process.

During the course of our earlier field work in the southern Ituri, J. Hart once stayed with about 30 Mbuti in remote forest who subsisted for 8 days on meat and mbau seeds collected from streams and rain puddles, and from which, apparently, tannins had been leached. When traders arrived in camp, the Mbuti switched to cassava and rice as dietary staples.

Although wild plant foods comprise only a small part of their current diet, Mbuti are, nevertheless, always on the lookout for edible, or otherwise useful, plants. Only in the case of special resources such as honey, however, is gathering the apparent motivation of their movements through the forest. In the central and southern Ituri, Mbuti tend either to be in camps near villages, where they provide garden labor in exchange for agricultural food, or else they are in forest hunting camps where they acquire meat to exchange for cassava, plantains, or rice.

Gathering of wild plant foods is done by both males and females. Both sexes participate in the net hunt and in the course of a day's hunt, they are likely to walk 5–10 km and will stop briefly to gather as opportunity presents itself. Mushrooms, net-making fiber, or leaf thatch are frequently gathered. Yams or other high-energy substitutes for agricultural foods are less frequently gathered.

Some gathered plant foods such as honey, *C. schweinfurthii* fruits, *Irvingia* nuts, edible fungi, termite alate, and oil palm fruits are highly prized by villagers and Mbuti alike. Special trips will be made to gather these foods. These gathering activities are instructive in that they illustrate how high dispersion and rarity of valued wild food plants make it difficult for Mbuti to locate camps near concentrations of specific food resources.

For example, in 1982, several Mbuti families collected fruits of *C. schweinfurthii* to sell to villagers. From their base camp at Epulu, the two nearest trees with fruit crops were 5 and 6 km away in different directions. Two people, working together, could collect and carry all ripe fruit available at a given tree in a single day. This crop would almost certainly not have been an adequate source of calories for more than a few people during the intervening days while they waited for more fruit to ripen on the tree.

Many wild plant foods gathered by Mbuti demand extensive processing before they can be eaten. This is particularly the case with yams, which are also labor intensive to extract. Most edible yam species are either deep-rooted and/or contain toxins (Burkill, 1939; Hladik et al., 1984). Excavation may entail hours of digging, and pits may extend down more than a meter. Most tubers, and all stem bulbils, must be soaked and some boiled repeatedly before they become edible.

Wild foods are widely exploited as "famine foods" throughout Africa during periods of crop failure and starvation (Dalziel, 1937; Coursey, 1976). Many species reported as commonly utilized are those we have discussed here, including yams, seeds of *R. heudelotti,* and fruits of *C. schweinfurthii.*

Nadine Peacock (personal communication) recently recorded exploitation of yams and the seeds of *T. conophorum* and *Treculia africana* by both Mbuti and villagers during food shortage after crop failure in the northern Ituri. She noted that yams were frequently dug from fallow gardens and secondary forest rather than from mature forest. She also reported that many people left, moving to areas not affected by famine. Most use of wild foods as famine staples in the Ituri appears to be on a short-term basis.

The only time we found Mbuti to subsist voluntarily for extended periods (2 weeks to a month) without a continuous supply of agricultural food was during periods of abundant *A. mellifera* honey (see also Ichikawa, 1981). Large bands break up at this time and small groups disperse over the forest (Turnbull, 1965a). Net hunting is reduced but not eliminated. Honey and bee larvae become dietary staples with addition of some meat, fish, and occasional agricultural produce.

DISCUSSION

To summarize, the Mbuti today are hunters. Wild plant foods are gathered, but they are considerably less important than agricultural produce as a source of energy in the diet. While Mbuti can identify, and will gather, a large number of edible species, only a small number of these are carbohydrate or oil-rich species with an adequate energy density to possibly substitute for agricultural food in their diet. With the exception of *G. dewevrei*, all of these species are uncommon in primary forest of the Ituri region. Furthermore, most wild plant foods are available only on an irregularly seasonal basis. Annually, there is a period of 5 months, and sometimes more, when the only gathered foods available are yams and the fruits of oil palm, both restricted primarily to secondary forest. Wild meat and honey, principal forest foods acquired today, could not, apparently, provide a staple source of dietary energy during this period. Honey is seasonal, being uncommon or absent during the period of wild plant food scarcity, and meat is lean with little fat at this time.

Speth and Spielman (1983) speculate that hunter–gatherers faced with shortage of plant foods would avoid reliance on protein as a calorie source by selecting meat with high fat content, storing fat and carbohydrate-rich foods, or by exchanging meat for fat or carbohydrate. The latter strategy is practiced by the Mbuti today. We suggest that neither of the other strategies would have been feasible for hunter–gatherers of closed equatorial forest in the absence of agriculture. Even with iron acquired from forest-shifting cultivators, the Mbuti catch few animals of high fat content. It seems more likely that hunter–gatherers would have lived instead in environments where energy-dense plant foods were more abundant.

Most of the important food species gathered by the Mbuti do not regenerate in closed forest environments, but are associated instead with more open habitats. In the closed evergreen forest of the Ituri, open habitats are not naturally common. Environments suitable for regeneration of these species have become more widely available with the introduction of agriculture into the forest.

The pattern of shifting cultivation, in which small areas of forest are opened and then shortly thereafter abandoned to regrowth, may mimic natural disturbances favored by light-demanding species (T. Hart, 1985). In a very real sense, shifting cultivation has extended the forest–savanna ecotone into the forest interior (Bailey and Peacock, in press). Many gathered plant species have become more abundant as a result.

Our observations of wild food availability bring into question earlier assertions, such as those of Turnbull (1965a), that the closed evergreen forest could provide Mbuti with a continuously abundant food supply. Assumptions such as Tanaka's (1978) that the Caesalpiniaceous forests of the Ituri provide abundant resources for hunter–gatherers, are unsupported by evidence. Instead, the data indicate that human food availability is localized and limited in both types of closed Caesalpiniaceae-dominated forest of the Ituri region.

The ecological observations presented here do not directly answer questions about the history of human occupation of the Ituri region. Several other lines of evidence suggest that current ecological conditions have not been stable. An understanding of past vegetation changes may be helpful in elucidating human history in the region.

Human occupation may have occurred during periods when the Caesalpiniaceous forests as we know them today were not present, as is suggested by findings at Matupi Cave (Van Noten, 1977). Recent dry periods of forest retraction in Africa occurred 3000 to 1600 years BP (Livingstone, 1975).

In the Epulu area we have found buried charcoal dated at 2290 ± 90 years before present (BP; Beta Analytic Inc. Coral Gables, Florida). If the vegetation was able to fuel numerous or large scale blazes, it was certainly drier and more open than it is today. Desmond Clark (personal communication) notes that the data for the central Ituri charcoal is not incompatible with dates for similar buried charcoal horizons in northeast Angola and Zambia. He suggests that widespread fires may have been of human origin, perhaps fired in conjunction with specialist hunting practices. In any case, the charcoal may be evidence of the use by hunter–gatherers of more open deciduous forest or woodland during a recent dry period in an area which is now closed evergreen forest. Light-dependent food plants, rare in the evergreen forest, may have been more abundant under such conditions.

Cultivation of crops probably entered the central African forest area with the spread of Bantu-speaking people out of the southern Cameroun area, commencing about 4000 BP (Ehret, 1982; Saxon, 1982). It now appears that the forest itself may not have been an insurmountable barrier to the advance of agriculturalists. Movements, however, were apparently funneled along major waterways, leaving large blocks of upland forest uninhabited (Bailey, 1979; Ehret, 1982). Other groups moved along the forest perimeter. It was from these environments that agriculturalists presumably entered the forest interior. Today, we find Mbuti hunters in contact with many ethnic groups of shifting cultivators and speaking the languages of the particular groups with whom they have contact, be it Bantu, Ubanguian, or Sudanic (Thomas and Bahuchet, 1983). These historical considerations, coupled with data on the distribution of important food plants, suggest the hypothesis that evergreen forests of the Ituri were essentially uninhabited until recently. Small-scale shifting cultivation has permitted hunter–gatherers to occupy these environments on a permanent basis. Our studies indicate that agriculture has made the forest a more hospitable environment, both by providing a reliable source of energy-dense foods, available through exchange, and by producing patches of secondary forest in which hunter–gatherers could forage.

Although now largely degraded, semi-deciduous and deciduous forests were once extensive north of the closed forest zone (Devred, 1958). Based on the habitat requirements of major food species, these forest and the savanna ecotones would have been a more likely habitat for hunter–gatherers without access to agricultural crops.

The Babinga pygmies of the Lobaye Forest (Central African Republic) currently occupy semi-deciduous and secondary forests, and provide several interesting comparisons with the Ituri Mbuti. Caesalpiniaceae, the dominant plant family in the Ituri, is replaced in the Lobaye by Ulmaceae, Sapotaceae, and Meliaceae (Bahuchet, 1972). The Lobaye Forest contains important food species, notably *Panda oleosa* and *Antrocaryon micraster,* which are rare or absent from the central Ituri. Like the Mbuti, the Babinga have long-standing trade relations with forest agriculturalists (Bahuchet and Guillaume, (1982). During the dry season, however, the Babinga spend considerable time gathering yams (Bahuchet, 1975).

We never found wild yams to be a major component of Mbuti diet in the Ituri forest. Further work investigating the distribution and abundance of yams, in particular in microhabitats where they might be common, such as drier hill forests, secondary forest, and the forest edge, is clearly needed.

There are many difficulties in trying to reconstruct the economic history of a hunting and gathering group. Important contributions can be made from diverse approaches (Colchester, 1984). An ecological analysis can reveal the potential of a given environment for various types of subsistence economies. It is important not only to determine the density of food resources in various vegetation types, but also to establish whether these habitats have been modified by agriculture or other human activities. In some cases, the use of secondary vegetation is obvious, but at other times, the imprint of past agriculture on the forest becomes obscure with age. In the case of the Mbuti, the ecological interpretation presented here may contribute to a reconstruction of Mbuti history as more archeological information becomes available from the Ituri Forest.

ACKNOWLEDGMENTS

Our study in the central Ituri Forest was supported by the United States Man and the Biosphere Program, federal grant numbers 4789-4 and 4789-6. We wish to thank the Institut Zairois pour la Conservation de la Nature for their aid and cooperation. We are particularly grateful to H. Breyne of the National Herbarium (Zaire) and L. Libens of the Jardin Botanique National (Belgium) who aided in plant identifications. Our colleagues in the field. R. Wrangham, N. Peacock, R. Bailey, and D. Wilkie generously shared ideas and unpublished data. R. Wrangham, R. Bailey, R. Hames, D. Livingstone, A. Millard, T. Miller, L. Robbins, T. Struhsaker, and D. Wilkie constructively criticized earlier drafts of this paper. We also wish to acknowledge our three anonymous reviewers, many of whose suggestions were incorporated into the final version. Our greatest thanks and appreciation are due the peoples of the Ituri Forest who, over the 5 years we have lived with them, have advanced our research and helped us in innumerable ways.

REFERENCES

Abruzzi, W. S. (1979). Population pressure and subsistence strategies among the Mbuti Pygmies, *Human Ecology* 7: 183–189.

Bahuchet, S. (1972). Etude écologique d'um campement de pygmées Babinga. *Journal d'Agriculture Tropicale et de Botanique Appliquée* 19: 509–559.

Bahuchet, S. (1975). Rapport sur une mission effectuée en saison seche en Lobayé. *Journal d'Agriculture Tropicale et de Botanique Appliquée* 22: 177–197.

Bahuchet, S., and Guillaume, H. (1982). Aka-farmer-relations in the northwest Congo Basin. In Leacock, E., and Lee, R. (eds.), *Politics and History in Band Societies.* Cambridge University Press, Cambridge, pp. 189–211.

Bailey, R. (1979). The early Bantu expansion: Alternate routes. Unpublished manuscript.

Bailey, R., and Peacock, N. (1988). Efe pygmies of northeast Zaire: Subsistence strategies in the Ituri Forest. In de Garine, I., and Harrison, G. (eds.), *Coping with Uncertainty in the Food Supply.* Oxford University Press, New York.

Bamps, P. (1948). *Flore d'Afrique Central.* Jardin Botanique National de Belgique, Domaine de Bouchout, Meise, Belgium.

Bose, S. (1964). Economy of the Onge of Little Andaman. *Man in India* 44: 298–301.

Bourlière, F., and Verschuren, J. (1960). *Introduction à l'Ecologie des Ongulés du Parc National Albert.* Institut des Parcs Nationaux du Congo Belge, Brussels.

Bultot, F. (1971). *Atlas Climatique du Bassin Congolais, Première Partie.* Publications de l'Institut National pour l'Etude Agronomique du Congo Belge, hors série. Brussels.

Burkill, I. (1939). Notes on the genus *Dioscorea* in the Belgian Congo. *Bulletin du Jardin Botanique de i'Etat, Bruxelles* 15: 345–392.

Cavalli-Sforza, L. (1972). Pygmies, an example of hunter–gatherers, and genetic consequences for man of domestication of plants and animals. In deGrouchy, J., Ebling, F., and

Henderson, I. (eds.), *Human Genetics: Proceedings of the Fourth International Congress of Human Genetics*. Excerpta Medica, Amsterdam, pp. 79–95.

Cavalli-Sforza, L. (1977). Biological research on African Pygmies. In Harrison, G. (ed.), *Population Structure and Human Variation*. Cambridge University Press, Cambridge, pp. 273–284.

Colchester, M. (1984). Rethinking stone age economics: Some speculations concerning the pre-Columbian Yanoama economy. *Human Ecology* 12: 291–314.

Coursey, D. (1967). *Yams*, Longmans, London.

Coursey, D. (1976). The origins and domestication of yams in Africa. In Harlan, J., Duvet, J., and Stemler, A. (eds.), *Origins of African Plant Domestication*. Mouton, Paris, pp. 383–408.

Dalziel, J. (1937). *The Useful Plants of West Tropical Africa*. Crown Agents for the Colonies, London.

Devred, R. (1958). La Végétation forestière du Congo Belge et du Ruanda-Urundi. *Bulletin de la Société Royale Forestière de Belgique* 6: 408–468.

Dieterlen, F. (1978). Zur phanologie des aquatorialen regenwaldes im Ost-Zaire (Kivu). Dissertations Botanicae 47, J. Cramer, Vaduz.

Eder, J. (1978). The calorie returns to food collecting: Disruption and change among the Batak of the Phillipine tropical forest. *Human Ecology* 6: 55–69.

Ehret, C. (1982). Linguistic inferences about early Bantu history. In Ehret, C., and Posnansky, M. (eds.), *The Archaeological and Linguistic Reconstruction of African History*. University of California Press, Berkeley, pp. 57–65.

Emmons, L., Gautier-Hion, A., and Dubost, G. (1983). Community structure of the frugivorous-folivorous forest mammals of Gabon. *Journal of Zoology, London* 199: 209–222.

Endicott, K. (1984). The economy of the Batek of Malaysia: Annual and historical perspectives. *Research in Economic Anthropology* 6: 29–52.

Frankie, G., Baker, H., and Opler, P. (1974). Comparative phenological studies of trees in tropical wet and dry forests in the lowlands of Costa Rica. *Journal of Ecology* 62: 881–919.

Gardner, P. (1972). The Paliyans. In Bicchieri, M. (ed.), *Hunters and Gatherers Today*. Holt, Rinehart and Winston, New York, pp. 404–447.

Gerard, P. (1960). Etude écologique de la forêt dense à *Gilbertiodendron dewevrei* dans la region de l'Uele. L'Institut National pour l'Etude Agronomique du Congo Belge, Série Scientifique No. 87, Brussels.

Hamilton, A. (1981). *A Field Guide to Uganda Forest Trees*. University Printery, Makere University, Kampala.

Hamilton, A. (1982). *Environmental History of East Africa: A Study of the Quaternary*. Academic Press, New York.

Harako, R. (1976). The Mbuti as hunters: A study of ecological anthropology of the Mbuti pygmies (I). *Kyoto University African Studies* 10: 37–99.

Harako, R. (1981). The cultural ecology of hunting behavior among Mbuti Pygmies in the Ituri Forest, Zaire. In Harding, R., and Teleki, G. (eds.), *Omnivorous Primates*. Columbia University Press, New York, pp. 499–555.

Hart, J. (1978). From subsistence to market: A case study of the Mbuti net hunters. *Human Ecology* 6: 325–353.

Hart, J. (1979). Nomadic hunters and village cultivators: A study of subsistence interdependence in the Ituri Forest of Zaire. Unpublished masters thesis in geography, Michigan State University, East Lansing.

Hart, J. (1985). A study of feeding ecology in a guild of African forest duikers. Unpublished Ph.D. doctoral dissertation in fisheries and wildlife, Michigan State University, East Lansing.

Hart, T. (1985). The ecology of a single-species dominant forest and a mixed forest in Zaire, equatorial Africa. Unpublished doctoral dissertation in botany and plant pathology, Michigan State University, East Lansing.

Hartley, C. (1977). *The Oil Palm* (2nd ed.). Longman, New York.

Hayden, B. (1981). Subsistence and ecological adaptations of modern hunter/gatherers. In Harding, R., and Teleki, G. (eds.), *Omnivorous Primates*. Columbia University Press, New York, pp. 344–421.

Hiernaux, J. (1977). Long-term biological effects of human migration from the African savanna to the equatorial forest: A case study of human adaptation to a hot and wet climate. In Harrison, G. (ed.), *Population Structure and Human Variation*. Cambridge University Press, Cambridge, pp. 187–217.

Hill, K. (1982). Hunting and human evolution. *Journal of Human Evolution* 11: 521–544.

Hill, K., Hawkes, K., Hurtado, M., and Kaplan, H. (in press). Seasonal variance in the diet of Ache hunter–gatherers in eastern Paraguay. *Human Ecology*.

Hladik, A., Bahuchet, S., Ducatillion, C., and Hladik, C. M. (1984). Les plantes à tubercules de la forêt dense d'Afrique centrale. *La Terre et La Vie* 39: 249–290.

Ichikawa, M. (1981). Ecological and sociological importance of honey to the Mbuti net hunters, Eastern Zaire. *African Studies Monographs (Kyoto)* 1: 55–68.

Ichikawa, M. (1983). An examination of the hunting-dependent life of the Mbuti Pygmies, Eastern Zaire. *African Study Monographs (Kyoto)* 4: 55–76.

Janzen, D. (1967). Synchronization of sexual reproduction of trees with the dry season in Central America. *Evolution* 21: 620–637.

Lebrun, J., and Gilbert, G. (1954). Une classification écologique des forêts du Congo. L'Institut National pour L'Etude Agronomique du Congo Belge, Série Scientifique No. 63, Brussels.

Lee, R. (1973). Mongongo: The ethnography of a major wild food resource. *Ecology of Food and Nutrition* 2: 307–321.

Livingstone, D. (1975). Late quaternary climatic change in Africa. *Annual Review of Ecology and Systematics* 6: 249–280.

Livingstone, D. (1980). History of the tropical rain forest. *Paleobiology* 6: 243–244.

Milton, K. (1984). Protein and carbohydrate resources of the Maku indians of northwestern Amazonia. *American Anthropologist* 86: 7–27.

Moore, H. (1973). Palms in the tropical forest ecosystems of Africa and South America. In Meggers, B., Ayensu, E., and Duckworth, W. (eds.), *Tropical Forest Ecosystems in Africa and South America: A Comparative Review*. Smithsonian Institute Press, Washington, D.C., pp. 63–88.

Nelson, R. (1975). Implications of excessive protein. In White, P., and Selvey, N. (eds.), *Proceedings of the Western Hemisphere Nutrition Congress IV*. Publishing Sciences Group, Acton, Massachusetts, pp. 71–76.

Peterson, J. (1978). Hunter–gatherer/farmer exchange. *American Anthropologist* 80: 335–351.

Putnam, P. (1948). The pygmies of the Ituri Forest. In Coon, C. (ed.), *A Reader in General Anthropology*. Yale University Press, New Haven, pp. 322–342.

St. Moulin, L. (1976). *Atlas des Collectivités du Zaire*. Universitaires du Zaire, Kinshasa.

Saxon, D. (1982). Linguistic evidence for the eastward spread of the Ubangian peoples. In Ehret, C., and Posnansky, M. (eds.), *The Archaeological and Linguistic Reconstruction of African History*. University of California Press, Berkley, pp. 66–77.

Schebesta, P. (1933). *Among Congo Pygmies*. Hutchinson, London.

Schebesta, P. (1936). *Revisiting My Pygmy Hosts*. Hutchinson, London.

Schnell, R. (1957). *Plantes Alimentaires et Vie Agricole de l'Afrique Noire. Essai de Phytogéographie Alimentaire*. Larose, Paris.

Schnell, R. (1976). *Introduction à la Phytogéographie des Pays Tropicaux (Vol. 3). La Flore et la Vegetation de l'Afrique Tropical.* Gauthier-Villars, Paris.

Schweinfurth, G. (1874). *The Heart of Africa* (2nd ed.). Marston, Low and Searle, London.

Sinha, R. (1972). The Birhors. In Bicchieri, M. (ed.), *Hunters and Gatherers Today.* Holt, Rinehart & Winston, New York, pp. 371–403.

Speth, J., and Spielman, K. (1983). Energy source, protein metabolism, and hunter–gatherer subsistence strategies. *Journal of Anthropological Archaeology* 2: 1–31.

Stanley, H. (1990). *In Darkest Africa.* Charles Scribner's Sons, New York.

Stefansson, V. (1956). *The Fat of the Land.* Macmillan, New York.

Tanaka, J. (1978). A study of the comparative ecology of African gatherer-hunters with special reference to San (Bushmen-speaking people) and Pygmies. *Senri Ethnological Studies* 1: 189–212.

Tanno, T. (1976). The Mbuti net-hunters in the Ituri Forest, Eastern Zaire. Their hunting activities and band composition. *Kyoto University African Studies* 10: 101–135.

Tanno, T. (1981). Plant utilization of the Mbuti pygmies. *Kyoto University African Study Monographs* 1: 1–53.

Terashima, H. (1983). Mota and other hunting activities of the Mbuti archers: A socio-ecological study of subsistence technology. *African Study Monographs (Kyoto)* 3: 71–85.

Thomas, J., and Bahuchet, S. (eds.) (1983). *Encyclopédie des Pygmées Aka: L'Introduction à lEncyclopédie Fasicule l.* Langues et Civilization à Tradition Orale (50), Etudes Pygmées IV, Centre National de la Recherche Scientifique, Paris.

Turnbull, C. M. (1965a). *Wayward Servants.* The Natural History Press, New York. Turnbull, C. M. (1965b). The Mbuti Pygmies: An ethnographic survey. *Anthropological Papers of the American Museum of Natural History* 50: 139–282.

Turnbull, C. M. (1965c). The Mbuti Pygmies of the Congo. In Gibbs, J. (ed.), *Peoples of Africa.* Holt, Rinehart & Winston, New York, pp. 279–317.

Van Noten, F. (1977). Excavation at Matupi cave. *Antiquity* 51: 35–40.

Vincent, A. (in press). Plant foods in savanna environments: A preliminary report of tubers eaten by the Hadza of northern Tanzania. *World Archaeology.*

Wu Lueng, W.-T. (1968). *Food Composition Table for Use in Africa.* U.S. Department of Health, Education and Welfare, and U.N. Food and Agriculture Organization.

3

Batak Foraging Camps Today: A Window to the History of a Hunting–Gathering Economy

James F. Eder

Hunter–gatherers rarely existed in total isolation, and since the advent of farming, most, like the Mbuti, had close contact with agriculturalists. Nevertheless, the prevalent assumption has been that as hunting and gathering societies take up farming, they (1) become more integrated with and often dependent upon the wider social system almost immediately and that (2) they make a sharp transition from mobility to sedentism.

Eder suggests that the nature and direction of the changes a hunter–gatherer society undergoes as it becomes increasingly incorporated into the wider society are to some extent determined by its own cultural characteristics. Using historical accounts, interviews with the oldest Batak, and comparative observations of other hunter–gatherer societies, he examines how, on Palawan Island in the Philippines, Batak hunting and gathering practices have changed over the past hundred years as they incorporated other practices into their subsistence system. He also shows that the Batak become more, not less, mobile as they become integrated into the wider society.

Eder's findings are based on seven criteria against which he measured changes in Batak hunting and gathering practices: Seasonality, encampment duration (mobility), encampment size, resource utilization,

Originally published in *Human Ecology: An Interdisciplinary Journal*, 16(1)(1988): 35–55.

James F. Eder, Department of Anthropology, Arizona State University, Tempe, Arizona 85287.

Case Studies in Human Ecology, edited by Daniel G. Bates and Susan H. Lees. Plenum Press, New York, 1996.

division of labor, hunting technology, and length of workday. He concludes that despite the fact that the overall yields of hunting and gathering for the Batak today ought to be higher than in the past (fewer Batak forage in the same location and they stay for shorter periods of time) they are in fact lower. Because the Batak are now engaging in a range of economic activities, no one activity will be as remunerative as if it had been pursued full time. However, the Batak successfully maintain themselves and have been quick to incorporate new technologies into their subsistence system.

This chapter concerns the impact that incorporation into wider social and economic systems has had upon the hunting–gathering economy of the Batak of the Philippines, a tropical forest foraging people inhabiting the mountains of central Palawan Island. Like most contemporary hunting–gathering peoples, the Batak no longer earn their subsistence exclusively by hunting and gathering. Rather, trade, shifting cultivation, and wage labor have come to be important sources of cash and subsistence, reflecting growing articulation with lowland Philippine economy and society over the past one hundred years. At the same time, however, the Batak do continue to earn about half their total subsistence from forest foraging, and they remain capable of retreating to forest camps in the more remote parts of their territory, there to subsist as full time hunter–gatherers for days, and even weeks, at a time.

That, in these circumstances, Batak hunting and gathering has somehow declined in importance relative to other economic activities during the past century is an obvious, but not very illuminating, observation. More interesting is the issue of the precise changes that such incorporation has brought to the practice of hunting and gathering itself. A direct focus on change promises, on the one hand, to contribute to a better understanding of what aboriginal Batak life—or at least Batak life one hundred years ago—was in fact like. This same focus, on the other hand, should also contribute to a greater understanding of the process of incorporation, of non-state societies into state societies, and of why that process has been so variable in outcome.

A openness to the range of possibilities for change in a hunting–gathering economy is particularly appropriate to the study of hunter–gatherers such as the Batak, whose continuing, part-time ability to live off the land full time may be deceiving. Certainly an air of authenticity appears to surround contemporary Batak hunting and gathering, which is largely pursued at transitory forest camps, geographically separate from the settlements where they today nominally reside. Batak camps, consisting of a small number of temporary leaf shelters, are characteristically remote in location and pristine in setting. Only the presence of a few consumer durables and some occasional agricultural or purchased foods hauled to camp suggests that Batak hunting-gathering in the past was not otherwise simply a larger version of what survives in the present. Such leaps of faith are abetted by the Batak themselves, who readily assure camp visitors (and may themselves believe) that, "This is how we used to live all the time."

While forest camp life is arguably the most traditional component of contemporary Batak subsistence economy, my aim in this chapter is to call attention to systematic and profound demographic, economic, and social organizational differences between the hunting–gathering way of life that can be observed in such camps today and the hunting–gathering way of life that existed among the Batak as recently as fifty years ago. But if contemporary Batak forest camps hence do not provide a clear window to the past of an undisturbed foraging economy, they do nevertheless provide a useful arena in which to observe (or at least to speculate about) the historical distortions engendered in that economy by incorporation into the Philippine nation-state. Using fragmentary but revealing turn-of-the-century historical accounts, memory data from the oldest Batak, inference, and comparative observations of other foraging peoples, I explore below how Batak hunting and gathering may have changed over the past one hundred years along the following dimensions: Seasonality, encampment duration, encampment size, resource utilization, division of labor, technology, length of workday, and labor productivity.

In this enterprise, I will eschew discussion of such collateral issues as when, precisely, the Batak joined some outside social system, or what the precise boundaries of that social system are. Concerning the first issue, however, I certainly do not maintain that the Batak were "pristine" hunter–gatherers down through 1880 (my baseline). My position is simply the pragmatic one, that until about 1880 the Batak appear to have been demographically and culturally intact, relatively isolated, and largely self-sufficient. After about 1880, in contrast, and particularly after about 1930, intensification of contact with wider Philippine society—seen most visibly in growing immigration of lowland Filipino settlers to Palawan Island—extensively restructured Batak subsistence economy. This chapter hence concerns one aspect of my continuing research on the process of change among the Batak themselves, change that has so overwhelmed their individual and collective adaptive capacities as to threaten them with physical and cultural extinction (Eder, 1987).

THE BATAK

The Batak are distributed in a series of eight local groups, each group identified with a particular river valley on the east side of Palawan island north of Puerto Princesa City. Local groups today range in size from 3 to 24 households and are located 3–10 km. upstream from a coastal lowland, "Filipino" village. These villages were, in turn, founded beginning in the late 19th century by land-seeking settlers from neighboring Cuyo Island and elsewhere in the Philippines. Before this process of coastal settlement began, the Batak may have numbered 500–600 individuals; today they number less than 400 individuals, and many of these are the offspring of recent Batak marriages with lowlanders.

It may be presumed (but only presumed) that at some time in their aboriginal past, the Batak were pure hunter–gatherers, isolated from other populations. Certainly, according to their own folklore, the Batak were once exclusively hunter–gatherers. They lived only, it is said, in temporary forest camps, exploiting the same forest foods that they utilize today: Wild pig, flying squirrel, jungle fowl, wild honey, wild yams, wild greens, and an assortment of fish, mollusks, and crustaceans. Hunting–gathering remains today a major component of Batak subsistence economy; indeed, they retain the capability to pursue this activity on an exclusive basis for an extended period of time. Not only do small groups of households still regularly gather in forest camps to live off the land, but during recent periods of severe social stress, such as World War II and an unsuccessful government effort at forced relocation in 1970, entire local groups have retreated to the forest for a year or more.

Trade, horticulture, and wage labor, however, are also characteristic Batak economic activities today. Actually, trade in commercially valuable forest products, a mainstay of tribal subsistence economies throughout insular Southeast Asia, is probably not new at all to the Batak. They collect and sell honey, rattan, and Manila copal in order to purchase rice, clothing, tobacco, salt, and other consumer wants; their dragon jars, brassware, and porcelain heirloom goods testify that they have traded for some time. By some estimates (e.g., Kress, 1977: 46) the Chinese have traded directly or indirectly with Palawan for a thousand years; Batak contact with sea-going traders, whether Chinese or Muslim, is likely in the hundreds of years, at least.

Batak agriculture may also be of some antiquity. Batak swiddens today are planted almost exclusively in upland rice and are not the idylls of ecological diversity described by Conklin (1957), Geertz (1963), and others for Southeast Asian tribal societies. Some case may be made that upland rice

**Table 1. Proportional Contributions of Different
Subsistence Activities to Total Annual Food Supply
and Cash Income of Langogan Batak (1981)**

Activity	Food Supply[a]	Cash income[b]
Hunting and gathering		
Subsistence consumption	25	—
Sales/exchange	25	50
Agriculture		
Subsistence consumption	25	—
Sales/exchange	5	10
Wage labor	20	40
Total	100	100

[a] Valued in calories.
[b] Includes cash spent for food.

is a recent acquisition, one conceivably only brought to the Batak at the
end of the 19th century by the first lowland migrants to Palawan. Swiddening itself, however, is likely older.

Contact between the Batak and wider socioeconomic systems intensified after the first lowland settlers began to arrive, apparently during the
latter half of the 19th century. As Batak involvement with lowlanders increased, their desires for lowland foods and manufactured goods grew
apace. Lowlanders who could provide such goods became a new—and
essential—resource to the Batak. Everywhere, patron–client ties evolved,
tying individual Batak to individual lowlanders.

The earliest historical accounts of the Batak (Miller, 1905; Venturillo,
1907) show that all of the economic activities reviewed here were present
by 1900. Hunting–gathering has probably declined somewhat in relative importance in recent decades, although I estimate that it still provides about
50% of the diet, either directly or through the trade of honey and Manila
copal. Shifting cultivation and wage labor provide the remainder; see
Table 1, which shows the sources of food and cash income for one particular group of Batak during 1981.

These various post-1880 changes in Batak subsistence economy reori-
ented Batak economic affairs and social relationships toward greater participation in lowland Filipino society, even as they reflected incremental
land alienation and other threats to Batak resources by Filipino settlers.
These circumstances underlaid two fundamental changes in Batak settlement pattern, discussion of which will in turn help illuminate the more
specific changes in Batak hunting and gathering. The first settlement pattern change, dating to the closing decades of the nineteenth century, was

the emergence of a pattern of seasonal residence in upland rice fields. Only after the arrival of lowland settlers in Palawan, it is said, did Batak commitment to agriculture increase to the point that they actually constructed houses and lived in their rice fields. Previously, particularly when root crops still dominated Batak agriculture, periodic visits to swidden fields were accommodated to a pattern of year-round residence in temporary forest camps. Today, during the agricultural season, the reverse is true; a Batak's field house is a base from which periodic foraging visits to the forest are made.

A second settlement pattern change occurred during the early decades of the 20th century, when settlers and government officials began to encourage the Batak to come down out of the mountains and establish permanent, lowland-style settlements on the coastal plain. In a pattern of movement begun after World War II and continuing to the present, each local group has, on several occasions, relocated its settlement site further up its respective river valley, moving just ahead of advancing lowland populations. This stepwise series of movements has provided the Batak with a modicum of isolation while allowing them to maintain convenient spatial access both to forest resources and to lowlanders themselves. The map of central Palawan Island in Figure 1 shows the locations of the eight present-day Batak settlements, relative to the five 1930s reservations and to contemporary lowland Filipino villages in the region.

Despite the wrenching experience of lowland colonization and associated, fundamental changes in subsistence economy and settlement pattern, the Batak still inhabit the same territory—indeed, the same river valleys—that they inhabited in 1880. But now that outsiders also reside in this territory, there is a pervasive insecurity about the Batak's own tenurial status. Legally, the Batak are indigenous inhabitants on public forest land not yet officially released for settlement by the Bureau of Forest Development. If this land is released, the Batak face an unequal competition with lowland settlers for private ownership. Batak land has been alienated in the past and, with considerable justification, they fear that more will be alienated in the future.

BATAK HUNTING AND GATHERING: THEN AND NOW

This section examines what appear to be the principle demographic, economic, and social organizational differences between Batak hunting–gathering today and as it may have been in the past.

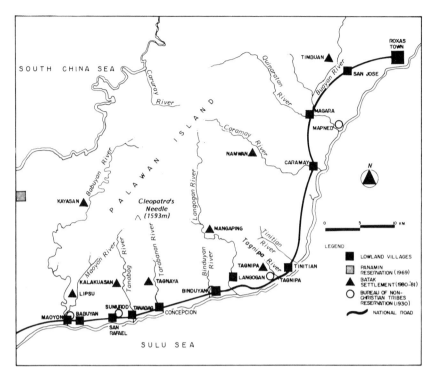

Figure 1. Batak territory today.

Seasonality

While it has become a truism that few or none of the world's surviving hunter–gatherers still hunt and gather on a full-time basis, rarely has the displacement of hunting and gathering in favor of other subsistence activities been uniform across the seasons. Thus, while it might be that a particular foraging people still derive 50% of their total subsistence from hunting and gathering, it is unlikely that during each week of the year (or even during each month of the year), foraging accounts for exactly (or even approximately) 50% of subsistence activities. If only because the newer economic activities, such as agriculture, are often themselves seasonal, hunting–gathering becomes seasonal as well, waxing and waning in importance over the course of the year.

To explore possible seasonalities in contemporary Batak hunting and gathering, it is useful to return to a focus in settlement pattern, moving from the longer-term evolutionary changes discussed above to short-term cyclical changes. During 1981 I studied the activities of one local group of Batak, composed of sixteen households residing along the Langogan River. Over the course of the year, I tracked their separate movements between settlement houses, swidden field houses, and a variety of transitory camps: The forest foraging camps discussed above; settlement camps, which appear during the height of the dry season, particularly in April, when warm nights and mosquitos drive the Batak out of their settlement houses and into cooler, open sleeping areas at the river's edge or short distances inside the forest; swidden camps, which appear during the same period and provide a temporary residence during the slash-and-burn phase of the swidden cycle, until swidden field houses are constructed in May; and lowland camps, established downstream to take advantage of wage labor opportunities on lowland farms.

Table 2 shows the percentage of time the sixteen households at Langogan allocated to each of these various residential locations during 1981, classified by month. Data for May, November, and January are estimated.[1] During the six months from May to October, from rice planting to rice harvesting, the swidden field house is the primary residential location. During the leisurely, postharvest months of November, December, and January, the settlement is the focus of activity. During February, March, and April, the Batak are primarily on the move between encampments of various kinds. Overall, Table 2 shows that the Batak spend about 60% of their time in settlement or swidden houses and about 40% in encampments.

Table 2 shows that forest camps in particular are clearly more important during the first six months of the year (which are primarily dry and non-agricultural) than during the last six (which are primarily rainy and swidden-oriented). Given that the bulk of contemporary hunting and gathering occurs during residence at forest camps, these data suggest a marked seasonality in the present importance of hunting and gathering.

Encampment Duration

Emerging seasonalities in the importance of hunting and gathering in turn had important implications for camp duration and camp size.

[1]Knowledge of where a Batak spends the night, of course, is only a partial indicator of what he or she is doing. Hence Table 2 provides only a crude measure of how Batak allocate their time to different subsistence activities over the course of the year. In particular, subsistence tasks are not specific to particular residential locations. Thus hunting–gathering is a more important component of Batak subsistence economy than the percentage of days spent in forest camps might indicate, because all residential locations afford some opportunity for nearby foraging. Similarly, the Batak commute to some of their wage labor and coffee-picking jobs from their swidden or settlement houses.

Table 2. Batak Settlement Pattern: Percent of Time Allocated to Various Residential Locations Classified by Month

Month	Houses		Camps				Visiting other local groups
	Settlement	Swidden	Settlement	Swidden	Forest	Lowland	
January[a]	50.0				30.0	20.0	
February	6.3		13.4	31.3	48.2		
March	10.7		9.8	50.0	19.2	10.7	
April	3.6		58.9	26.8	4.0	1.3	
May[a]	5.0	45.0		5.0	45.0		
June	9.8	45.5			34.8	5.4	4.5
July	10.7	62.5			25.9		1.8
August	14.3	82.1			2.7	0.9	
September	6.7	92.4			0.9		
October	20.5	63.4			4.5		11.6
November[a]	79.5	11.6			8.9		
December	79.5	11.6			8.9		
	24.7	35.0	6.8	9.4	19.4	3.2	1.5

[a] Estimated.

Occupation periods at a given location are considerably shorter today than in the past, being a matter of days (two to seven, in my observations) rather than weeks (up to three or four, in the memories of older informants). The reason is that the Batak simply have a lot of other important things going on in their lives which demand their attention besides hunting and gathering.

In the past, it is said, when a group of Batak camped at a particular location began, after two to three weeks, to deplete local resources or to tire of the area, it simply moved elsewhere in the forest and established a new camp. This memory estimate of past forest camp mobility, equivalent to about 17–26 residential moves per year, is consistent with ethnographic observations of other, more isolated Southeast Asian hunting–gathering populations.

Among the Batak today, however, individuals must reconcile the demands of hunting and gathering against the demands of shifting cultivation and the market economy. In the face of such scheduling considerations, it is said, a Batak is only in camp a few days before he starts remembering the fresh batteries he ordered from a lowland settler, the chickens he left behind at his settlement house, or his unguarded swidden. Even more pressing may be the need to deliver some newly found wild honey to an impatient creditor or to locate lowland buyers for some highly marketable (but perishable) wild pig meat. Hence, not only are contemporary forest encampments of limited duration, but Batak (with occasional exceptions) leave them not to establish other forest camps but to return to their settlement or swidden houses.

Encampment duration today is relatively short, and yet the Batak spend 20% of their time in forest camps and another 20% in other kinds of camps (Table 2). This apparent paradox calls attention to a wider change in Batak subsistence economy as a whole: Residential mobility is more frequent now than in the past, a phenomenon also noted by Endicott (1979) among the Batek, a foraging people of peninsular Malaysia undergoing broadly similar processes of change. Hence, the demands of subsistence multidimensionality and a high level of social stress in the Batak environment lead the Batak to move back and forth between their various contemporary residential locations (settlement and swidden houses, forest, and lowland camps) more frequently than they had changed camp residence under the aboriginal foraging regime. This finding raises obvious serious questions about the accuracy and conceptual utility of evolutionary models which postulate a linear transition from mobility to sedentism as hunting–gathering societies take up agriculture and are incorporated into wider social systems (Eder, 1984).

Encampment Size

Similarly, encampments today are a lot smaller than they were before. Rarely, today, will more than seven households camp together at a particular location; in the past (and even as recently as the 1930s), encampments of up to 30 or 40 households were common. In part this change has occurred because of secular demographic processes (population decline, local group retreat to the interior) which do not concern subsistence or seasonality per se—although similar demographic changes have also been experienced by other hunting–gathering groups.

Encampments were larger in the past, however, not simply because there were more Batak, but because entire local groups of Batak often encamped together. Indeed, on occasion two entire local groups would encamp together. Today, the two largest local groups still total 24 and 16 households, respectively, but never in recent memory have the members of either one of these groups all encamped together as a group. Instead, as we have seen, encampments of two to seven households are customary. Underlying this shift to smaller encampments are some of the same scheduling considerations affecting camp duration. Just as contemporary encampments are relatively short because those camped together have other subsistence activities that require attention, relatively few people camp together to begin with because the scheduling considerations in question are somewhat different for each Batak household. Thus each household's swidden field is in a different location, the timing of each household's agricultural cycle is somewhat different, each household has a different set of ties and obligations to lowlanders, and so on. In effect, not everyone can get away to the forest at the same time.

Resource Utilization

The Batak today utilize a narrower range of forest plant and animal resources than they say they did in the past. Whenever I visited an encampment I routinely recorded all subsistence foods brought into camp while I was there, and I also inquired about other such foods obtained since the camp was established. Animal foods obtained and consumed at Langogan forest camps during my 1981 stay were wild pig, gliding squirrel, Palawan tree shrew, Palawan peacock pheasant, wild chicken, turtle, fish, eel, mollusks, shrimp, land crabs, and honey. The plant foods consumed were wild yams, greens, mushrooms, and rattan and palm pith. I no doubt missed some foods (certain wild fruits, for example, that may be consumed along the trail), but the foregoing are certainly the major wild foods consumed today.

Wild resource utilization likely has narrowed for two reasons. First, as argued earlier, wild resources which are themselves seasonally available may no longer be utilized if their seasons of availability coincide with a season when hunting and gathering is today of little importance to the Batak. The common tuber abagan, for example, said to have once been a major carbohydrate source during September, October, and November, is now virtually ignored at Langogan, because its period of greatest availability coincides with the rice harvest. Second, a variety of latter-day cultural circumstances and values influence Batak decisions about wild resource utilization. On the one hand, the Batak are acutely aware that their continued use of many forest foods helps mark them as "primitives" in the eyes of lowland Filipinos (although a few such foods, like wild pig, honey, and mushrooms, are highly valued by lowlanders). On the other hand, the Batak themselves routinely obtain a variety of lowland foods, such as coffee, sugar, and baked goods, and it seems reasonable to assume that access to such foods may have altered Batak preferences for some traditional foods (wild fruits, for example).

Division of Labor

Subtle changes in the organization and division of labor have occurred as well. First, certain traditional foraging activities that required the participation of large numbers of people are now no longer possible. In one such activity, a group pig hunt, a line of women would ascend a mountainside, shouting and beating the brush, driving any pigs in the area toward a line of waiting archers at the top. A group of at least 15–20 men and women was required, with groups of 50–60 men and women said to be optimal. Similarly, group fish stunning, today still practiced on tributary streams, was one practiced on entire rivers, when 30 or 40 adults could be still mobilized to gather and pound sufficient quantities of the tree bark that contained the stunning agent.

Other group foraging activities have become less common due to game depletion. In decades past, when wild pigs were more commonly encountered (and when hunting dogs were more numerous and better nourished), two or three men would often go out to hunt together with their spears and dogs. Such tactics have today lost ground to a more traditional hunting strategy, in which men go out singly to ambush pigs from blinds with bows and arrows or, more recently, with homemade guns. In fact, in the entire Batak population, only a few men remain who still hunt pigs using dogs.

Finally, during the swidden harvest months of August, September, and October, forest camps tend to be occupied by men only; women stay behind in the rice fields to harvest. Over the entire year, and largely because of such divisions of labor between two different economic activities, husbands and wives sleep separately almost 10% of the time, a phenomenon with no apparent aboriginal counterpart.

Hunting Technology

While bow and arrow hunting is unquestionably Batak, other hunting weapons, like the just-noted homemade guns, appear to have come (or gone) in this century. Monkeys and other small animals were apparently taken in the past with the blowgun—also once used to repel would-be Muslim slave raiders. How important the blowgun may have been for subsistence purposes, in comparison to the bow and arrow, is impossible to know, for the weapon fell into disuse after World War II. It may be that changing dietary preferences and growing market involvement led the Batak to abandon the blowgun about the time they began using spears and hunting dogs and, perhaps, became more preoccupied with hunting wild pigs.

Length of Workday

Time allocation was studied using a sort of all-day follow of the precise subsistence, domestic, and leisure activities pursued by a group of Batak residing at forest foraging camps and elsewhere (see Eder, 1987: 72-73). Table 3 displays pooled time allocation data for three forest camps studied in this fashion. It shows that men and women devote an average of 4.8 hours per day to subsistence, in my coding, activities such as fishing, honey collecting, jigging for eels, looking for turtles, and so on, which generally took a Batak away from camp (and hence include travel times). Men and women devote an additional 3.6 hours per day to such domestic activities as processing food, cooking and eating, bathing, and collecting firewood. Finally, they devote one hour per day to manufacturing or repairing various weapons and implements. While these particular conclusions are based on a total of only seven days of observations, I visited and observed informally numerous other forest camps in the course of my fieldwork, and time allocation at the three camps described here appears to be fairly representative of contemporary camp life in general. In any case and depending, or course, on one's notions about what constitutes work, the Batak would appear to keep fairly busy while at their camps today.

Table 3. Time Allocation at Batak Forest Camps (1981)

Camp location	Dates	Number of observations[a]		Percent of adult time (24-hour day)					
		Adults	Hours	Subsistence	Domestic activities	Tool manufacture and repair	Leisure	Illness	Childcare
Papandayan	3/15-3/17	7	48	21.6	15.4	2.0	56.9	2.9	1.2
Kaybacong	4/7-4/9	13	48	15.0	13.1	7.1	60.7	0.8	1.3
Ganed	5/23-5/26	2	77	23.7	15.9	3.1	57.3	—	—
Mean[b]				20.1	14.8	4.1	58.3	1.2	0.8
Mean expressed as hours in a 24-hour day				4.8	3.6	1.0	14.0	0.3	0.2

[a] Coded observations made at 15-minute intervals.
[b] Weighting data for each case equally.

In the absence of comparable data on time allocation at forest camps in the past, no firm conclusions can be drawn about possible changes in this regard. An inferential case can be made, however, that the Batak work longer hours, i.e., devote a greater proportion of their time to productive activities, under contemporary forest-dwelling conditions than in the past. First, at least some of the contemporary foraging effort of men is directed at the market as well as at subsistence; all households would like to return from a forest camp to the settlement not only with the night's meal but with some honey or pig meat to sell. Second, some of the work activities of women at contemporary camps involve weaving such agriculturally related articles as harvesting baskets and rice-drying mats.

DISCUSSION

It is now widely noted that hunter–gatherers, no less than other non-state peoples, have long been subject to the influence of—if not actually incorporated into—wider social and economic systems (e.g., Schrire, 1984). Less well appreciated is the active role that incorporated peoples of all sorts themselves play in influencing the direction of the incorporation process, and hence their own futures (Hall, 1986: 399). In the case at hand, the sorts of changes that occurred in Batak subsistence economy over the past one hundred years, in camp size, in resource utilization, in labor organization, and the like, clearly reflect growing market articulation with lowland Filipino society. Equally clearly, however, the nature and direction of these same changes is grounded in the characteristic economic, social, and cultural attributes of the Batak themselves (see Hall, 1983: 589–591). The discussion here has been limited to changes in hunting and gathering, but this same interplay of endogenous and exogenous factors has influenced the directions of change in all subsistence activities, and, therefore, the relative appeal of those activities. Hence I close, somewhat speculatively, by suggesting how the changes discussed here, in the practice of hunting and gathering, may slowly be eroding the overall appeal of hunting and gathering itself.

Taking the returns to hunting and gathering, whether measured in calories or in protein, as a surrogate for the overall appeal of hunting and gathering, it would seem at first glance that such returns ought to be higher today than before: Fewer Batak forage at a given location, and they don't stay as long. On energetic grounds, in other words, hunting and gathering should be as remunerative a subsistence choice as ever for the Batak, and if its practice has slowly declined in this century (as indeed it has), then the explanation must either be that alternative economic activities are even more remunerative, or that factors other than levels of remuneration (e.g., political necessity; cultural preferences) explain choice-making in subsistence activities.

These are complex issues which cannot be pursued in their entirety here. Elsewhere, however, I have argued that none of contemporary Batak subsistence activities are very remunerative. Thus, if the precise mix of foraging, shifting cultivation, trade, and wage labor that the Batak pursue today is the outcome of some sort of optimization calculus, it is only optimization in the sense of making the best of a very bad deal—a deal colored by clientage and land insecurity and in which a Batak's subsistence behavior is as responsive to the demands of outside peoples and social systems as it is to his own needs (Eder, 1987: 52–102).

Here, I will simply explore one aspect of this issue by suggesting why, the first glance argument offered above notwithstanding, the returns to hunting and gathering today may well be lower than in the past. First, the shorter duration of camp occupation makes round trip travel more costly; i.e., the energetic costs of getting there and back from the settlement must be amortized over several days, rather than several weeks. It may be, of course, that the Batak do not locate their camps as far away from the settlement and from one another as they once did, but any energetic advantage here is likely more than offset by lower returns due to resource depletion in oft-visited areas. Certainly, the return to eel fishing and mollusk gathering, for example, are dramatically lower in the vicinity of the settlement (itself often a base for short foraging trips) than they are upriver (Eder, 1987: 79–81). More importantly, the wild pig population, as just noted, appears badly depleted in the more accessible areas. As mobile as the Batak continue to be, if they do not make as full a use of their traditional territory that they once did, the returns to their foraging efforts may have suffered apace.

Second, regardless of location, the energetic costs of travel to and from forest camps are high because the Batak bring along more baggage than they used to. Pots and pans, flashlights, radios and even radio-phonographs are among the items that Batak take to camp today.

Third, the relatively small number of individuals foraging in the vicinity of contemporary forest camps may in fact be too small for optimal resource exploitation. The more men who are off hunting pigs, for example, the more likely that at least one will encounter and kill a pig—a pig large enough to feed the entire camp. At contemporary camps, however, only a few adult men are available to hunt pigs.

Finally, the narrowed diet breadth of camps is not necessarily in the direction of greater energetic efficiency in foraging. Cultural factors, themselves sensitive to outside influences, help determine, as we have seen, diet choice and hence, foraging strategies. The large amount of time that Batak men continue to devote to wild pig hunting, for example, may have less to do with any relative abundance of pigs or any Batak success in obtaining them than with the fact that pig meat is a very tasty—and marketable—food. Such behavior, furthermore, could conceivably be abetted by the circumstance that the Batak appear to be less risk aversive in their foraging activities than they may have needed to be in the past, given that a Batak today can draw upon lowland traders and his own agricultural stores for part of his food supply. Again, in some areas Batak are accustomed to collecting and selling Manila copal and using the proceeds to purchase milled rice. At least during some months of the year, such Batak would obtain about 50% percent more food calories per hour of work expended if they instead simply dug and processed the most common species of wild yam (Eder, 1978).

In any case, it is certainly possible in principle that Batak hunting and gathering today is not as remunerative or successful as it once was; nothing else the Batak do on a parttime basis appears to be as remunerative or successful as when that same activity is pursued full time. This is a sort of "jack of all trades, master of none" argument, but I think that it has some merit. The case is most readily made with agriculture. The Batak are widely stereotyped as lazy by lowlanders precisely because, in the eyes of lowlanders, they are lazy farmers. Stripped of its ethnocentrism, there is some truth to this observation. Because of the competing demands of other economic activities on their time, the Batak do not invest the amount of labor in agriculture that lowlanders do. More particularly, they do not invest enough labor in agriculture, e.g., in weeding, in guarding, to realize the returns to land and labor that lowlanders do (see Eder, 1988). Hence we should at least entertain the possibility that, because of competing demands on their time, the Batak are not as successful at hunting and gathering as they might be—and as they perhaps once were.

ACKNOWLEDGMENTS

Fieldwork among the Batak during the summer of 1972 was supported by an N.I.M.H. Predoctoral Research Grant; during the summer of 1975, fieldwork was supported by an Arizona State University Faculty Grant-in-Aid; and from August 1980–December 1981, fieldwork was done while on sabbatical leave from Arizona State University and supported by a Wenner-Gren Foundation Grant-in-Aid. A preliminary version of this paper was presented at the 82nd annual meeting of the American Anthropological Association, Chicago, IL, November 16–20, 1983. I would like to thank Tom

Headland for helpful comments on an earlier draft of the present manuscript, and I also acknowledge permission from the University of California
Press and *American Anthropologist* to use previously published material.

REFERENCES

Conklin, H. C. (1957). *Hanunoo Agriculture.* Food and Agricultural Organization, Rome.
Eder, J. F. (1978). The caloric returns to food collecting: Disruption and change among the
    Batak of the Philippine tropical forest. *Human Ecology* 6: 55–69.
Eder, J. F. (1984). The impact of subsistence change on mobility and settlement pattern in
    a tropical forest foraging economy: Some implications for archaeology. *American Anthro-
    pologist* 86: 837–853.
Eder, J. F. (1987). *On the Road to Tribal Extinction: Depopulation, Deculturation, and Maladap-
    tation among the Batak of the Philippines.* Berkeley: University of California Press.
Eder, J. F. (1988). Hunter–gatherer/farmer exchange in the Philippines: Some implications
    for ethnic identity and adaptive well-being. In Rambo, T., Gillogy, K., and Hutterer, K.
    (eds.), *Ethnic Diversity and the Control of Natural Resources in Southeast Asia.* Center for
    South and Southeast Asian Studies, University of Michigan, Ann Arbor, pp. 37–57.
Endicott, K. M. (1979). The impact of economic modernization on the *Orang Asli* (Aborigines)
    of northern peninsular Malaysia. In Jackson, J. J., and Rudner, M. (eds.), *Issues on
    Malaysian Development.* Heinemann Educational Books, Singapore: pp. 167–204.
Geertz, C. (1963). *Agricultural Involution.* University of California Press, Berkeley.
Hall, T. D. (1983). Peripheries, regions of refuge, and nonstate societies: Toward a theory of
    reactive social change. *Social Science Quarterly* 64: 582–597.
Hall, T. D. (1986). Incorporation in the world-system: Toward a critique. *American Sociological
    Review* 51: 390–402.
Kress, J. H. (1977). Contemporary and prehistoric subsistence patterns on palawan. In Wood,
    W. (ed.), *Cultural-Ecological Perspectives on Southeast Asia.* Southeast Asia Series No. 41,
    Center for International Studies, Ohio University, pp. 29–47.
Miller, E.Y. (1905). The Bataks of Palawan. *Philippines Department of the Interior, Ethnological
    Survey Publications* 2: 179–189.
Schrire, C. (1984). Wild surmises in savage thoughts. In Schrire, C. (ed.), *Past and Present in
    Hunter-gatherer Studies.* Orlando, FL: Academic Press, pp. 1–25.
Venturillo, M. H. (1907). Manners and customs of the tagbanuas and other tribes of the
    island of Palawan, Philippines. Mrs. Edward Y. Miller, trans. *Smithsonian Miscellaneous
    Collections* 48: 514–558.

4

Northern Islands, Human Error, and Environmental Degradation

Thomas H. McGovern, Gerald F. Bigelow, Thomas Amorosi, and Daniel Russell

While we worry today about the environmental crises resulting from industrialization and the use of fossil fuels, in the preindustrial past, humans did not always live in harmony with their environments, and have caused destruction of the resources upon which they depended, to their own detriment. A case of such a process is documented for the North Atlantic offshore islands of the eighth through eleventh centuries AD *by McGovern, Bigelow, Amorosi, and Russell. In this instance of medieval colonization by Scandinavian settlers, mixed farming was brought into an environment rich in forests and natural pastures. The settlers, however, overstocked domestic animals, depleted stands of trees, and caused soil erosion with their farming practices. This environmental degradation, the authors suggest, may have played an important role in changing social relationships and in the economic decline of these colonies.*

Why did the colonists fail to change their ways in the face of this degradation? The authors discovered that the settlers are very likely to have been aware of the dangers of overstocking and overpopulation, but that there were many impediments to change. For one thing, climatic changes might have made the impacts of their management practices

Originally published in *Human Ecology: An Interdisciplinary Journal,* 16(3)(1988): 225–270.

Thomas H. McGovern, Thomas Amorosi, and Daniel Russell, NABO, Department of Anthropology, Hunter College, City University of New York, New York, New York 10021. **Gerald F. Bigelow,** Peary-MacMillan Arctic Museum and Arctic Studies Center, Bowdoin College, Brunswick, Maine 04011.

Case Studies in Human Ecology, edited by Daniel G. Bates and Susan H. Lees. Plenum Press, New York, 1996.

*difficult to interpret; for another, social organization was changing in the
context of increasing economic and political inequality. Eventually, the
once-rich islands became incorporated into the larger northern European
economic system as impoverished dependencies.*

INTRODUCTION

An important recent trend in prehistoric human ecology is its expansion
from wholly prehistoric cases to include the analysis of more recent, more
complex, and more fully documented past cultures (Ogilvie, 1981a, 1981b,
1985; Parry, 1978; Smith and Parry, 1981; Parry et al., 1987; Ingram et al.,
1981). Climatic change and the unplanned consequences of human environmental impact had significant effects upon large, complex, recent societies as well as upon small, simple, prehistoric ones (Cronon, 1983; Osborne,
1985). The interaction of the ecology and politics of past agricultural systems is increasingly a primary focus of paleoeconomic–paleoecological
analyses, just as in modern development studies (Green, 1980; Lennihan,
1984; Vayda, 1983). Such integrated approaches require an abundance and
quality of data that has drawn many prehistorians into investigation of the
more recent past (Randsborg, 1980). The powerful combination of documentary, paleoecological, and archaeological evidence available to the historical cultural ecologist often allows detailed and effective modeling of
such complex interactions over a genuinely useful time span. This paper
attempts to contribute to this growing field of historic human ecology by
presenting a preliminary analysis of the processes and causes of environmental degradation in the medieval North Atlantic. Before we move to the
analysis itself, some culture–historical background may prove helpful.

BACKGROUND

Between AD 800–1000, Viking-age Scandinavian populations expanded
into the North Atlantic, probably colonizing the eastern islands (Shetland,
Faroe, Orkney, N. Hebrides) and the Scottish mainland by ca. 850. The
more distant western islands (Iceland, Greenland, Vinland) were settled
within the next three generations (Iceland c. 874, Greenland c. 985, Vinland
c.1000; see Arge, 1988; Jones, 1984, 1985; Bigelow, 1984; McGovern,
1980/81; Wallace, 1987). This wave of sea-borne migration carried an initially homogeneous culture, technology, and economy into the western

hemisphere and (briefly) to the shores of North America. The first settlers shared a hierarchical, chiefly political organization, a well-developed seafaring tradition, and a subsistence economy based primarily upon domestic animals (cattle, sheep, goat, pigs, dogs, horses) and cereal cultivation (mainly barley and oats) but with an opportunistic readiness to exploit available wild resources of both sea and land.

In Orkney, Shetland, and Faroe, historical, archaeological, and palynological evidence indicate that limited grain agriculture (mainly barley, but possibly supplemented locally with oats) was carried out (Johansen, 1975, 1979, 1982, 1985; Hallsdottir, 1982, 1984, 1987; Donaldson et al., 1981). In Greenland, documentary sources indicate that grain-growing never proved economically viable, and by the 13th century most Greenlanders "had never seen bread" (*King's Mirror,* trans. Larsen 1917: 65). Rotary querns, which were common artifacts in the eastern colonies (Bigelow, 1984), have been found on only a few Greenlandic farms (Nørlund, 1936), and they may have been used for milling imported grain or local lyme grass (*Elymus sp.,* see Griffin and Rowlett, 1981). In Iceland, barley-growing was definitely pursued along the South coast well into the mid-14th century (Eldjarn, 1961) and may have survived into recent times in a few localities (cf. Thorarinsson, 1956; also Gunnarson, 1980). However, it is clear that locally-produced grain was economically marginal in Iceland by later medieval times. Icelanders and Greenlanders thus shared an elevated trophic level on the terrestrial food chain.

During the subsequent medieval period, the various island communities became less homogeneous in subsistence and trading economies, while at the same time undergoing political integration into a Norwegian Atlantic realm (eastern islands were taken over before AD 1000; Iceland and Greenland lost their political independence AD 1262–1264). In Iceland, the period between the end of the initial settlement phase (ca. 930) and the absorption by Norway (1262–64) is known as the Commonwealth Period. It has long been regarded as a literary and economic golden age in which most of the rich and varied saga literature was written and which combined political independence with relative prosperity.

The increasing diversification of economic strategy in the later Middle Ages partly reflected local adaptation to significantly different local environments, but also seems tied to the relative distance from, and integration with, continental economies (cf. Bigelow, 1987a, 1987b; McGovern, 1985a; Durrenberger, 1988; Gelsinger, 1981; Wallerstein, 1974). Some of the eastern islands experienced an archaeologically visible transition around 1150–1200 from Viking period architecture and artifact assemblages to a Late Norse pattern incorporating a greater number and range of imported artifacts, elaboration of fishing technology, adoption of domestically produced pottery, and some less well understood alterations in butchery pattern and site layout (cf. Hamilton, 1956; Bigelow, 1985, 1987a). A late Norse transition in Iceland is less evident, and it now seems doubtful that the somewhat isolated Greenlandic colony ever underwent the same sort of transition as can be documented in the eastern island communities (McGovern, 1981a, 1985a).

Beginning about 1250–1300, the climatic cooling known as the "Little Ice Age" (LIA) began to have a varied, but significant, impact on local subsistence economies all across the North Atlantic. While the coldest portion of the LIA seems to have occurred at the end of the 17th century (Lamb, 1977), most of the Scandinavian North Atlantic communities felt major effects by the early 14th century. The entire region is marginal to submarginal for cereal agriculture (Parry, 1978), and many other components of the transported continental agricultural system were at the edges of their climatic tolerance limits. The region as a whole is thus particularly vulnerable to relatively small-scale shifts in northern hemisphere climate (Lamb, 1977).

A general decline in the prosperity of the Norwegian state, growing influence of German Hanseatic traders, and the impact of the Black Death, all had varied effects on the individual island groups, with the more distant western settlements being most adversely affected. Political absorption of Norway by Denmark after 1380 likewise had diverse, but often unfavorable, effects on the former Norwegian Atlantic possessions.

The later Middle Ages and Early Modern period saw the complete extinction of the Greenlandic colony (ca. 1450–1500; cf. Gad, 1970) and major loss of population in Iceland (Thorarinsson, 1961; Rafnsson, 1984), while the eastern settlements in Shetland and Orkney (Bigelow, 1985; Fenton, 1978) apparently experienced modest prosperity and population stability or increase. The available evidence thus suggests that the eastern island communities were more successful in their long-term adaptation to changes in their natural and social environments.

ENVIRONMENTAL IMPACT AND ENVIRONMENTAL DEGRADATION

While all analysts are agreed that changing trade flows and the onset of the Little Ice Age profoundly effected the fate of the North Atlantic communities, a growing number of scholars have focused their research upon the local impact of Norse settlement and subsistence systems upon particular island ecosystems as a major factor affecting farm and community abandonment. Unplanned consequences of overexploitation of flora and soils have been suggested as significant factors leading to both population decline in Iceland (Thorarinsson, 1961, 1970; Fridriksson, 1972; Sveinbjarnardottir, 1982; but cf. Adalsteinsson, 1981) and complete extinction in Greenland (Albrethsen and Keller, 1986; Krogh, 1982; Berglund, 1986).

Deforestation

The medieval colonists themselves noted their impact on native woodlands of scrub birch, willow, and alder (which can grow in dense thickets 1.5–2m tall in favored areas). The often-quoted statement by Ari Thorgillsson in the *Book of the Icelanders* (ca. 1125) that "At that time [first settlement] Iceland was covered with forests between mountains and seashore" (*Islendingabok* Ch. 1, trans. Hermannson 1930: 60) clearly reflects an awareness of an altered contemporary landscape.

Our Biological and Geological Evidence

Much of the natural science data presented here has been kindly supplied to the authors by Stefan Adalsteinsson, Paul Buckland, Bent Fredskild, Margaret Hallsdottir, and Johannes Johansen, as Norse environmental impact has grown considerably in recent years, and new indicators and fresh data are continually being added.

The effect of the Norse *Landnam* (pioneer settlement) is visible in many of the pollen samples investigated to date. The Greenlandic profiles show a marked decline in willow and birch at landnam, which is mirrored by a parallel decline during the 1920s and 1930s, when sheep herding was reintroduced to parts of South Greenland. While the Icelandic and Faroese sequences are complicated by the earlier (ca. AD 600) settlement of small communities of Celtic monks, they too indicate a decline of arboreal pollen and a rise of Gramineae pollen. The Shetlands have been occupied by humans since at least Neolithic times, but most analysts agree (Spence, 1979; Berry and Johnston, 1980) that the essentially treeless modern landscape is the product of grazing pressure by human domesticates (especially sheep).

While sheep and goat grazing has clearly been a major agent locally in reducing the scrub woodlands and in preventing their regeneration, other human activities also had a direct effect upon native plant communities. The Norse extracted and smelted bog iron throughout the North Atlantic region, and their relatively soft iron implements must have regularly required resmithing. Definite smithies dating to the first periods of Norse settlement have been identified in Newfoundland, Greenland, and Iceland,

and iron slag has been widely recovered there and elsewhere in the Norse world (A. S. Ingstad, 1977; Roussell, 1936, 1941; Eldjarn, 1961; Bigelow, 1984; Curle, 1939; Hunter and Morris, 1981). Smelting requires a large volume of charcoal, which could have been partially supplied by driftwood. However, Icelandic saga references to systematic charcoal-making in the dwarf forest and to destructive effects of accidental wildfires resulting from charcoaling (*Ale-hood,* trans. Palsson 1971: 82–83) indicate that native woodlands were subject to pressure from this source and that forest rights were jealously guarded.

More deliberate burning of woodlands may have been a feature of the initial Norse landnam in Greenland. Archaeological test excavations in widely scattered sites in the Western Settlement made during a survey project in 1981 (McGovern and Jordan, 1982) revealed a consistent pattern of a dense band of ash and charcoal (some plainly willow) at the interface of the earliest Norse cultural deposit and the sterile subsoil. A similar basal burned layer was observed in some of the bio-archaeological transects dug as part of the 1984 investigations at V 51 Sandnes in the Western Settlement (Fredskild and Humle, 1991). While some of these burned layers may be the result of natural fires or accidentally spreading of Paleo-Eskimo camp-fires, their wide distribution in the Western Settlement and their stratigraphic context within the Norse deposits suggests a more direct association with the Norse landnam. It would thus seem likely that fire was deliberately used as a land-clearing tool by the first settlers in this part of Greenland.

Surviving stands of scrub timber were later regularly used as fuel, as carbonized willow and alder fragments are common components of Norse hearth deposits in Greenland. Such carbonized local woods were recovered in appreciable quantity right through the stratified midden sequence investigated at Sandnes in 1984 (D. Layendecker, n.d.). Willow, Alder, and probably mosses were also collected for fodder, floor insulation, and probably bedding (Buckland et al., 1983; McGovern, Buckland et al., 1983; Buckland, personal communication, 1985; Sadler and Buckland, n.d.), and thick "twig layers" are commonly found both *in situ* on the floors of Greenlandic Norse structures (Roussell, 1936) and as widespread house cleaning layers in the middens (McGovern, 1979). As noted by Keller (1983), some of the woodlands also may have been consumed by fires built for cheese production as part of the normal dairying process.

Pasture Impacts

Norse economic activities must have had local effect on nonarboreal plant communities as well. Since domestic cattle, sheep, and goats were both major sources of nutrition and measures of wealth and status throughout the region, there may have been a recurring temptation to overstock, or delay in reducing grazing intensity in response to lowered pasture productivity. Trampling by both animals and humans likewise may have had a locally significant effect on groundcover growth and regeneration (such trampling impact is rapidly apparent during Greenlandic archaeological excavations). The yard walls and homefield enclosures so frequently associated with ruins throughout the region may have acted as much to restrict human and animal trampling as to control grazing access.

Turf was a major building material for houses, byres, and other structures throughout the region, and the turf and stone buildings required steady maintenance and regular rebuilding. The best quality building material came from the uppermost portions of tightly knit sod from established grass-sedge pastures (Olafsson, 1983a, 1983b; Roussell, 1934). The regular cutting and removal of high quality construction turves would thus place steady pressure on prime pasture communities.

Turf cut or "flayed" from outfields and placed on meadows closer to the home farm to fill bare spots and boost infield productivity was also a common agricultural practice in 18th and 19th-century Orkney and Shetland, and the resulting deflation scars are still visible (Fenton, 1978: 280–281). If the medieval Norse colonists made regular use of such turf manure, they may have inflicted lasting damage on the productivity of distant grass communities and promoted soil erosion fronts that could spread rapidly to more productive areas (Fridriksson, 1972; Slicher van Bath, 1963).

Norse Conservation Measures

However, it is important that we clearly distinguish the evidence for environmental *impact* of Norse economies from evidence for environmental degradation, in the sense of an alteration in natural ecosystems that effectively reduced the productivity of the land for the Norse settlers. After all, many of the changes recorded in the pollen rain (promoted by deliberate and accidental forest clearance) may have effectively raised the productivity of the predominate floral cover for the Norse economy, shifting it toward the grass-sedge communities that produced the most useful pasture for domestic animals.

Recent research has indicated other pasture-conserving and productivity-enhancing farming strategies practiced by the Norse settlers. While deliberate, intensive, large-scale manuring was not a widespread practice in the early medieval world, there definitely was both conscious and accidental use of manure and other midden debris as fertilizer in the medieval

North Atlantic (Fenton, 1981: 210–217 for discussion). Many Norse middens in Greenland are deep, rich in dung, and closely concentrated near building entrances, suggesting that the full fertilizing value of the manure went unrecognized. Icelandic middens are often further from structures (usually downwind), but are also occasionally deeply stratified (Amorosi, 1988). However, other midden deposits are more diffuse, suggesting deliberate or accidental spreading of the organic material during deposition (McGovern, 1979a). Whatever the intent, there is no question that the disposal of dung and garbage greatly enriched local soils and promoted the lush modern plant cover typical of Norse ruins.

Survey work in the Eastern Settlement (Krogh, 1982) and at Sandnes in 1984 has documented another, clearly intentional, measure to raise and maintain pasture productivity: Irrigation channels. The most elaborate system yet documented is at the Greenlandic bishops' manor of Gardar in the Eastern Settlement, which acted to draw off and distribute water from a small lake above the manor. The Sandnes system would also have distributed water from a stream over a wide area through a radiating network of small feeder channels. While some channels may have served to drain waterlogged areas, the general intent seems to have been to extend the area of wet-meadow (which greens up earliest in spring and remains more resistant to early frost). More work on such systems is needed, but it seems clear that the Norse very purposefully attempted to improve the productivity of pastures in the homefields near the farms.

Management of Impact

Norse land use practices were thus not wholly destructive of northern plant communities and topsoil. Partial or complete deforestation was only one aspect of a complex interplay of planned and accidental impacts upon the natural ecosystem. Perceptive analyses by Green (1980) and Rindos (1985) have indicated that the interactions of agricultural and natural ecosystems are not usefully modeled by simple linear cause and effect chains of either economic or environmental determinism. As Green suggests, we may better conceive of such interactions as a cycle of human management decisions which have direct impacts upon components of a natural environmental system, which then undergo alterations, which in turn provide feedback signals to human managers, who may then choose to alter or retain their strategy of exploitation (Green, 1980: 343–345).

Thus, all agricultural systems will produce some environmental impact: Its assessment as adverse or positive can only be made with reference to a particular economic strategy and specific time scale. Short-term observations and highly generalized studies are thus inadequate to investigate the balance of favorable and unfavorable environmental impact, or to accurately assess the success or failure of management response. A more effective analytic approach requires an investigation of the specific characteristics of the impacted natural system and the human management of that system's response that resulted in improved yield, homeostasis, or degraded yield for a given resource and a given economy over a substantial period of time (cf. Lees and Bates, 1984; Vayda and McCay, 1977; Parry, Carter and Konijn, 1987).

In order to identify a significant degradation of resources in the Norse case, we must address the following questions:

- Were Norse land use practices in fact causing adverse ecological impact locally, outweighing the effects of measures promoting favorable changes (thus altering a homeostatic balance in an unfavorable direction)?
- Were the impacts of Norse land use sufficiently widespread to cause significant, sometimes irreversible *large-scale* degradation of ecosystem components important to Norse economy?
- If Norse land use practices were indeed destructive of such vital economic resources, why did Norse farmers fail to perceive and correct the problem?
- What impediments to management blocked effective response to culturally recognized warning messages from the natural ecosystems?

The first two questions relate to both the natural viability of the impacted ecosystem components and to the intensity of Norse exploitation of these resources. A type of carrying capacity argument thus must be developed that allows for some measurement of relative productivity and demand. As many have pointed out, carrying capacity assessments are meaningless without case-specific linkage of particular resources with particular elements of a particular economic strategy (see Glassow, 1978 for review). Therefore, we will attempt to model the specific interaction of Norse domestic animal husbandry and pasture resources, comparing patterns in Shetland, Iceland, and Greenland.

MODELING PASTURE COMMUNITY VULNERABILITY

We may begin by firmly identifying pasture as a major determinate of Norse settlement location and density throughout the North Atlantic. Generations of fieldworkers have used patches of greenery to locate Norse farm ruins, and the rule of thumb that grass and sites are associated still holds true in most areas. The strength of the association of pasturage and site location is greatest in Iceland and Greenland (cf. McGovern and Jordan, 1982; Nørlund, 1936), but it is clear that access to both arable and pasture was a critical determinate of site location in Shetland (Small, 1969) and Faroe (Arge, 1988). While zoo archaeological data indicate wide divergence in overall subsistence economy (Amorosi, 1988; Bigelow, 1984; McGovern, 1985b), analysts agree that pastoralism formed a central core of the Norse economic strategy throughout the region. Thus, a concentration upon factors affecting the viability and resilience of pasture communities seems empirically justified.

North Atlantic pasture plant communities differ considerably in productivity and in patchiness (both between island groups and within individual islands), but species composition remains reasonably uniform. Thus, it seems reasonable to directly compare the potential of these island plant communities for withstanding pressure from human economic impact. While length of summer sunlight (latitude), soil type, precipitation, and exposure all clearly have significant effects on the viability and resilience of plant communities in the region, temperature during the growing season is normally the most important single limiting variable in this northern zone (Parry, 1978; but see also Bergthorsson et al., 1987; Bergthorsson, 1985, who argue the importance of winter temperatures as well). Accumulated temperature (measured in day-degrees) must exceed a critical level during the growing season if the plant taxon is to complete its life-cycle. Estimates of the baseline temperature (at which the plant taxon begins growth) and the critical total of day-degrees vary with different authors (Parry, 1978; Smith, 1975; Bergthorsson, 1985) but a reasonable estimate suitable for gross comparison would be a baseline temperature of 4.4°C and a critical accumulated temperature level of 1050 day-degrees for barley , and a baseline of 5°C and critical accumulated temperature of approximately 350 day-degrees for pasture grasses. Holding other variables equal, the difference between these critical accumulated temperature levels and the observed accumulated temperatures should provide a rough index of the overall viability of plant community members in different areas (though probably presenting a worst-case estimate in most situations).

Figure 1 presents such an assessment for Shetland, Iceland, and West Greenland, comparing the day-degrees accumulated for barley and pasture grasses during the growing seasons based on modern instrumental data. The modern (baseline) Shetlandic temperature averages come from the station at Baltasound (1931–47, 1953–60) on the northernmost island of Unst (Irvine, 1968). Similar data for Iceland comes from Vik (1931–60), on the south coast (Eythorsson and Sigtrygsson, 1971). Greenlandic data comes

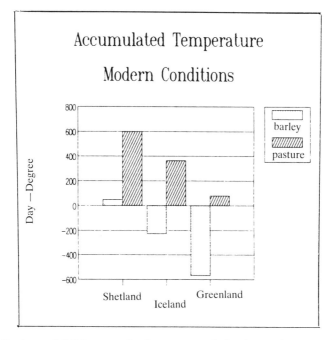

Figure 1. Surplus or deficit in accumulated temperature during the growing season for barley and pasture grasses. Baseline temperatures for barley estimated at 4.4°C, pasture grasses at 5°C. Critical level of accumulated temperature estimated at 1050 day degrees for barley and 350 day degrees for pasture grasses. Shetlandic data from Baltasound on Unst (1931–1947, 1953–1960), Icelandic data from Vik (south coast, 1931–1960, Greenland data from Kapisigdlit (inner parts of Nuuk District, 1939–1956). Note from increasing apparent marginality from east to west.

from the modern village of Kapisigdlit (1939–56), in the center of the former Norse Western Settlement (Orvig, 1968, table LXXIII). At each modern station, pasture communities would seem to be secure (though with major differences in climatic margin of security), while barley growing should be economically feasible only at the Shetlandic station. While it is not commercially produced, barley can be grown in sheltered locations in Southern Iceland today (Bergthorsson, 1985), so the 226 day-degree deficit recorded at Vik may not actually constitute a biologically prohibitive threshold for the region as a whole. Thus these figures do not provide a precise cut-off point for plant survival, but rather reflect relative degrees of viability and indirectly may serve as proxy indicators of probability of cereal and hay harvest failure.

Contrasting Vulnerability

Despite the clear limitations of this simple quantitative model, it underlines potentially significant differences in climatically-controlled natural viability of key plant species common to the region. Even allowing for many factors not being held equal, the 55% difference in pasture grass accumulated temperature between Kapisigdlit and Baltasound, and the 75% difference in barley accumulated temperature between Vik and Baltasound, appears to signal a major contrast in inherent community resilience in the face of stresses from any source. As noted above, the documentary, paleobotanical, and archaeological record makes clear that the early settlers in the western islands had very different luck with barley than their relatives in the eastern communities.

Thus it is justifiable to expect that overgrazing, trampling, and excessive turf cutting, as well as any climatic cooling, would have most adverse impacts (and pasture conservation techniques would be least effective) in the western island communities. Within these settlements, pastures subject to further local reduction in accumulated temperature (at higher elevations, on north-facing slopes, on knolls exposed to windchill) would be still more vulnerable to stress. We will thus concentrate upon the western hemisphere settlements of Iceland and Greenland, as these should provide the best examples of impact leading to resource degradation.

INTENSITY OF LAND USE

The calculation of the absolute size of past human populations is an exercise fraught with uncertainty and error in prehistoric contexts (Hassan, 1978) and similar calculations in the medieval North Atlantic context are equally problematic. Estimates of Commonwealth period Icelandic population range from less than 30, 000 to over 75, 000 (Thorarinsson, 1961; Gelsinger, 1981; Fridriksson, 1969, 1972 for discussion), depending on different authors' assessment of the number of dependents associated with each tax paying farmer. Estimates of medieval Greenlandic population are still more difficult, and must be based entirely on an assessment of the number of people per farm ruin (calculated from floor area measurements or estimated from size of the ruin). Most such estimates place the maximum Greenlandic Norse population at between 4,000 and 6,000 individuals (ca. 1000–1500 for the Western Settlement and ca. 3000–4500 for the Eastern Settlement, McGovern, 1979a; Krogh, 1982).

These estimates are clearly imprecise, and require improvement through ongoing survey and excavation work. However, even fairly accurate estimates of past population size tell us nothing directly about population pressure upon resources, and it may prove more productive to consider settlement distribution patterns in selected, well-surveyed areas, rather than wrestling with total population figures.

LOCAL LAND USE MODELS—DATA AND ASSUMPTIONS

One of the archaeologically best-known regions of Iceland is the inner portions of the Thjorsa river valley (Thjorsardalur) in Arnessysla in the south-central portion of the country (Stenberger, 1943; Eldjarn, 1961; Vilhjalmsson, 1983, 1984). Originally containing at least 15 farms, it has been thought that the valley was abandoned after a massive ash fall from the volcano Hekla, normally dated to AD 1104 (Thorarinsson, 1961). Recent work by Vilhjalmsson (1983, 1984) has documented additional sites and suggests that depopulation may have been more gradual than catastrophic. Farm ruins in this valley are roughly 1–3 km apart, and a recent study by Russell (1985) employing site territory analyses indicates that the average estimated territory per site is between approximately 450–160 hectares. These are only rough estimates, and additional fieldwork is likely to raise the number of known sites considerably and allow refinement of pasture area estimates in the future (Vilhjalmsson, personal communication).

The most thoroughly investigated portion of the Greenlandic settlement is the Ameralla drainage in the Western Settlement, probably comprising most of the medieval parish centered on the church farm at V 51 Sandnes (Bruun, 1918; Roussell, 1936, 1941; McGovern, 1979a; Andreasen, 1980, 1981; Pedersen, 1985). This region contains over 25 farms, about a third of the Western Settlement, spaced at roughly 3–5 km intervals.

Fodder Consumption

The Icelandic agricultural scientist Sturla Fridriksson (1972) has produced a series of working estimates for pasture productivity and stock fodder requirements based on his experience with modern Icelandic farming, which should be directly relevant to medieval conditions. (Icelandic stock today are mainly descended from medieval breeds, see Adalsteinsson, 1981;

Russell, 1985; Russell et al., 1985; Amorosi, 1988). While noting a wide range of observed pasture productivity (from less than 100 kg hay/ha to over 3,000 kg hay/ha), Fridriksson uses the figure of 300 kg hay/ha as a useful working figure for unfertilized traditionally-managed hayfields. He further proposes an annual consumption rate of 700 kg of hay for each fertile ewe, and implies that a cow would need roughly six times as much (or about 4200 kg/yr). Nørlund (1936) estimated that a traditional cow would require approximately 4563 kg/yr under traditional Icelandic management practice of the early 20th century.

A passage from the 12th century Icelandic lawcode *Gragas* (Gragas Ib, p. 87, kindly pointed out and translated by William Miller and Stefan Adalsteinsson) seems to indicate that ten old sheep were roughly equivalent in grazing impact to one legal cow (mature and fertile), which would apparently imply a hay consumption rate of approximately 420–450 kg/ewe/yr. However, this grazing pressure assessment may not be directly convertible to total yearly fodder demand, given the more destructive grazing pattern of sheep compared to cattle. For the purposes of this study, we will employ Fridriksson's sheep feeding estimate (which may be effectively a worst-case) and use the yearly consumption figures of 700 kg per sheep and 4400 kg per cow (rounded mean of the Fridriksson and Nørlund estimates), assuming all animals are adult and maintained in lactating condition (a simplification to be rectified in later, more realistic models).

A massive study of modern sheep-grazing potential prepared for the sheep-raising Greenlandic communities located in what was the old Norse Eastern Settlement (*Detail plan for Faarealven i SydGrønland*, K. Egede ed., 1982) also provides data for the calculation of average pasture productivity. Using the Fridriksson estimate of 700 kg hay/yr/fertile ewe, the mean of 41 grazing zones in this part of Greenland produces an estimate of 233 kg/ha (range 91 kg/ha–350 kg/ha).

STOCKING LEVELS

Our estimate of stocking levels is based upon the size and number of stalls present in the byres excavated at several of the excavated frams from the Thjorsardalur and from Greenland, which should give a roughly accurate assessment of the number of cattle normally housed on each farm (for a discussion of architectural measures of farm productivity see McGovern, 1985a). The architectural data provide some basis for estimating the usual number of cattle kept of individual farms, but a reasonable cattle to caprine ratio is needed to convert this cattle estimate to a rough assessment of the farm's total stock. Our sources for such conversion ratios are both documentary and zooarchaeological. The comprehensive 18th century Icelandic livestock surveys are generally regarded as accurate for major economic species (Rafnsson, 1984), and are recognized as a major resource for Icelandic economic and social history. They reveal a cattle to caprine ratio far different from recent sheep-dominated stocking patterns.

LOCAL LAND USE MODEL—RESULTS

Table 1 presents such rough stocking estimates for three sites in the Thjorsardalur and three in the Ameralla drainage. The Icelandic sites of Stong (Roussell in Stenberger, 1943) and Samsstadir (Rafnsson, 1974) are large to moderate sized farms, while Gjaskogar (Eldjarn, 1961) is smaller and certainly poorer. The Greenlandic sites include one major church farm at V51 Sandnes (Roussell, 1936; McGovern, 1987), a moderate sized holding at V54 (Andreasen, 1982; McGovern et al., 1983), and a small farm (probably typical of most Western Settlement holdings) at V35 (Roussell, 1936; McGovern and Jordan, 1982). The estimated fodder requirements for the major domesticates and the farm total are presented in the last three columns.

Table 2 compares these estimates of total fodder requirement to the area (in hectares) required to fulfill this requirement at four different productivity levels (200–1000 kg/ha). The final column on the right gives the estimated site territory pasture area (note that the estimates for Thjorsardalur are based upon map assessments, while the Greenlandic estimates are actual field assessments of vegetation distribution). It should be noted that this site territory approach ignores the contribution of distant high altitude hayfields outside the valley-bound Von Theissen polygons, and the possible importation of fodder (such as seaweed and shore grasses) from the coast. These are surely significant omissions, especially for larger and politically more powerful farms controlling access to distant resources. Survey work in the richest portion of the Eastern Settlement in Greenland has documented saeters (shielings: Summer livestock stations) at over 300 m (Albrethsen and Keller, 1986; Keller, 1983). Clearly, more work in the uplands of both island communities needs to be carried out (especially as the more northerly Western Settlement seems to lack evidence of high altitude saeters, McGovern, 1987; Christensen, 1987).

Therefore, the site territory pasture assessments used here undoubtedly underestimate the total pasture exploited by each farm (the consumption figures are probably also underestimates, as they exclude

Table 1. Estimates of Major Domestic Livestock Numbers and Required Fodder at Selected Sites from the Thjorsardalur in Iceland and the Ameralla Drainage in West Greenland

	Architectural estimate of cattle	Ratio of cattle to caprines	Estimated proportionate number of caprines	Estimated cattle fodder	Estimated caprine fodder	Estimated total fodder
Iceland: Thjorsardalur						
Strong	20	ca. 1:5.13[a]	103	88000	71826	159826
Samsstadir	20	ca. 1:5.00	100	88000	70000	158000
Gjaskogar	12	ca. 1:6.00	72	52800	50400	103200
Greenland: Western settlement						
V51 Sandnes	25	ca. 1:1.12[a]	28	110000	19600	129600
V54 Sandnes	8	ca. 1:3.75[a]	30	35200	21000	56200
V35 Sandnes	4	ca. 1:4.50[a]	18	17600	12600	30200

[a] Based on bone ratios with allowance for Payne Effect (ratio rounded upward 30% for unsieved, 10% for sieved collections).

Table 2. Estimated Fodder Requirements of the Selected Sites in Iceland and Greenland Compared to the Pasture Area Required at Different Productivity Levels[a]

Site	Estimated total fodder required	100 kg/ha	Pasture required			Estimated site territory pasture
			500 kg/ha	300 kg/ha	200 kg/ha	
Iceland: Thjorsardalur						
Strong	159826	160	320	533	799	314
Samsstadir	158000	158	316	527	790	314
Gjaskogar	103200	103	206	344	516	ca 450
Greenland: Western settlement						
V51 Sandnes	129600	130	259	432	648	350
V54 Sandnes	56200	56	112	187	281	160
V35 Sandnes	30200	30	60	101	151	113

[a] The last column on the right presents the estimated actual site territory (not including distant fields or uplands).

horses, pigs, and domestic fowl who would also have taken a small, but potentially significant, share of the fodder). However, at this initial stage of modeling, we will assume that least-effort principles operated to induce a rapid fall-off of fodder exploitation efficiency with increasing distance from the farm.

Allowing for some underestimation, Table 2 thus suggests that farms the size of Stong, Samsstadir, V 54, and Sandnes (V 51) would require an average pasture productivity level of between 300 and 500 kg/ha if their pasture territories were close to the 300–400 ha as suggested by our von Theissen polygons.

Thus both larger farms at lower elevations and smaller farms at higher elevations apparently were able to support their reconstructed stocking level at pasture sizes and productivity levels which seem at least reasonable according to Fridriksson's estimates and the existing archaeological survey data for these two parts of Iceland and Greenland. Applying the lower Detail plan (Egede, 1982) pasture production levels to the Greenlandic sites yields results suggesting either significant overstocking by the larger farms or a successful attempt to locally raise pasture productivity well above levels now normal for the more productive Eastern Settlement. The model also suggests that the landscape in these two regions was effectively full, as little unused, spare pasture could have existed without an improbably marked increase in pasture productivity levels.

Evidence for a Full Landscape

This admittedly rough quantitative model's depiction of a fully exploited landscape is supported by results of archaeological excavations in both the Ameralla drainage of the Western Settlement and in the Thjorsardalur. In the Ameralla, sites are commonly found on what are today genuinely marginal locations (on 30–45% slopes, in extensive areas of boulder-scree and bare rock, with only discontinuous grass pastures, isolated from boat landing sites, from upland pasture, and from caribou trails). One of the most marginal of these small farms was investigated in 1977-1978 (McGovern, 1979a; McGovern et al., 1983). Deeply stratified midden deposits from V48 Niaquussat produced a series of basal radiocarbon dates clustering around AD 1000, and terminal dates which suggest it was occupied to the end of the Western Settlement ca. 1350. The somewhat larger farm V54 Nipaitsoq excavated during the same project (Andreasen, 1982), also produced basal radiocarbon dates clustered around AD 1000. These two farms, one clearly marginal, were thus first settled within a generation of landnam in Greenland (ca. AD 985).

The small Gjaskogar farm in Thjorsardalur is at 300 m (100m higher than Stong and Samsstadir). As its excavator Eldjarn comments (1961: p. 14), the ruin is also nearly 100 m higher than any modern farm in southern Iceland. The site was originally a small smithy, apparently a detached, special-purpose bog iron smelter for one of the more prosperous valley farms. Later, the site was converted into a small farm, very similar in layout (though on smaller scale) to the Thjorsardalur valley farms documented in 1943 and 1974. Stratigraphic excavation revealed that the farm was abandoned some time *before* the Hekla ashfall of ca. 1104. Eldjarn estimated that as much as 50 years elapsed between desertion and the ashfall, and suggested that over-grazing and rapid soil erosion was the cause for abandonment.

Thus it appears that present quantitative models and available archaeological data support the view that even the most marginal grazing resources in the western islands were indeed fully in use by ca. 1000–1100. In this full landscape, Norse pressure upon pasture and woodland would have been both widespread and relatively intense, causing marked environmental impact. Under such circumstances degradation of resources important to the Norse economy would become a realistic possibility.

Evidence for Environmental Degradation

The late Dr. Sigurdur Thorarinsson, in a series of well-supported articles (Thorarinsson, 1956, 1961, 1970), has forcefully argued for an initial overexpansion of Icelandic settlement into the subarctic interior and into the higher elevations occurred prior to 1104, followed by rapid and irreversible erosion of soils and a subsequent retreat of settlement. In several different study areas in Iceland, Thorarinsson used documentary, archaeological, and geological data to demonstrate a progressive loss of soil and contraction of both pasture plant communities and human settlement. Subsequent work (Sveinbjarnardottir et al., 1982; Sveinbjarnardottir, 1982, 1983; Buckland et al., 1986; Fridriksson, 1972; Ogilvie, 1981, 1985; Hallsdottir, 1987) by archaeologists, natural scientists, and historians has generally supported Thorarinsson's model, and modern Icelandic agricultural policy has erosion reduction as a primary goal (Bergthorsson, 1985). While the most rapid and intense degradation of soils and groundcover seems to have occurred in the post-medieval period, there seems little doubt that Thorarinsson was correct in asserting that significant damage occurred locally well before the end of the Commonwealth period (Buckland et al., 1986: pp. 50–51; Hallsdottir, 1987: pp. 34–37). Dr. Stefan Adalsteinsson (1981: pp. 58–76) has argued that much of this erosion has been the result of long-term geomorphological processes, and is not attributable entirely to overgrazing by sheep. In Greenland, there are also direct indications that land use patterns did result in both impact and degradation. Fredskild (1978 and in Krogh, 1982: pp. 180–181) noted a significant increase in the siltation rate in a pond (a measure of soil erosion within its catchment) in one of the most favored zones of the former Eastern Settlement during the Norse occupation, with an apparent peak in the later phases of the colony, and a decline in siltation rate after the end of Norse settlement. Recent research by Jakobsen (1991) and Hansen (1991) in the central Vatnahverfi district of the Eastern Settlement suggest a rapid and accelerating impact of Norse agriculture on plant communities and soils around a large number of farm sites in this heavily settled area. Current evidence thus indicates that soil erosion may have been as serious a problem in parts of Norse Greenland as it was in contemporary Iceland.

Causes of Adverse Impacts

If Scandinavian colonists in the western hemisphere islands of Iceland and Greenland did inflict such adverse impacts upon a portion of the natural ecosystem vital to their own economic survival so as to cause degradation of both ecosystem component and human prosperity, then we should search for the causes of this evidently maladaptive behavior. Why would any group skilled in the arts of sub-arctic farming continue practices that produced neither riches nor stability for the community as a whole? To use Green's (1980) terms, why did environmental feedbacks fail to trigger appropriate management responses?

To address these difficult questions, we must consider the amount and nature of the environmental information available to the agricultural decision-makers, the cognitive framework to which this information was fit, and the political goals and status enhancing strategies of the actual decision-makers. Short-term political expediency and the expression of divergent class interests are critical factors in modern land use decisions, and changing the [locus] of decision-making authority in a hierarchy clearly can affect not only the scale of a decision's consequences, but also the content of individual managerial choices. Bender (1981) correctly points out that environmental archaeologists routinely ignore such social factors in prehistoric contexts, and tend to impose a mechanistic thermostat model on ancient decision-makers, limiting them to passive response to external (mainly climatic) pressures. Gunnarson (1980) has levelled similar criticisms at climatologists. Archaeologists working in historic periods thus have a special obligation to attempt to bridge the gap between what we can directly observe in modern cases and what we have been willing to infer in prehistoric ones.

Humans react not to the real world in real time, but to a cognized environment filtered through traditional expectations and a world view which may or may not value close tracking of local environmental indicators. Humans are also not always willing or able to forego short-term personal advantage for long-term common benefit.

It may thus be useful to identify some factors causing information flow pathologies that may have operated in this case:

- *False Analogy:* The managers' cognitive model of ecosystem characteristics (potential productivity, resilience, stress signals) may be based on the characteristics of another ecosystem whose surface similarities mask critical-threshold differences from the actual local ecosystem.
- *Insufficient Detail:* The managers' cognitive model is overgeneralized, and fails to sufficiently allow for the actual range of spatial variability that in an ecosystem whose patchiness is better measured in resilience than initial abundance (Moran, 1984).
- *Short Observational Series:* The managers lack a sufficiently long memory of events to track or predict variability in key environmental factors over a multi-generational period and are subject to chronic inability to separate short-term and long-term processes.
- *Managerial Detachment:* The managers are socially and spatially distant from agricultural producers who both carry out managerial

decisions at the lowest level, and are normally in closest contact with local-scale environmental feedbacks (Rappaport, 1977).

- *Reactions Out of Phase:* Partly as a result of the last two factors, the managers' attempts to avert unfavorable impacts are too little and too late, or apply the wrong remedy.
- *Someone Else's Problem* (S. E. P.):* Managers at many levels may perceive a potential environmental problem, but do not feel obligated to take action as their own particular short-term interests are not immediately threatened.

Some of these information processing problems will be most prevalent in a pioneering situation, in which immigrating populations lack both a long-tested and locally relevant body of traditional environmental lore and established native populations from whom such long-term observational data can be acquired (Thorarinsson, 1961). The first three pathologies would thus seem most serious during the initial phases of colonization, and should decline in importance as the population learns the new ecosystem.

Environmental Impediments to Management

North Atlantic islands may have proved particularly deceptive cases, with surface similarities masking very different sets of critical thresholds. Were the Scandinavian settlers of the Viking age prone to act on information distorted by false analogy and insufficient detail?

Cognitive Models

We have good documentary evidence that the Norse colonists did indeed notice many differences between the western hemisphere islands and those closer to home. Success or failure of barley growing was noted; all five species of seals found in Greenlandic waters were identified and named; and differences in the role of wild species in islanders' diets were all discussed by the well-informed author of *Kings' Mirror* (Larsen, 1917). We have good archaeological evidence that the Norse Greenlanders rapidly developed their characteristic integration of seal and caribou hunting with domestic animal husbandry within the first few years of settlement (McGovern, 1985a), taking advantage of the rich wild resources of their new home.

---

*We are indebted to Dr. P. C. Buckland for the introduction of this most useful concept to North Atlantic studies (Buckland 1988: p. 7); cf. D. Adams 1982.

We also have reason to believe that the Scandinavian settlers were well aware of the perils of overstocking and human overpopulation. In his *Book of the Settlements,* Ari Thorgillsson stated that by ca. 930 the country of Iceland (traditionally first settled 874) was *albyggt,* or fully inhabited (trans. follows Hastrup 1985: p. 8). There has been some controversy over whether Ari meant that the country had in fact been fully occupied up to some culturally cognized level, or if he meant only that the country had been fully claimed, and that land was no longer free for the taking (Jones, 1985; Sveinsson, 1953). As suggested above, the available archaeological data indicate that Ari was not speaking in an entirely figurative manner. In any case, the *albyggt* condition of the country did spur the formal organization of a specifically Icelandic law code and the gradual adoption of a multi-tiered *thing* (assembly) system. According to the later law code *Gragas* (codified AD 1117, V. Finsen, 1974; Hastrup, 1985), participation in the political system required that a farmer be a follower of a particular chieftain (*godi*), that he pay a thing tax, have (free of debt) a cow for each of his dependents (or property of equal value), and a debt-free horse or ox and all necessary farm implements (Sveinsson, 1953: p. 49). For a farmer supporting a nuclear family of 3–5 people, this would require him to own at least 4–5 cattle (or a mix of possessions of equal worth). Such property restrictions indirectly placed a ceiling on the number of fully independent farmers who could establish themselves in a given area, and thus may have acted to discourage high settlement densities.

A more explicit legal limit on settlement is provided by the Faroese code of *Sedabraevid* (1298), which stated that "from now on no man who owns less than 3 cows is to set up a house of his own" (Young, 1979: pp. 140-153). Such legal limits to local carrying capacity may have been made equally explicit in other North Atlantic codes now lost to us. The regular spacing of farmsteads in Greenland (McGovern, 1980b) certainly suggests some sort of formal cultural mechanism at work.

Thus there is evidence that the Scandinavian Atlantic communities were aware of the dangers of overpopulation and excessive settlement density, and that they were also aware of some major differences between island resources. Was this awareness sufficient to avoid the first three cognitive pathologies noted above?

Interpretation of Environmental Feedback

The rapid pace of colonization indicates that the simple recognition of major demographic and environmental constraints could not alone ensure effective long-term adaptation. While gross differences in the resources of the old and new settlements were understood and integrated into traditional knowledge, the more subtle feedback messages of critical plant communities may have been significantly harder to decode. As we have seen (Figure 1), modern climatic data indicate that it is the resilience and stress-resistance of pasture communities that would be most altered as Norse farmers sailed north and west—not gross species composition or initial resistance to grazing pressure. As modern experience suggests (Egede, 1982: pp. 15–17), it is not easy to judge pasture resilience until damaging overgrazing has already occurred. Stocking levels appropriate to wind-sheltered areas may be disastrous on nearby exposed slopes, as small holes in groundcover are rapidly widened, soon turning into a swiftly advancing erosion front (Fridriksson, 1972) that is difficult to halt. Calculation of sub-arctic pasture regeneration time is still a tricky task, and many modern managers have seriously misjudged stocking levels (Zhigunov, 1961). Norse experience gained in central Norway, the British Isles, or the even the eastern Atlantic islands may have provided disastrously false analogies after a few seasons of hopeful farming, especially in poorly watered uplands and exposed slopes.

The problem of short observational series may have also proven particularly significant in the western hemisphere islands, as Iceland and Greenland are significantly more exposed to the effects of relatively small-scale (and short-term) climatic fluctuations than are islands more squarely in the path of the ameliorating North Atlantic Drift (Lamb, 1977; Gunnarson, 1980). A number of thorough studies have convincingly demonstrated the vulnerability of pasture and other major components of medieval economy to comparatively small-scale climatic change in the North Atlantic as a whole (Bergthorsson 1985, Ogilvie 1980).

Climatic Change

Climatic change must have been a particular liability for Icelandic and Greenlandic managers in the later Middle Ages, as the onset of the Little Ice Age (LIA) was to produce irregular reductions of temperature and growing season of very considerable magnitude. The initial Viking period expansion seems to have taken placed during a warming period now generally called the Little Climatic Optimum (LCO) which is usually estimated to have had mean temperatures roughly 1°C higher than present means; the later medieval LIA is usually estimated to have produced temperatures at least 1–2°C colder than modern means (Lamb, 1977: pp. 279, 436–437; Dansgaard et al., 1975; Ogilvie personal communication 1988).

Turning once more to our simple day-degree model for accumulated temperature, we can get a rough idea of the scale of impact of such appar-

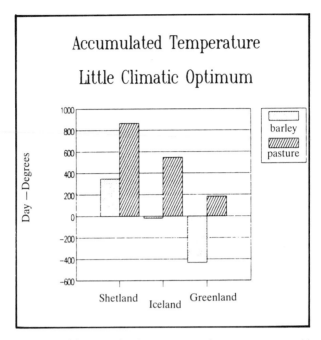

Figure 2. Surplus or deficit accumulated temperatures for pasture communities and barley for "Little Climatic Optimum" conditions (+1°C throughout the growing season). Baseline data as in Figure 1.

ently minor variations in mean temperature. Figure 2 presents LCO (+1°C) temperature effects for the three stations in Shetland, Iceland and W. Greenland (Baltasound, Vik, and Kapisigdlit). As the documentary data suggest, the possibilities for cereal agriculture would have been significantly expanded in both Shetland and Iceland during the first centuries of settlement.

Figure 3 presents a LIA (–1.5°C) temperature effect model for the same modern stations. The impact of LIA temperatures on the probability of barley harvest even in Shetland would appear significant. Pasture communities seem much further from a viability threshold, except in Greenland. In the former Western Settlement area the potential impact on pasture community viability seems severe. We must again note that these crude models probably considerably underestimate the actual biological hardiness of the plant taxa and the variable effects of local exposure and drainage involved, and are used here primarily to provide a comparative yardstick.

In this comparative mode, it is interesting to note that the pasture grass accumulated temperature estimate for the Little Ice Age in Shetland is slightly higher than the figure for the Western Settlement station's Little

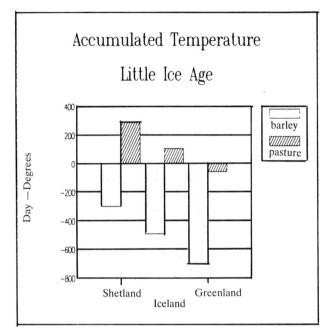

Figure 3. Surplus and deficit accumulated temperatures for pasture communities and barley recalculated for "Little Ice Age" conditions (–1°C throughout the growing season). Baseline data as in Figure 1.

Climatic Optimum estimate. Also note the extent to which LCO conditions might establish false expectations of pasture productivity and resilience in the minds of the early farm managers. It would be easy to imagine a disastrous series of management responses based upon an LCO cognized environment to ecosystemic signals generated by the onset of LIA conditions. Even if this crude accumulated temperature model proves unrealistically simple, it still seems very likely that environmental impediments to accurate and timely management response would have been considerable, and probably most serious in the more exposed western island communities.

Cultural Impediments to Management

However, natural impediments to appropriate managerial response to early signals of environmental degradation were not the sole cause of maladaptive destruction of critical resources. We can identify several additional cognitive maladies at work in the western settlements, and these are less easily ascribed to short observation period and false analogy by pioneering early settlers. At the same time that the comparative mildness of the Little Climatic Optimum may have drawn to a close, major social changes that were to directly affect land ownership and land management also took place in the western islands.

Social Change

One major change was the decline and virtual disappearance of slavery (Hastrup, 1985; Durrenberger, 1985) in Iceland and, apparently, in Greenland. The increasing availability of freeborn labor and the declining access to sources of foreign slaves are factors usually cited to explain this shift (Foote and Wilson, 1970; but see Durrenburger, 1985 for a more sophisticated treatment). It would appear that moderately prosperous farmers of the twelfth century had little problem finding poorer colonists willing to work for them as household servants or to rent land as tenants. As time passed, more and more colonists seem to have fallen from land-owning to land-renting status. Sveinsson (1953: 55) estimates that circa 1100 the great majority of farmers owned their farms and could meet the minimum thing tax requirements allowing them participation in the political process on the local or national level. Shortly after 1300 he estimates that the number of landowning taxpayers had dropped by 20%, and by ca. 1400 the majority of the population had been reduced to tenant status.

Differential Impact Model

Another simple quantitative model may help clarify the process by which environmental decay and variable pasture yields led to decreasing economic and political independence for the smallholders. While we believe that this spreadsheet model has relevance to other parts of the medieval North Atlantic (especially Iceland), the present version has been based on our best current data set from West Greenland. In Greenland, second-rank farms (like Sandnes: The Greenlandic settlements' only first-rank farm is the episcopal manor at Gardar, cf. McGovern, 1985b) were generally *landnamsmann's* (first settler) farms claimed during the initial colonization.

These sites' territories included the richest original pasture communities. These early, central farms thus began with a natural advantage in pasture quality and a social advantage in the ability to claim wider pasture area. Their greater labor resources and larger herds also provided them with a greater possibility for local improvement by irrigation and manuring. The effects of such natural and social advantages are plainly visible today in marked differential richness of plant communities around the larger farm ruins (Christensen, 1987; McGovern and Jordan, 1982; Nørlund, 1936).

Using data from the comparatively well-documented Ameralla drainage in Greenland, we have compiled a spreadsheet model of the different resources and requirements of three sites typical of different levels of prosperity (Table 3). Although the three farms listed are hypothetical ideal types, they are based upon actual cases, and figures used here represent current best estimates for the variables involved. This simplified model includes only adult cattle and caprines, and uses the same fodder consumption figures employed previously.

The lower panel illustrates different consumption requirements, with estimated household sizes drawn from floor area calculations (McGovern, 1979), and human consumption figured in "sheep units" following Fridriksson (1972). Fridriksson calculates that 9 sheep units are minimally required to support 1 adult for a year, assuming subsistence based mainly on domestic animal products.

While this simple model includes a number of unrealistic assumptions (including an absence of rents or tithes due the larger farm), it brings together variables that can be reasonably estimated with current data and (unlike some prehistoric optimization models) attempts to use probable native categories of cost and benefit. While no great precision should be expected from such an initial formulation, it still may suggest gross differences in economic status and possible response to adversity. Note for example that the second-rank farm (V51) generates something like thirty-eight times the fodder surplus of the fourth-rank farm under optimal conditions, despite its greater fodder consumption.

If we recalculate with a 30% drop in pasture productivity affecting all farms and pasture types equally (in practice, the smaller farms at higher elevation would be much more severely affected), the model may illustrate the differential impact on the different farm types (Figure 4). Recall that the modern Greenlandic sheep-farm managers (Egede, 1982) regularly include a 30% reduction in their worst-case stocking plans, so that this order of fluctuation may well represent normal inter-annual variability under climatic regimes similar to today's. The transition from LCO to LIA conditions may have been accompanied by even more extreme variability.

Figure 4 indicates a fodder deficit for all three farm types, but note the difference in magnitude. A "normal" preceding year would have left the second-rank farm with a surplus three times the size of its deficit (stored fodder might thus still retain enough residual nutrition to bring the

Table 3. Spreadsheet Model of Differential Impact on Three Idealized Norse Farms of Different Size (Based on the Actual Western Settlement Sites V51, V54, and V35)[a]

	Second-rank farm (V51)	Third-rank farm (V54)	Fourth-rank farm (V35)
Animals			
Cattle	25 (1.12)[b]	8 (3.75)[b]	4 (4.50)[b]
Caprines	28	30	18
Fodder required (kg)			
Cattle	110000	35200	17600
Caprine	19600	21000	12600
Total	129600	56200	30200
Pasture area (ha):			
1.00% of maximum estimated size (× 100)	400	175	120
Pasture quality (kg/ha):			
1.00% of maximum estimated yield (× 100):			
1200	48000 (10)	10500 (5)	0 (0)
400	56000 (35)	21000 (30)	2400 (5)
300	4000 (5)	5250 (15)	10800 (45)
200	4000 (5)	5250 (15)	10800 (45)
Total fodder yield	168000	63000	31200

Fodder required	129600	56200	30200
Yield required	38400	6800	1000
Fodder: reserve/shortfall (%)	22.86	10.79	3.21
Estimated human household (adult = 1, child = 25)	19.75	8.50	4.50
"Sheep units" (+ cows)	178	78	42
Human "sheet units" required	178	77	41
Sheep units required	0	2	2
Sheep unit			
Reserve/shortfall (%)	0.14	1.96	3.70
Adult rations	0.03	0.17	0.17

[a] Optimal conditions; no rents or tithes included. This crude model incorporates estimates of stocking levels of major domesticates, their fodder requirements, the available pasture area for each farm type, the rough mix of pasture quality available to each, and the resulting fodder production compared to estimated fodder demand. The bottom panel presents the estimated household provisioning situation given the number of domesticates and the estimated human population on each farm type.

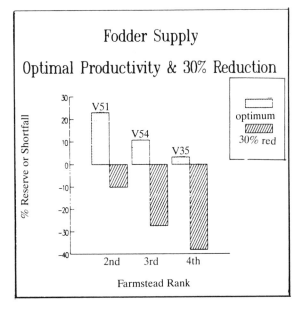

Figure 4. Based on the spreadsheet model of Table 3, this graph compares the effect of a 30% drop in pasture productivity on the fodder supplies of the three farm types. All show a fodder deficit, but note the gap between "good year" and "bad year" production on the smaller (3rd- and 4th-rank) farms.

farm's own stock through). The third and fourth-rank farms would have been forced to either borrow fodder or slaughter stock.

If we assume that all farms would have to bring stocking levels down to the reduced pasture productivity level (ignoring any stored fodder or elite extractive power), then we must adjust our spreadsheet model. Table 4 illustrates the result of a strategy that culls animals (caprines first) to bring stocking levels down to the approximate break-even point with available fodder. The middle panel again calculates the effect of this culling on sheep units available for human consumption, and the bottom panel presents the pattern of stock reduction for the three farm types.

Figure 5 illustrates the impact of such stock culling as a percentage decline from optimal conditions. Figure 6 presents the same data in actual numbers of animals slaughtered. Both measures indicate a disproportionate impact on the wealth of middle and low ranking farms and the greater difficulty such holdings would have in rebuilding flocks and herds.

Figure 7 illustrates some of the costs of such a stock reduction in terms of household provisioning (measured in sheep units and not taking

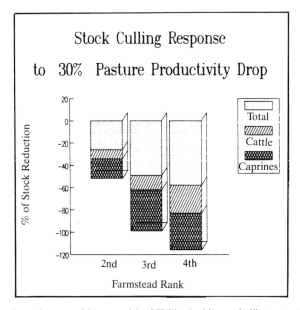

Figure 5. Based on the spreadsheet model of Table 4, this graph illustrates the impact of stock-culling decisions on the herds of the three farm types as a percent of the total stock normally maintained.

into account any diversion of dairy produce from human consumption). While all farm types would see provisioning deficits, the impact would clearly be greatest on the middle and lower ranking households. The second rank farm could balance its deficit by simply discharging one or two adult servants and cutting rations to the rest (adding a few more homeless paupers to the population), but middle and lower ranking households would have no such easy solution to their provisioning short-fall.

In reality, we know that all households in Greenland greatly augmented their available "sheep units" with large amounts of seal and caribou meat, and that whales, birds, and other wild species also contributed to nutrition on all farms. However, it is interesting to note that the bones of seals (the most important wild resource in Greenland) are much more common in the archaeofauna of small farms than large ones (McGovern, 1985a). Where abundant wild resources were absent (or when hunting failed), the model indicates that impact on small holders' domestic economy would be severe.

Table 4. The Spreadsheet Model of Table 3 Recalculated to Allow for a 30% Reduction in Pasture Producitvity[a]

	Second-rank farm (V51)	Third-rank farm (V54)	Fourth-rank farm (V35)
Animals			
Cattle	23 (1.00)[b]	7 (2.71)[b]	3 (4.00)[b]
Caprine	23	19	12
Fodder required	129600	56200	30200
Cattle	101200	30800	13200
Caprine	16100	13300	8400
Total	117300	44100	21600
Pasture area (ha):			
1.00% of maximum estimated size (× 100)	400	175	120
Pasture quality (kg/ha):			
0.70% of maximum normal estimated size (× 100)			
840	33600 (10)	7350 (5)	0 (0)
280	39200 (35)	14700 (30)	1680 (5)
210	42000 (50)	18375 (50)	12600 (50)
140	2800 (5)	3675 (15)	7560 (45)

Total fodder yield	117600	44100	21840
Fodder required	117300	44100	21600
Yield required	300	0	240
Fodder: reserve/shortfall (%)	0.26	0.00	1.10
Estimated human household (adult = 1, child = .25)	19.75	8.50	4.50
"Sheep units" (+ cows)	161	61	30
Human "sheep units" required	178	77	38
Sheep units available–required	-17	-16	-8
Sheep unit			
Reserve/shortfall (%)	-9.42	-20.26	-21.57
Adult rations	-1.86	-1.72	-0.92
Stock reduction required by fodder shortfall			
Cattle	2	1	1
Caprines	5	11	6
Total stock loss (%)			
Cattle	7	12	7
Caprines	8	13	25
	18	37	33
Total stock loss (%)	26	49	58

[a] Reduction unrealistically affecting all farm types equally; in practice, smaller holdings would be harder hit. Stock has been culled to bring fodder demand down to the lower production levels (culling preferentially removed caprines, but attempted to balance consumption and production with minimum number of animals slaughtered). The middle panel reflects the household provisioning shortfalls, while the bottom panel presents the stock reduction options taken.
[b] Ratios in parentheses.

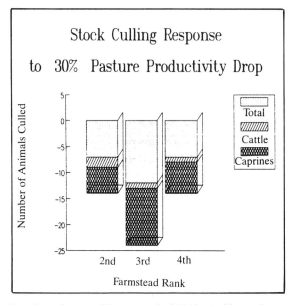

Figure 6. Also based on the spreadsheet model of Table 4, this graph presents the actual number of animals culled to reduce herd size after a 30% reduction in pasture productivity. Note the relatively large number of animals requiring slaughter on the middle ranking farm.

Traditional Cost Accounting

Did medieval North Atlantic farmers really weigh stock mix and fodder supply as carefully as our model assumes? Is the current formulation simply another example of 20th century cost accounting imposed on a premodern situation by the mechanics of an optimization model (Jochim, 1983)? Fortunately for our modelling, we do have anecdotal evidence that at least some remodern North Atlantic farmers were quite capable of just such fine-grained cost–benefit analysis as our analysis requires.

A 17th century Faroese folk tale has the stock figure of the foolish landowner order the equally stock figure of the clever hired hand to keep one additional yearling ram through the winter rather than slaughtering it as the hired man requests. The foolish landowner insists that one more immature animal will "make no difference" to fodder supplies. The hired man quietly kills the young ram anyway, and regularly puts aside the hay it would otherwise have been issued each day. When spring comes late (snow on the ground after May 3rd) the despairing landowner prepares to

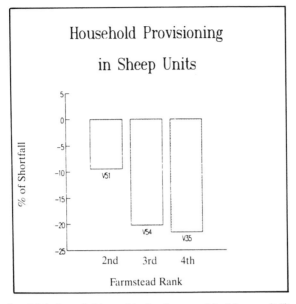

Figure 7. The shortfall in household provisioning (measured in "sheep units") resulting from the stock culling required to balance fodder demand with a 30% reduction in pasture productivity. Note the greater demand for wild resources to be expected on lower ranking farms. Archeofauna from these type sites do indicate a much higher consumption of seals on the smaller holdings (McGovern, 1985a).

kill his starving cows. The hired man then reveals the hidden hay store (which proves enough to carry the cattle through) and asks the landowner "now to tell him if it made no difference" (quoted and translated in Wylie 1987: pp. 35–36). We may expect that successful medieval North Atlantic farmers were equally careful accountants of fodder supply and demand.

Pasture Productivity and Political Power

Even if we maintain our deliberately unrealistic assumptions that all farmsteads would begin as fully independent units (owing no rents, tithes, or other payments to larger holdings) and that climatic fluctuation would effect all pastures equally, the model still strongly suggests that the middle and lower ranking farms would find it hard to avoid incurring obligation for borrowed fodder, household provisions, and replacement stock. If these lesser households were again victimized (by recurring bad seasons; by human labor shortages due to family life-cycle changes, accident, death or maiming in battle; by stock infertility, random animal mortality or epidemic murrain; or by simple bad luck and poor judgement) they would find such largess hard to repay.

Such persistently asymmetric economic relations could be quickly converted to political asymmetry in the Scandinavian North Atlantic. Note that the fourth rank farm's reduced cattle herd would be just at the legal minimum for independent status under the Faroese code. While this Greenland-based impact model requires recalibration for Iceland, its general assumptions and predicted outcomes of different stock management strategies probably remain valid.

Iceland's often more favorable grazing conditions may have been somewhat offset by the limited wild resources available in comparison with Greenland. In both settlements, the existing political and legal structure would tend to place maximum grazing stress upon those marginal holdings least likely to possess highly resilient local pasture communities. The heirs of the landnamsmen retained a consistent advantage over other farmers in the same area, and this ecological advantage would ensure continuation or enhancement of their political and economic dominance if overall yields dropped.

Periodic reductions in pasture productivity, even if they were spread as unrealistically evenly as we have assumed, would bear most strongly upon the third and fourth rank farmers. According to our model, only the second rank farm would be able to rapidly replace stock and take full advantage of a return of favorable weather during the following year. Sharp oscillations in climate could thus be tracked far more closely by the great farmers, with the smallholders' responses much more likely to be out of phase. A succession of poor years, or marked interannual variability, would leave small and moderate farmers little choice but to borrow fodder and replacement stock from the larger land holders, while desperately attempting to maximize their own fodder production in order to avoid permanent loss of political independence. Even this highly simplified model may suggest how easy it would be for the increasing numbers of small holders to fail in this race, losing control of both agricultural and political independence. What could a farmer forced into tenantry expect?

Consequences of Tenantry

Hastrup's analysis (1985: pp. 100–120) of the Icelandic *Gragas* law code of ca. 1117 indicates that three classes of farmer were recognized by the early twelfth century: *bondi* (landowning yeoman), *leiglendingr* (tenant farmer), and *budsetumadr* (shack-man, or cottager). The tenant was "a free-born man, whose freedom was, however, limited by the contractual relationship with the *bondi*" (Hastrup 1985: p. 110). The tenant rented land and buildings for a year (leases expiring at the same season each year), and had to pay a rent of a maximum of 10% of the total capital value of the property (not 10% of the year's produce, which would normally be much less). The cottager rented land on the same terms, but was additionally subject to labor service to the landlord, and required consent of the local community (*hreppr*) before he could settle in the district. Below the status of cottager were the totally impoverished (often wandering) paupers, who played an increasing role in sagas set in the 13th century (Sveinsson, 1953).

The tenant was obligated to maintain the value of the land, but could not allow it to lie fallow: ". . . if he does not work the land as he ought to and leaves meadows unmown he shall be punished as for breach of contract" (*Gragas* II: pp. 145–146, trans. Hastrup 1985: p. 111). He could not sublet the land or extract wood, fish, or wildfowl beyond his own subsistence requirements. In the event that the tenant failed to harvest enough hay for his animals or became totally impoverished in the course of the year, the landlord was obligated to supply hay and to support the tenant's family until the year-contract could be terminated. On the other hand, the landlord had the right to determine the number of livestock tenants could keep, and in later times at least was able to compel tenants to provide fodder and shelter for one or more of the landlord's cattle (J. Johannesson, 1974: p. 348).

Thus a tenant was hardly free to make his own agricultural decisions. Failure to maximize production would almost certainly result in a failure to renew the yearly lease, and might result in ruinous fines as well. The number and probably the mixture of animals kept would ultimately be someone else's decision, a decision that the tenant would have to carry out as best he could.

The landlords' legal obligation to provide fodder and human food to a failing tenant would certainly have provided the landlord an incentive to ensure the maximum extraction of hay and maximum summer stocking levels by the tenant, and to promptly evict any tenant who failed to pursue a maximizing strategy. The careful provisions for transfer or retention of specific improvements by an evicted tenant found in *Gragas* suggest that such evictions were not uncommon even in the early 12th century, and in any case a tenant could have had no legal remedy to an eviction at the end of the yearly contract.

Note also that the rental fees apparently were calculated on the basis of total assessed value of the property, not on a percentage of a particular yearly income. Christian Keller (personal communication) suggests that the *de jure* assessed value rent may have been replaced in practice by a *de facto* income-based rent, but we have no direct evidence for this in Iceland or Greenland. In any case, data from Shetland suggest that rents, tithes, taxes, and fines would have placed an increasing burden on the middle and lower rank farmers from the 12th century onward, necessitating significant changes in household economy (Bigelow, 1987b).

If hard-pushed pastures began to require reduction of grazing pressure or begin to show the first (initially subtle) signs of erosion, the tenant would have been caught between the proverbial rock and hard place. This situation could have produced a high turnover rate in the actual landworker, so long as the supply of poorer farmers seeking tenant contracts remained ample.

As we have seen, the tenant was by no means the lowest-ranking member of this farming society (cottagers could not even control their own labor during peak seasons), and there appears to have been no shortage of potential renters. A high tenant turnover and interdistrict mobility would have tended to replace the long-term, meadow-by-meadow knowledge of past yields and response to particular farming strategies available to a longtime resident with the hasty and overgeneralized choices of a short-term worker battling a harsh season and a large rental payment. Clearly, the loss of freeholding status had serious implications for the local environment as well as for the farm family involved.

Even temporary or permanent farm abandonment may not have allowed pastures a complete fallow. *Gragas* (Ib, p. 92, reference and translation kindly supplied by William Miller) provides for mandatory rental of vacant estates to neighboring farmers. As Miller notes, this provision was probably intended to force the neighbors to pay for grass and hay they would have had expropriated anyway, but would have had the effect of ensuring continued groundcover exploitation.

Stable rents (or too-slowly readjusted rents) and strong incentives for maximization of short-term output, combined with declining yield and rapid turnover of the landworking agricultural manager would thus appear to be a prescription for environmental degradation—unless the landowning agricultural managers carefully monitored local environmental feedbacks and were willing to reduce rental income to adjust to new fallow requirements. However, the evidence suggests that such undemanding landlords were increasingly scarce just at this point in Iceland, and probably also in Greenland.

Management Hierarchy and the Locus of Land Use Decisions

Above the freeholding *bondi* were the chiefly *godar*, who effectively controlled the political process and who seem to have often acted more like rapacious extra-legal predators than the pillars of justice the law codes envisaged (see Durrenberger and Palsson, 1988 for a thorough analysis of the breakdown of law-enforcement). The late 12th to mid-13th centuries saw escalating competition between *godar* in Iceland, and the emergence of a few great families who controlled multiple valley systems. These great chieftains carried on increasingly savage warfare among themselves, and often showed scant concern for local interests. While increasing number of *bondi* fell below the minimum legal property levels for political representation in the mid-13th century, the great chieftains of the major families became wealthy indeed. The 13th century *godi* and litteratus Snorri Sturlasson accumulated the equivalent value of nearly 10,000 cattle, and his was only the largest of several comparable fortunes at the time (Sveinsson, 1953). As predicted by our differential impact model, it is a harsh wind indeed that blows none good, and those with political authority and an ecologically favored set of holdings were likely to get relatively richer while the society as a whole became poorer.

Both local farmers and local *godar* became increasingly subordinated to regional and national powers. Their ancient right to freely withdraw support once freely given (discouraging excessive concentrations of power and acting as a self-conscious levelling device) became empty as their economic dependence on the ambitious great families increased. The pauperization of middle-ranking *bondi* and lesser chieftains thus simultaneously subverted enforcement of previously effective social mechanisms restraining stratification and shifted land-use decisions up a rank in the newly renegotiated social heirarchy. The ultimate landowner (secular or ecclesiastical) of this period might only occasionally have visited his more marginal holdings, and then seems to have been mainly concerned with collecting additional, extra-traditional exactions and recruiting often unwilling local farmers for his warband. While 10th through 11th century godar had fought with bands of a few hundred on a side, armies of 1400 men were not unknown by the mid-13th century (Sveinsson, 1953: p. 56). Elites locked in this sort of escalating power-struggle were very likely to be rather detached managers of distant ecological feedbacks, and may have been counted on to show little sympathy for strategies involving reduction of present production levels in favor of long-term conservation.

The malady of S. E. P. may also have operated with a vengeance: Not only would small holders' economic distress have been "some one else's problem" to these lawless great landowners, but impoverishment of smaller *godi* and former freeholding thingmen would actually directly strengthen the great chieftains both economically and politically—in the short-term. In the bloody turmoil of the end of the Commonwealth, short term payoffs may have been all that mattered to the leadership of the day, and the early warnings of Little Ice Age and progressive environmental degradation may have been heard only by the politically powerless.

After the submission of Greenland and Iceland to the Norwegian state in 1262–1264, the church and the crown became major island landowners. The scale of church holdings in later medieval Greenland is indicated both by the disproportionate size and richness of church buildings in this tiny colony (McGovern, 1981, 1985a; Berglund, 1982), and by the report of the episcopal steward Bardsson of ca. 1350–1370 (Jonsson, 1930) which lists nearly two-thirds of the best land of the Eastern Settlement as church property or owing rents to the church. In Greenland, all of the bishops and most of the episcopal stewards were foreign-born appointees, who themselves owed tax and tithe payments to the European center (Gad, 1970).

With these social and political developments in the 13th-15th centuries, the Atlantic Islands became integrated into the growing North European economic system (Wallerstein, 1974; Gelsinger, 1981; McGovern, 1985b; but cf. Keller, 1988). Their political independence ended, the peoples of the western hemisphere colonies became impoverished peripheries of a distant and increasingly disinterested core. The Greenland colony perished entirely by 1500, and Iceland's groundcover and human population faired badly indeed in early modern times. By the end of the 17th century, some 94% of the farmers of Iceland were tenants (Gunnarson, 1980: p. 10) and the pasture area of the country had been reduced by over 40% (Fridriksson, 1972). Managerial detachment, out of phase response, and S. E. P. are well-documented in this grim period, as may be evident in a quote of the venerable Icelandic bishop Hannes Finnsson (writing just after a major demographic crisis of the 1780's in which 21.5% of the total population died): "I cannot consider it to be far from the truth which I have heard some people say that deaths due to the small-pox had been far more damaging for the country than deaths due to hunger." (While during epidemics some of the best and most promising people died. . .) "The people who primarily died during periods of starvation were the irresponsible, the pithless, the indulgent and the vagrants and those who due to illness were unable to participate in the production." (quotation and translation from Gunnarson, 1980: p. 10)

AFTERWORD

Since this article was written in 1986–1987, a great deal of new research on the problems of human impact and climate impact on the North Atlantic Islands has been carried out by a growing number of scholars (for an overview, see McGovern, 1991; Buckland, 1991; Morris and Rackham,

1992; Morris et al., 1993). New investigations in the inland Vatnahverfi District in the Eastern Settlement of Greenland have revealed massive erosion resulting from Norse grazing pressures, with impacts beginning soon after first settlement (Hansen, 1991; Jakobsen, 1991). In Iceland, multidisciplinary projects have greatly refined and expanded our understanding of the rate and extent of soil erosion and human impact upon whole landforms (Buckland and Dugmore, 1991; Buckland et al., 1991).

Theory and organizational research structure have also progressed in the past half-decade. A growing movement variously labelled "Political Ecology" or "Historical Ecology" (Crumley, 1991) is now rapidly broadening and expanding some of the ideas advanced in early papers like this one—linking the development of particular cultural landscapes and particular human-environmental trajectories to interactions of human cognition, soils, changing weather, and changing politics. In 1992 a regional research cooperative called the North Atlantic Biocultural Organization (NABO) was formed with the support of the U.S. National Science Foundations Arctic Social Science Program, Arctic System Science Program, and Global Change program. NABO works to coordinate multi-disciplinary research on the complex interactions of humans and changing landscapes in this climatically sensitive region, involving over 180 active participants from ten nations. Cooperative projects are now underway all across the region, and NABO is working with the GISP2 ice core project and the PALE (paleoclimates of arctic lakes and estuaries) program to better integrate the new annual scale and decadal scale high resolution climate data now becoming available. Despite its prevailing weather, the North Atlantic has become a hot research area, and its many investigators can be expected to make far more sophisticated contributions than this one in the coming years.

ACKNOWLEDGMENTS

The authors gratefully acknowledge the many scholars who contributed data, criticism and ideas to this paper. We would particularly like to thank Stefan Adalsteinsson, Paul Buckland, Coleen Batey, Paul Durrenberger, William Fitzhugh, Bent Fredskild, Margret Hallsdottir, Kirsten Hastrup, Johannes Johansen, Richard Jordan, Susan Kaplan, Christian Keller, Dosia Layendecker, Morten Meldgaard, William Miller, Gudmundur Olafsson, Gisli Palsson, Sveinbjorn Rafnsson, Jon Sadler, Gudrun Sveinbjarnardottir and the anonymous reviewers for *Human Ecology*. Research reported here was generously supported by the U. S. National Science Foundation, The National Geographic Society, the Wenner-Gren Foundation for Anthropological Research, the American-Scandinavian Foundation, the Shetland Islands Council, the Scottish Development Department (Historic Buildings and Monuments), British Petroleum Development Ltd., NATO Scientific Grants Program, and the Research Foundation of the City University of New York. The authors are wholly responsible for any errors of fact or interpretation.

REFERENCES

Adalsteinsson, S. (1981). *Saudkindin, Landid og Thojodin,* Reykjavik.
Adams, D. (1982). *Life, the Universe, and Everything,* Penguin, New York.
Albrethsen, S. E. (1982). Traek af den norrone gaards udvikling paa Grønland. In Myhre, B., Stoklund, B., and Gjaeder, P. (eds.), *Vestnordiske Byggeskikk Gjennom To Tusend Aar,* Stavanger Museum Press, Stavanger, Norway.
Albrethsen, S. E., and Keller, C. (1986). The use of the saeter in medieval Norse farming in Greenland. *Arctic Anthropology, 23*(1&2): 91–109.
Amorosi, T. (1986). Report of 1986 Field Activities, Hunter College Icelandic Zooarchaeology Project. Preliminary report on file, Icelandic National Museum and Hunter College Bioarchaeology Facility.
Amorosi, T. (1987a). Report of 1987 Field Activities, Hunter College Icelandic Zooarchaeology Project. Preliminary report on file, Icelandic National Museum and Hunter College Bioarchaeology Facility.
Amorosi, T. (1987b). Icelandic Zooarchaeology, paper presented at the session *Economic and Ecological Approaches to the Medieval North Atlantic,* Society for American Archaeology meetings, Toronto.
Amorosi, T. (1988). Icelandic Archaeofauna: A preliminary review. Paper presented at the *Norse in the North Atlantic* conference, Peary MacMillan Arctic Center, Brunswick, Maine, April 18–21, 1988.
Amorosi, T. (1989). Contributions to the Zooarchaeology of Iceland: Some preliminary notes. In Durrenburger, P., and Palsson, G. (eds.), *The Anthropology of Iceland,* University of Iowa Press, Iowa City.
Andreasen, C. (1980). Nordbosager fra Vesterbygden paa Grønland. *Hikuin, 6,* 135–146.
Andreasen, C. (1981). Langhus-ganghus-centraliseret gaard: Nogle betragtninger over de norre Ønegaardtyper. *Hikuin, 7,* 179–184.
Andreasen, C. (1982). Nipaitsoq og Vesterbygden. *Grønland,* 5-6-7, 177–188.
Arge, S. (1988). Om landnamet paa Faer-rne. *Hikuin,* 15.
Bailey, G. N. (ed.) (1983). *Hunter–gatherer Economy in Prehistoric Europe.* Cambridge University Press, Cambridge.
Bates, D., and Lees, S. (1979). The myth of population regulation. In Chagnon, N., and Irons, W. (eds.), *Humans in Evolutionary Perspective,* North Scituate Massachusetts, Duxbury.
Bender, B. (1981). Gatherer–hunter intensification. In Sheridan, A., and Bailey, G. (eds.), *Economic Archaeology: Towards an Integration of Ecological and Social Approaches* BAR Int. Series 96, Oxford, pp. 149–157.
Bender, B. (1978). Gatherer–hunter to farmer: A social perspective. *World Archaeology, 10*: 204–222.
Berglund, J. (1973). Paa den yderste nogne Ø. *Skalk* 4: 23–25.
Berglund, J. (1982). Kirke, hal, og status. *Grønland1982* 9: 310–342.

Berglund, J. (1986). The decline of the Norse settlements in Greenland. *Arctic Anthropology* (1&2): 109–137.

Bergthorsson, P. (1985). Sensitivity of Icelandic agriculture to climatic variations. *Climatic Change* 7: 111–127.

Bergthorsson, P., Bjornsson, H., Dyrmundsson, O., Gudmundsson, B., Helgadottir, A., and Jonmundsson, J. V. (1987). The effects of climatic variations on agriculture in Iceland. In Parry, et al. (eds.), *Assessment of Climatic Variations on Agriculture,* Reidel, Dordrecht, Netherlands Part III.

Berry, R. J. and Johnston, J. L. (1980). *The Natural History of Shetland.* Collins, London.

Biddick, K. (1984). *Archaeological Approaches to Medieval Europe.* Medieval Institute, Kalamazoo, MI.

Bigelow, G. F. (1984). *Subsistence in Late Norse Shetland: An Investigation into a Northern Island Economy of the Middle Ages.* Ph. D. dissertation, Dept. of Archaeology, University of Cambridge, Cambridge.

Bigelow, G. F. (1985). Sandwick, Unst and the Late Norse Shetland economy. In Smith, B. (ed.), *Shetland Archaeology: New Work in Shetland in the 1970's.* The Shetland Times Ltd., Lerwick, pp. 95–127.

Bigelow, G. F. (1987a). Domestic architecture in Medieval Shetland. *Review of Scottish Culture* 3: 23–38.

Bigelow, G. F. (1987b). Taxation, nutrition, and trade. Paper presented at the session *Economic and Ecological Approaches to the Medieval North Atlantic,* Society for American Archaeology meetings, Toronto.

Bigelow, G. F. (ed.) (1991). The Norse of the North Atlantic, *Acta Archaeologica* 61, Copenhagen.

Binford, L. R. (1968). Post-Pleistocene adaptations. In Binford, S. R. and Binford, L. R. (eds.) *New Perspectives in Archaeology,* Chicago, Aldine, pp. 313–341.

Binford, L. R. (1981). *Nunamiut Ethnoarchaeology.* Academic Press, New York.

Bruun, D. (1918). The Icelandic colonization of Greenland and the finding of Vineland. *Meddel. om Grønland* 57(3).

Buckland, P. C. (1988). North Atlantic faunal connections—introduction or endemics? *Entomologica Scandinavica* Supplement 1988: 8–29.

Buckland, P. C. and Dugmore, A. (1991). If this is a refugium, why are my feet so bloody cold: The origins of the Icelandic biota in the light of recent research. In Maizels, J. K. and Caseldine, C. (eds.) *Environmental Change in Iceland: Past and Present.* Kluwer, Netherlands, pp. 107–125.

Buckland, P. C., Dugmore, A. J., Perry, D. W. D., and Savory, Sveinbjarnardottir, G. (1991). Holt in Eyjafjallasveit Iceland, a paleoecological study of the impact of Landnam. In Bigelow, G. F. (ed.), The Norse of the North Atlantic. *Acta Archaeologica* 61: 14–21.

Buckland, P. C. and Perry, D. W. (1985). Ectoparasites of sheeep from Storaborg, Iceland and their interpretation. Paper presented at the British Association for the Advancement of Science, annual meetings, symposium *North Atlantic Faunal Connections—Introductions or Endemics?* Aug. 26–30, 1985.

Buckland, P. C., Perry, D., Savory, D., Sveinbjarnardottir, G. (1988). Holt in Eyjafjallasveit, Iceland: A paleoecological study of the impact of Landnam. Paper presented at the *Norse in the North Atlantic* conference, Peary MacMillan Arctic Center, Brunswick, Maine, April 18–21 1988.

Buckland, P. C., Sveinbjarnardottir, G., Savory, D., McGovern, T. H., Skidmore, P., and Andreasen, C. (1983). Norsemen at Nipaitsoq, Greenland: A paleoecological investigation. *Norwegian Archaeological Review* 16(2): 86–98.

Buckland, P. C., Gerrard, A. J., Larsen, G., Perry, D. W., Savory, D. R., and Sveinbjarnardottir, G. (1986). Late Holocene paleoecology at Ketilsstadir in Myrdalur South Iceland.
Jokull 36: 41-55.

Butzer, K. W. (1982). *Archaeology as Human Ecology,* Cambridge, University Press, Cambridge.

Christensen, K. M. (1987). Patterns of landuse in Norse Greenland, paper presented at the
session *Economic and Ecological Approaches to the Medieval North Atlantic,* Society for
American Archaeology meetings, Toronto.

Clark, J. G. D. (1952). *Prehistoric Europe, the Economic Basis.* Methuen, London.

Clark, J. G. D. (1954). *Excavations at Star Carr.* Cambridge University Press, Cambridge.

Clark, J. G. D. (1975). *The Earlier Stone Age Settlement of Scandinavia.* Cambridge University
Press, Cambridge.

Coe, M. W. and Flannery, K. (1964). Microenvironments and Mesoamerican prehistory. *Science* 143(3607): 650–654.

Cohen, M. N. and Armelagos, G. (eds.) (1984). *Paleopathology at the Origins of Agriculture.*
Academic Press, New York.

Crosby, A. W. (1986). *Ecological Imperialism: The Biological Expansion of Europe 900–1900.*
Cambridge University Press, Cambridge.

Cronon, W. (1983). *Changes in the Land.* Hill and Wang, New York.

Crumley, C. L. and Marquardt, W. H. (eds.) (1987). *Burgundian Landscapes in Historical Perspective.* Academic Press, New York.

Crumley, C. (ed.) (1991). *Historical Ecology: Cultural Knowledge and Changing Landscapes.*
School of American Research press, Santa Fe, NM.

Curle, A. O. (1939). A Viking settlement at Freswick, Caithness. *Proceedings of the Society of
Antiquaries of Scotland* 73: 71–110.

Dansgaard, W., et al. (1975). Climatic changes, Norsemen, and modern man. *Nature* 255: 24–
28.

Donaldson, A. M., Morris, C. D., Rackham, D. J. (1981). The Birsay Bay project: Preliminary
investigations into the past exploitation of a coastal environment at Birsay, Mainland,
Orkney. In Brothwell, D. and Dimbleby, G. (eds.), *The Environmental Aspects of Coasts
and Islands,* BAR Internat. Series 94. pp. 65–85.

Dunnell, R. C. (1980). Evolutionary theory and archaeology. In Schiffer, M. L. (ed.) *Advances
in Archaeological Method and Theory.* Vol. 3, Academic Press, New York, pp. 38–100.

Durrenberger, E. P. (1985a). Sagas, totems, and history. *Samfelagstidindi* 5: 51–80.

Durrenberger, E. P. (1985b). Stratification without a state: The collapse of the Icelandic commonwealth, MS.

Durrenberger, E. P. (1987). Text and Transactions in Commonwealth Iceland. Paper presented
at the session *Economic and Ecological Approaches to the Medieval North Atlantic,* Society
for American Archaeology meetings, Toronto.

Durrenberger, E. P. (1988). Production in Medieval Iceland. Paper presented at the *Norse of
the North Atlantic* conference, Peary-MacMillain Arctic Center, Bowdoin College, Maine.

Durrenberger, E. P. and Palsson, G. (eds.) (1988). *The Anthroplogy of Iceland.* University of
Iowa Press, Iowa City.

Dyson, S. (1985). *The Creation of the Roman Frontier.* Princeton University Press, Princeton.

Egede, K. (ed.) (1982). *Detailplan for Faarealven i Sydgrønland.* Progress report by Uper-
naviarssuk Research Station, Qaqortoq Kommune, Greenland.

Einarsson, T. (1963). Pollen-analytical studies on the vegetation and climate history of Iceland
in late-and pot-glacial times. In Love, I. A. and Love, D. (eds.) *North Atlantic Biota and
Their History,* Pergamon Press, New York, pp. 355-365.

Eldjarn, K. (1961). Baer i Gjaskogum. *Arbok hins Islenzka Fornleifafelags* 1961: 7–46.

Eythorsson, J. and Sigtryggsson, H. (1971). The climate and weather of Iceland. *The Zoology of Iceland*, Vol 1, Reykjavik.

Fenton, A. (1978). *The Northern Isles*. John Donald, Edinburgh.

Fenton, A. (1981). Early manuring techniques. In Mercer, R. (ed.), *Farming Practice in British Prehistory*, Edinburgh University Press, Edinburgh, pp. 210–217.

Finsen, V. (ed.), (1852–1883). *Gragas: Islaendernes Lovbog i Fristatens Tid.* (4 Vols.), reprinted 1974, Odense University Press, Odense.

Fitzhugh, W. W. (1972). Environmental archaeology and cultural systems in Hamilton Inlet, Labrador. *Smithsonian Contributions to Anthropology* 16.

Fitzhugh, W. W. and Lamb, H. F. (1985). Vegetation history and culture change in Labrador prehistory. *Actic and Alpine Research* 17(4): 357–370.

Flannery K. V. (ed.) (1976). *The Mesoamerican Village.* Academic Press, New York.

Foote, P. and Wilson, D. (1970). *The Viking Achievement.* Duckworth, London.

Fredskild, B. (1973). Studies in the vegetational history of Greenland. *Meddel. om Grønland* 198(4).

Fredskild, B. (1978). Paleobotanical investigations of some peat deposits of Norse age at Qagssiarssuk, South Greenland. *Meddel. om Grønland* 204: 1–41.

Fredskild, B. (1981). The natural environment of the Norse settlers in Greenland, *Proceedings of the International Symposium on Early European Exploitation of the Northern Atlantic 800-1700*, Groningen, pp. 27–42.

Fredskild, B. (1982). Vegetationen i norron tid. *Grønland* 1982 (5-6-7): 189–196.

Fredskild, B. (1983). The Holocene vegetational development of the Godthabsfjord area, West Greenland, *Meddel. om Grønland.* Geoscience, 10: 1–28.

Fredskild, B. (1986). Agriculture in a marginal area: S. Greenland AD 985–1985. In Birks, H. J. B. (ed.), *The Cultural Landscape—Past, Present and Future.* Botanisk Institutt, Rapport 41, Bergen, p. 28.

Fridriksson, S. (1969). The effects of sea ice on flora, fauna, and agriculture. *Jokull* 19: 146–157.

Fridriksson, S. (1972). Grass and grass utilization in Iceland. *Ecology* 53(5): 785–796.

Gad, F. (1970). *A History of Greenland*, Vol. 1, D. Hurst, London.

Gelsinger, B. E. (1981). *Icelandic Enterprise: Commerce and Economy in the Middle Ages.* University of South Carolina Press, Columbia, SC.

Glassow, M. A. (1978). The concept of carrying capacity in the study of culture process. In Schiffer, M. L. (ed.), *Advances in Archaeological Method and Theory*, Vol. 1 Academic Press, New York, pp. 32–44.

Grayson, D. K. (1984). *Quantitative Zooarchaeology: Topics in the Analysis of Archaeological Faunas.* Academic Press, New York.

Green, S. W. (1980). Broadening least-cost models for expanding agricultural systems. In Earle, T. K. and Christenson, A. L. (eds.), *Modeling Change in Prehistoric Subsistence Economies*, Academic Press, New York. pp. 209–242.

Griffin L. C. and Rowlett, R. (1981). A "lost" Viking cereal grain, *Journal of Ethnobiology* 1(2): 200–207.

Gunnarson, G. (1980). A study of causal relations in climate and history with emphasis on the Icelandic experience. *Meddelande Fraan Ekonomisk-Historiska Inst., Lunds Universitet, 17,* Lund, Sweden.

Hallsdottir, M. (1982). Frojgreining tveggja jardvegssnida ur Hrafnkelsdal. In Thorarinsdottir, H. et al. (eds.) *Eldur er i Nordri*, Reykjavik, pp. 253–266.

Hallsdottir, M. (1984). Frjogreining tveggja jardvegssnida a Heimaey. *Arbok híns Islenzka Fornleifafelags* 1983: 48–68.

Hallsdottir, M. (1987). *Pollen Analytical studies of human influence on vegetation in relation to the Landnam tephra layer in southwest Iceland*, Ph.D. thesis, University of Lund, Sweden.

Hamilton, J. R. C. (1956). *Excavations at Jarlshof, Shetland*. Edinburgh, Her Maj. Stat. Office.

Hansen, B. U. (1991). Using climate and vegetation studies in southern Greenland to estimate the natural resources during the Norse period. *Acta Borealia* 1: 20–55.

Hastrup, K. (1985). *Culture and History in Medieval Iceland: An Anthropological Analysis of Structure and Change*. Oxford, Clarendon Press.

Hastrup, K. (1981). Cosmology and society in medieval Iceland: A social anthropological perspective on world-view. *Ethnologica Scandinavica* 1981: 64–78.

Helle, K. (1981). Norway in the High Middle Ages, *Scandinavian Journal of History* 6(3): 161–189.

Hermannson, H. (ed. and transl.) (1930). *The Book of the Icelanders (Islendingabok)* Islandica 20, Ithaca, New York.

Higgs, E. S. (ed.) (1972). *Papers in Economic Prehistory*. Cambridge University Press, Cambridge.

Higgs, E. S. (1975). *Paleoeconomy*. Cambridge University Press, Cambridge.

Hodder, I. (ed.) (1987). *Archaeology as Long-Term History*. Cambridge University Press, Cambridge.

Holm Olsen, I. M. (1981). The archaeological results. In Mathiesen, *et al.* (eds.) The Helg-y Project, *Norwegian Arch. Review* 14: 77–177.

Hunter, J. and Morris, C. D. (1981). Recent excavations at the Brough of Birsay, Orkney. In Bekker-Nielsen, H., Foote, P. and Olsen, O. (eds.) *Proceedings of the Eigth Viking Congress, Aarhus 1977*, Odense University Press, Odense, pp. 245–258.

Ingram, M. J., Farmer, G. and Wigley, T. M. L. (1981). Past climates and their impact on man: A review, In Wigley, *et al.* (eds.) *Climate and History*. Cambridge University Press, Cambridge, pp. 3–50.

Ingstad, A. S. (1977). *The Discovery of a Norse Settlement in America*. Columbia University Press, New York.

Irvine, S. G. (1968). An outline of the climate of Shetland. *Weather* 23: 392–403.

Jakobsen, B. H. (1991). Soil Resources and soil erosion in the Norse Settlement area of Osterbygden in southern Greenland. *Acta Borealia* 1: 56–67.

Jochim, M. (1979). Breaking down the system: Recent ecological approaches in archaeology. in M. L. Schiffer (ed.) *Advances in Archaeological Method and Theory*, Vol. 2: 77–117.

Jochim, M. (1983). Optimization models in context. In Moore, J. and Keene, A. (eds.) *Archaeological Hammers and Theories*, Academic Press, New York, pp. 157–171.

Johansen, J. (1975). Pollen diagrams from the Shetland and Faroe Islands. *Danmarks Geologiske Undersøgelse* 1974: 369–387.

Johansen, J. (1979). Cereal cultivation at Mykines, Faroe Islands AD 600, *Danmarks Geologiske Undersøgelse* 1978: 93–103.

Johansen, J. (1982). Vegetational development in the Faroes from 10,000 BP to the present, *Danmarks Geologiske Undersøgelse* 1981: 111–136.

Johansen, J. (1985). *Studies in the Vegetational History of the Faroe and Shetland Islands*. Foyoya Frodskaparfelag, Thorshavn.

Johannesson, B. (1960). *The Soils of Iceland*. Rekjavik.

Johannesson, J. (1974). *Islands Historie i Mellomalderen*. Universitetsforlaget, Oslo.

Jones, G. (1984). *History of the Vikings*. Oxford University Press, Oxford.

Jones, G. (1985). *The Norse Atlantic Saga*. Second ed. Oxford University Press, Oxford.

Jones, R. (1978). Why did the Tasmanians stop eating fish? In Gould, R. A. (ed.), *Explorations in Ethnoarchaeology*. New Mexico Press, New Mexico, pp. 11–49.

Jonsson, F. (ed.). (1930). *Det Gamle Grønlands Beskrivelse af Ivar Bardarsson*. Copenhagen.

Keene, A. (1983). Biology, behavior, and borrowing. In Moore, J. and Keene, A. (eds.), *Archaeological Hammers and Theories.* Academic Press, New York, pp. 135–156.

Keller, C. (1983). Gaard og seter paa Grønland-et førsøk paa a analysere ressurstilgangen i middelalderen ved hjelp av satelittbilder. In Olafsson, G. (ed.), *Hus Gaard och Bebyggelse.* Rekyjavik, pp. 59–66.

Keller, C. (1988). Vikings in the West Atlantic: A model for Norse Greenland medieval society. Paper presented at the *Norse of the North Atlantic* conference, Peary-MacMillan Arctic Center, Bowdoin College, Maine.

Kirch, P. V. (1980). The archaeological study of adaptation: Theoretical and methodolological issues. In Schiffer, M. L. (ed.), *Advances in Archaeological Method and Theory,* Vol. 3 Academic Press, New York, pp. 101–158.

Krogh, K. J. (1982). *Eirik den Rødes Grønland,* Nationalmuseet.

Lamb, H. H. (1977). *Climate: Past, Present, and Future.* Vol. 2, London, Methuen.

Larsen, L. M. (tran.) (1917). *The King's Mirror.* American–Scandinavian Foundation, New York.

Lees, S. and Bates, D. (1984). Environmental events and the ecology of cumulative change. In Moran, E. F. (ed.), *The Ecosystem Concept in Anthropology.* AAAS Symposium Series no. 92, Westview Press, Boulder, CO, pp. 133–159.

Lennihan, L. (1984). Critical historical conjunctures in the emergence of agricultural wage labor in northern Nigeria, *Human Ecology* 12 (4): 465–480.

Layendecker, D. (n.d.) Wood remains from Sandnes, West Greenland. Unpublished research report on file Hunter College and Greenland Museum.

Mellars, P. (ed.) (1978). *The Early Post-Glacial Settlment of Northern Europe,* Duckworth, London.

McGovern, T. H. (1980a). Cows, harp seals, and churchbells: Adaptation and extinction in Norse Greenland, *Human Ecology* 8 (3): 245–277.

McGovern, T. H. (1980b). *Site catchment and maritime adaptation in Norse Greenland.* In Findlow, F. and Eriksson, J. (eds.), *Site Catchment Analysis: Essays on Prehistoric Resource Space,* UCLA Press, Los Angeles, CA, pp. 193–209.

McGovern, T. H. (1980/81). The Vinland adventure: A North Atlantic perspective, *North American Archaeologist,* 2 (4): 285–308.

McGovern, T. H. (1981). The economics of extinction in Norse Greenland, In Wigley, T. M. L., *et al.* (eds.) *Climate and History,* Cambridge University Press, Cambridge, pp. 404–434.

McGovern, T. H. (1985a). The arctic frontier of Norse Greenland In Green, S. and Perlman, S. (eds.), *The Archaeology of Frontiers and Boundaries,* Academic Press, New York, pp. 275–323.

McGovern, T. H. (1985b). Contributions to the Paleoeconomy of Norse Greenland, *Acta Archaeologica,* Vol 54: 73–122.

McGovern, T. H. (1987). Trade and subsistence in Norse Greenland: Some results of the 1984 Sandnes excavations. Paper presented at the session *Economic and Ecological Approaches to the Medieval North Atlantic,* Society for American Archaeology meetings, Toronto.

McGovern, T. H. (1988). A comparison of the Eastern and Western Settlements in Greenland. *Hikuin* 15, Aarhus.

McGovern, T. H. (1991). The archaeology of the Norse North Atlantic. *Annual Review of Anthropology* 19: 331–351.

McGovern, T. H. and Jordan, R. H. (1982). Settlement and land use in the inner fjords of Godthaab District, West Greenland. *Arctic Anthropology* 19(1): 63–80.

McGovern, T. H., Buckland, P. C., Sveinbjarnardottir, G., Savory, D., Skidmore, P. and Andreasen, C. (1983). A study of the faunal and floral remains from two Norse farms in the Western Settlement, Greenland. *Arctic Anthropology* 20(2): 93–120.

McGovern, T. H. and Bigelow, G. F. (1984). The archaeozoology of the Norse site Ø17a, Narssaq, Southwest Greenland. *Acta Borealia* 1(1): 85–102.

Miller, W. I. (1987). Some aspects of householding in the medieval Icelandic Commonwealth with special reference to complex households. Paper presented at the *Anthroplogy of Iceland* conference, University of Iowa, Iowa City.

Moore, J. A. (1983). The trouble with know-it-alls: Information as a social and ecological resource, In Moore, J. and Keene, A. (eds.), *Archaeological Hammers and Theories*, Academic Press, New York, pp. 173–192.

Moran, E. (ed.) (1984). *The Ecosystem Concept in Anthropology*, American Association for the Advancement of Science Symposium Series No. 92, Westview Press, Boulder, CO.

Morris, C. D. and Rackham, J. (eds.) (1992). *Norse and Later Settlement and Subsistence in the North Atlantic*. Glasgow University Press/NABO occ. publ. No. 1, Glasgow.

Morris, C. D., Batey, C. and Jesch, J. (ed.) (1993). *The Viking Age in Caithness, Orkney, and the North Atlantic*, Edinburgh Uuniversity Press, Edinburgh.

Nørlund, P. (1936). *Viking Settlers in Greenland*, Munksgaard, Copenhagen.

Ogilvie, A. (1981a). Climate and economy in eighteenth century Iceland, In Smith, C. D. and Parry, M. (eds.), *Consequences of Climatic Change*. University of Nottingham Press, Nottingham, pp. 54–69.

Ogilvie, A. (1981b). *Climate and Society in Iceland from the Medieval Period to the Late Eighteenth Century*, Ph.D. dissertation, University of East Anglia, Norwich UK.

Ogilvie, A. (1985). The past climate and sea-ice record from Iceland. Part I: Data to AD 1780, *Climatic Change* 6: 131–152.

Olafsson, G. (1983a). *Torfbaerinn, Fra Eldaskala til Burstabaejar*, National Museum of Iceland, Reykjavik.

Olafsson, G. (ed.) (1983b). *Hus, Gaard, och Bebyggelse*, National Museum, Reykjavik.

Orvig, S. (ed.) (1968). *Climates of the Polar Regions*. World Survey of Climatology 14.

Osborne, A. R. (1985). Agricultural intensification vs. ecological stability in Qing China. Paper presented at the 1985 American Anthropology Association meetings, session on historical ecology.

Parry, M. (1978). *Climatic Change, Agriculture, and Settlement*. Dawson Archon.

Parry, M. L. (ed.) (1985). The sensitivity of Natural Ecosystems and Agriculture to Climatic Change. Special issue of *Climatic Change* 7(1).

Parry, M. L. and Carter, T. R. (1985). The effect of climatic variations on agricultural risk. *Climatic Change* 7(1): 95–110.

Parry, M. L., Carter, T. R. and Konijn, N. T. (eds.) (1987). *The Impact of Climatic Variations on Agriculture*, Vol. 1: *Assessments in cool temperate and cold regions*. Reidel, Dordrecht, Netherlands.

Perry, D. W., Buckland, P. and Snaesdottir, M. (1985). The application of numerical techniques to insect assemblages from the site of Storaborg, Iceland. *Journal of Archaeological Science* 12: 335–345.

Pahlson, I. (1981). A pollen analytical study on a peat deposit at Lagafell, Southern Iceland. *Striae* 15: 60–64.

Palsson, H. (1971). *Hrafnkel's Saga and Other Icelandic Stories*. Penguin Books, Harmondsworth.

Parsons, J., Sanders, W. and Santley, R. (1979). *The Basin of Mexico*. Academic Press, New York.

Pederssen, J. A. (1985). Sandnes Archaeological Rescure Project 1984, *Forskning i Grønland* 1/85: 23–30.

Rafnsson, S. (1976). Samsstadir i Thjorsardal. *Arbok hins Islenzka Fornleifafelags* 1976: 39–120.

Rafnsson, S. (1984). Bufe og byggd vid lok Skaftarelda og Moduhardinda. *Skaftareldum 1783–1784,* Reykjavik.

Randsborg, K. (1980). *Viking Denmark.* Duckworth, London.

Rappaport, R. A. (1968). *Pigs for the Ancestors: Ritual in the Ecology of a New Guinea People.* Yale University Press, New Haven.

Rappaport, R. A. (1971). Ritual, sanctity, and cybernetics. *American Anthropologist* 73(1): 59–76.

Rappaport, R. A. (1977). Maladaptation in social systems. In Friedman, J. and Rowlands, M. (eds.), *The Evolution of Social Systems,* London, Duckworth.

Rindos, D. (1984). *The Origins of Agriculture: An Evolutionary Prespective.* Academic Press, New York

Roussell, A. (1934). *Building Customs in the Scottish Isles.* Munksgaard, Copenhagen.

Roussell, A. (1936). Sandnes and the neighboring farms. *Meddel. om Grønland* 88(3).

Roussell, A. (1941). Farms and churches in the medieval Norse settlements of Greenland. *Meddel. om Grønland* 86(1).

Russell, D. (1985). *A Biogeographical Model for Island Dwarfism of Domestic Livestock in the Scandinavian North Atlantic: A Comparative Metrical Analysis of Bos and Ovicaprid Metapodials,* M. A. thesis on file, Hunter College, New York.

Russell, D. Amorosi, T., and McGovern, T. H. (1985). *An Archaeofauna from Storaborg, Southern Iceland.* Preliminary report on file, Icelandic National Museum and Hunter College Bioarchaeology Facility.

Sadler, J. and Buckland, P. C. (nd.). *Twig Layers.* Unpublished research report, on file, Hunter College Bioarchaeology Facility and Grønlands Landsmuseum.

Small, A. (1969). The distribution of settlement in Shetland and Faeroe in Viking times. *Sagabook of the Viking Society* 17 (2-3): 145–155.

Smith, C. D. and Parry, M. L. (eds.) (1981). *Consequences of Climatic Change.* Nottingham University Press, Nottingham.

Smith, L. P. (1975). *Methods in Agricultural Meteorology,* Elsievier, Amsterdam.

Smith, E. A. (1984). Anthropology, evolutionary ecology, and the explanatory limitations of the ecosystem concept. In Moran, E. F. (ed.), *The Ecosystem Concept in Anthroplogy,* AAAS Selected Symposium 92, Washington, DC.

Spence, D. H. N. (1979). *Shetland's Living Landscape: A study in Island Plant Ecology.* Thule Press, Sandwick.

Sørensen, I. (1982). Pollenundersogelser i moddingen paa Niaqussat. *Grønland* (8–9).

Stenberger, M. (ed.) (1943). *Forntida Gardar i Island.* Copenhagen.

Sveinbjarnardottir, G. (1982). *Farm abandonment in Eyafjallasveit,* S. Iceland Department of Geography, University of Birmingham Working Paper 14.

Sveinbjarnardottir, G. (1983). Paleoekologiske undersogelser paa Holt i Eyafjallasveit, Sydisland. In Olafsson, G. (ed.), *Hus Gard och Bebyggelse.* Reykjavik, pp. 241–250.

Sveinbjarnardottir, G., *et al.* (1981). Excavations at Storaborg: A paleoecological approach. *Arbok hins Islenzka Fornleifafelags* 1981: 113–129.

Sveinbjarnardottir, G., (1982). Landscape change in Eyafjallasveit, Southern Iceland. *Norsk Geolog. Tidskrift* 36: 75–88.

Sveinbjarnardottir, G., (1983). An uninvited guest. *Antiquity* 57: 127–130.

Sveinsson, E. O. (1953). The age of the Sturlungs, *Islandica* 36, Yale University Press, New Haven.

Thorarinsson, S. (1956). *The Thousand Years Struggle Against Ice and Fire.* Museum of Natural History, Reykjavik.

Thorarinsson, S. (1961). Population changes in Iceland. *Geographical Review* 51(4): 519–533.

Thorarinsson, S. (1970). Tephrochronology and medieval Iceland. In Berger, R. (ed.), *Scientific Methods in Medieval Archaeology,* pp. 295–328, UCLA Press, Los Angeles.

Vayda, A. P. and McCay, B. J. (1975). New directions in ecology and ecological anthropology, *Annual Review of Anthropology* 4: 293–306.

Vayda, A. P. and McCay, B. J. (1977). Problems in the identification of environmental problems. In Bayless-Smith, T. P. and Feachem, E. G. A. (eds.), *Subsistence and Survival: Rural Ecology in the Pacific.* Academic Press, New York.

Vayda, A. P. and Rappaport, A. P. (1968). Ecology, cultural and non-cultural. In Clifton, J. A. (ed.), Introduction to Cultural Anthropology: *Essays in the Scope and Methods of the Science of Man,* Houghton Mifflin, Boston.

Vilhjalmsson, V. O. (1983). Arkaeologiske Undersogelse paa Stong i Thorsardalur i Junimaaned 1983, research report on file, National Museum of Iceland.

Vilhjalmsson, V. O. (1984). Fornleifarannsokn a Stong 1984, research report on file National Museum of Iceland.

Wallace, B. (1987). L'Anse Aux Meadows: The Final Outpost. Paper presented at the session *Economic and Ecological Approaches to the Medieval North Atlantic,* Society for American Archaeology meetings, Toronto.

Winterhalder, B. and Smith, E. A. (eds.) (1981). *Hunter–Gatherer Foraging Strategies.* University of Chicago Press, Chicago.

Wallerstein, I. (1974). *The Modern World-System: Capitalist Agriculture and the European World Economy in the 16th Century.* Academic Press, New York.

Wylie, J. (1987). *The Faroe Islands: Interpretations of History.* University Press of Kentucky, Lexington.

Young, G. V. C. (1979). *From the Vikings to the Reformation.* Shearwater Press, Douglas, Isle of Man.

Zhigunov, P. S. (ed.) (1961). *Reindeer Husbandry.* 2nd ed., Moscow.

II

Pastoralism

Pastoralism is animal husbandry—the breeding, care, and use of herd animals such as sheep, goats, camels, cattle, horses, llamas, reindeer, and yaks. When animal husbandry is pursued as a primary adaptation it is a highly specialized strategy of land use, which in certain respects resembles hunting and gathering but in terms of productivity is more comparable to intensive farming. Like most hunter–gatherer groups, pastoralists use lands whose vegetation they only minimally manage: They graze their animals on wild grasses, shrubs, and, sometimes, fallow crop lands. Like agricultural populations, pastoralists invest time and energy in the management of productive resources—their livestock.

Many pastoralists are, like the herders of Kenya and Zimbabwe described in Chapters 5 and 6, nomadic, moving their herds from pasture to pasture on a seasonal schedule within a well-defined territory. The degree of mobility varies from group to group, and even from year to year within a group, depending on such environmental factors as rainfall, vegetation, and the availability of water holes. Economic and political constraints also affect the pattern of nomads' movements. Pastoralists must deal with the demands of other groups, including governments, in order to gain access to pastures and to the markets where they can exchange animals and animal products for clothing, tools, weapons, and food.

The extent of specialized pastoralism, exclusive reliance on animal husbandry, varies with environmental and market conditions (Bates and Lees, 1977). Few groups rely exclusively on their herds for day-to-day subsistence. To do so would entail heavy risks in two respects. In order to keep their animals alive, pastoralists have to adjust to the vagaries of the environment—temperature, availability of water, availability of pasturage, and so forth. At the same time they must deal with the existence of other groups with whom they may be in competition. Given these complications, it is no surprise that when the environment permits, pastoralists tend to pursue a more generalized subsistence strategy, raising at least some crops along with their animals (Schneider, 1964; Salzman, 1971; Berleant-Schiller and Shanklin, 1983).

Pastoralism is more productive than hunting and gathering. Hunters do not try to increase the numbers of animals or use the products of animals still living. Pastoralists invest labor in breeding and caring for their animals and so increase their reproduction and survival rates. Tim Ingold notes that apart from reindeer herders, pastoralists are usually concerned with the production of milk, hair, blood, or wool and with traction, using animals as vehicles or sources of work energy (1980: p. 87). By investing human labor in the production of milk rather than meat, the herder gains a greater net return. The animal need not be killed to be useful. In fact, successful herders can generally increase their holdings at a faster rate than farmers, for as the animals reproduce, the offspring can be incorporated into their herds. Of course, this advantage is partially offset by the precarious nature of herding in most areas: Animals are susceptible to disease, drought, and theft, any of which can reduce a rich household to poverty overnight.

Full-time pastoralism may be a less efficient use of land than farming in areas where cultivation is possible, such as the areas of the Himalayas and the Alps described in Chapters 7 and 8. People can produce approximately ten times as much food, measured in calories yielded per acre of land, by raising grains instead of livestock. But in areas where agriculture is risky or impossible, pastoralism is a useful strategy for converting forage—sources of energy that humans cannot use directly—into milk, blood, and meat. These foods are stored in the form of animals until the people need them either to eat or to trade for agricultural foods, clothing, and other items they cannot otherwise obtain. The fact that animals can move themselves permits herders to move the production system to the resources. Pastoralism is a relatively efficient way of extracting energy from an environment not suited to agriculture. But since it produces much less food energy per acre of land than agriculture, specialized pastoralists necessarily have low population densities.

Pastoralism, then, may have developed hand in hand with intensive agriculture (Lees and Bates, 1974). Whatever the reasons for its development, pastoralism is predicated on agricultural surplus and on regular interaction between herders and farmers. Pastoralism may be an alternative to agriculture, but it is almost never independent of it.

In nonindustrial societies, sedentary pastoralism, or animal husbandry that does not involve mobility—ranching, say, or dairy farming—is relatively rare. The practice more generally followed is nomadic pastoralism—moving the herds that are one's livelihood from pasture to pasture as the seasons and circumstances require. Land that is rich enough to support a herd indefinitely in one location will yield far more output if it is given over primarily to crops. By taking advantage of the mobility of herd animals and their own ability to group and regroup, however, pastoralists can adapt to marginal areas by moving as conditions dictate. Mobility is the key that unlocks widely dispersed resources and allows a population to gain a living from an environment that could not sustain a settled community.

Issues that have more recently concerned scholars studying pastoralists are: common land-use and its regulation (McCay and Acheson, 1987; Bromley, 1992); changing environmental conditions, particularly due to environmental degradation resulting from development (Horowitz and Nyerges, 1987); government policies and their impacts (see Horowitz and Painter, 1986); how herders respond to droughts and other environmental hazards (see for example, Browman, 1987); the impact of changing market conditions on herding practices; and the impact of changing division of labor assignments in pastoralist societies, particularly related to gender. (see *Human Ecology,* Special Issue, 1996).

The question of how nomadic pastoralists regulate access to pastures themselves, especially pastures used sequentially, has long been a subject of interest to human ecologists. This was a central theme of Frederick Barth's work (1961), in which he ascribed the role of chiefs in nomadic pastoral society to the complex functions they served as "traffic regulators" and liaisons with sedentary populations.

The use of common land pastures has received attention more recently among those human ecologists concerned with issues of common property. In fact, debates on "the tragedy of the commons" initially focused upon common grazing ground. The tragedy of the commons presumably arises when a group of resource users have common access to a single resource, for example, a pasture, which they may use for personal gain. If all users attempt to maximize gain without consideration of others, the resource will be quickly degraded and then destroyed; thus, for example, profit-motivated overgrazing will destroy the pasture. But individual resource-users have no inducement (theoretically) to hold back for the sake of the future while their fellow users do not. Short-term profits pay off in the short term, while long-term conservation efforts require enforcement because they require sacrifice. Recent studies have examined the systems that regulate access to and use of common property such as pasture to show how some have succeeded historically while others have not, and what were the conditions that produced either outcome (see Hardin and Baden, 1977; McCay and Acheson, 1987; Bromley, 1992). Netting, in Chapter 8, provides a classic illustration.

Central governments have sought to control the movements of nomadic pastoralists throughout their existence, in part because they are often regarded as a threat along a frontier (Lattimore, 1940); in modern times, in part also to deliver services such as health and education (Gradus, 1985);

and, finally, to increase productivity of herding. Controlling the activities of herders generally involves a reduction in their mobility and their flexibility. In the short run, the result is often an increase in productivity per unit of land and labor, making the technological shifts entailed in such change very attractive to many pastoralists. But there is also generally a concomitant environmental degradation indicating long-term costs of a serious nature (see, for example, Bedoian, 1978).

The introduction of new techniques in response to desertification often entails a clash of competing interests (see, for example, Horowitz and Salem-Murdock, 1987). Human ecologists have tended to be highly critical of policies of economic development aimed at pastoralists that reflect ignorance of or false preconceptions about their management of resources (Horowitz, 1986; Fratkin, 1991).

The most significant consequences for pastoralists experiencing the effects of both development and the emergence of modern nation-states and concomitant constraints upon their mobility have been in the ways they cope with environmental hazards such as drought. Earlier, traditional strategies do not always work under new contexts, or have different outcomes. Fratkin and Roth (Chapter 5) and Scoones (Chapter 6) deal with this very important issue in pastoralist research.

Shifts in rainfall or temperature are not the only environmental events pastoralists confront: the human environment may turn out to be the more challenging variety. Beyond government policy and ethnic and state boundaries, there are markets, and these regulate the lives of pastoralists to an increasing degree as they grow more and more dependent on cash and what it can buy. Bishop (Chapter 7) provides one example of the changing assignment of labor and other shifts resulting from responses to changing market conditions in transhumant agropastoralism.

REFERENCES

Barth, F. (1961). *Nomads of South Persia: The Basseri Tribe of the Kamseh Confederacy.* Humanities Press, New York.

Bates, D., and Lees, S. (1977). The role of exchange in productive specialization. *American Anthropologist.* 79(4): 824–841.

Bedoian, W. (1978). Human use of the pre-saharan ecosystem and its impact on desertization. In Gonzalez, N. (ed.), *Social and Technological Management in Dry Lands: Past and Present, Indigenous and Imposed.* Westview, Boulder, CO, pp. 61–109.

Berleant-Schiller, R., and Shanklin, E. (eds.) (1983). *The Keeping of Animals.* Allenheld, Osmun, Totowa, New Jersey.

Bromley, D. W. (ed). (1992). *Making the Commons Work: Theory, Practice and Policy.* Institute for Contemporary Studies, San Francisco.

Browman, D. (ed). (1987). *Arid Land Use Strategies and Risk Management in the Andes: A Regional Anthropological Perspective.* Westview, Boulder, CO.

Gradus, Y. (1985). *Desert Development: Man and Technology in Sparselands.* D. Reidel Publishing Company, Boston.

Hardin, G. (1968). The tragedy of the commons. *Science* 162: 1243–1248.

Hardin, G. and Baden, J. (eds.). (1977). *Managing the Commons.* W.H. Freeman, San Francisco.

Horowitz, M. (1986). Ideology, policy, and praxis in pastoral livestock development. Horowitz, M. and Painter, T. (eds.), In *Anthropology and Rural Development in West Africa.* Westview, Boulder, CO., pp. 249-272.

Human Ecology, Special Issue: "Gender and Livestock Management," (24) 2 (1996).

Horowitz, M. and Salem-Murdock, M. (1987). The political economy of desertification in White Nile Province Sudan. Little, P., Horowitz, M., and Nyerges, A. C. (eds.). In *Lands At Risk in the Third World: Local-level Perspectives.* Westview, Boulder, CO, pp. 95–114.

Lattimore, O. (1962). *Inner Asian Frontiers of China.* Beacon Press, Boston.

Lees, S. and Bates, D. (1974). The origins of nomadic pastoralism: A systemic model. *American Antiquity.* 39(2): 187–193.

Little, P., Horowitz, M., and Nyerges, A. E. (eds.). (1987). *Lands at Risk in the Third World.* Westview, Boulder, CO.

McCay, B. and Acheson, J. (eds.) (1987). *The Question of the Commons: The Culture and Ecology of Communal Resources.* University of Arizona Press, Tucson.

Salzman, P. (1971). Movement and resource extraction among pastoral nomads: The case of the Shah Nawazi Baluch. *Anthropological Quarterly* 44: 185–197.

Schneider, H. K. (1964). Economies in East African aboriginal societies. In Herskowitz, M. and Harwitz, M. (eds.), *Economic Transition in Africa.* Northwestern University Press, Evanston, pp. 53–75.

5

Who Survives Drought? Measuring Winners and Losers among the Ariaal Rendille Pastoralists of Kenya

Elliot Fratkin and Eric Abella Roth

In some respects nomadic pastoralists resemble most of our descriptions of hunter–gatherers. Like most hunter–gatherer groups, pastoralists use lands whose vegetation they only minimally manage: They graze their animals on wild grasses, shrubs, and, sometimes, fallow crop lands. On the other hand, like agricultural populations, pastoralists invest time and energy in the management of productive resources—their livestock. In 1984 northern Kenya was hit by severe drought which decimated herds. Fratkin and Roth describe how one population, the Ariaal, coped with drought and, more important, coped with governmental agencies that intervened to help them. The 1984 drought offered an opportunity to test the assumption that natural disasters or catastrophes level or diminish wealth inequalities among pastoral households. Moreover, the study offers insight into why many pastoralists try to maintain herds well above what is needed for subsistence.

The key to Ariaal subsistence strategy is herd diversity and mobility; herd diversity allows a family to use different pastures and ensures against loss due to epidemics. Mobility, perhaps even more important, allows them to cope with the fact that, in an arid environment,

Originally published in *Human Ecology: An Interdisciplinary Journal*, 18(4): 385–402, under the title "Drought and Economic Differentiation among Ariaal Rendille Pastoralists of Kenya."

Elliot Fratkin, Department of Anthropology, Smith College, Northampton, Massachusetts 01063.   **Eric Abella Roth,** Department of Anthropology, University of Victoria, Victoria British Columbia V8W 2Y2 Canada.

Case Studies in Human Ecology, edited by Daniel G. Bates and Susan H. Lees. Plenum Press, New York, 1996.

vegetation deteriorates very rapidly, requiring that herds be moved regularly. Moreover, vegetation is only rich in protein and carbohydrates during the limited growing season.

Following the 1984 drought, there was a great amount of livestock loss, which was differentially experienced by members of the population. Rich households lost more units of productive livestock than did others; however, they were buffered by their wealth from declining to the point where they owned fewer units than they needed for self-sufficiency. Moreover, they owned a larger percentage of drought-resistant camels. Thus the drought had the effect of forcing a larger percentage of poor herders to settle and has amplified wealth differentials.

Governmental agencies intervened, but considered the local people, their herding practices, and their animals as problems to be corrected rather than a key to exploiting the very arid environment. In fact the Ariaal system of production was entirely conservationist in effect: Animals were moved regularly to follow the major peaks in vegetative production. By making the pastoralists dependent on handouts and subject to restrictions on when and where they can move their animals, government policies have made them not only dependent on others but also encouraged overgrazing near settlements.

Ariaal Rendille are livestock pastoralists numbering about 8,000 persons, who subsist off the milk, meat, blood, and trade of their large herds of camels, cattle, goats and sheep in the desert region of Marsabit District, northern Kenya. Although this area receives less than 250 mm of rain per year, its varied topography allows Ariaal to exploit different microenvironments, including highland mountain pastures for their cattle, lowland deserts that bloom in the wet season and are utilized by camels and small stock (goats and sheep), and lowland plateaux used by camels and small stock as the foliage gets drier. The entire area of northern Kenya is too dry for extensive agriculture and it is populated almost exclusively by pastoral peoples including Turkana, Pokot, Samburu, Rendille, Gabra, Boran, Somali and Mukugudo Maasai (see Figure 1).

Pastoralists have long adapted to periodic drought, a standard feature of the environment. Because Kenya lies in the Intertropical Convergence Zone (where northeast monsoon winds bring hot air from Arabia, while southeast monsoons bringing moist air from the Indian Ocean), the area is subject to seasonal rainfall when these winds converge in April and October. The short rainy periods are broken by extensive dry periods

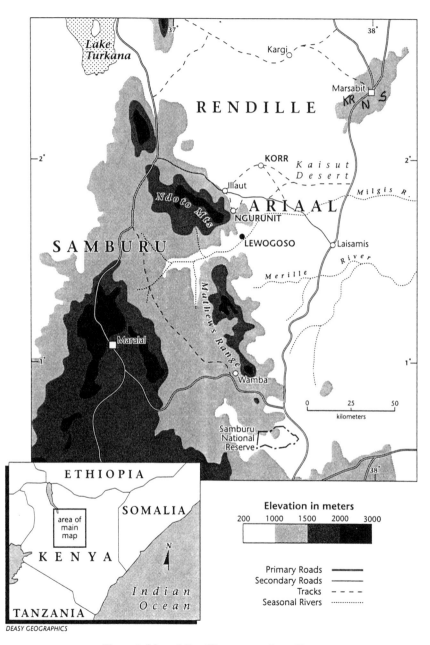

Figure 1. Map of Rendille area, northern Kenya

appropriately termed by the Ariaal "the long hunger" (November to March) and the "short hunger" (May to September). However, long term rainfall patterns tend to fluctuate. Kenya received higher than average rainfalls throughout the first half of the 20th century, which, combined with improved health and veterinary care in the 1950s and 1960s, led to growth of both human and livestock populations. Since 1968, however, much of Africa north of the equator has been subject to extensive drought, particularly in 1971 (resulting in the Sahelian famine), 1984 (the Ethiopian famine), and 1990 (the Somali famine).

African pastoralists have historically responded to extensive drought through a variety of mechanisms, including herd diversity (keeping different types of livestock) and herd mobility (moving both their herds and human populations to better pastures where some rain has fallen). Herd diversity is important, as camels can exploit one type of environment (drier lowlands), small stock another (watered lowlands), and cattle yet another (watered highlands). However, the ability to move to distant pastures is social as well as physical, and is only possible by maintaining social ties to kinsmen or friends living in different areas. One can seldom move one's animals to occupied pastures, particularly during drought periods, unless related by marriage, descent, or friendship to people already living there. Resident pastoralists moreover welcome kinsmen as further protection against cattle raids and stock rustling by traditional enemy groups (Fratkin and Smith, 1994).

Married Ariaal men and women and their small children live in semi-sedentary settlements located near permanent water, subsisting on their milk animals. Surplus stock (juveniles, males, and non-lactating female animals) are grazed in mobile and independent livestock camps orbiting around the main settlements, with members of the warrior age-grade herding cattle in the mountains, adolescent males grazing camels in the lowlands, and young boys and adolescent girls herding small stock near the main settlements (Fratkin, 1987).

While the mechanisms of herd diversity, mobility, and the maintenance of extensive kinship and friendship ties have ensured the survival of the Ariaal in the past, today they are finding it more and more difficult to herd their animals. This is due to several factors, most notably population growth of pastoral as well as agricultural peoples expanding on highland resources important for dry season grazing, but also to political insecurity where Ariaal Rendille face traditional pastoralist enemies (Turkana, Boran, and Somali) now armed with automatic weapons obtained from war-torn Ethiopia, Sudan, and Somalia. Increasingly, Ariaal Rendille households are moving closer to towns and fixed water points, where they seek the safety and security provided by police, hospitals, schools, and shops (Fratkin 1989; 1991).

This paper describes the effects of the severe drought of 1984 on one community of Ariaal Rendille pastoralists in Marsabit District, Kenya. Comparing the post-drought herd losses to pre-drought herd counts in 38 households, we show that the extensive drought of 1984, combined with the development of towns and distribution of famine relief foods, has accelerated a process of economic differentiation, dividing the Ariaal Rendille into a society of "haves" and "have-nots." Although the wealthier households lost proportionally more of their animals than poor households, they had a sufficient number of animals to recover from the loss, while poorer families did not have enough livestock to recover, forcing many to leave the nomadic community to seek jobs or famine relief in the growing towns.

ARE PASTORALISTS EGALITARIAN?

Livestock, unlike land, constitutes fluid capital for pastoral producers, subject to both natural increases but also to large-scale loss. An Ariaal ideal is that anyone can become wealthy, or at least sufficient in livestock through a combination of hard work and good fortune. Lugi Lengesen, an Ariaal elder, tells us, "Give me a piece of land (to farm), and I wouldn't know what to do with it. But give me two goats (a male and female) and I can become a rich man in time." Maintaining large herds of animals is important to the Ariaal Rendille for several reasons. Camels, cattle, and small stock of goats and sheep provide daily food in the form of milk, meat, and trade for grains. Seventy percent of the Ariaal diet consists of milk in the wet season, while small stock are consumed or traded for grains (principally maize meal) in the dry season. Furthermore, cattle and camels are the essential media of brideprice, where multiple marriages among polygynous Ariaal are the direct way to build large household membership necessary to herd their animals. Finally, the Ariaal assert that the maintenance of large herds of animals is the best protection against catastrophic losses due to livestock epidemics, droughts and famines, and raids, none of which are uncommon. While some environmentalists blame pastoralists for overgrazing and degrading the environmental due to their attempts to maximize herd size (Hardin, 1968), other studies show that there are limits to how large herds can grow due to leveling mechanisms of disease and labor shortages (Coughenour et al., 1985; Dahl and Hjort, 1976; Homewood and Rodgers, 1991; McCabe et al., 1988).

The events of the severe drought of 1984 in northern Africa showed that, indeed, wealthier households had a much greater probability of surviving drought than poor households. Moreover, it showed that the division of pastoral society into wealthy and poor may be more institutionalized than the ideal of self-made wealth indicates. These economic divisions have been observed among Middle Eastern pastoralists, where Daniel Bates (1973:134) writes for the Yoruk of Turkey, "while fortunes fluctuate . . . , life histories of influential men show little of this," and as Dan Bradburd (1982:96) notes of the Kommachi of Iran, "although shifts of wealth may occur they are not generally great enough to make the rich poor or the poor rich." The Ariaal ideal of the self-made man may, as in our own society, be more an ideal type than a predictable reality.

HOUSEHOLD ORGANIZATION IN LEWOGOSO LUKUMAI COMMUNITY

Ariaal live in a variety of community arrangements, ranging from small and permanent cattle-keeping settlements in the highlands to large and mobile settlements that raise camels and small stock in the desert lowlands. Settlements are typically patrilineal and patrilocal, made up of brothers or clan agnates whose wives come from other clan settlements. Lewogoso Lukumai, our study community, is named after the subclan Lewogoso of the larger patrilineal section of Lukumai, to which most of its members belong. Lewogoso is a large community, even by Rendille standards, consisting in 1976 of a large circle of 52 houses (total population 269), which separated into three smaller settlements following the drought of 1984. Settlement composition now was largely determined by the number of pack animals to carry water, where households owning more camels lived farther distances from the water holes, while those with more cattle and small stock moved closer to the permanent water sources (Roth and Fratkin, 1991).

While lineage and clan affiliation determines settlement composition, production within the community is based on autonomous household organization. A household is defined as the smallest domestic unit with its own independent herd and which can make independent decisions over the allocation of its members' domestic and herding labor. A typical household consists of a married male stockowner, his wife or cowives and their children, with an occasional dependent such as widowed mother or wife's brother. Each women builds and maintains her own house, and a household may range from one to five houses.

Households vary considerably in the composition and size of their livestock herds. Wealthier households tend to be polygynous, have large herd sizes, and greater numbers of camels and cattle than small stock. Wealth also tends to be concentrated in certain lineages, while impoverishment appears to be associated with Ariaal households owning small stock rather than large stock, and with poor Rendille immigrants who recently moved or married into the Ariaal community.

LOSS THROUGH DROUGHT: METHODS AND MATERIALS

To quantify Ariaal livestock losses related to the drought, herd counts obtained in 1976 for 38 households in Lewokoso Lukumai settlement were compared to livestock censuses of the same household herds in 1985. While the original 1976 Lewogoso community had, by 1985, grown to over 75 households in three settlements, analysis was limited to the 38 households originally studied in 1976. Counting people's livestock is as difficult and rude as asking for people's bank balances. Nevertheless we managed to count household herds by direct observation and interview, particularly during the *almhado* ritual ceremony held annually, when all of the Ariaal's livestock return to the main settlements for blessings. These interviews were often conducted in the presence of related herd owners who knew the general (and probably exact) histories and sizes of their kinsmen's herds.

We wished to know what Ariaal households had enough animals to support their members, and which did not. To do this, we standardized the livestock counts into tropical livestock units (or TLUs, a standard reference representing 250 kg of weight where 1 TLU = 1 cattle, or 0.8 camel, or 10 small stock). This standard unit enabled us to calculate changes in livestock ownership (as TLUs) for pre-drought (1976) and post-drought (1985) conditions. Figures 2–5 show changes in household herd size between 1976 and 1985, showing changes in total TLUs (Figure 2), camel ownership (Figure 3), cattle (Figure 4), and small stock ownership (Figure 5).

Next, we wished to know what is the minimum number of animals necessary to support an individual or household in the context of rural northern Kenya. We adopted Pratt and Gwynne's (1977: 34–43) estimate of 4.5 TLUs per person as the minimum level of livestock necessary to provide an individual with sufficient calories in a pastoral economy in arid lands. This calculation is made assuming a diet that is 75% milk and 25% meat (although we know that grains acquired from trade of livestock play an important role in pastoralist nutrition, particularly in the dry season when milk supplies are low).

We estimate that for Ariaal, 4.5 TLUs provides an individual with approximately 1.5 liters of milk, 20 grams of meat, and 70 grams of maize meal daily, yielding an estimated average of 1600 kcal and 105 grams of protein per day (Field and Simpkin, 1985: 171–72). This figure represents the minimum amount necessary to sustain an individual, and compares poorly to an American diet that typically provides over 2,500 kcal daily to adults. However, the figure of 4.5 TLUs per person provides a useful measure to compare households.

We established the following classification to scale household self-sufficiency and wealth for Ariaal:

1. POOR—TLUs/person < 4.5
2. SUFFICIENT—TLUs/person = 4.5–9.0
3. RICH—TLUs/person > 9.0

The first category represents less than the minimal per person nutritional requirements, while the second and third represent, respectively, up to and beyond two times the minimum. Because households vary in per person size, we use the TLU per person rather than per household to determine wealth. At the same time it focuses on individual household members' nutritional requirements.

RESULTS

The drought resulted in a dramatic decline in herd size for all species of animals and for all Lewogoso households, as seen in Table 1, which presents pre- and postdrought household herd size by species and per person TLUs. Differential mortality is apparent, however, with camels, the most drought resistant animals, suffering the least amount of loss (18.3%), cattle the highest (51.2%), and small stock, intermediate (49.8%). These losses are illustrated in Figures 2–5.

Households did not lose livestock equally, however. Table 2 shows specific types of livestock loss for each of the three economic levels, where rich and sufficient households (with greater numbers of camels and cattle) lost more absolute numbers of animals than poor households, which concentrate on small stock production. In Ariaal society, as among other East African pastoralists, wealth and prestige are measured by ownership of large animals, related both to their copious supplies of milk and their role in bridewealth and ritual consumption.

Most importantly, Table 2 shows there is a graduated loss of TLUs per level, with the rich losing the highest proportion (51.5% of their TLUs), sufficient households, an intermediate amount (43.0%), and the poor classification, the least (37.8%). The fact that wealthy families lost proportionally more animals than poor households is probably due to a reverse

Table 1. Pre- and Postdrought Household Herd Size by
Species, Per Person TLUs, and Mean Percentage Loss

Species	Predrought	Postdrought	Mean percentage loss
Camels			
x	11.5	9.4	18.3
S.D.	17.2	16.3	
C.V.	149.6	173.4	
Cattle			
x	32.4	15.8	51.2
S.D.	31.5	17.8	
C.V.	97.2	112.7	
Small stock			
x	134.0	67.3	49.8
S.D.	128.0	66.4	
C.V.	95.5	98.7	
TLUs			
x	12.7	6.4	49.6
S.D.	10.9	5.4	
C.V.	85.8	84.4	

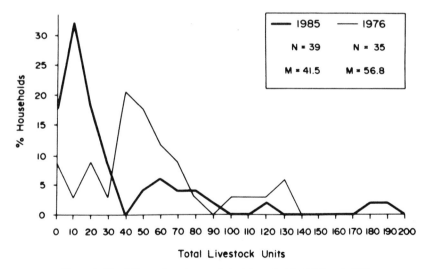

Figure 2. Total livestock units per Ariaal households, 1976 and 1985.

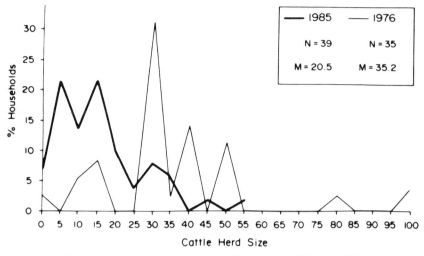

Figure 3. Cattle ownership per Ariaal households, 1976 and 1985.

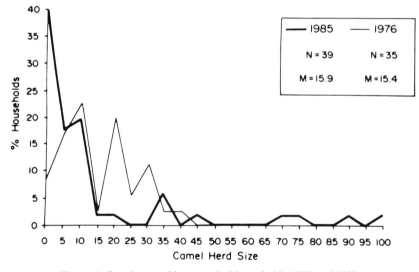

Figure 4. Camel ownership per Ariaal households, 1976 and 1985.

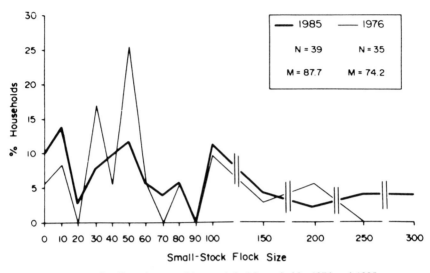

Figure 5. Small stock ownership per Ariaal households, 1976 and 1985.

economy of scale, where pastoralists with fewer animals are able to provide better care than wealthy herders with many animals.

Since economic status is directly linked to absolute herd size, we next examined livestock loss by economic level, as shown in Table 3. Once again the pattern of rich households suffering the worst livestock loss emerges.

Table 2. Average Pre- and Postdrought Herd Sizes, Absolute and Percentage Loss by Species, and Economic Status

Status		Predrought	Postdrought	Loss	N	%
Rich	Camels	18.8	15.4	3.4	18.1
	Cattle	51.2	24.3	26.9	52.5
	Small stock	181.9	85.4	96.5	53.1
	TLUs	20.2	9.8	10.4	51.5
Sufficient	Camels	4.4	3.4	1.0	22.7
	Cattle	16.5	8.8	7.7	46.7
	Small stock	101.8	58.2	43.6	42.8
	TLUs	6.4	3.7	2.7	42.2
Poor	Camels	4.0	3.7	0.3	7.5
	Cattle	8.4	4.7	3.7	44.0
	Small stock	59.1	37.7	21.4	36.2
	TLUs	3.0	1.8	1.2	40.0

Table 3. Pre- and Postdrought Status, Based on Per Person TLU Scale

Status	Predrought N	Predrought %	Postdrought N	Postdrought %	Percentage change
Rich	19	50.0	8	21.0	-29.0
Sufficient	12	31.6	15	39.5	+7.9
Poor	7	18.4	15	39.5	+21.1
Totals	38	100.0	38	100.0	

Table 4. Status Change by Household

Predrought Status	Postdrought status	N	Percentage
Rich (19)	Rich	8	42%
	Sufficient	11	58%
	Poor	0	0%
Sufficient (11)	Sufficient	4	33%
	Poor	8	67%
Poor (7)	Poor	7	100%

In 1985, only eight of the original nineteen families remained in this classification. In contrast, the sufficient and poor groups increased in size, reflecting the general loss of TLUs for all households as a result of drought. Poor households increased from seven in 1976 to fifteen in 1985.

Finally, while Table 3 pertains to categorical change, it does not consider the fate of individual households. Table 4 depicts pre- and postdrought household economic statuses within each level. Combined with previous results, these data indicate that while rich households suffered the highest absolute loss of animals, the very size of their herds buffered them from falling below the minimum TLU per person level. Eleven of the predrought rich households (58%) did fall to the sufficient classification after the drought in 1985, but none became poor. In comparison, an even larger proportion of the households sufficient before the drought (67%) became poor by 1985.

SUMMARY AND DISCUSSION

The 1984 drought had differential impacts on Ariaal households , varying by household wealth, type of animals kept, and the household size and composition. Analyzing the effects of the 1984 drought upon individual households of Lewogoso Lukumai, the number of poor households doubled, while sufficient and rich pastoral households decreased by more than 50%. Nevertheless, eight of the ten wealthiest households of 1976 remained the only rich households in 1985. Furthermore, these rich households actually increased their ownership of camels, while poor and sufficient households took losses in all three livestock types. This finding of increases in wealth differences contradicts the view that drought or other catastrophes level or diminish household inequalities, and in fact contributed to a greater polarization between wealthy and poor in a supposedly egalitarian pastoral community.

These findings confirm what pastoralists consistently maintain as they strive to maximize their herds, that a rich man may lose half of one hundred animals and survive, where a poor man will lose half of ten animals and perish. As pointed out in an analysis of Turkman nomadic pastoralists by Irons (1979), maximizing economic strategies for pastoralists act as a buffer against environmental calamities, as well as providing surplus animals for ritual and social use such as age-set ceremonies and brideprice payments. Nevertheless, certain ecologists criticize pastoralists for purportedly herding 50 to 100% more animals than required for subsistence, citing such excesses as prime agents in rangeland degradation and desertification (Pratt and Gwynne 1977; Lamprey, 1983). While other ecologists dispute these findings (cf. Coughenour et al., 1985; Horowitz, 1979; Western and Finch 1986), the Ariaal example indicates that regardless of the long-term environmental impact maximizing strategies function well in times of ecological stress.

Rather than acting as an equalizing force of household wealth, drought increased disparities in both absolute and categorical livestock holdings, with the rich households remaining rich, the middle households becoming poor, and the poor households becoming even poorer. In the absence of enough animals to survive, the poorest households have three alternative economic strategies available. One is the long-standing tradition of herding for other, more affluent households in return for the loan of milk animals to feed their households. A second, more recent, avenue is increased reliance on the cash economy through the sale of remaining livestock. Often, however, these poorer households sell of all their stock and end up impoverished, while rich households only sell their surplus animals. A third strategy is to abandon the pastoral economy altogether, where increasingly impoverished pastoralists are migrating to towns and cities in search of wage paying jobs as laborers or watchmen.

It is not clear whether pastoral impoverishment is permanent or whether individuals can recover and re-enter the pastoral economy. McCabe (1987) observed that of four Turkana households suffering drought-related livestock loss, one was able to achieve predrought levels in only three years. However, Hogg (1986) describes the fate of Kenya Boran, who, deprived of their livestock by the political turmoil in the 1960s, led to a permanent settling of stockless families in the towns of Isiolo District.

Regardless of the long-term fate of these pastoralists, the immediate stresses of large scale loss to drought must be significant, both in social and nutritional terms. The frequent recurrence of drought in this region and the effectiveness of maximizing economic strategies argue for the persistence of household wealth differentials as a consequence of social and environmental factors. The recent development of famine-aid communities among the Rendille and growth in urban migration of Rendille and Ariaal seeking wage-labor suggests a shrinking and transformation of their subsistence pastoral economy to include new alternatives (Fratkin, 1991). It remains to be seen whether town life and the settling of pastoralists leads to improvements or disadvantages in their quality life, particularly in terms of health and nutrition, and whether permanent classes of rich and poor develop among the Ariaal as they have among other pastoral societies.

ACKNOWLEDGMENTS

Data on Ariaal was collected at Lewogoso Lukumai settlement, Marsabit District, Kenya between July 1974 and February 1976 and between August 1985 and March 1986. We are grateful to Mr. Larion Aliaro, Mr. Lugi Lengesen, and the people of Lewogoso community for their assistance in the fieldwork, and to the Office of the President, Republic of Kenya, and the Institute of African Studies, University of Nairobi, for their permission to conduct research and their assistance in this project. Funding was provided with grants from the Smithsonian Institution, the National Geographic Society, and the Social Science Research Council.

REFERENCES

Bates, D. (1973). *Nomads and Farmers; A Study of the Yoruk of Southeastern Turkey.* Museum of Anthropology, Anthropological Papers 52. University of Michigan, Ann Arbor.
Bradburd, D. (1982). Volatility of animal wealth among southwest Asian pastoralists. *Human Ecology* 10(1): 85–106.
Coughenour, M., Ellis, J., Swift, D., Coppock, D., Galvin, K., McCabe, T. and Hart, T. (1985). Energy extraction and use in a nomadic pastoral ecosystem. *Science* 230: 619–625.
Dahl, G. and Hjort, A. (1976). *Having Herds: Pastoral Herd Growth and Household Economy.* Stockholm Studies in Social Anthropology 2. University of Stockholm, Stockholm.

Field, C.R. and Simpkin, S. P. (1985). *The Importance of Camels to Subsistence Pastoralists in Kenya.* IPAL Technical Report E-7, Nairobi: UNESCO, pp. 161–192.

Fratkin, E. (1986). Stability and resilience in East African pastoralism: The Ariaal and Rendille of Northern Kenya. *Human Ecology* 14: 269–286.

Fratkin, E. (1987). Age-sets, households and the organization of pastoral production. *Research in Economic Anthropology* 8: 295–314.

Fratkin, E. (1989). Two lives for the Ariaal. *Natural History* 98(5): 39–49.

Fratkin E. (1991). *Surviving Drought and Development: Ariaal Pastoralists of Northern Kenya.* Westview Press, Boulder, CO.

Fratkin, E. and Smith, K. (1994). The organization of pastoral production. In Fratkin, E., Galvin, K. and Roth, E. A. (eds.), *African Pastoralist Systems,* Lynne Rienner Publishers, Boulder, CO.

Hardin, G. (1968). The tragedy of the commons. *Science* 162: 1243–1248.

Hogg, R. (1986). The new pastoralism: Poverty and dependency in northern Kenya. *Africa* 56(3): 319–333.

Homewood, K. M. and Rodgers, W. A. (1991). *Maasailand Ecology: Pastoralist development and wildlife conservation in Ngorongoro, Tanzania.* Cambridge University Press, Cambridge.

Horowitz, M. M. (1979). *The Sociology of Pastoralism and African Livestock Projects.* AID Program Evaluation Discussion Paper No. 6, The Studies Division, Office of Evaluation, Bureau for Program and Policy Coordination. United States Agency for International Development, Washington.

Irons, W. (1979). Political stratification among pastoral nomads. In Equipe Ecologie (eds.), *Pastoral Production and Society,* Cambridge University Press, Cambridge, pp. 361–374.

Lamprey, H. F. (1983). Pastoralism yesterday and today: The overgrazing problem. In Bourliere, F. (ed.), *Tropical Savannas,* Ecosystems of the World, Volume 13. Elsevier, Amsterdam, pp. 643–666.

McCabe, T. (1987). Drought and recovery: Livestock dynamics among the Ngisonyoka Turkana of Kenya. *Human Ecology* 15(4): 371–390.

McCabe, J. T., Dyson-Hudson, R., Leslie, P. W., Dyson-Hudson, N. and Wienpahl, J. (1988). Movement and migration as pastoral responses to limited and unpredictable resources. In Whitehead, Hutchinson, Tinnmann, and Varady (eds.), *Arid Lands Today and Tomorrow,* Westview Press, Boulder, CO, pp. 727–734.

Pratt, D. and Gwynne, M. (1977). *Rangeland Management and Ecology in East Africa.* Hodder and Stoughton, London.

Roth, E.A. and Fratkin, E. (1991). Rendille herd composition and settlement patterns. *Nomadic Peoples* 28: 83–92.

Western, D. and Finch, V. (1986). Cattle and pastoralism: Survival and production in arid lands. *Human Ecology* 14(1): 77–94.

6

Coping with Drought: Responses of Herders and Livestock in Contrasting Savanna Environments in Southern Zimbabwe

Ian Scoones

Rather than assuming environmental stability over time, human ecologists have placed a great deal of emphasis in the past two decades upon the ways people respond to the pressures of environmental stress such as is caused by earthquakes, floods, and frosts. Among those problems that have elicited the most attention are droughts, the subject of Scoones' paper. Scoones shows the importance of attention to the details of difference in the environment, in the characteristics of the problem over time, and the means that people employ to cope. His study of herding practices in southern Zimbabwe, which has adopted extensive herding only in the past century, differentiates between grasslands on contrasting soils, which are affected by drought in different ways and recover at different rates. The intensity and duration of droughts varies as well, posing different problems to farmers, which change through time. Environmental variation is not sufficient, however, to account for the herding practices Scoones observed; he also looked at socioeconomic factors that regulated herd movement by the pastoralists, including labor management, the influence of wealth, loaning arrangements, institutional constraints, and conflict over access to

Originally published in *Human Ecology: An Interdisciplinary Journal,* 20(3)(1992): 293–314.

Ian Scoones, Drylands and Sustainable Agricultural Programmes, 3 Endsleigh Street, London WC1H 0DD, England.

Case Studies in Human Ecology, edited by Daniel G. Bates and Susan H. Lees. Plenum Press, New York, 1996.

territory. Scoones concludes with the advice that policymakers consider these factors so as not to impede local herders' implementation of their own knowledge and experience to respond to drought.

INTRODUCTION

Drought is a recurrent phenomenon in dryland Africa. Herders and farmers must continually adjust their practices in order to cope with variability. No drought is the same, some are localized, some widespread; some affect grass production, others crops. Local strategies must therefore be flexible and responsive to a range of uncertain contingencies. For this reason it is vital that field research examines the details of herder and livestock response, rather than offering aggregate insights. This requires a comprehensive analysis of the interaction of livestock biology and herder resource management at the local level that can inform livestock development planning.

Dryland savanna environments in southern Zimbabwe are subject to enormous variations in rainfall, with coefficients of variation of annual rainfall ranging between 20% and 35%. Uncertainty dominates herding practice; herders and livestock must respond to high levels of spatial and temporal variation of available fodder. Seasonal variation occurs with regular deficits in the late dry season. Interannual variation is marked also, with long-term cattle population dynamics being highly influenced by episodic events, notably drought (Scoones, 1993). The result is a largely non-equilibrium dynamic system, where rainfall variability is so high that livestock and grass populations rarely reach a stable level. Under such conditions, notions of fixed "carrying capacity" and predictable, regular, and conservative management interventions are irrelevant (Ellis and Swift, 1988; Westoby et al., 1989; Behnke and Scoones, 1993). Herders must adaptively respond to spatial and temporal variability through "opportunistic" management (Sandford, 1982; Scoones, 1994).

This paper presents a case study that explores opportunistic management in the face of drought. The contrasting responses to short- and long-term droughts are shown by examining cattle populations in two different savanna ecosystems in a communal area in southern Zimbabwe. Biological and socioeconomic responses unfold through droughts, resulting in a diversity of complex drought coping strategies. Biological responses are modified by differential management inputs–herding, transhumant movement, and supplementary feeding. The impacts of drought on cattle herds can

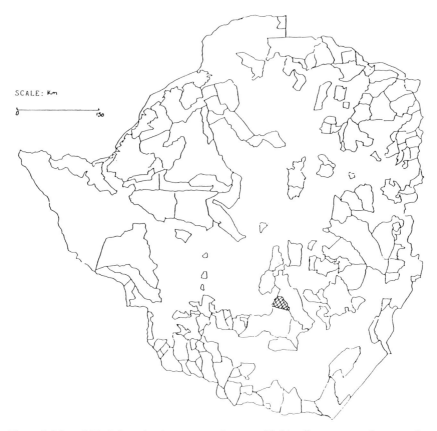

Figure 1. Map of Zimbabwe showing communal areas, with Mazvihwa communal area study area highlighted.

thus only be understood with insight into this interaction of ecological and socioeconomic factors.

THE STUDY AREA: PATTERNS OF SPATIAL AND TEMPORAL VARIATION

The study area is centered on Mazvihwa communal land in Zvishavane district, southern Zimbabwe (Figure 1). The area is typical of many communal areas in the drier regions of Zimbabwe. A high population density of around 30 persons/km² is supported by a mixed farming system of dryland cropping and livestock keeping. Small amounts of gardening and irrigated farming supplement food and incomes. Of more significance are remittance incomes from off-farm employment; these supply a major proportion of income flows in the rural areas (Jackson et al., 1987).

The area is populated by Shona speaking Karanga people who have, since the onset of colonial rule in the late 1890s, spread out from their original hilltop settlements and come to inhabit both the sandy soil hills and clay soil plains areas. Cattle keeping has only become a major economic activity over the past century. Previously, relatively small numbers of stock were kept in guarded mountain sites, as the area was subject to intensive raiding by the Ndebele people.

Today, people live in scattered household clusters, with older men's families being surrounded by the households of male kin. It is on the basis of these shallow lineage networks, reinforced by the Shona pattern of patriarchal and patrilocal inheritance, that important sharing relationships, of cattle, labor and food, are usually based (Scoones and Wilson, 1988). Settlement and land-use patterns in the area have been highly influenced by state intervention over the past 60 years, with villages, in some areas, planned in lines separating distinct agricultural and grazing blocks. This has been particularly the case in the plains area of the Mazvihwa study area. The sandy-soil hilly area has been, by comparison, relatively untouched by colonial and post-independence intervention (Scoones, 1990).

The data presented in this paper is based on a detailed field study carried out between 1986 and 1988, with follow-up visits since then.[1] Two major data sources are drawn on for information on cattle populations. First, veterinary cattle-dip data for nine dips in Mazvihwa communal land provides monthly records of a range of biological and economic parameters. The second source of data was a detailed survey of 385 cattle owned by a subset of 71 households in a stratified cluster-based sample in Mototi ward of Mazvihwa communal land.[2]

Two droughts during the 1980s are examined in detail in this chapter—a two- to three-year drought between 1982 and 1984, and a single year drought in the season between 1986 and 1987. Some reflections on the contrasts with the very severe 1990 to 1992 drought are also included. Spatial variation in fodder resources is influenced particularly by soil type. Two contrasting savanna types are evident in the Mototi ward study area (total area c. 100 km²): the clay soil savanna zone, the sandy soil

---

[1]The main period of fieldwork was carried as part of a doctoral study between 1986 and 1988. This work was carried out in collaboration with Ken Wilson. Since 1988, return visits for shorter periods have been made in 1989, 1990, 1991, and 1992.

[2]The household survey data was collected in conjunction with Ken Wilson who originally established the sample group. The sample was stratified according to ecological zone (clay, edge, sand) and wealth (according to wealth rank—see footnote).

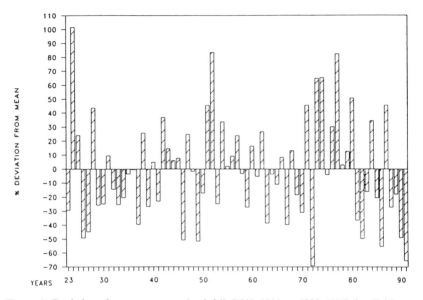

Figure 2. Deviations from mean annual rainfall (1923–1924 to 1990–1991) for Zvishavane Town (ca. 40 km from study area).

savanna zone, and in between an edge zone where both savanna types can be identified.

Within each savanna type further spatial variation at the more local level can be discerned. Of particular importance for grazing management is catenary variation across slopes, as different portions of the landscape respond differently (in terms of biomass production and its variability) to the impact of drought. In the clay soil zone, upland savanna grassland has high potential productivity and grass quality due to the good nutrient content of the soil type, but grass production is highly variable between years. Only with heavy rainfall is infiltration sufficient on these clay soils to provide for grass growth. Lower down the slope on the river and stream banks, or in transition zones where pans and sinks form, infiltration is higher and grass growth is more certain. A similar pattern of catenary variation is observed in the sandy soil zone. By contrast, sandy soil savanna upland grass production is less variable in quantity but is lower in quality than in the clay soil zone, because of the nutrient and infiltration properties of the granitic sandy soil. Run-on portions of the landscape are equally important in providing stable and high quality grass production. These valley-bottom lands (dambos or vleis) are key grazing resources in the sandy soil savanna areas (Scoones and Cousins, 1994).

Local drought coping strategies are keyed into responding to the patterns of spatial and temporal variability that exist at different scales in savanna environments. The ability to respond to this variability is dependent on a range of socioeconomic factors. These include: herding labor availability, kin support networks, cattle loaning and sharing relationships, cash income for labor hire or fodder purchase, and tenurial restrictions on herd movement. These factors were investigated with a stratified sample (by ecological zone and wealth) of 71 households. These households (defined in terms of residence units) are situated within a series of household clusters which are based on labor and cattle-sharing relationships (Scoones and Wilson, 1988).

RESPONSES TO DROUGHT

An understanding of the contrasting dynamics of savanna ecology in clay and sandy soil zones suggests a number of human ecological hypotheses about livestock and herder response in the different zones (Bell, 1982; Walker, 1985; Frost et al., 1986; Scoones, 1990):

- The phases of drought (population movement, collapse and recovery) will be different in the different ecological zones; drought will affect the clay zone populations first because of the early collapse in grass production. This will be reflected in population parameters (birth and death rates) and population numbers.
- The percentage cattle mortality will be highest in the clay zone areas, less in the edge zone, and lowest in the sandy soil zone. This is because drought has a lesser impact on grass production in the sandy soil zone. In addition, the availability of key resource grazing patches, notably dambos, is more extensive in the sandy soil zone.
- The movement pattern of cattle will be away from the clay soil zone to the edge zone and on to the sandy soil zone areas. Movement will at first be local, and will later involve movement out of the area to sandy soil zone areas with higher available fodder. This movement will also depend on patterns of water availability in the different zones.
- Recovery of cattle populations following drought will be especially rapid in the clay soil savanna areas, as grass production responds quickly to the return of rainfall. Grass is also of good quality and so rapidly boosts the condition of animals.

These hypotheses, derived from an understanding of savanna ecology, can be tested against the available data.

Savanna ecology is clearly insufficient to explain the whole range of responses seen; socioeconomic factors are also important in modifying the ecological patterns of drought response (cf. Homewood and Rodgers, 1991; Fratkin and Roth, 1990; Herren, 1990; McCabe, 1987; Homewood and Lewis, 1987; Campbell, 1984, for east African cases). A number of hypotheses can be proposed:

- The survival of livestock will depend critically on the ability of households to respond to spatial and temporal variation in fodder resources. Flexible movement responses will be vital.
- Movement options will be constrained by available labor. The availability of household labor will be positively correlated with herd survival.
- Drought response options will be constrained by available cash income, particularly income unaffected by drought, to hire labor or purchase supplementary feeds. The cash income of households (particularly remittance income) can be expected to be positively correlated with herd survival.
- The ability to arrange loaning sites for cattle suffering local drought shortages will be key. This will be assisted by strong kin and friendship networks; especially linkages that spread to other ecological zones.
- The ability to move animals will be affected by tenure rules that regulate access to common grazing resources in nearby areas. The strength of local and state institutions in ensuring exclusion of outsiders' cattle or restricting cattle movement will be important in affecting herd survival. These hypotheses will be examined with data derived from household and group interviews in the study area.

CATTLE POPULATION RESPONSES

This section examines the contrasting responses of cattle populations during two droughts—1982–1984 and 1987–1988. Two sets of data examine the patterns of livestock population collapse and recovery: first, veterinary department dip records, and second, the detailed monitoring of sample herds.

Population Collapse and Recovery

Table 1 shows the patterns of collapse and recovery of cattle populations around three groups of dips in different ecological zones. The data

Table 1. Cattle Population Collapse and Recovery

Zone	Dip	N	Collapse, 1982–1984 (%)	Collapse, 1987–1988 (%)	Recovery, 1984–1986 (%)
Clay	Makovora	2082	68.3	30.5	228.3
	Gwamadube	2988	81.4	27.6	111.3
	Mazvihwa	1679	82.5	38.8	108.3
Edge	Gwenombe	1705	80.4	22.8	90.5
	Solomon	8211	61.4	12.2	57.7
Sand	Kwata	1766	63.4	18.9	69.7
	Zerubi	2055	73.6	20.3	77.8
	Murowa	2819	63.8	8.3	36.0
	Chibvumba	950	72.6	14.4	24.7

Note: Collapse indicates percentage reduction of starting population at end of period. Recovery indicates percentage increase in cattle population over period (see text for details). N refers to the maximum cattle population at each dip during 1982, prior to the drought.

Table 2. Percentage of Original Cattle Numbers Present Following Drought by Ecological Zone

Zone	Survival, 1982–1984 (%)	Survival, 1987–1988 (%)
Clay	17.8	68.6
Edge	28.4	80.5
Sand	35.7	104

show that clay soil savanna cattle populations had higher percentage reductions in populations in both droughts. This reflects the more severe impact of drought on fodder resources in the clay soil zone. However, recovery (through both reproduction and in-migration) is faster following the 1982–1984 drought in the clay soil savanna. The rapid bounce-back of grass biomass in clay soil savannas is important in this recovery.

These patterns of collapse and recovery are reflected in the sample herds (Table 2). The changes in herd size are lowest in the sandy soil zone and highest in the clay soil zone, with the edge zone showing an intermediate level.

Mortality Rates

Dip data show that in the 1982–1984 drought, clay zone populations show peak mortality before the sandy soil zone does. Clay soil zone mortality reaches a maximum twice the size of the sandy soil zone mortality in March 1983, some two months earlier than in the sandy soil zone. By contrast, in the 1987–1988 drought, the peaks are coincident in January 1988, but the clay soil mortality rate was four times higher than the sandy soil mortality. Detailed examination of the sample herds during the 1987–1988 drought showed that peak mortality was in November 1987 for the clay zone and January 1988 for the edge zone. There was no increased mortality in the sandy soil zone.

The data on the timing and scale of mortality for herds in the different zones bears out the hypothesis suggested earlier. Clay zone biomass production collapses earlier and more dramatically in serious droughts than in the sandy soil zone (Scoones, 1990; see above). This changed availability of forage is reflected in patterns of herd mortality.

Cattle mortality is felt differentially within herds. In both droughts the highest mortality rate was suffered by mature cows. In 1982–1984 only 16% survived, while in 1987–1988 71% survived. Since over 50% of the total herd were cows or heifers, the impact on the breeding population of this differential mortality was severe.

Birth Rates

In all dipping areas in Mazvihwa the birth rates rapidly picked up following drought (Table 3), showing birth rates (numbers of calves born/total population in October) of 35% (clay zone) and 24% (sandy soil zone) in the year following the 1984–1985 drought (October 1984 to September 1985) and 24% (in both zones) following the 1987–1988 drought (October 1988 to September 1989). If the proportion of cows in the sample cattle

Table 3. Births (%B) and Deaths (%D) in Clay and Sandy Soil Savanna Dips, Mazvihwa. Numbers as Proportion of Total Cattle Census at October

Period	Clay soil		Sandy soil	
	%B	%D	%B	%D
Oct. 83–Sept. 84	0	0.4	0.4	0.5
Oct. 84–Sept. 85	35	0	24	0
Oct. 85–Sept. 86	16	0	20	0
Oct. 86–Sept. 87	13	0	14	1
Oct. 87–Sept. 88	7	18.5	5.6	8.5
Oct. 88–Sept. 89	24	0.4	24.3	0.9
Oct. 89–Sept. 90	15	0.4	17.6	0.3

population is representative of the dip population, this represents a calving rate approaching 100%.

The late decline and rapid recovery in birth rates shown by the data for both ecological zones probably reflects the physiology of local breeds and crosses which are well adapted to stress, showing rapid reconception following drought.

These data, from both dipping records and household sample data, have established that there are different dynamics of cattle population change evident in the different ecological zones identified. The patterns observed are in line with the expectations proposed in the ecological hypotheses outlined above. The data on population parameters demonstrate that the higher variability of primary production potential in the clay soil zone (see above) results in earlier collapse, but faster recovery, of populations exposed to drought.

HERD MANAGEMENT AND LIVESTOCK SURVIVAL

This section examines the various management responses employed in the Mazvihwa area during the two drought periods and analyze how these have affected livestock survival.

Movement

The movement of cattle to alternative grazing areas dominates the management strategies used by farmers to ensure cattle survival. Movement is an important component of herd management in normal years; this involves localized movements to key resource grazing patches within the landscape (Scoones, 1994). Movement in response to drought-induced shortages of fodder occurs at different scales and in relation to the availability of different savanna types. Local movement occurs between clay and sandy soil zone savanna and from upland grazing resources to lowland key resource areas. Larger scale movements to areas with fodder surplus can occur under conditions of severe drought.

The pattern of movement in the 1982–1984 drought (Figure 3) initially involved localized movement away from the clay soil savanna areas into the sandy soil areas, where grazing was available on mountains and in the lower parts of the catena (dambos). Browse from miombo trees was also important in this period. However, the available fodder was insufficient to support the growing influx of cattle into the sandy soil zone and by

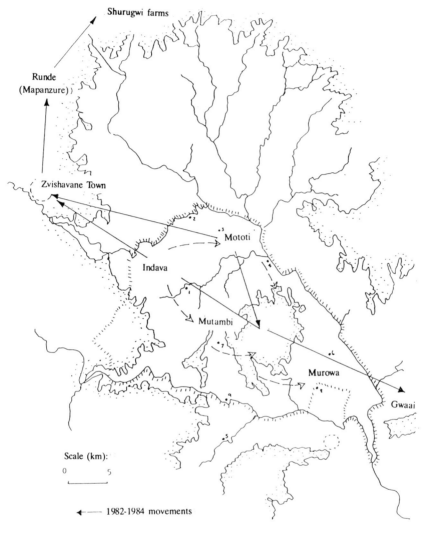

Scale (km):

0   5

◄—— 1982-1984 movements

1987-1988 movements

1 = Makovora; 2 = Gwamadube; 3 = Mazvihwa; 4 = Gwenoabe; 5 = Solomon;
6 = Kwata; 7 = Zerubi; 8 = Murowa; 9 = Chibvumba

Figure 3

November 1982 some cattle were beginning to die. It was at this stage that some owners decided to move their cattle out of the area. Others followed during the dry season of 1983. Cattle were moved initially to the outskirts of Zvishavane town, where they grazed on nearby hills.

Movement during 1987–1988 was less dramatic. Localized movement was important for some herd owners, and cattle were moved from the clay soil savanna to the sandy soil areas, largely as a result of organized loaning arrangements. Forage was scarce in parts of Indava ward as early as April 1987 and cattle were moved to the sandy soil areas of Mutambi and Murowa, where grazing was found on the low-lying dambo areas. Fodder shortages hit Mototi ward later, and movement to Murowa area occurred beginning in August 1987. However there was some resistance to large-scale movements from the clay soil zone expressed by sandy soil area inhabitants. They did not want to repeat the devastation of their grazing experienced because of a huge influx of animals during the 1982–1984 crisis.

The drought period of 1991–1992 has caused major mortality in the Mazvihwa area.[3] Between October 1991 and April 1992, some attempts at local movement, along the lines described for the previous two droughts, were attempted. However the availability of grass was so low over such wide areas, that there were relatively few advantages to extensive movement. Instead, investment in supplementary fodder supply was more evident than in previous drought periods. However, this was only an option for a few herd owners and proved insufficient to keep livestock alive. The 1991–1992 drought has been so extensive and so severe that the "traditional" mechanisms of opportunistic movement to offset localized fodder shortages have proven inadequate.

The impact of large scale movement out of Mototi ward on herd survival can be examined for the 1982–1984 drought (Table 4). During the 1982–1984 drought, the adoption of a movement strategy significantly increased the probability of cattle survival ($X^2 = 82.13$; Sig = 0.000). The cattle belonging to the 21 herd owners who did not move their cattle during the drought suffered very high levels of mortality. Although they were well aware of the potential advantages of cattle movement, their options were constrained by a range of factors that will be discussed below. The various characteristics that affect the ability of households to engage in large-scale movement, localized grazing responses, or supplementary feeding in order to respond to drought are discussed in the following sections.

---

[3]By May 1992 drought mortality for Chivi and Zvishavane was estimated by the Veterinary Department to be as high as 50–60% of total pre-drought cattle populations.

Table 4. Movement Strategies During the 1982–1984 Drought and the Impact on Cattle Survival

Strategy	Description of movement	Survival %	N (herds)
A	Out of Mototi ward, ca. Nov., 1982	40.1	287 (17)
B	Dry season, 1983 (Aug.–Oct.)	22.9	402 (18)
C	No movement outside area	3.3	181 (21)

Note: Survival relates to the percentage of the starting population (N) alive at the end of the drought. The number of herds following each strategy is shown in parentheses.

Labor

Labor availability at the household level does not appear to relate strongly to cattle survival in drought. Correlations of adult equivalent unit[4] household size measures with cattle survival in the two drought periods were insignificant, although the relationship for the prolonged drought of 1982–1984 was stronger ($r = 0.2$; 1-tailed significance $= 0.1$).

However it may not be labor availability at the household level that is key. Herding labor may be shared among a cluster of households. In the case of the 1982–1984 drought, households shared labor to move stock over long distances. Someone would accompany the animals and stay with them for a week or more away from home. Increased survival of cattle through movement in 1982–1984 may have, in part, been due to increased labor availability. However, during the 1987–1988 drought, there was no obvious advantage to be gained from cooperative herding, as in this case cattle survival was 77% (compared to 79% for individual herding and 75% for hired herding labor.

Labor is an important consideration in the supplementary feeding of animals. All herd owners reported having fed animals crop residues or lopped trees for fodder during the severe 1982–1984 drought. The same was true during the 1991–1992 season. During the less severe 1987–1988 drought, 83% of cattle owners interviewed fed cattle crop residues (maize, pearl millet, sorghum, groundnuts) and some 15% lopped trees for fodder.

---

[4]Adult equivalent unit (see Collier et al., 1987) is a weighted measure for household size. The measure used takes account of varied presence and absence of migrant laborers. It is more related to consumption requirements than herding labor, however, other measures of labor availability (e.g., total household size, adult labor, etc.) were also insignificant.

Table 5. Cattle Survival Rates According to Wealth
Ranks for Two Droughts[a]

Wealth Rank	1	2	3	4
Survival %, 1982–1984	30.4	15.4	16.5	21.3
Survival %, 1987–1988	81.8	69.9	74.6	77.3

[a] Statistcs: 1982–1984: χ^2 = 21.84; significance = 0.0001; 1987–1988: χ^2 = 5.04; significance = 0.16.

Wealth

Drought requires the mobilization of labor and capital resources. With larger herds, wealthier households can be expected to have a higher return per animal from investing in the maintenance of their herds during drought. At least for the longer drought of 1982–1984, there appears to have been a significant relationship between cattle survival and wealth, as defined by local people during a wealth ranking exercise (Table 5).[5]

Access to sources of income that are independent of drought allows animals to be kept alive through the purchase of supplementary feeds. However for the 1987–1988 drought, there are no significant correlations between cattle survival and either household cash income levels or remittance levels.[6] This may reflect the lack of cash investment in drought response strategies during 1987–1988. Indeed only 1 out of 46 herd owners purchased extra feed for the supplementation of young calves during this period.

Loaning Arrangements

The cattle loaning system (*kuronzera*) enables grazing pressure within the communal areas to be redistributed. Cattle may be loaned on a temporary basis for the duration of a local crisis, or on a longer-term arrangement. Cattle are loaned to both relatives and friends and often at some

[5] Wealth ranking was carried out by several groups of locals associated with the research (men, women, and the research team). They classified the existing sample into four groups according to their own perceptions of wealth, using their own criteria. The wealth ranking used in the analysis is a composite of these three ranking exercises. For a discussion of methods see Grandin, 1988, and Scoones, 1988.
[6] Cash income and remittance levels were assessed for the household sample on the basis of regular repeat surveys of income and expenditure estimates. Discrepancies were small and the results were thought to reflect a reasonably accurate estimate of cash flows to and from this small group of households (Scoones, 1990).

distance from the owner's home (e.g., 10 kms), in order to relieve grazing pressure. Large herd owners rarely keep more than ten to fifteen animals in their own kraal, and prefer to loan out to a number of sites (*miraga*). Loaning lowers the risk of local overgrazing, reduces herding and management requirements and assists stockless relatives and friends.

Incidences of loaning increased during both the 1982–1984 and the 1987–1988 droughts. A common pattern was for clay soil zone herd owners to loan animals to stockless friends and relatives in the sandy soil or edge zone, typically 5–10 km distant. Kinship connections across ecological zones were a distinct advantage in establishing loans. This was particularly possible for the chiefly VaNgowa clan, originally residents of the sandy soil hill areas, who later moved out into the edge zone and plains during the colonial era. Other immigrant groups, established for a relatively shorter period in the area, were less fortunate. They had to rely more on friendships and pleas, than on kinship obligations, for mutual aid.

During the 1982–1984 drought, the loaning system could not cope with the huge demands from livestock owners in the clay soil zone. Movement was no longer regulated through agreements between households (or clusters), but herders moved their animals *en masse* to areas with grazing. Later, a transhumant lifestyle was adopted as animals were moved on to areas outside Mazvihwa communal area, often with herders camping out with animals for extended periods.

Tenurial Conflict

Movement between areas is regulated by tenurial arrangements. Within the communal areas a common property grazing regime exists where access to local grazing territories (usually a village area) is open to local inhabitants' animals (including those borrowed from others), but not to other animals from outside the area, unless some agreement is reached between local village headmen (Scoones and Wilson, 1988; Cousins, 1992). Under conditions of extreme pressure, as were faced in 1982–1984, this kind of agreement did not work; the people of the sandy soil areas of Mototi, Murowa, and Mutambi wards were unable to stop large numbers of cattle from moving into the area. As relatives and friends of people living in the clay soil plains, they were unable to watch these cattle die. The common property regime's codes, established for normal years, were inadequate, and pastures were open to all comers.

In 1987–1988 and 1991–1992, a comparable situation arose in many areas. However in some areas, higher authorities were called in (village committees and councillors) to ensure that cattle coming into a particular area were restricted to those animals loaned to individuals in the community. With a strengthened negotiating position, the sandy soil savanna communities were able to apply more strings to the loaning package and a number of individuals insisted that animals be loaned on a long-term basis, rather than just for the duration of the drought.

Movement outside the boundaries of communal areas is more difficult. Movement to commercial ranches during 1982–1984 involved, for the most part, illegal trespass on private land, resulting in impoundment of animals and arrest of herders. In a few instances, grazing was hired from private landowners. In other cases, the landowners accepted that the movement of cattle from the communal areas was inevitable, and in the interests of "good neighborliness," no action was taken.

Institutional and Legal Constraints

Local movement is generally arranged through informal institutions, with networks of individuals, households, or clusters setting up loans. When problems arise, local institutions such as the village committee, the councillor, the chief or headmen are called in.

However, these local level institutions have proved inadequate to deal with large-scale movements. For a start, movement of animals outside their dip area is illegal without a permit from the Veterinary Department. Such permits are quite complex to acquire, requiring a series of visits to official offices and the signing of a number of forms. Movement is further restricted by specific veterinary regulations related to the control of foot and mouth disease and required by the European Community. These regulations restrict virtually any movement between disease zones,[7] thus reducing the options for long distance movement in response to variable grazing conditions.

It is difficult for small-scale herders to negotiate access to grazing with private ranch owners (including government). Attempts by community leaders to encourage the Zvishavane District Administration or the agricultural extension service to mediate failed both during 1982–1984 and 1991–1992. Policy restrictions on movement thus hamper flexible drought responses and local attempts at opportunistic management. The result is, inevitably, that higher drought mortalities are incurred.

[7]These regulations have been established as part of the terms of a Lome trade agreement for beef export from Zimbabwe. Movement is restricted between "infected," "buffer," and "disease free" zones.

CONCLUSIONS

The case study presented in this chapter highlights an evolving sequence of drought responses that start with local herd management to alleviate seasonal food shortages, with cattle herded to key resource areas, such as dambos or river banks. This is often combined with increased browsing activity during the dry season. This is followed by movement, particularly away from the highly variable fodder resources of the clay soil zone toward the more stable resources of the sandy soil zone. In severe droughts transhumant movements over longer distances may follow.

Biological responses show a more rapid drop in livestock condition in the clay soil zone, with earlier mortality than in the sandy soil zone. In all areas, birth rates do not drop until well into the drought, reflecting the stress-adapted physiology of indigenous cattle breeds. Drought impacts appear to be cumulative with proportionately higher mortalities in a two-year drought, of which most occur in the second year. Homewood and Lewis (1987) found a similar pattern differentiated by agroecological zone during the 1983–1985 drought in Baringo, Kenya.

Under most drought conditions, flexible movement appears an effective strategy in offsetting mortality. Recovery of populations, both through reproduction and in-migration, was rapid in all zones, particularly in the clay soil zone. This pattern of movement in response to drought impact, and subsequently rapid recovery of livestock populations, is found equally in other pastoral areas (Campbell, 1984; Fratkin, 1986; McCabe, 1987; Toulmin, 1994).

This study highlighted the differential ability of herders to effectively cope with drought, and with labor and cash constraints limiting the capacity of poorer households to respond to drought stress through movement or supplementary feeding, especially in the longer drought of 1982–1984. Drought mortalities resulted in increased differentials in cattle ownership in the two-year drought of 1982–1984, when a dramatic increase in stockless households was noted. This was not the case in the one year drought of 1987–1988. Stocklessness did not increase significantly during this period; indeed, some households acquired the use of cattle due to loaning arrangements. Increased stock ownership differentials following drought have been reported in east African studies (Fratkin and Roth, 1990; Herren, 1990), but contrasting impacts due to the degree of drought severity have not been emphasized.

The picture that emerges from this case study is one of a resilient system able to bounce back from the impact of drought. Biological factors contribute to this resilience. These include the availability of a spatially diverse grazing landscape, the existence of a range of browse trees in both clay and sandy soil savanna types, and the hardy physiology of local cattle breeds and crosses. Herd management strategies, particularly mobility, are also very important.

Government policy and institutions need to facilitate flexible and opportunistic patterns of management. Currently they do not. Veterinary restrictions on movement of livestock have a serious, damaging impact on small herders' coping strategies. Underutilized private or government ranch land is rarely made available to help in drought; instead farmers are beseeched to destock through sales at low prices. Farmers bear in mind the considerable costs of restocking and the devastating impact of stocklessness on agricultural production, and are understandably reluctant to sell all their animals (Scoones, 1990). There has been limited institutional support to grazing associations and village committees in order to assist the negotiation of coordinated access rights to different grazing resources at times of drought. Most investment in grazing management has focused on technical recommendations for grazing rotation (Cousins, 1992).

Understanding the complexities of drought responses at the local level provides insights into the opportunities and limitations of existing drought response strategies. Policymakers would do well to consider how to build upon farmers' and herders' coping strategies and make them more effective.

ACKNOWLEDGMENTS

The research would not have been possible without the assistance of many people in Mazvihwa communal area, notably my hosts over two years, the Mukamuri family. Johnson Madyakuseni, Abraham Mawere, Billy Mukamuri, Florence Shumba, and Ken Wilson all contributed to the field research. The research was carried out while I was research associate of the Department of Biological Sciences, University of Zimbabwe, and the Renewable Resources Assessment Group, Imperial College, University of London. Various versions of this paper have benefitted from the comments of Camilla Toulmin. Funding was from the SERC/ESRC of the UK government and the International Institute for Environment and Development.

REFERENCES

Bell, R. H. V. (1982). The effect of soil nutrient availability on community structure in African ecosystems. In Huntley, B. J. and Walker, B. H. (eds.), *Ecology of Tropical Savannas,* Springer Verlag, Berlin, pp. 193–216.

Behnke, R. and Scoones, I. (1993). Rethinking range ecology: Implications for rangeland management in Africa. In Behnke, R., Scoones, I., and Kerven, C. (eds.), *Range Ecology at Disequilibrium. New Models of Natural Variability in African Savannas.* Overseas Development Institute, London.

Campbell, D. (1984). Response to drought among farmers and herders in Southern Kajiado District, Kenya. *Human Ecology* 12: 35–64.

Collier, P., Radwan, S., Wangwe, S. and Wagner, A. (1986). *Labour and Poverty in Rural Tanzania: Ujaama and Rural Development in the United Republic of Tanzania.* Clarendon Press, Oxford.

Cousins, B. (1992). *Managing communal rangeland in Zimbabwe: Experiences and lessons.* Commonwealth Secretariat, London.

Ellis, J. and Swift, D. (1988). Stability of African pastoral ecosystems: Alternate paradigms and implications of development. *Journal Range Management* 41: 450–459

Fratkin, E. (1986). Stability and resilience in east African pastoralism: The Rendille and Ariaal of northern Kenya. *Human Ecology* 14: 269–286.

Fratkin, E. and Roth, A. E. (1990). Drought and economic differentiation among Ariaal pastoralists of Kenya. *Human Ecology* 18: 385–402.

Frost, P., Menault, J., Walker, B., Medina, E., Solbrig, O. and Swift, M. (1986). Responses of savannas to stress and disturbance: A proposal for a collaborative programme of research. Report of IUBS Working Group on Decade of the Tropics Programme/Tropical Savanna Ecosystems. *Biology International,* International Union for Biological Sciences, Paris.

Grandin, B. (1988). *Wealth Ranking in Smallholder Communities: A Field Manual.* Intermediate Technology Publications, London.

Herren, U. (1990). Socioeconomic stratification and smallstock production in Mukogodo division, Kenya. *Research in Economic Anthropology* 12: 111–148.

Homewood, K. and Lewis, J. (1987). Impact of drought on pastoral livestock in Baringo, Kenya, 1983–1985. *Journal of Applied Ecology* 24: 615–631.

Homewood, K. and Rodgers, W. (1991). *Maasailand Ecology. Pastoralist Development and Wildlife Conservation in Ngorongoro, Tanzania.* Cambridge University Press, Cambridge.

Jackson, J., Collier, P. and Conti, A. (1987). *Rural development policies and food security in Zimbabwe.* Part II. Rural Employment Policies Branch, International Labour Organisation, Geneva.

McCabe, J. T. (1987). Drought and recovery: livestock dynamics among the Ngisonyoka Turkana of Kenya. *Human Ecology* 15: 371–390.

Sandford, S. (1982). Pastoral strategies and desertification: Opportunism and conservation in drylands. In Spooner, B. and Mann, H. (eds.), *Desertification and Development: Dryland Ecology in Social Perspective.* Academic Press, London, pp. 61–80.

Scoones, I. (1988). Learning about wealth: an example from Zimbabwe. *RRA Notes,* 2. International Institute for Environment and Development, London.

Scoones, I. (1990). *Livestock populations and the household economy: A case study from southern Zimbabwe.* Ph.D. thesis, University of London.

Scoones, I. (1993). Why are there so many animals? Cattle population dynamics in the communal areas of Zimbabwe. In Behnke, R., Scoones, I., and Kerven, C. (eds.), *Range Ecology at Disequilibrium. New Models of Natural Variability and Pastoral Adaptation in African Savannas.* Overseas Development Institute, London.

Scoones, I. (1994). Exploiting heterogeneity: Habitat use by cattle in dryland Zimbabwe. *Journal of Arid Environments* (in press).

Scoones, I. (1994). New directions for pastoral development in Africa: An overview. In Scoones, I. (ed.), *Living with Uncertainty: New Directions for Pastoral Development in Africa.* Intermediate Technology Publications, London.

Scoones, I. and Cousins, B. (1994). The struggle for control over dambo resources in Zimbabwe. *Natural Resources and Society* (in press).

Scoones, I. and Wilson, K. (1988). Households, lineage groups and ecological dynamics: Issues for livestock research and development in Zimbabwe's communal lands. In Cousins, B. (ed.), *People, Land and Livestock*. Centre for Applied Social Sciences, Harare.

Toulmin, C. (1994). Tracking through drought: options for destocking and restocking in the small-scale pastoral sector in dryland Africa. In Scoones, I. (ed.), *Living with Uncertainty: New Directions for Pastoral Development in Africa*. Intermediate Technology Publications, London.

Walker, B. (1985). Structure and function of savannas: An overview. In *Management of the World's Savannas* Tothill, J. and Mott, J. (eds.), Australian Academy of Sciences, Canberra, pp. 83–91.

Westoby, M., Walker, B., and Noy-Meir, I. (1989). Opportunistic management for rangelands not at equilibrium. *Journal of Range Management* 42: 266–274.

7

From *Zomo* to Yak: Change in a Sherpa Village

Naomi H. Bishop

Bishop documents a major shift in transhumant herding in a high-altitude Himalayan community. In a village in east-central Nepal, many families are shifting from transhumant agropastoralism involving zomo, *a cow–yak hybrid, to herding cows and yaks in order to produce* zomo. *Zomo are suited to middle altitudes, 7,000 to 11,000 feet, where they produce large quantities of rich milk for butter production. However, the transhumant lifestyle of* zomo *herders involves living at pastures for much of the years and the constant work of butter production is hard. The new approach utilizing cattle and yak involves change—new management skills, new migration routes, and different marketing strategies.*

The "traditional" pattern of herding zomo *was to purchase females from elsewhere (since the hybrid* zomo *itself cannot produce a first-quality offspring) and to herd them in a transhumant pattern, between high pastures (14,000 feet) and low ones at village level (8,500 feet). Animals are milked twice daily, butter and cheese made every day, and firewood and fodder has to be secured. Economically,* zomo *herds can generate a good income from butter sales but also require a great deal of cash investment as the herd is not self-replicating. Moreover, aged* zomo *are a burden since, for religious reasons, they may not be slaughtered or sold for meat.*

Originally published in *Human Ecology: An Interdisciplinary Journal,* 17(2): 177–204.

Naomi H. Bishop, Department of Anthropology, California State University, Northridge, California 91330.

Case Studies in Human Ecology, edited by Daniel G. Bates and Susan H. Lees. Plenum Press, New York, 1996.

The cow–yak herd innovation consists of cows, a male yak, and their hybrid calves (zomo). The purpose of this herd is to generate cash through the sale of hybrids. While they do not need to be milked, labor demands are still high as they must be grazed separately. Generally, households that have made the shift to the new herding strategy are headed by older men. Why do people decide to change their livelihoods? Bishop suggests several factors, which vary by household circumstance. As children are drawn to wage labor in India, households headed by the elderly may lack the labor needed to milk twice a day. Also, older people may not wish to spend so much of the year at high pastures away from the village. Finally, selling zomo *babies is an easier source of cash income than butter production, nor does it require leaving the village as does wage labor in India. Shifting forms of animal husbandry had potential implications for the ecological and social environment of the village, in addition to the economic fortunes of the herding families.*

INTRODUCTION

Transhumant agropastoralism, which combines agriculture in settled communities with livestock herding away from the village to high and low pastures over an annual cycle, is a flexible strategy for adaptation in middle and high altitude Himalayan communities. Although these villages are at the upper limits for agriculture, the proximity of subalpine and alpine grasslands suitable for grazing sheep, goats, and bovids (cows, yaks, and their hybrid offspring, *zomo*) provides opportunities for additional sources of food and income. Pastoralism in these high zones, in combination with settled agriculture, has become the specialization of Bhotia[1] (Tibetan-derived) groups such as Sherpa, with other groups, e.g., Tamang and Gurung, participating to a lesser extent in the lower elevations. In order to be successful pastoralists in these zones, herders must have the zootechnical expertise, access to pastures, access to livestock appropriate to the available pasturage, and trade or market relationships for sale and barter of livestock and products. Therefore, not everyone in a village nor every village at these altitudes will engage in herding. However, the presence of this mixed sub-

---

[1]Bhotia is used here to refer to people speaking Tibeto-Burmese languages in Nepal; it can also refer to Nepalese populations of Tibetan origin. It is a term which can have negative connotations when used by the dominant ethnic groups in Nepal.

sistence complex across the Nepal Himalaya attests to the resilience and potential productivity of mixed agriculture and pastoralism.

Mountain ecosystems are fragile (Thomas, 1979), and life is hazardous for the humans who inhabit them. Shifts in climate over very short altitude spans, the unpredictable nature of the weather, shallow topsoil, and geomorphological instability all contribute to the heightened vulnerability of those dependent on mountain environments for subsistence. Added to this are the normal vicissitudes of agriculture and pastoralism: disease, predation, shifts in the market, and access to fertilizer (organic or chemical), seed, etc. Guillet (1983) discusses the number of ways that mixed agropastoralism provides safeguards against the vagaries of this environment. Combining agriculture with pastoralism provides a broader subsistence base than either strategy separately, thus compensating for the possibility of failure in either sphere. Furthermore, this type of subsistence increases the possibility for cash income. Utilization of several vertical zones over the year (for example, growing different or staggered crops in fields at different altitudes, or growing crops in villages while moving herds in and out of the village) increases the possibility for intensification and thus enhances self-sufficiency. Finally, as noted by Alirol (1979), as well as others, the practice of mixing and changing herd composition over time permits individuals to maximize the efficient utilization of pastures and fields as environmental changes dictate. In a changing and unpredictable environment, the possibility of buying and selling whole herds easily, or changing the combination of animals in a herd from year to year, is one key to the success of this adaptation. Bonnemaire and Tessier (1976, p. 115) point out that in Langtang, herd diversity ("the utilization of a whole palette of varied genetic types"; my translation) permits Langtang herders to maintain large productive herds at high altitudes with only a minimum of fodder supplementation in winter, since each component of the herd can utilize a slightly different niche.

This paper examines transhumant large animal husbandry in a middle altitude village in east-central Nepal. Over the past 15 years there has been substantial interest shown in this type of subsistence strategy throughout Nepal (Bonnemaire and Tessier, 1976; Palmieri, 1976; March, 1977; Alirol, 1976; Alirol, 1979; Cox, 1985; Brower, 1987). Several ethnic groups are included (Tibetan, Sherpa, and Tamang), with villages ranging from 7000 to 11,000 feet in central and east Nepal. Herd composition, social organization of herding and pasture management, as well as types of economic strategies pursued by communities and by individuals within communities vary from location to location. On the other hand, zootechnical aspects of handling the animals and their products are quite similar throughout the Himalayas, regardless of location or ethnicity. All these studies are, at some level, examining the factors that contribute to the successful management of large animals under these conditions in order to both evaluate the impact of this subsistence strategy on mountain environments past and present, and to predict its future viability in this region.

Transhumant bovid husbandry is part of an ancient Eurasian tradition of herding cattle (Kawakita, 1983). However, the herding of yak and their hybrids is unique to the Central Asian region. Hybrid husbandry, in particular, provides some special difficulties as well as benefits for those Himalayan herders who attempt it. The balance between those difficulties and benefits, in light of the alternatives available in the past and present, will be the focus of this paper, as it describes a village changing from the longstanding pattern of herding hybrids to an alternative pattern of producing them. This change has ecological, social, and economic implications for the residents of this village and can be related to changes in the larger political and economic spheres that affect them as well as others in Nepal. By examining the context and potential implications of this change, insight can be gained into the past as well as the future of these inhabitants of the middle altitude Himalayas.

MELEMCHI: A BRIEF DESCRIPTION

The village of Melemchi lies at an altitude of approximately 8,500 feet, in the east-central Nepal region known as Yolmo or Helambu (Bishop and Bishop, 1978). The residents are agropastoralists, pursuing a mixed strategy of farming and herding. Wheat, high altitude barley, potatoes, radishes, and, in some years, corn are grown in the fields surrounding the houses of Melemchi, supplemented in summer months with small vegetable gardens. In addition, many families own corn fields in the satellite village of Tarke Tau 1,000 feet below, where they may have a second house. Today, most families in the village own some milk-producing animals, either cows or buffalo, which they keep in the village as much for fertilizer as for milk. Other families live away from the village in *goths* (portable quonset-type huts made by spreading bamboo mats over a substructure of sticks; Figure 1), and herd mixed groups of cows, yak, hybrids, goats, or sheep. These herds move in transhumant fashion over the mountainsides between an altitude 7,000 to 14,000 feet. Phillipe Alirol has said, "The word *goth* has a greater meaning than that of a simple shelter. To own a *goth* is to have a herd, to be a herdsman, and thus to identify oneself with a cultural group (Sherpa, Gurung), traditionally dedicated to herding" (my translation, Alirol, 1981; p. 197).

Whether in a *goth* or in the village, all family members contribute to the family's subsistence: Women and men together perform agricultural

Figure 1. A *zomo goth* made of bamboo mats placed over a frame of sticks (9000 feet altitude). The Tibetan mastiff dog is chained nearby to warn the family of any approach. He sits on a pile of manure which has sprouted vegetation in the damp weather; the manure is collected into piles and is neither scattered over the pasture nor carried to fields back in the village.

tasks and care for the livestock, while children assist in various ways. Between the ages of 5–12 years, children help with household tasks, such as carrying water, tending chickens and baby animals, caring for younger siblings, and assisting their mothers with chores. By age 12, children are able to participate in adult work, albeit with lighter loads. At this age, children may be hired within the village to carry manure to the fields or to carry loads of firewood. Fodder gathering, which involves climbing high in trees to lop off branches and then carrying the huge bundles with headstraps, is generally the work of 15 to 18-year-old boys, as well as adults. In *goths*, girls in their late teens can tend the cattle alone, bearing responsibility for milking and feeding the animals. Some tasks fall to adults; for example, wood cutting is the purview of adult men, while women usually make the butter and cheese, or in the village, distill the *rakshi* (liquor).

The closest major market or bazaar is the capital city, Kathmandu, some 50 miles or 2–3 days walk away. In summer 1986, there were approximately 220 people residing in Melemchi—165 in the village and 55 living in *goths*. Between 100–200 additional Melemchi residents (including

Figure 2. Two bovids at 12,000 feet altitude; on the left, a yak-cow hybrid female (*zomo*); on the right, a male yak (*Poephagius grunniens*).

children) were living in India at that time circular migrants engaged in wage labor in high altitude regions.

Since 1971, Melemchi has undergone substantial change: the number of houses has doubled (although not the number of actual residents because of increased outmigration), increasing numbers of people of both sexes and all ages are moving back and forth between the village and India, and residents have increased access to cash and the consumer goods that it buys. There is also greater contact with the central government of Nepal both via Radio Nepal and participation in local panchayat affairs. A government-sponsored, Nepali-medium primary school has been established in the village, and adult literacy classes are underway. And incorporation into the Langtang National Park has changed the villagers' relationships with tourists and tourism.

ZOMO HERDS: THE TRADITIONAL PATTERN

According to the oldest residents, Melemchi people have always herded *zomo* (Figure 2), a female hybrid bovid produced by crossing a male yak with a female cow. Although other types of crosses are found in Hi-malayan herds, Melemchi *zomo* are of this type. A typical herd consists of a number of *zomo,* a bull (preferably a Tibetan dwarf bull [*Bos taurus*]) to service them, and a minimal number of male or female offspring (ideally none). Herds may also include sheep and/or goats, or these ruminants may be herded alone. Nearly all residents of Melemchi from 1971 to 1986 had lived in a *zomo goth* at some time in their lives, and for most of the middle and older generations it was a lifetime pattern.

Transhumant Herd Management

Goth life is a life of transhumant migration; families spend summers at very high pastures (up to 14,000 feet), move down to the village level at 8,500 feet for the winter months, then reverse the process beginning in March. Summer pastures are often a full day's walk from the village, even for an adult, and women and young children may stay in the high pastures all summer without returning to the village until October.

The work of a *zomo goth* revolves around dairying. Herds must be sent out to pasture, animals must be milked twice daily, butter and cheese must be made every other day, and herds must be protected against pre-dation. *Zomo* graze without direct supervision, and once retrieved for eve-ning milking, they cluster around the *goth* at night. A *goth* requires a minimum of two adults to manage the work, and there is no question that older children ease the workload and make it possible for a family to main-tain a *goth* on into middle age and later. Young men start their *goths* si-multaneously with their marriage. When wives or husbands die, the *goths* are usually sold because the surviving spouse has difficulty managing alone. Men's work in a *goth* involves taking the herd to the grazing areas and retrieving them, climbing trees to cut fodder, supplying the household with wood, moving the loads when the *goth* shifts locale, supervising the breeding of the animals, traveling between the *goth* and the village to fetch supplies, and transporting and selling butter to markets outside the village, e.g., Kathmandu. Women remain at the *goth,* where they milk and make butter and cheese, care for the children, maintain the household (cook and fetch water), watch the animals around the *goth,* spin wool, and weave jackets. While men are away, which is frequently and can be for periods of up to a week or two, women must do all the men's tasks as well as their own. Young children must be watched carefully in this environment, and it is not until they are 5 or 6 years old that they are able to help with even small tasks. Older children can be of real assistance to their parents, helping them with chores, and even substituting for them while they are in the village tending crops or attending festivals. The predominance of large family size in Melemchi, especially prior to widespread availability of contraception, has no doubt contributed to the possibility for economic diversification found in Melemchi agropastoralists, as elsewhere (Fricke, 1986).

Life in a *zomo goth* is hard. Families live with only a bamboo mat and a barking dog between them and a variety of wild animals, as well as a host of natural disasters. Living quarters are cramped; whole families of up to 12 individuals live in a tiny enclosure, often sharing it with several baby bovids, sheep, goats, and chickens. In winter, temperatures drop, snowstorms can last several days, and there is the added chore of cutting fodder daily. In monsoon summer at high pastures, the areas around the *goths* become muddy and leech-infested, and family members are especially vulnerable to skin and respiratory infections. Always, women are isolated and miss out on the activities in the village, even when there are other *goths* sharing the pasture. And the chore of moving the *goth* occurs from five to ten times a year, depending on an individual's route, placing an especially heavy burden on men. Moving a *goth* involves at least eight to nine adult loads, and some of the locations are over half a day's walk apart. One man with a *zomo goth* for his entire adult life (19 years) complained that he would like to sell his *zomo goth* because with so many people in India, there is no one to help him move it.

Men inherit their first herd from their fathers when they marry or begin to live in a separate household (anticipatory inheritance). If the parents are elderly, they may split their herd among their sons and take up residence in the village or in Tarke Tau. If they are not ready to abandon herding themselves, they may give a few animals from their herd to each son when he leaves home and retain the rest for themselves. *Kharkes,* or pastures, are inherited, as well as the animals, when the family herd is passed on. Brothers generally share the family *kharkes,* although they may have individually owned stone shelters (*pathis*) on the shared pastures. Over an annual cycle, brothers may use the family pastures sequentially, or may occupy them simultaneously. One man split his *zomo* herd between two of his sons but retained the *kharkes* for his own cow–yak *goth*; his sons had to rent *kharkes* from an uncle whose sons were in India.

Zomo Herding and the Agricultural Cycle

The transhumant cycle in Melemchi is intimately tied in with the agricultural one. Householders have to maintain both their animals and their crops. Labor must be available at the right time and place throughout the year to make agriculture possible. Two major crops are planted in Melemchi village: wheat/barley and potatoes. A third crop, corn, is usually planted in Tarke Tau.

The agricultural cycle places demands on the *zomo goth* owner in that if he owns fields, someone from the family must be available to work on crops in the early fall (wheat/ barley), in winter (corn), in early spring (potatoes), in late spring (wheat/ barley), in midsummer (corn), and late summer (potatoes). Furthermore, manure must be available; transhumant *zomo* herds are not sources of manure except for the period in late September when they come to the village for 1–2 weeks. However, sheep *goths* are commonly taken to Tarke Tau for the winter months to fertilize the corn fields. Animals from transhumant herds are never used to plow fields. Although *goth* families are close to fields in winter, in summer they may be a full day's walk away from the village. It is significant that young *zomo goth* owners, who have no house, also have few fields in the village. This mirrors the historic situation in Melemchi, when nearly everyone had *goths* and there were few houses and no farming within the village at all. Some men inherit fields at marriage; most often, these are corn fields below the village or potato fields within the village, rather than wheat or barley fields. Young *goth* owners may help with their parents' fields, sharing the harvest as well as the labor, or they may buy grain using cash or butter. As families mature and houses and fields are acquired, the children grow, and there is additional labor available to make an agropastoral strategy possible.

ECONOMICS OF *ZOMO* HERDING

A *zomo goth* is maintained to produce cash income from the sale of milk products, particularly butter. As hybrids, *zomo* show heterosis (hybrid vigor): they are larger than either parent, and females produce twice as much milk as either purebred yak or cow (Bonnemaire and Tessier, 1976). *Zomo* have an extended altitude range, from 7,000–14,000 feet, making them perfect animals for the middle altitude zone encompassing villages like Melemchi.

Economically, *zomo* have great potential for generating good income from butter sales; however, maintaining a *zomo goth* also involves a major expenditure of cash. As a *zomo* herd ages, or when expansion of the herd is desirable, a herder must purchase new *zomo,* often from some distance away. *Zomo* must be purchased from breeders; since they are hybrids, they cannot be recruited from within the herd. The offspring of *zomo,* F2 hybrids or backcrosses, show no hybrid vigor. F2 males, like F1 males, are sterile,

Figure 3. A woman preparing to milk a *zomo.* The *zomo* is staked and drinks whey from a pan resting on the hide from her calf. Behind the woman is the milking pail and a small basket of salt. It is believed that feeding *zomo* salt increases milk production, by causing the animal to eat more grass.

but they differ from them in that F2 males are small and weak. While F2 females can produce offspring, and therefore milk, their milk production is meager and they too are small and weak. Although F2 calves must be born in order for their *zomo* mothers to produce milk, they are inferior to their parents in every way and are permitted to die after birth[2] unless the mother needs their presence for the lactation response. Female *zomo* vary in this respect; some need no stimulation from their calf to let down milk, some require suckling by their own calf, and still others are content merely to see the skin of their baby waved from the *goth* entrance door, once it has become a floor mat (Figure 3).

[2]As Buddhists, Melemchi herders are proscribed from killing living creatures; furthermore, there is the additional constraint that the *zomo's* calf is partly cow, and therefore falls under the general sanction against harming cows in this Hindu country. For these reasons, the F2 calves are neglected by the herders from birth, allowed only the most minimal opportunities to suckle, and so, rarely survive. Informants explain that it is common to stake out the newborn calf for several days allowing it only to graze (it cannot digest grass at this age), and then let it nurse. The calf then kills itself through the resulting colic.

While F2 and subsequent back crosses are universally considered inferior with regard to productivity, they are found in higher frequencies elsewhere in Nepal. In Melemchi, F2s are kept only out of necessity; most herds have one or two females who will not give milk without the presence of their calf. Current *goth* owners take one of two tacks in handling this problem: they sell the F2 or, most recently, they attempt to breed it back to either a yak or a Tibetan bull in order to revert to the "pure stock," especially the rare and hard to obtain *Bos taurus.*

Aged *zomo* are also an economic liability for *goths.* Since *zomo* are half cow, they will not be killed, and herders frequently must maintain a number of nonproductive aged animals in their herds which compete for forage and resources with the productive animals. Overall, the economic aspects of herding *zomo* are complex, with high profits possible if butter prices are high and predation/illness low, but also the real possibility of a lot of hard work for very little gain. Many who have given it up say it is because of the financial pressures of a bad year, and it is notable that those who didn't inherit *zomo goths* never have one.

A NEW ALTERNATIVE: COW–YAK *GOTHS*

In 1986, seven families in Melemchi were engaged in a new form of animal husbandry. They had transhumant herds, in many cases using the same kharkes, but instead of *zomo* and Tibetan bulls, these *goths* were composed of cows, a male yak, and their hybrid calves. Unlike the traditional *zomo goth,* none of these include sheep or goats. The purpose of these herds is to generate cash through the production of F1 hybrid offspring, either females (*zomo*) to sell to Melemchi herders or within the region, or males (*zobo*) which are desired as beasts of burden by people of Langtang. Since the production and raising of calves is the primary activity, most of the milk goes to the young offspring and only enough to supply the needs of the family itself is retained by the herder. This reduces the dairying chores considerably, while at the same time increasing the numbers of animals being grazed. Since hybrids are not sold until the age of three, this increases pressure on pasture resources.

Another difference observed in cow–yak *goths* is their pattern of transhumance, which must accommodate two species who diverge widely in their altitude tolerance. Cows have no resistance to cold stress and generally range no higher than 12,000 feet; even in Melemchi village at 8,500 feet or in *goths* as low as 7,600 feet, lowland cows can fail to thrive. Yaks, on the other hand, are able to withstand high altitude and extremes of cold, but have no resistance to lowland diseases; they cannot descend easily below 9,000 feet.

Breeding is more complicated in a cow–yak *goth*. Bulls breed easily with *zomo* and require no assistance from the herder, but not all yak are interested in cows. Cows are definitely intimidated by yak, so that they must be tied to be bred. Ideally, breeding should be timed so that births coincide with maximum food availability in spring and summer (Alirol, 1979; Brower, 1987), i.e., they should breed in early summer. But cows may not be in prime breeding condition at high altitudes in summer. Breeding, therefore, may conflict with the desire to maintain the two species in optimal altitude zones throughout the year.

The essential incompatibility of the two species of a cow–yak herd, drawing as it does from the two extremes of the bovid altitude range, poses difficulties for the herders who must stress their species at both ends, or manage the herd in two parts, except for the several months during which breeding occurs.[3] Each herder has handled this in a different way, depending on the location of his *kharkes,* the possibilities for managing his herd in two parts, and his access to lower altitude pastures or fodder. Regardless of the individual patterns, one result is that herds of cows are being pastured nearer (and in some cases within) the village for much more of the year than occurs with the *zomo* pattern of summers spent at high pastures.

Like a *zomo goth,* cow–yak *goths* suffer losses from disease and predation. In addition, there is the substantial financial investment in the yak that must be balanced by good calf production. In 1986, a yak cost Rs. 4,000–5,000, compared with Rs. 500–600 for a lowland bull. Calf production continues to be poor, with only a small percentage of females being bred by the yak, and a small percentage of those actually giving birth. Finally there is the delay in profit, as well as the sporadic income of these *goths,* compared with a *zomo goth* which produces butter on a fairly regular basis, beginning with the appearance of the first baby. The owner of a cow–yak *goth* must raise the calves for 3 years before they are sold, and there may be months or even years between sales.

CAUSES OF THE SHIFT

The numbers of *goths* in Melemchi dropped by one-fourth between 1971–1989: In 1971 there were 24 *goths,* while there were 20 in 1986, and 18 in 1989. In this same period, the number of houses more than doubled,

---

[3]Perhaps this is part of the reason that cow–yak *goths,* unlike *zomo goths,* do not include sheep and goats; managing two species is enough!

and it is clear that an increasingly smaller proportion of adult householders are maintaining this way of life.

A major difference occurred over the 17-year period in the type of *goth* maintained: in 1971, all *goths* but one were *zomo goths* (the other, a sheep *goth*), while in 1989 there were eight *zomo,* six cow–yak (down from a high of eight), and four sheep/goat *goths.* It was also notable in 1989 that those who had adopted the new cow–yak pattern were older (mean age = 53), owned houses in the village, had wives living in the village or no wife at all, and had older children assisting with the *goth.* The same was true for men who had sheep/goat *goths.* In contrast, those with *zomo goths* were either quite young (23–26 years) or middle aged (39–44). Only one of the *zomo goth* owners had a house in the village.

This difference suggests that there may be distinct advantages to a cow–yak *goth* for those who are older. When asked why they switched, the answers were uniform: a *zomo goth* is too much work, the life is too hard, and the *goth* is uncomfortable. All pointed out that with cows you could live closer to the village for more of the year and still make money. A comment from a *zomo* owner confirms this: "If I get too old to follow *zomo,* I might breed them." This was reminiscent of other comments that young people nowadays are not willing to put up with the discomforts of *goth* life *or* village life, but want to go to India where they can earn good money. There was a shared sense that young or old, *zomo goth* life was a hard one, particularly because of the isolation and the distance from the village.

A second factor in the appeal of cow–yak *goths* was economic. All who were trying this anticipated greater profits from sales of hybrids than from sales of butter. It is true that selling hybrids, at Rs. 4,000–5,000 each, would be very lucrative, but in 1986, only one man had realized any success in producing offspring; the rest had suffered (in some cases, repeated) losses of animals and produced almost no *zomo* calves. Yet, only two men quit. By 1989, those with cow–yak *goths* were beginning to see modest success, and maintained that this is all they had ever hoped for. They recognized that breeding success would be lower with cow–yaks. For example, one man said his yak bred six of his nineteen cows, and produced three babies; if that were a *zomo goth,* he could expect twelve babies from nineteen *zomo.* Some were selling their calves at the age of 1 or 2, at lower prices than anticipated, rather than waiting until they were 3 years old as planned. Several acknowledged that they had bought cows or yak that were too young, and were having to wait excessively long to realize any profit.

Unfortunately, it is not easy to compare the relative economic potential of these two *goth* types. Alirol (1979) provides some data on expenses and income from individual households with different types of herds in

Kalingchowk, but it is still not possible to generalize about the profitability of any herd type due to the difficulty of obtaining complete and accurate information on people's financial status, the frequency with which households sell and buy animals, the fluctuations in the market for livestock and butter, and heterogeneity of the herds in terms of age and productivity.

It is possible to compare the initial cost of a herd of 12 females and a male: 12 *zomo* at Rs. 4,000 each plus one bull at Rs. 600 would cost a total of Rs. 48,600, compared with 12 cows at Rs. 600 each and one yak at Rs. 5,000, costing only Rs. 12,200. Initially, it is cheaper to start with cows and a yak. If each of the *zomo* produced the maximum amount of butter per year, the herder could earn Rs. 51,000 from the sale of butter. If each of the cows produced a *zomo* baby, Rs. 48,000 could be realized from the sale of calves, but only after 3 years, i.e., ultimately, the productivity would be quite comparable. However, the productivity of both of these animals alters with age. In fact, in Kalingchowk region, Alirol found it was only the most wealthy who could borrow the money to purchase prime animals, which enabled them to maximize their productivity so that the loans could be repaid. Others had to maintain herds of much lower productivity, buying aged animals, and never accumulating the capital to pursue an optimal plan (Alirol, 1979). Age and conditions of the animals are only two of many factors that affect the profitability of a particular herd type.

It is possible to suggest several hypotheses to account for the appeal of a cow–yak *goth* to older, rather than younger, men:

1. *Comfort:* Older men and women no longer will tolerate the hardships of high pasturing in the monsoon rains, but want to be close to friends, fields, and have the possibility of more time in a house.
2. *Risk:* Older men are financially better able to take the risk of a new venture. They may have accumulated capital or be supplemented by children doing wage labor.
3. *Novelty:* Older men may be looking for a change.
4. *Money:* Older men may have the cash to invest in a new set of animals and wait for profits to come as the calves mature to selling age; young men begin with an inheritance but no cash, and they inherit *zomo*.
5. *Challenge:* Rearing a yak is perceived as something requiring skill and experience; older men may see themselves as able to meet the challenge.
6. *Investment:* Older couples may want to maintain a herd to retain their pasture rights, but desire the easier husbandry tasks of breed-

ing stock rather than dairying. *Kharkes* that are unused will decline in quality, and it is believed that they may be usurped by others.

7. *Lack of help:* Older couples have grown children who have gone to India or set up their own households. Adults who abandoned *goth* life completely said it was because there was no help. A cow–yak *goth* does not have the twice-daily dairying chores; wives can stay in the village and leave the work to the husband and one son or daughter, as occurred in several cases.

8. *Need or desire for cash:* Older men may be unable to find employment in India, yet need or desire cash money, which has become increasingly necessary in maintaining life in the village.

It is, and has been, possible for men over the age of 50 to herd *zomo*; today there is a couple in their seventies from a nearby village who maintain their *zomo* herd with the help of a grandson. However, among Melemchi residents living today, most gave up their *zomo goths* when they reached their thirties or forties, although a few hung on into their early fifties. There are two factors that promote early retirement from *zomo goth* life: (1) the desire to give a herd to sons at marriage, which would come some 20–30 years after the start of the father's herd, and (2) the difficulty of the work and life in a *zomo goth.* Someone who starts at age 20 will have been running a *zomo goth* for 30 years by the time he reaches the age of 50.

The predominance of men over the age of 50 with sheep *goths* or cow–yak *goths* emphasizes the point that *zomo* herding with its daily work *plus* difficult living conditions is a younger couple's occupation. Five of the six men with cow–yak *goths* had sold their *zomo goths,* gone for a period of time to India, and returned to invest in a cow–yak *goth.* While there are exceptions, it was commonly acknowledged that it was difficult for older men to be hired in India, especially men without specialized skills. Unskilled work is very hard and pays relatively little. Men said they started up a *goth* again, both because they wanted to make money, and they wanted to keep their *kharkes* in use and available for their sons.

Men do not begin the easier life of a cow–yak *goth* herder because their children have left home and there is no one to help; in all cases, there were older children still helping their parents. Nor does the presence or numbers of children in India predict whether and what kind of *goth* a family will have. No doubt this is due to the variability in amounts and kinds of support afforded by family members in India.

The younger men, who had chosen to herd *zomo* in 1986, say that they and their wives like the life; they enjoy the isolation, don't want to live in the village, feel it is a good life, like the ready supply of milk, cheese, and yogurt, and expect to do it for their entire lives. Of the alternatives, none wanted to go to India ("work is too hard there" and they "can't speak the language"), and they said that handling yak was too difficult. One middle aged man in his twentieth year herding *zomo,* said it was too hard to keep both yak and cows happy at the same time. All of them were especially proud of the quality of care they gave their *zomo* and bulls, on their knowledge of husbandry, and of their success as *zomo* herders. By 1989, however, several were planning to sell their *goths*; those without houses said they wanted to work in India, while one man with a house as well as other assets (rice fields) said he wanted to live in the village so that his only son could be educated in the school. The recent incorporation of Melemchi into the Langtang National Park was cited as a reason to sell, but more clearly at issue was the desire to participate in the changes going on in the village itself.

ALTERNATIVES

Alternative sources of cash income in Melemchi are few, and there were even fewer in the past. In interviews, Melemchi residents said that with the exception of wage labor in India, they have always relied on *zomo goths* plus village agriculture for their subsistence. Cash from butter and wool, plus bartering of products and services within the village and the region, served the needs of this community. Local products were bartered with lowlanders, for example, corn or bamboo mats for rice, and cash was used to buy cloth, oil, salt, and tea in Kathmandu. Unlike many Bhotia agropastoralist communities elsewhere in Nepal (Furer-Haimendorf, 1975), Melemchi residents, for geographic and historical reasons, were never involved in major trading activities between Tibet and India, nor were they recruited as mountaineering or tourist guides. However, today, cash is becoming increasingly necessary as both interest in, and opportunities for, obtaining market goods reaches Melemchi.

The major alternative source of cash for Melemchi residents is wage labor in Kathmandu or India. Often accompanied by their families, men go to work on high altitude road gangs or construction projects; wives set up lodging and food establishments if their children are too young to work, or the whole family works on the roads. Young people may also go alone, without their families, in the company of a relative or with other villagers. Most people go and come back many times in their lives, some never return, while still others have never left the village. Householders who go to India sell their *goth* before leaving and buy a new set of animals when they return. In this way families may alternate *goth* life and wage labor over their lifetimes (Bishop, 1993). One final source of income that has emerged in the last ten years with the increase in tourist trekking is providing lodging for trekkers who come through the village. Although lucrative in trekking season, the householder must be able to speak Nepali and have a house appropriately located within the village. It has been slow to develop, but by 1989, there were four lodges in the village and three villagers had lodges at Tharepathi as well, 4 hours walk above the village. Access to tourist dollars may expand in future with the National Park presence in the area.

IMPLICATIONS OF THE SHIFT

Whether there is a complete shift from *zomo* herds to cow–yak herds or, as at present, the co-existence of both options, the introduction of cow–yak herds in Melemchi has several potential consequences for the physical environment, as well as the social lives, of residents.

New Patterns of Transhumance

Cow–yak *goths* exhibit different patterns of transhumance, which could alter the impact of this subsistence system on the surrounding environment in the future. If cow–yak *goths* become widely adopted, it is possible there will be a shift from the use of high pastures to an intensification in the middle altitude zones closer to human habitation. This could have serious repercussions on the environment surrounding the villages at this level, which is more intensively used both for cultivation and for maintenance (fodder, forest litter, wood) than higher elevations. Alirol (1979) argues that the limitation on the transhumant subsistence system in general is the availability of *winter* forage, because it is during this season that transhumant herds are down in the lower altitudes in direct competition with household bovids. In Melemchi, for example, there are a large number of bovids kept at households. In winter, these are either tied at the houses or grazed on land adjacent to the village or below in Tarke Tau. All are fed dried grass as well as daily fresh fodder cut from the areas around their shelters. Alirol further points out that in Kalingchowk region where he studied, pasturing in winter is unsupervised and unregulated, in contrast to the strict controls kept on summer pastures. Winter grazing in village forests and nearby land can decimate areas through negligence and free-ranging of animals. A shift from *zomo* to cows could extend the pressure on these lower altitude forests and pastures beyond the tolerable level, by increasing the length and intensity of exposure (*goth* cows competing with household cows and buffalo for more months), as well as through the absence of regulations and controls. On the positive side, cow–yak *goths,* as well as sheep *goths,* make major contributions to agriculture through the production of manure during the winter months in and around the villages of Melemchi and Tarke Tau.

Changes in Animal Numbers

It is possible that herd size will increase with a shift to cow–yak *goths,* since cows are less expensive to buy than *zomo* (Rs. 400/lowland cow, Rs. 700-1,000/highland cow as compared with Rs. 4,000–5,000/*zomo*; 1986 prices). In addition, calves are retained in cow–yak *goths* for up to 3 years, swelling herd size by their presence. Larger herds would place larger burdens on the middle altitude environment to support them. While cow–yak and *zomo* herds in 1986 were roughly comparable in size (17–18 animals/*goth*), by 1989, cow–yak *goths* averaged 23 animals/*goth* compared with 18 *zomo*/*goth.* The increase came from the presence of immature animals. There is probably a limit to the number of bovids that can be managed by a single family unit. Most herders said that they didn't like more than about 17 animals, although one man said he would like 40 if he had some extra help. Another factor that limits herd size is the capital invested in the herd. A number of people expressed the concern that it was dangerous to have too much invested in animals, that it would be difficult to sell them if you needed to. With the price of *zomo* so high, it is considered foolish to have too many. In addition to the cow *goths* brought to the village during summer months, there is also the possibility of household cows being used for *zomo* production outside the *goth* system. Four village households are breeding their household cows with a yak, in hopes of producing *zomo* to sell at high prices. They are having success, so that despite the high stud fee, rearing village *zomo* for sale may become as viable as maintaining village buffalo and cows. A parallel situation was reported by Brower (1991) in Khumbu, where increased tourism made it viable to have one or two male hybrids, or *zopkio,* to rent out to tourists as pack animals at high daily rates. Families near trekking routes who never had herds discovered they could maintain a few *zopkio* for a good cash income. The new-found presence of *zopkio* in these villages is placing a burden on the traditional pasturage system, as well as having a potentially detrimental impact on the land closely surrounding villages. In Melemchi, while it is not clear that absolutely more cows will be kept in the village if they are bred to yak rather than bulls, it would represent an expansion of the traditional *zomo goth* pattern and add *zomo* to the mix of bovids kept in the village year round.

Change in the Social Structure of Herding

The introduction of cow–yak *goths* carries the potential to alter the system of individual and community management of herds and pasturing. Transhumance involves the coordination of people and animals over time and space; together with an agricultural regime with conflicting demands on household time and labor, it requires "communal institutions including a ritual complex, communal decision making, and delegation of authority" (Guillet, 1983, p. 566). Such institutions exist in Melemchi to coordinate the arrival and departure of livestock in the village, to adjudicate disputes over *kharke* ownership, and to collect taxes on pastures, grass fields, and animals. Melemchi herds are privately owned, as are the *kharkes*. This pattern of individual ownership of pastures and herds contrasts strongly with transhumant herders elsewhere in Nepal. It is possible that the cow–yak herds of Melemchi will bring about increased communalization of herds in this village, as herds are split up, with yak and *zomo* yearlings being "boarded" with zomo herds at high pastures while the cows are kept together at lower pastures. Furthermore, as herds spend more time in the vicinity of the village utilizing shared resources there, new mechanisms for communal control over livestock and their pasturing may need to be developed. For example, as *zomo goths* have declined in number, rules delineating times for all animals to move up to higher pastures have ceased to be enforced. Such rules may be resurrected or modified as the animal population changes and grows.

New Expertise Required

There is substantial zootechnical expertise in managing, breeding, and pasturing *zomo,* the heritage passed along over generations in Melemchi. No one in Melemchi has experience with yak husbandry. One problem is that a yak must be purchased when young, so that it will grow up used to its owner and adjusted to the pasturage. However, it is difficult to tell how such a young yak will develop and whether it will breed with cows. Even with a willing yak and cow, successful breeding requires knowledge of reproductive physiology as well as skill in managing a large intact yak. The variable success of the yaks in Melemchi herds suggests that it may take time for successful management skills to develop.

Shortage of Butter

Another potential outcome of a shift to cow–yak *goths* is the possibility of a severe shortage of butter. Cows produce less milk, with lower butterfat content, but more importantly, their milk will go toward raising *zomo* calves, not butter production. In 1986 and 1989, people had difficulty obtaining butter for household use, even in months of greatest butter production. *Goth* owners acknowledge that they no longer need to sell butter outside the local area. So far, no one is raising the price or holding back the supply to force the price up; one herder explained that such behavior would make him very unpopular in the village. Butter is crucial for both diet and ritual. It is consumed daily in every household in the form of butter tea, and when there is butter to spare, it is used in cooking. Butter lamps are burned on all ritual occasions, and butter is both consumed and used in preparation of ritual statuary (*torma*) and foods for both shamanic and Buddhist ceremonies. For example, at the Nara festival held every summer for five days in each Yolmo Sherpa village, butter is used for constructing *torma,* for butter lamps, and for frying the special braided Nara bread. In Melemchi, 15 gallons of melted butter were used in the 1972 Nara festival to fry the bread alone. Although with expanded access to the markets of Kathmandu it is conceivable that butter could be purchased, there is a strong preference among Sherpas and Tibetans for *zomo* or yak butter. In fact, butter from Yolmo and Kalingchowk region to the east is purchased by Sherpas and Tibetans in Kathmandu, and it has been argued that the increased demand for butter resulting from the arrival in Kathmandu of 6000 Tibetan refugees was instrumental in maintaining transhumant herders in Kalingchowk (Alirol 1979), where they increased the proportion of *zomo* in their herds in response to this market demand.

Alteration in Residence Patterns

Widespread adoption of cow–yak *goths* would increase the possibility for extended social interaction in the village, through a pattern of transhumance that permits women to remain in the village year round, or at least for longer periods. One resident reported that in 1924 when he got his first *zomo goth,* there were only one or two people living in the village during summer; everyone else was out with the herds. Around 1964, some people began living in the village year round, keeping household animals such as buffalo for manure. Today, the village has a lively social life during summer, peopled by the many households not involved in *goths* and those with cow herds not in high pastures. Opportunities for visiting, consulting the *bombo* (spirit medium), and drinking distilled liquor were many, as were fights and disagreements.

THE FUTURE

It is too soon to tell just what will happen with the cow–yak herding pattern in Melemchi. It began in 1982 with one herder, whose yak has produced regularly and with great success, both for his cows and for others. He maintains it is due to the quality of his yak, his skill at managing his herd, and the high quality of his *kharkes* (his family is one of the most wealthy, and he inherited prime pasturage when he was a young man). Others have been less fortunate. Several yak have died and the success rate with breeding is still low.

The possibility of cow–yak *goths* in an area that traditionally practiced a different form of transhumance constitutes a new option for these stock farmers. It may or may not become established and expand. There are still more *zomo goths* than cow–yak *goths,* and in terms of animal numbers, cow–yak *goths* in 1989 account for only 46% of the large animals maintained in *goths.* Also, as already indicated, cow–yak *goths* have been less successful than anticipated in producing offspring, healthy herds, and income. Finally, it must be remembered that sheep and/or goat herds are another option which exists in Melemchi. Like *zomo* herding, it involves high summer pastures, but unlike *zomo* herding, the daily work is much less demanding and requires only the herder and one helper. Wives of sheep herders live in the village year round.

It is not clear why cow–yak *goths* appeared at this time. No one in Melemchi mentioned any ecological changes such as pasture degradation or an increase in predator pressure that might stimulate a shift away from *zomo goths.* From the standpoint of market forces, it would seem a better time than ever before to herd *zomo* and make butter. There is a shortage of butter locally, the price is good, and there is livestock available at falling prices. The most probable explanation for the interest in trying cow–yak *goths* lies in the changes that have occurred over the past 10 years in this village, resulting in the necessity for cash money. Younger people go to work for wage labor in India; for older men a cow–yak herd can be viewed as one way to stay in the village where they have family and property, while retaining the possibility of making cash money. They are protecting and maintaining the property they inherited. They have limited expectations of the amount of money they will make, although each clearly hopes to do well enough to make it worth their while. All are hoping that their youngest sons, who are now in their late teens and early twenties, will want to take over, but that looks less and less likely.

Shifts in herd composition and transhumant strategies such as have been described for Melemchi are not anomalous, but rather constitute an integral aspect of the Himalayan transhumant agropastoral subsistence strategy. Alirol (1979) points out that the succession of different types of livestock over the life of a single herder represents adaptability on his part, not inconsistency. In defining the three basic elements of mountain adaptation, Guillet (1983) includes "a potential for change in strategy" as one of the three. There are a limited number of options for subsistence and income for mountain people in the Himalayas. Messerschmidt in his ethnohistory of the Gurung, tells of how they shifted from pastoral nomadism with cattle and sheep, swidden agriculture and hunting to settled agriculture, transhumant sheep herding and migrant labor in the Ghurka Army (Messerschmidt, 1976). Melemchi has adopted a different combination of these elements: transhumant cattle herding, settled highland agriculture, and migrant wage labor on high altitude road projects. Single factors such as altitude, ethnicity, or geographic location are not adequate to predict or explain the particular complex of factors in any one village. A major key to understanding mountain adaptations will be provided when we understand how decisions are made, both at the individual and group level: what do people perceive their options to be, what factors do they consider when making decisions about herd management, and how they view short-term and long-term outcomes.

ACKNOWLEDGMENTS

This research was sponsored by grants from the National Institutes of Health (1971–1972: NIH Training Grant No. 1224 for the investigation of the socioecology of langur monkeys), the National Geographic Society (1986), Wenner-Gren Foundation for Anthropological Research (1989), and The Joseph P. Healey Endowment Fund (1989).

REFERENCES

Alirol, P. (1976) Le milieu et l'elevage dans la region du Ganesh Himal (Nepal). In *Le Yak: Son Role Dans la Vie Materielle et Culturelle des Eleveurs d'Asia Centrale. Ethnozootechnie No. 15,* Societe d'Ethnozootechnie, Paris, pp. 119–125.

Alirol, P. (1979). *Transhuming Animal Husbandry Systems in the Kalingchowk Region (Central Nepal)*. Swiss Technical Assistance, Bern.

Alirol, P. (1981). Habitat des pasteurs transhumants nepalais. *L'homme et la maison en Himalaya* pp. 187–189.

Bishop, J. and Bishop, N. (1978) *An Ever-Changing Place*. Simon and Schuster, New York.

Bishop, N. (1993). Circular migration and families: A Yolmo Sherpa example. *South Asia Bulletin*, 8(1/2): 59–66.

Bonnemaire, J. and Tessier, J. H. (1976). Quelqeus aspects de l'evage en haute altitude dans l'Himalaya central: Yaks, bovins, hybrides et metis dans la valle du Langtang (Nepal). In *Le Yak: Son Role Dans la Vie Materielle et Culturelle des Eleveurs d'Asia Centrale. Ethnozootechnie No. 15,* Societe d'Ethnozootechnie, Paris, pp. 91–119.

Brower, B. (1991). *Sherpa of Khumbu: People, Livestock, and Landscape.* Oxford University Press, Delhi.

Cox, T. (1985). Herding and socioeconomic change among Langtang Tibetans. *Contributions to Nepalese Studies* 12(3): 63–74.

Fricke, T. (1986). *Himalayan Households: Tamang Demography and Domestic Processes.* UMI Research Press, Ann Arbor, Michigan.

Furer-Haimendorf, C. von (1975). *Himalayan Traders.* John Murray Publishers, London.

Guillet, D. (1983). Toward a cultural ecology of mountains: The central Andes and the Himalayas compared. *Current Anthropology* 24(5): 561–574.

Kawakita, J. (1983). Comment. *Current Anthropology* 24(5): 568.

March, K. (1977). Of people and yaks: The management and meaning of high altitude herding among contemporary Solu Sherpas. *Contributions to Nepalese Studies* 4(2): 83–97.

Messerschmidt, G. (1976). Ecological change and adaptation among the Gurungs of the Nepal Himalaya. *Human Ecology* 4(2): 167–185.

Palmieri, R. (1976). Domestication and Exploitation of Livestock in the Nepal Himalaya and Tibet: An Ecological, Functional, and Culture Historical Study of Yak and Yak Hybrids in Society, Economy, and Culture. Ph.D. dissertation in Geography, University of California, Davis.

Thomas, R. B. (1979). Effects of change on high mountain adaptive patterns. In Webber, P. (ed.), *High Altitude Geoecology.* AAAS Selected Symposia Series No. 12, pp. 139–188.

8

What Alpine Peasants Have in Common: Observations on Communal Tenure in a Swiss Village

Robert McC. Netting

The successful social regulation of land use reflects both a sensitivity to local social conditions and to the characteristics of the system of exploitation and the resource itself. In this instance of communal land tenure in the Swiss Alps, Netting examines an ancient and apparently very stable system of land management through communal tenure combined with private individual land ownership. Netting raises the question, "what variables promoted and effectively maintained the continued balance of individual and communal rights to resources?" He examines the characteristics of several types of communal holdings to explore the features of exploitation which particularly lend themselves to communal management: alpine grazing lands, forests, rugged waste lands, paths and roads. This example makes the useful point that persistence of a cultural practice of resource management through time requires explanation just as much as change does.

This chapter is a revised version of a paper originally presented at the symposium, Cultural Adaptations to Mountain Ecosystems, given at the Annual Meeting of the American Anthropological Association, New Orleans, Louisiana, November 28, 1973, and was originally published in *Human Ecology: An Interdisciplinary Journal* 4(2)(1976): 135–146.

Robert McC. Netting, Late of the Department of Anthropology, University of Arizona, Tuscon, Arizona, Tuscon, Arizona 85721.

Case Studies in Human Ecology, edited by Daniel G. Bates and Susan H. Lees. Plenum Press, New York, 1996.

Although land tenure of a particular type has not been a characteristic defining feature of peasant society, anthropologists have placed a certain emphasis on communal forms of landholding among peasants. However, little effort has been made to analyze the agricultural functions of both individual and collective land rights as they are exercised in specific contexts. In the popular mind there may still linger a presumed evolutionary sequence in which peasants fall somewhere between an earlier stage of cooperative and egalitarian access to resources and a more recent emphasis on private property ownership. Students of peasantry have paid particular attention to the model of the closed corporate community as a landholding body in a dual society where peasants are subject to powerful outsiders.

Although few social scientists would now subscribe to 19th century notions of an inevitable progress from ancient tribal communism through clan holdings to individual ownership in severalty (Morgan, 1963: 551), there remains some sense that individual ownership of land has become dominant among peasants only in the recent past.

> Peasant proprietorship in many Western European countries is a product of the 19th century, and landownership is no part of immemorial peasant tradition. It has, in fact, weakened it because the old peasantries were attached to cooperative schemes of land use, and private ownership of the soil as we understand it was not found. (Evans, 1956)

An earlier evolutionary transition in German land tenure was noted by Engels; to account for the change from collective ownership of land by the gens and later by communistic household communities to individual family holdings, he cited the increasing pressure of population on land resources and the lack of sufficient territory to sustain shifting cultivation. In such circumstances, disputes over land interfered with the common economy. Not all types of productive resources, however, became private. "The arable and meadowlands which had hitherto been common were divided in the manner familiar to us, first temporarily and then permanently among the single households which were now coming into being, while forest, pasture land, and water remained common" (Engels, 1972: 202). Historical studies have emphasized the absence of any irreversible direction of change in European land tenure. The early medieval peasant holding (*Hufe* or *mansus*) appears to have combined individual property with rights of usufruct in common lands (Pfeifer, 1956). Communal rights and organizational mechanisms coexisted with individually heritable and alienable rights in parcels of obviously scarce and valuable arable land (Homans, 1960).

The influential concept of the closed corporate peasant community as proposed by Eric Wolf (1957) embodies "outright communal tenure" with varying degrees of periodic land redistribution, restriction of landholding to community members, and communal jurisdiction over inheritance and sale of land. Wolf makes clear the fact that corporate land tenure is neither a simple survival nor the result of some putative tendency to conservatism. In the type cases of both Mesoamerica and Java, closed corporate communities result from conquest and the attempt by an occupying power to seize resources, concentrate population, and make village units responsible for tribute and corvée labor. Both the mechanisms to level differences among members by periodic reallotments of land and the equal distribution of rent in labor, kind, or money may be seen as means to maintain the internal order of a community subjected to outside political and economic constraints (Wolf, 1966: 86).

A somewhat different perspective on the problem of communal vs. individual tenure is provided by alpine communities in Western Europe, where both types of landholding have persisted in relatively stable association over a long and well-documented period of time. In the case of one Swiss village with local records beginning in the 13th century, different kinds of resources have remained under contrasting types of ownership to the present day. Although various external demands for rent, taxes, and military service have been enforced over the centuries by church, nobility, and state, the community has continued to make a large share of the important decisions affecting its own economy and resource allocation. Such local autonomy suggests that corporate features may be less oriented to resisting external domination and more closely related to environmental conditions and subsistence requirements. My contention will be that, in the absence of decisive legal or military controls from the larger society, the system of property rights in the peasant community will be directly related to the manner in which resources are exploited, the competition for their use, and the nature of the product produced—more specifically, land use by and large determines land tenure.[1]

There is little doubt that the initial year-round settlement of alpine areas by Celtic populations following 500 BC represented an intensification in the use of the mountain environment in what is now southern Switzerland.[2] Areas that had probably supported only seasonal transhumance were made sites of permanent villages with large clearings on the forested slopes. It seems clear that a considerable increase in labor was required to provide

---

[1]The same point has been forcefully made by Ester Boserup (1965: 77–87) in her discussion of precolonial land tenure systems with a worldwide distribution.

[2]Grave goods (Sauter, 1950) and place names (Zimmermann, 1968) suggest permanent pre-Christian occupation of sites high on valley slopes in the Rhone drainage. The Alemmanic infiltration from the ninth to the eleventh century AD may well have increased population pressure to the point in the thirteenth century when German speakers from Valais emigrated to found new alpine communities in Austria and Italy (Gutersohn, 1961: 28).

hay for the animals' winter forage, shelter and heating during the cold months for men and beasts, grain crops on the steep fields, and irrigation on the drier slopes. Favored spots where these subsistence requirements could be met attracted resident populations, and the building of substantial log houses, terraced fields, and artificial water courses within clearly defined village territories indicates the continuing pressure of a population to make the most of available resources (Netting, 1972, 1974). Scarcity of land or water in the face of demographic requirements makes adaptive the investment of labor and capital to increase production per unit area and render the yield more dependable through time.[3] A corollary of such intensification is the claiming of individual rights in resources which are (1) necessary to survival, (2) so scarce that community members must compete for them, and (3) so productive naturally or through improvement by the investment of labor or capital that they provide a reasonably secure, long-term return.[4] Although we have no direct evidence of a change in this area from communal pasture rights among transhumants to individual or family rights in land among sedentary mixed farmers, the tendency has been noted frequently in other parts of the world (Barth, 1964; Manners, 1964; Stenning, 1959).

The first written sources concerning Törbel, a village in the Vispertal of Valais, southern Switzerland, suggest both individual ownership and corporate holding of land. A document dated 1293 refers to one man's sale of land in four named meadow localities to the community as a whole. Since the seller who received cash was granted use of the property in return for annual payments, it is possible that the transaction was equivalent to the mortgaging of the land. Similar cases in the 14th century suggest that the community was acting as a banker for its members who pledged land as security for loans, but there is no indication that communal ownership of these lands was permanent or that they were worked by communal labor. Although the church[5] and absentee landlords had feudal claims to portions of village land (Via 330, 1989: 265), it is obvious that several freemen and the corporate community itself also possessed rights in land which could be traded, mortgaged, or sold. The village was treated as a group with joint

[3]Chayanov (1966: 115) has cited the Swiss peasant farm as characterized by demographic pressure and a low degree of mobility of land, leading to a much higher level of agricultural intensity than that found in relatively less crowded areas of rural Russia.

[4]"There is a large and growing theoretical literature in economics on this point, the point, that is, that as a resource becomes more valuable it becomes profitable to decide who exactly owns it" (McCloskey, personal communication; cf. also McCloskey, 1975, footnote 30).

[5]A tribute roll of scattered parcels in Törbel on which feudal dues were owed to the cathedral chapter in Sion is reproduced in von Roten (n.d.). These lands appear to have been gifts to the church by pious individuals in the village.

responsibility for its tithe to the parish church at Visp as early as 1224.[6] During the 14th century, five noble families are mentioned as having land rights in Törbel, but also listed are nine resident peasants whose combined property equals three-fifths of that belonging to the nobles (von Roten, n.d.). A notarized instrument dated 1392 transferred three grain fields from a seller in Törbel to two different buyers in return for cash. The sale included access and water rights, and the plots are designated by reference to adjoining fields of three other named owners. Similarly detailed private transactions occur regularly in public records thereafter (Törbel Gemeindearchiv, Section H), and a number of Törbel residents preserve comparable bills of sale from as early as 1642. As in many parts of the Alps, the general tendency in Törbel during medieval times appears to have been toward relaxation and early disappearance of feudal obligations owed to both spiritual and temporal lords and the emergence of a relatively autonomous community of free peasant proprietors.

An agreement formally drawn up in Latin on parchment makes clear the existence of several types of community property in Törbel during the 15th century and probably codifies customary usage of long standing. A local political body of 22 named Törbel residents came together on February 1, 1483, in Visp as a voluntary *Gemeinschaft* (collective or association) for the purpose of better regulating the use of the alp, the waste lands, and the forest. The law specifically forbade a foreigner (*Fremde*) who bought or otherwise occupied land in Törbel from acquiring any right in the communal alp, common lands, or grazing places, or permission to fell timber. Ownership of a piece of land did *not* automatically confer any communal right (*genossenschaftliches recht*). The inhabitants currently possessing land and water rights reserved the power to decide whether an outsider should be admitted to community membership. The closing of the community to immigration appears here to have been an internal decision based on population pressures rather than a decree promulgated by outside authorities. That customary rights to the common lands of the alp were largely unchallenged is suggested by the absence of any documents reflecting disputes or litigation over it between the village and any noble or ecclesiastical lords (*cf.* Bloch, 1970: 182–189).

An inventory of 1507 lists the alps and waste lands (*Alpen und Allmeinen*) that belong to the community. Written alp use rights specified in 1517 that no citizen could send more cows to the alp than he could feed during the winter, thus effectively limiting individuals to the number of ani-

---

[6]I am indebted for translation and commentary on several of the relevant documents to Herr U.-D. Sprenger (n.d. and personal communications).

mals which their own hay meadows could support, and severely fining them for any attempt to appropriate a larger share of community grazing privileges.[7] This rule continues to be enforced to the present day. In 1519, a further agreement set boundaries on the communal lands and forests as well as defining the width and use of horse roads, foot and cow paths, and logging tracks. A major code promulgated in 1531 by the Citizenry or Peasant Corporation of the Communities of Törbel and Burgen (*Burgerrecht oder Bauernzunft der Gemeinde Törbel und Burgen*)[8] listed 24 statutes regulating immigration to or emigration from the community, hunting on the alp, stock damage to private plots, the spread of cattle disease, dispute settlement, participation in village government, alp pasturage rights, and compulsory communal house building. Sixty named males representing their own and nine additional families subscribed to this charter.

Historical evidence is entirely consistent with the assertion that both individual and communal rights in resources have been present for at least 500 years, and that they have regularly associated private control with meadows, grain fields, gardens, vineyards, and buildings, and community tenure with the alp, the forests, certain waste lands, and access routes. This is not to say that rights were *always* allocated to a single type of administration. The community could enlarge its holdings by purchase from other collectives, as in the 1514 acquisition of the Oberaaralp, some 70 km distant

---

[7]The "tragedy of the commons," in which the rational herdsman increases his herd without limit to the eventual economic detriment of all, as the cattle overgraze and degrade the pasture environment, (Hardin, 1968) was thus avoided by democratic decision based on a sound awareness of the ecological consequences. Commons were sustained for centuries in European communities without permanent damage to resources. A similar traditional limit on the number of animals a person could graze on the open fields was termed a "stint" in medieval England and was usually proportional to the quantity of arable land occupied (McCloskey, 1975). Hardin's contention that only private property or government control of land could prevent the tragedy of the commons has been disputed in recent years by anthropologists, political scientists, and biologists (McCay and Acheson, 1987; Ostrom, 1990; Berkes, et al., 1989). It is now apparent that comparable common property institutions are used by local communities to regulate and protect woodlands, grazing grounds, water sources, irrigation systems, hunting territories, and in-shore fisheries in a great many societies, both traditional and modern. Explicit rules prevent use of the commons by outsiders, thus eliminating the open access that can lead to resource over-exploitation. The products that members can appropriate from the commons are also restricted. Rule making by an assembly of members, settlement of disputes, enforcement of communal decisions, provision for maintenance, monitoring, and recognition by government generally characterize successful common property regimes (Ostrom, 1990). Because such rights can provide valuable benefits to the present holders and to their heirs through time, it is to the advantage of members to practice active conservation of the renewable natural resource base and to strive for environmental sustainability. The Swiss case (Netting, 1981) is one model of the successful management of common property over perhaps a millennium of use.
[8]Burgen, although independent at the time, later became a hamlet incorporated into Törbel.

from Törbel above the Grimsel Pass.[9] It also bought or traded for private parcels within or bordering the alp in 1400, 1632, 1726, 1768, 1772, and 1833, received a gift of forest from several owners in 1762, and acquired rights of way in various parts of its territory in 1666, 1711, 1727, and 1832. These changes reflect little in the way of altered land use. High, dry meadows that produced poor and irregular hay harvests for their owners could be perhaps more productive when incorporated into adjoining communal grazing grounds, and it was only pieces of this sort that were transferred to public hands.

In a stable, highly self-sufficient alpine village with environmental factors of altitude, slope gradient, isolation, and water supply largely dictating land use, what variables promoted and effectively maintained the continued balance of individual and communal rights to resources? A review of the major classes of communal holdings may clarify their common features.

1. The alp can be grazed only in summer when it is free from snow. Because of its altitude (able 2000 m), with a limited growing season and thin soils, it cannot produce sufficiently dense stands of grass for haying. Irrigation is also not practical. The alp can afford grazing for milk cows, heifers, and sheep at successively higher levels, but no single section can support the animals continuously, and the best pasturage may vary in its occurrence. In order to use widely distributed grasslands in an optimal manner while remaining within reach of water and forest shelter for the stock during spring and fall storms, a large, fenceless area of range is necessary.[10] Overgrazing that would decrease the alp's carrying capacity must be rigidly prohibited, because alternative pastures are not available. A decline in the quantity or quality of grass would be readily apparent in lower milk, and therefore cheese, production per animal. Cattle owners carefully monitor the condition of their cows by Sunday visits to the alp, and deterioration

[9]The substantial cash price of 850 Bernese pounds was collected by a number of individuals who lacked grazing rights on the Torbjer alps, but within 50 years the added land became communal property.

[10]Similar factors promoting efficiency of grazing and control of cattle in areas segregated from arable and meadow lands are apparent in the classic open-field system of Europe. Strip parcels that were individually tilled and administered under a three-field rotation were opened during the fallow period for common pasturage on stubble with free rights of way across neighboring plots (Uhlig, 1971: 107). The same land thus alternated between individual and communal tenure according to its use for either crops or grazing. Where land was more plentiful and the emphasis was on a livestock economy, communal pasture was periodically redistributed into individual plowing strips. Temporary individual rights to cultivation of this kind are found in the former Russian *mir* system and the *muscha'a* of the Near and Middle East, Persia, and northwest India (Uhlig, 1971; 104). Redistribution also occurred all over Scotland, Wales, and Ireland (Baker and Butlin, 1973).

of the pasture or the effects of longer than average treks to the grazing grounds are a topic of immediate discussion.

Labor economies also make common grazing lands a viable option. A handful of men can herd the animals of an entire village, milk them, and produce cheese in bulk. The rest of the population is thereby freed for the vital summer task of haying. Maintenance of the alp such as keeping access paths open, renewing avalanche-damaged corrals, cleaning springs, and redistributing manure can be effectively performed by the cooperative labor of all cattle owners in a few days each year. Decisions on protecting the alp from encroachment by other villages, organizing the herding and dairy activities, allotting equitable use rights, preventing overgrazing, and making necessary improvements can be made democratically by an alp association (*Burgerschaft*) that is often coterminous with the village citizenry. A diffuse resource such as an alp both loses productive value if it is split into private parcels and requires a considerably increased labor input due to the duplication of effort. The cost of fencing alone might seriously reduce the profits of summer grazing.

There are private alps belonging to individuals or groups that can dispose of the property at will, but these are rare. In Valais, 95% of all alpine pasture has been under communal ownership (Carrier, 1932: 205). Although a number of Swiss alps may have been at one time claimed by great ecclesiastical or secular lords and rented for payment in cheese, they seem to have been taken over during the middle ages by the peasants who used them.

2. Forests occurring at various elevations of the Törbel territory, up to 2200 m, especially on steeper, shaded slopes, provide materials necessary for every inhabitant. They are the source of firewood used for heating the houses through large stone stoves, and formerly necessary for cooking in open fireplaces. Heavy squared logs were basic to the construction of houses, barns, granaries, and storage buildings. Until recently, the forest floor was scraped to supply needles for strewing the cattle stalls in winter (Stebler, 1922: 98–99). Growing timber also anchors mountain soil, preventing erosion and rapid runoff of melt waters. Woodlands above the cultivated area lessen the danger of destructive avalanches and provide shelter for livestock on the alp. Much of the Törbel timber is relatively slow-growing larch, and maintenance of fuel and lumber supplies plus watershed protection enjoins strictly limited and selective cutting through the entire forested area. Private ownership of woodland would interfere with obtaining controlled continuous yields and present problems in filling the minimal needs of each household due to intergenerational demographic changes. Communal administration of the forest allows annual cutting to be decided on by the elected village council. These officials further divide the marked trees into equal shares that are allocated by lot to teams of three households. These self-selected teams provide the necessary cooperation for felling and snaking the logs down the mountain. Since little

can be done to increase timber production, the emphasis is on restricting resource use to the renewal rate of forest growth, leaving undamaged the protective function of the woodland, and giving equal shares to all households. Communal forest ownership would appear to meet these requisites most efficiently. Although individuals might put aside part of their timber allotment for building repairs, it appears that major construction over at least the last century has necessitated buying logs in other communities.

3. Waste lands or *Allmeinen* tended to be bare, rocky, or otherwise minimally productive lands scattered through the village territory. Those areas thus designated in Törbel are cliffs, steep ravines, and mountain peaks where little or no grass grows. Such rugged slopes, too precipitous for cattle, could afford sparse browsing for goats, and it was to them that the village goat herd was taken in summer. Wild grass was pulled from the crags to supplement the hay supply at the end of winter. Villagers could freely take stone for foundations and roofing slate from these common lands. Moreover, such areas were protected from outsiders, who might occupy them to the detriment of inhabitants. The high mountain catchment basin of Törbel's principal irrigation stream also was treated as common land, thus guarding the vital water rights of the village.

4. The need for communally owned and maintained paths and roads is obvious. With intense competition for every scrap of meadow and arable land, access routes could become a source of contention. In 1402, Johann Ester publicly threatened all trespassers on his land. To this day, lack of an agreed-upon right of way can render land useless to its owner. Thus, the community must specify the width and type of traffic on its traveled ways, resist infringement or rerouting, and keep the paths in repair.

In contrast to the strongly communal character of rights to the alp, forests, waste lands, and pathways, most meadows, lower-altitude pastures, gardens, grain fields, and vineyards in Törbel have been subject to individual tenure.[11] They may be rented, worked on shares, traded, or sold, and

[11]The assumption that peasants in pre-industrial corporate communities held significant resources of annually tilled arable land as a group, assigned temporary use rights to member households for their subsistence, and reallocated land according to need, thereby maintaining relative equality among domestic units, now appears to be questionable. Wolf (1981) later pointed to persistent inequality in peasant villages, despite various ceremonial redistributions of goods. It is apparent that the long-term, intensive cultivation of highly productive improved lands such as wet rice paddies, terraced hillsides, orchards, vineyards, gardens, and irrigated plots is accompanied by well defined, heritable private or household rights of ownership (Netting 1993: 157–185). Such communities very frequently also have common property rights, but these may include differential and unequal access by member households to resources including grazing grounds and irrigation water (Netting 1993: 196).

they are passed on through partible inheritance. Spouses retain separate title to their lands, even though these are worked cooperatively by the family. Alienation of land appears to have required major cash payments and elaborate contracts during the entire course of recorded village history. The acquisition of land evidently became so expensive by 1672 that a special enactment forbade sales at a price higher than that determined by civic appraisers. Buildings or fractional shares in such structures as barns, granaries, and multifloored apartment houses are also owned, and maintenance is provided for in condominium-like agreements. All such property rights show certain similarities: (1) They cover resources for which there is high value in the subsistence economy. (2) The production from or occupation of such resources is relatively frequent and dependable (e.g., two hay harvests plus several weeks of tethered grazing are the assured annual return from a good meadow). (3) The resources may be used effectively in small, fixed portions (e.g., garden plots may average less than 70 m² each, and a total vineyard holding consisting of several parcels is usually 500 m² or less). (4) The resources may be improved or their production intensified. Yields are regularly increased in privately owned lands in Törbel by irrigation, manuring, erosion control, crop rotation, and careful horticulture (Netting, 1972). (5) The resource may be exploited effectively by individual or family labor and capital investment within the capability of a single household.

It seems possible to differentiate an emphasis on communal, as opposed to individual, rights in land resources according to the nature of land use (Table 1). The remarkable stability of both types of land rights in a Swiss alpine village reflects the relatively unchanging patterns of resource use within rigid environmental constraints, as well as the comparative freedom of this

Table 1

Nature of land use	Land tenure type	
	Communal	Individual
Value of production per unit area	Low	High
Frequency and dependability of use or yield	Low	High
Possibility of improvement or intensification	Low	High
Area required for effective use	Large	Small
Labor- and capital-investing groups	Large (voluntary association or community	Small (individual or family)

area from external political domination. Changes in technology or economic organization might alter the present balance of private and communal right to agree with new kinds of land use. For instance, a shortage of labor due to industrial work and outmigration plus the creation of a feeder road network may make year-round communal dairying and ultimately corporate control of meadow land desirable. On the other hand, decline in the use of wood for fuel and high demand for vacation chalet sites may lead to subdividing of the communal forest among private owners or long-term leaseholders.

The comparative advantages of alternate land usage and the desirability of altering related tenure practices may not be immediately apparent. Peasant farmers may indeed display some reluctance to alter tenurial arrangements that have proved effective in the past. Certainly more important in introducing potentially maladaptive factors into the system would be the legal arrangements decreed by an outsider power structure as a means of exploiting the peasant community. In an alpine situation where environmental parameters of altitude and topography largely determine agricultural potential, where technology is essentially unchanging, and where community boundaries have remained fixed for a long period of time, the maintenance of a single integrated system of communal and individual tenure suggests an ecological interpretation. Communal tenure promotes both general access to, and optimum production from, certain types of resources while enjoining on the entire community the conservation measures necessary to protect these resources from destruction. The persistence of communal rights should not be dismissed as a historical anachronism or credited solely to external domination of the closed corporate community.

ACKNOWLEDGMENTS

This research was supported by a Guggenheim Fellowship, a grant from the University Museum, University of Pennsylvania, and National Science Foundation Grant No. GS–3318. Gemeinde Präsident Otto Karlen kindly gave me permission to consult the village archives currently in the charge of the priest, Hochwürdiger Herr Pfarrer Markus Jossen. I especially appreciate the comments made by Donald N. McCloskey on an earlier version of this article.

REFERENCES

Baker, A. R., and Butlin, R. A. (1973). *Studies of Field Systems in the British Isles,* Cambridge University Press, Cambridge.

Barth, F. (1964). *Nomads of South Persia,* Humanities Press, New York.

Berkes, F., Feeney, D., McCay, B. J., and Acheson, J. M. (1989). The benefits of the commons. *Nature* 340: 91–93.

Bloch, M. (1970). *French Rural History,* University of California Press, Berkeley.

Boserup, E. (1965). *The Conditions of Agricultural Growth,* Aldine, Chicago.

Carrier, E. H. (1932). *Water and Grass,* Christophers, London.

Chayanov, A. V. (1966). In Thorner, D., Kerblay, B., and Smith, R. E. F., (eds.), *The Theory of Peasant Economy,* Richard D. Irwin, Homewood, Ill.

Engels, F. (1972). In Leacock, E. B., (ed.), *The Origin of the Family, Private Property and the State,* International, New York (orig. 1884).

Evans, E. E. (1956). The ecology of peasant life in Western Europe. In Thomas, W. L. (ed.), *Man's Role in Changing the Face of the Earth,* University of Chicago Press, Chicago, pp. 217–239.

Hardin, G. (1968). The tragedy of the commons. *Science* 162: 1243–1248.

Homans, G. C. (1960). *English Villagers of the Thirteenth Century,* Russell and Russell, New York (orig. 1941).

Manners, R. A. (1964). Colonialism and native land tenure. In Manners, R. A. (ed.), *Process and Pattern in Culture,* Aldine, Chicago.

McCay, B. J., Acheson, J. M., (eds.) (1987). *The Question of the Commons: The Culture and Ecology of Communal Resources.* University of Arizona Press, Tucson.

McCloskey, D. N. (1975). The persistence of English open fields. In Parke, W. N., and Jones, E. L. (eds.), *Economic Issues in European Agrarian History,* Princeton University Press, Princeton.

Morgan, L. H. (1963). In Leacock, F. B., *Ancient Society* (ed.), World, Cleveland (orig. 1877).

Netting, R. McC. (1972). Of men and meadows: Strategies of alpine land use. *Anthropological Quarterly* 45: 132–144.

Netting, R. McC. (1974). The system nobody knows: Village irrigation in the Swiss Alps. In Downing, T. E., and Gibson, M. (eds.), *Irrigation's Impact on Society,* University of Arizona Press, Tucson, pp. 67–75.

Netting, R. McC. (1981). *Balancing on an Alp: Ecological Change and Continuity in a Swiss Mountain Community.* Cambridge University Press, Cambridge.

Netting, R. McC. (1993). *Smallholders, Householders: Farm Families and the Ecology of Intensive, Sustainable Agriculture.* Stanford University Press, Stanford.

Ostrom, E. (1990). *Governing the Commons: The Evolution of Institutions for Collective Action.* Cambridge University Press, Cambridge.

Pfeifer, G. (1956). The quality of peasant living in Central Europe. In Thomas, W. L. (ed.), *Man's Role in Changing the Face of the Earth.* University of Chicago Press, Chicago, pp. 240–277.

Sauter, M. R. (1950). Préhistoire du Valais, *Vallesia* 5: 1–165.

Sprenger, U.–D. (n.d.). Besprechung einer Walliser Urkunde aus dem 13, Jahrhundert. Unpublished manuscript.

Stenning, D. J. (1959), *Savannah Nomads.* Oxford University Press, London.

Uhlig, H. (1971). Fields and field systems. In Buchanan, R. H., Jones, E., and McCourt, D. (eds.), *Man and His Habitat.* Routledge and Kegan Paul, London, pp. 93–125.

Viazzo, P. P. (1989). *Upland Communities: Environment, Population and Social Structure in the Alps since the Sixteenth Century.* Cambridge University Press, Cambridge.

von Roten, P. (n.d.), Untersuchungen über die Verteilung und die rechtlichen Verhältnisse des Grundbesitzes in der Vispertälern im 13 und 14. Jahrhundert. Ms. in Staatsarchiv Sitten, SA 1081.

Wolf, E. R. (1966). *Peasants,* Prentice–Hall, Englewood Cliffs, New Jersey.

Wolf, E. R. (1981). The vicissitudes of the closed corporate community. *American Ethnologist* 13: 325–329.
Zimmermann, J. (1968). *Die Orts und Flurnamen des Vispertales im Wallis,* Juris Druck–Verlag, Zürich.

III

Subsistence and Intensive Agriculture

Modern human existence depends on the production of plant food (grains, tubers, pulses, fruits, and vegetables), fiber (such as cotton), and fodder (to feed livestock, which in turn produce meat, milk, wool, and hide). Virtually all this production depends upon domesticated plants, species that characteristically cannot survive or reproduce without human intervention. The process of domestication of plants and animals by humans began more than 12,000 years ago and continues to the present (Redding, 1988; Bar-Yosef and Belfer-Cohen, 1989; McCorriston and Hole, 1991; Miller, 1992).

The labor requirements for the cultivation of plants display a broad range of variation. Generally speaking, people who engage in cultivation invest more time and energy in production of food and other necessities than do foragers, but the differences among cultivators are great, depending in a significant way on whether they are producing largely to support themselves and their families or on whether they are producing for a market (also, of course, to support themselves and their families, but with cash). If they engage in very little trade, the requirements of cultivation may be relatively light, leaving time for other activities such as hunting, making war, or simply resting (see Carneiro, 1960; Werner et al., 1979). Environmental limitations, such as a short growing season, low soil fertility, a profusion of pests, and other challenges to production may demand that cultivators work harder.

Cultivation oriented mainly to household consumption, using relatively small plots of land, with low-level technology (no plows, no tractors) and relatively low levels of labor input per unit of land has been conventionally labeled "horticulture," or gardening, as a subsistence type.[1] The day-to-day management of such subsistence gardens has generally been the domain largely of women, while men have been assigned the tasks of hunting, long-distance trading, making war, and engaging in ceremony and politics, except for the critical tasks of land preparation (such as clearing forests) and, sometimes, harvesting crops. However, this is a generalization, and societies

---

[1]Gardening may be important to family subsistence even in highly industrialized economies, including the United States (see Gladwin and Butler, 1982).

vary widely in their assignments of cultivation tasks by age and gender. The division of labor, in turn, has ramifications for fertility and other demographic characteristics of the local population (see Johnson, Chapter 9).

In relatively isolated prestate horticultural societies with few constraints on access to land, cultivators tended to shift to new fields as fertility declined in older ones (hence the term "shifting cultivation"); fallow periods in tropical forests, where soil fertility tends to be low, were very long. The main constraints to production were on availability of labor: Since most household needs were relatively easily satisfied by small gardens and supplemental hunting and gathering, there was little motivation for households to intensify their production through greater labor input. Ecological studies of the few remaining relatively isolated horticultural societies emphasized the bases of stability and persistence of such systems.

However, most horticultural societies today have become engaged in cash-crop production such as coffee, rubber, and other forest products, for national and international markets. The ecological consequences include not only changes in demography (see Johnson, Chapter 9), but dramatic impacts on basic resources, such as soil fertility (see Clay and Lewis, Chapter 11). The problem of sustainable development occupies many human ecologists who are studying changes due to the introduction of cash-cropping. It is clear that the immediate product of such a shift, an improvement in standards of living (see Conelly, Chapter 12, and Netting, Stone, and Stone, Chapter 14) is proving irresistible to local populations. The problem becomes one of learning to anticipate negative consequences and to avoid further damage to local resources. Some have suggested looking to the preindustrial past for models (see Dazhong and Pimentel, Chapter 13).

Intensification of plant production through the investment of more human (and later, animal, and still later, fossil fuel) energy per unit of land began occurring millennia ago, for reasons that are a source of lively controversy in the literature (see Lees, 1994). Some argue that population increase resulted in land scarcity in some areas, which necessitated more intensive agricultural practices (Boserup, 1965). Others argue that pressures to produce more for trade or to support an emerging elite arose for a variety of reasons (still contested). Whatever the original causes, there is indeed an association between trade, socioeconomic stratification, and intensification of production.

Class-stratified societies are complex by definition. Families may adopt different strategies of reproduction (see Folmar, Chapter 10), depending on whether they are rich or poor. They certainly are obliged to pursue very different means of livelihood. Agricultural producers tend to be at the base of the social pyramid in traditional agrarian societies (unlike modern industrial ones, where they usually consist of less than 10% of the total population, a tiny fraction cross-cutting more than one class). Their governments, and governments of conquering nations, harness their energy and local resources to serve nonlocal interests, with immense consequences for their land, their ways of making a living, and their future potentials.

Thus, while there has been a historical (if uneven) trend toward greater productivity on the part of cultivators, there has also been a trend toward greater dependency (Frank, 1966; Wallerstein, 1974; and Wolf, 1982). A classic work showing how incorporation into a world market system through colonialism influenced the human ecology of both extensive tropical forest cultivators and intensive irrigated rice agriculturalists is Clifford Geertz's study of "agricultural involution" in Indonesia (1963). Contemporary studies of changes in relations between people and their environments attend closely to the history of colonial interactions (see, for example, Lennihan, Chapter 15).

Dependency can be looked at in a different way. While dependent peoples are subject to exploitation, it is also often the case that they cannot survive, at least in numbers, in the environments they inhabit without large-scale and stratified organization. This is what Karl Wittfogel (1957) argued in making his case for explaining the emergence of what he called "agro-managerial totalitarianism" in the context of irrigated agriculture in China. Irrigation is the oldest known and most widespread means of intensifying agricultural production; by applying additional water to plants and regulating the timing of its application, farmers can substantially increase productivity per unit of land and secure more predictable harvests. Without irrigation, there is little that can be done to increase or secure productivity—many other inputs depend upon water. But irrigation requires great inputs of labor and organization for construction, regulation of water distribution, and maintenance. Farmers dependent upon irrigation have no choice but to obey the managers of the irrigation system or to starve.

This is not to say that irrigation managers need be despotic, exploitative, or totalitarian. As Abruzzi (Chapter 16) shows, even where rulers appear to be benevolent and supportive, farmers inhabiting a hostile terrain may be entirely dependent on them for survival. In this instance, the colonizing of new territory, we see how critical this dependence may become.

REFERENCES

Bar-Yosef, O. and Belfer-Cohen, A. (1989). The origins of sedentism and farming communities in the Levant. *Journal of World Prehistory* 3: 447–498.

Boserup, E. (1965). *Conditions of Agricultural Growth: The Economics of Agrarian Change under Population Pressure.* Aldine, Chicago.

Carneiro, R. (1960). Slash and burn agriculture: A closer look at its implications for settlement patterns. In A. Wallace (ed.), *Men and Cultures: Selected Papers of The International Congress of Anthropological and Ethnological Sciences.* University of Pennsylvania Press, Philadelphia.

Frank, A. G. (1966). The Development of Underdevelopment. *Monthly Review* 18: 17–31.

Geertz, C. (1963). *Agricultural Involution: The Process of Ecological Change in Indonesia.* University of California Press, Berkeley.

Gladwin, C. and Butler, J. (1982). *Gardening: A Survival Strategy for the Small, Part-time Florida Farm. Proceedings of the Florida State Horticultural Society* 95: 264–268.

Gladwin, C. and Butler, J. Is Gardening an Adaptive Strategy for Florida Family Farmers? *Human Organization* 43: 208–216.

Lees, S. (1994). Irrigation and Society. *Journal of Archaeological Research* 2: 361–378.

McCorriston, J. and Frank, H. (1991). The ecology of seasonal stress and the origins of agriculture in the Near East. *American Anthropologist* 93: 46–69.

Miller, N. F. (1992). The origins of plant cultivation in the Near East. In C. W. Cowan and P. J. Watson (eds.), *The Origins of Agriculture: An International Perspective.* Smithsonian Institution Press, Washington, DC, pp. 39–58.

Redding, R. W. (1988). A general explanation of subsistence change: From hunting and gathering to food production. *Journal of Anthropological Archaeology* 7: 56–97.

Wallerstein, I. M. (1974). *The Modern World-System: Capitalist Agriculture and the Origin of the European World-Economy in the Sixteenth Century.* Academy Press, New York.

Werner, D., Flowers, N., Ritter, M., and Gross, D. (1979). Subsistence Productivity and Hunting Effort in Native South America. *Human Ecology* 7: 303–315.

Wittfogel, K. (1957). *Oriental Despotism.* Yale University Press, New Haven.

Wolf, E. (1982). *Europe and the People Without History.* University of California Press, Berkeley.

9

Changing Household Composition, Labor Patterns, and Fertility in a Highland New Guinea Population

Patricia Lyons Johnson

Demography, the study of the characteristics of populations, is central to ecology. The size, distribution, and other characteristics of populations are assumed to reflect, respond to, and have an impact on other living things and the nonorganic factors that comprise the environment. However, when we study human populations, as Johnson demonstrates in this study of a Highland New Guinea community on which excellent demographic records have been kept over a period of time, we find that complex variables interact in complex ways to alter fertility. In this instance, Johnson tests a long-held belief that economic development results in a reduction in fertility. Presumably, this is a product of higher, more dependable family incomes, which depress the demand for labor and produce higher levels of health care, consequently lower infant and childhood mortality, as well as higher costs of investment in childrearing. In other words, since children are expected to survive, and to be expensive, families in the developed world plan to have fewer of them than families elsewhere, who anticipate high losses and need more children to work.

Johnson disputes the applicability of this general model in her case, and, by extension, in others. In highland Papua New Guinea among the

Originally published in *Human Ecology: An Interdisciplinary Journal,* 18(4)(1990): 403–416.

Patricia Lyons Johnson, Department of Anthropology and Women's Studies Program, Pennsylvania State University, University Park, Pennsylvania 16802.

Case Studies in Human Ecology, edited by Daniel G. Bates and Susan H. Lees. Plenum Press, New York, 1996.

Gainj, predevelopment fertility rates were comparatively low as a result of late ages at marriage, prolonged (and frequent) lactation patterns, prolonged absence of young husbands for distant wage labor, and cultural beliefs resulting in men's fear of sex with women. Development, bringing the introduction of cash crops (coffee, in this instance), may result in a change in the pattern of lactation for women, which will depress the contraceptive effectiveness of breast-feeding, which in turn will result in shorter birth intervals, which may well result in higher fertility for married women (who are assigned the labor of agricultural work in this society). On the other hand, the study also shows that families that engage in cash cropping are more likely to delay marriage for their young women, to keep them home, presumably, to provide labor in the fields. Thus, the fertility impacts of development may, as in this case, be contradictory.

Macrolevel economic development and subsequent modernization are often seen as the engines driving demographic change in the Third World. Some authors have proposed that the European demographic transition of the 19th century provides a model for 20th century developing nations, and that modernization will inevitably bring about a reduction in their fertility (Notestein, 1953; Coale and Treadway, 1986). According to proponents of this position: "The implication most frequently drawn for current population policy from the historical record of European fertility can be summed up in the slogan, 'Development is the best contraceptive'" (Knodel and van de Walle, 1986: 390). Other approaches to fertility in developing nations have emphasized the importance of variability in traditional societies and have questioned the applicability of demographic transition theory based on the European experience (Romaniuk, 1980, 1981; Watkins, 1986; Campbell and Wood, 1988). In this paper I want to suggest the following: first, that fertility change associated with development involves the complex interaction of a number of variables, second, that the effects of those variables may sometimes be contradictory, and third, that the effect of any variable may change as the society changes. Moreover, I suggest that household composition and the allocation of household labor may exert an important mediating influence in the relationship between development and fertility.

Since 1977 I have been part of a multidisciplinary team of researchers studying the Gainj, a small population who live in the northern fringe of

Papua New Guinea's central highlands.[1] Like many highland New Guinea peoples, the Gainj were contacted relatively recently. The initial entry of Europeans to the central highlands did not occur before 1930, and in many of the fringe highland areas, the difficulty of the steep and broken terrain postponed first contact even longer. It was not until 1953 that the Australian colonial administration entered the Gainj homeland, the Takwi valley of Madang Province's Eastern Schrader Mountains (Figure 1). The area was declared "pacified" in 1964, meaning that endemic tribal warfare had been abolished and, perhaps more importantly, that the valley was considered safe for European travel. Immediately, European labor contractors entered the Takwi to sign local men to 2 year wage labor contracts on coastal and island copra plantations. Returning migrants brought with them small amounts of cash and some manufactured items such as clothing and aluminum pots. Despite considerable male labor migration,[2] in 1977 when we began field work, the Gainj subsistence strategy was still classic slash-and-burn horticulture, combined with a small amount of hunting and gathering. Plots were cleared in primary or secondary forest, used for 1 or 2 years, then returned to long fallow and, ultimately, to the common fund of land. Their staples were starchy root crops such as sweet potato, taro, and yam, supplemented with crops of bananas, pumpkins, breadfruit, and pandanus.

In 1973, as part of a governmental development scheme, coffee was introduced to the area as a cash crop. At first, only a few households[3] were involved in coffee production. While many people talked eagerly of the benefits to be derived from a vaguely envisioned "development," most preferred to continue to concentrate on subsistence work until they had seen some tangible evidence that they would benefit from a change. The evidence came in 1978 when the first crop was marketed, with a return of

---

[1]The team has included, at various times, biological and cultural anthropologists, geneticists, a nutritionist, an endocrinologist, a physician, and several field assistants from the Papua New Guinea Institute of Medical Research. Dr. James Wood and I are the original and constant members of the team.

[2]Recruitment of this virgin labor force was so intense that the administration closed the area to further labor contracting in 1974. Although large numbers of men worked as wage earners, most of their wages were spent on commodity items on the coast. Local men cite as a reason for their subsequent eager acceptance of cash cropping their conviction that it will keep both men and money in the Takwi.

[3]The Gainj definition of a household includes all the people who regularly live and sleep under one roof, in one house. Thus, households may be made up of related individuals, as in the case of a nuclear family, of both related and unrelated individuals, or entirely of unrelated individuals, which is often the case in bachelor houses.

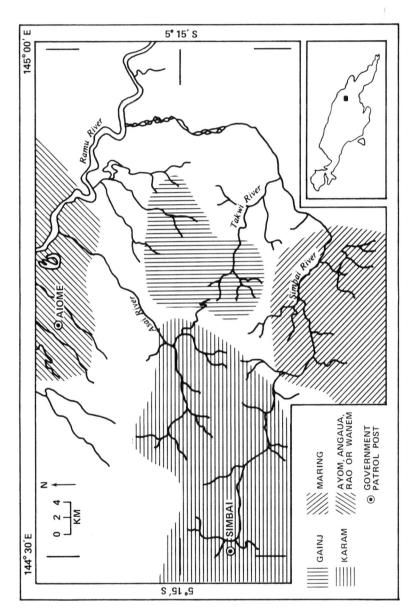

Fig. 1. Location of the Gainj and their neighbors.

K 2232,[4] or approximately U.S. $2900 for the growers. When we left the field that year, virtually every household had either begun growing coffee or was making plans to do so.

Because we were fortunate enough to have begun our work the year before the Gainj began marketing cash crops, we have excellent baseline data, and have been able to follow and document the process of socioeconomic change as it happens. We have particularly rich information about fertility, including behavioral, demographic, and endocrinological data. The Gainj do not employ any effective contraception, nor do they practice induced abortion. There is no indication of significant venereal disease (such as has affected fertility among many populations in the "infertile crescent" of Africa; see, for example, Howell, 1979, pp. 64–65), as evidenced by their low primary sterility rate, 1.1 ± 1.1%. Yet the Gainj have a remarkably low total fertility rate (TFR) of 4.3 ± 0.2, one of the lowest TFRs recorded for a non-contracepting population.

We know that the two major factors contributing to their low fertility are a late median age at first birth, 25.7 ± 0.6 years, and long median interbirth intervals, 36.5 months (Wood, 1994).[5] With an analysis of serum hormone profiles, we have shown that the most important factor in these long interbirth intervals is lactational anovulation, that period postpartum when lactation delays the return of ovulation and thus acts to delay conception and to increase the intervals between births. The median duration of lactational anovulation among the Gainj is 20.4 ± 4.7 months (Wood et al., 1985a). Given what we know, one of the major questions in our research agenda is what effect continuing economic development will have on these two important factors, age at first birth and lactational anovulation, and consequently on TFR. This paper will consider the possible effect on those variables of changes in household composition and household labor patterns generated by increasing involvement in production for the market.

When we returned to the Gainj in 1983, one of my goals was to compare coffee-growing and non-coffee-growing households on a number of household variables. As it turned out, it was impossible to find a significant number of households that were not growing coffee, while still pursuing subsistence gardening, and the comparison groups became households growing more coffee and households growing less. One hundred ten house-

---

[4]The kina (K) is the monetary unit of Papua New Guinea and in 1978 was roughly the equivalent to $1.30 U.S. The kina and the dollar are currently roughly at par.

[5]Simply put, if a woman begins reproducing at a late age and continues to reproduce at infrequent intervals, the number of children she can produce over her reproductive span will be small.

Table 1. Beta Coefficients and Their Standard
Errors, Regression of Number of Coffee
Gardens on Household Variables[a]

Variable	Coefficient	SE	t
Migration	0.003	(0.101)	0.03
Age	–0.032	(0.013)	2.36[b]
Wives (83)	0.628	(0.267)	2.35[b]
Dependents (78)	0.138	(0.062)	2.23[b]
Dependents (83)	–0.182	(0.059)	3.09[c]
Nonwives (78)	–0.291	(0.130)	2.23[b]
Nonwives (83)	0.964	(0.130)	7.40[d]

[a] R^2 = 0.458, F-stat = 9.43 ($p < .001$).
[b] $p < .05$.
[c] $p < .01$.
[d] $p < .001$.

holds representing 63% of all households from ten Gainj parishes were surveyed. Eighty-six of those households, or 78.2% of the sample, were what I call "conjugal family" households; they have as their focus a male head of household and at least one of his wives. The proportion of conjugal family households in the sample and in the larger population are the same. Indeed, this type of household is both the statistical and cultural norm among the Gainj, and other types, e.g., widow-headed households and bachelor houses, are considered temporary or aberrant and dependent upon and tied to the more permanent conjugal family households. The conjugal family household is also the basic unit of production and consumption and therefore is the appropriate unit to consider in any examination of economic success.

Table 1 shows the results for these 86 conjugal family households of a multiple regression of success in coffee growing on a number of household variables (the variables are defined in the Appendix). The largest and most significant positive effects were those of the number of wives and nonwives in the household in 1983. Further analysis of the data[6] shows that between 1978–1983 significant changes occurred in the dependency ratios of households. Less successful households increased their dependency ratios, the ratio of nonproducers to producers, while more successful households decreased their dependency ratios. Changes in dependency ratios can be effected by changing either the number of dependents, the number of producers, or both. The increase in the dependency ratio for less

[6] For a fuller explication of these data and analyses, see Johnson, 1988.

successful households was, in fact, attributable to both an increase in the number of dependents and a decrease in the number of producers. The decrease in the dependency ratio for more successful households, on the other hand, was entirely attributable to an increase in the number of producers; there was almost no change in the number of dependents in these latter households.

In both cases, the producers in question were nonwives, since the only change in the mean number of wives per household was a slight and nonsignificant decrease for more successful ones. To summarize the situation, between 1978–1983, less successful households lost nonwife producers, while more successful households added them. When we looked at who those additional producers were, we found that 54% of them were women of the household who were of marriageable age, but who had not been married out of their households. In other words, more successful households appeared to be retaining young women producers past the age when they would normally have left the household to become producers and reproducers, i.e., wives, in other households.

If successful households provide a model for economic success in cash-cropping, and if a pattern of later age at marriage for women, associated with these households, is emulated by households aspiring to similar success, what is likely to be the effect on the total fertility rate? The variable of interest is really age at first birth, but since premarital pregnancy is virtually unknown among the Gainj, increasing the age at marriage should also increase the age at first birth. What is not clear is how much an increase in age at marriage would increase age at first birth, for the following reason. There is an as yet unexplained lag of about 4.5 years between women's median age at marriage, 21.2 ± 0.5 years, and their median age at first birth, 25.7 ± 0.6 years. Possible explanations for this lag include both behavioral and physiological factors.

Once a marriage is recognized, there is a period during which husband and wife do not cohabit. He continues to live in a bachelor house where he has lived since about the age of 12, with unmarried males, and she moves from her natal family's home to live with her husband's resident female relatives. This represents a kind of "trial period" for a marriage, but what is being tested is not the compatibility of bride and groom, who will in fact spend little time together throughout their life in this highly sex- segregated society. What is being examined is how well a woman fits with the women with whom she will spend most of her time for the rest of her life. Once this period is over, it is still not clear how often sexual intercourse takes place, since it is considered potentially highly dangerous and debilitating for young men. It is not unusual for a man to enter into a migrant labor contract to forestall entering into sexual relations with his wife (Johnson, 1982).[7] Last, the median age at menarche for Gainj women is 18.4 ± 0.7 years.[8] It has been shown in some Western populations that late menarche is associated with very prolonged adolescent subfecundity (Apter and Vihko, 1983) and it may be that the same association applies among the Gainj. I should point out that other studies have not found this association (MacMahon et al., 1982), which makes the lag even more problematic.

Since the cause of the long interval before first birth is not clear, we can not assume that delaying marriage will necessarily delay first birth by an additional four and a half years, only that marriage will precede first birth. Figure 2 shows the total fertility rate as a function of age at first birth and duration of lactational anovulation, holding all other reproductive factors constant, and permits us to look at the results of changes in these two variables. If the age at first birth is increased from 25.7 years and the median duration of lactational anovulation, 20.4 months, remains the same, TFR decreases until, with a first birth at age 28, a woman could expect to produce fewer than four children over her reproductive span. Clearly, increasing the age at first birth would in fact reduce TFR, if the duration of lactational anovulation associated with traditional nursing did not change. However, given the new labor patterns associated with growing coffee, it seems highly unlikely that long lactational anovulation will continue to exert the influence on Gainj fertility that it has in the past.

It has been known for some time that the contraceptive effects of breastfeeding are highly dependent on the pattern of breastfeeding, that for lactation to exert an inhibitory effect, children have to suckle often and throughout the night and day, and that the effects of lactation are greater when there is little or no supplemental feeding (McNeilly, 1988). Traditional nursing among the Gainj follows just that pattern. There is, first, universal breastfeeding and children are fed on demand; since children under the age of six are rarely separated from their mothers, the breast is always available. No effort is made to wean children, and the median age at weaning is 38 months. Feedings are frequent and short, and while their frequency changes as the child ages, it changes very gradually from about twice an hour for newborns to once an hour for 3-year-olds (Wood et al., 1985a). Solid foods are not introduced until the child is about 9 months

[7]This fear of entering into sexual relationships with women is not unique to the Gainj. For similar reactions among neighboring Maring youths, see Buchbinder and Rappaport (1976).
[8]Gainj have, by current Western standards, a very high median age at menarche, but it falls well within the range observed among other highland groups: 17.5 for Simbu, 18.0 for Bundi, and in the neighboring Asai and Simbai Valleys, 19.7 and 18.5, respectively (Malcolm, 1970a,b, Buchbinder, 1973). It should be remembered that New Guinea highland populations are characterized by slow growth and late maturation.

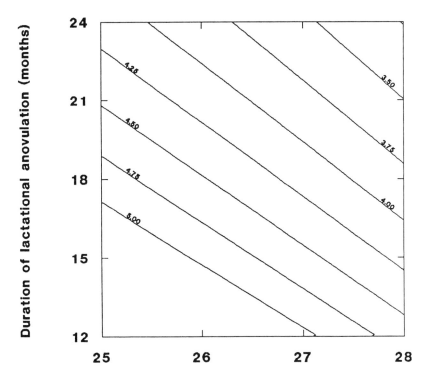

Age at first birth (years)

Fig. 2. Total fertility as a function of age at first birth and duration of lactational anovulation.

old, and traditional weaning foods are nutritionally poor, especially with respect to fat and protein. Mother's milk is a child's best and frequently only source of high quality fat and protein for a prolonged period.

This traditional pattern of frequent and prolonged nursing fits well with the traditional pattern of women's work as subsistence gardeners for their households. Since there is no effective storage technology in a very wet climate, women harvest food daily for immediate consumption. It makes no sense to harvest more food in one day than is likely to be eaten by a household in that day. Additionally, there are no constraints as to ripeness and seasonality; sweet potato and taro can stay in the ground almost indefinitely and be harvested virtually year-round. The daily constraint is simply in terms of daily need. So, while women's garden labor is arduous and continual, it is not tied to maximum production within a very limited time. These conditions make Gainj women's subsistence work highly

compatible with Gainj breastfeeding patterns that require frequent interruptions in the working day.

Women provide the major household labor force in cash cropping as
well as in subsistence gardening, but women's workday is differently structured in each enterprise. Once coffee is harvested, it is subjected to a preliminary drying process that permits stockpiling, so there is no theoretical
limit to the workday imposed by lack of storage techniques, as there is in
subsistence gardening. At the same time, there are both seasonal time constraints and daily ripeness constraints that actively encourage maximum
length workdays with as few interruptions as possible. Coffee labor, in contrast to subsistence labor, is tied to maximum production within a very limited time; frequent interruption becomes an economic drawback. As a
growing number of women become increasingly involved in cash crop production for their household units, it seems inevitable that nursing patterns
will shift to fewer nursing episodes and to earlier weaning, a pattern that
does not confer a delaying effect on the return of ovulation. As the inhibitory effects of lactational anovulation decrease, we can expect to see shorter
interbirth intervals, and, consequently, an increase in the total fertility rate.

Returning to Figure 2, if the age at first birth remained unchanged at
25.7 years but the period of lactational anovulation were decreased by only
5.4 months to a total period of 15 months, TFR would then exceed 5.0.
With that same period of 15 months of lactational anovulation, age at first
birth could be increased to 28 years with very little difference from the
observed TFR. To further suggest the profound importance of lactational
anovulation in any projection of Gainj fertility, it has been estimated that
if breastfeeding were to be totally abandoned, the mean birth interval for
Gainj women would be reduced to about 21 months, and TFR would more
than double, from 4.3 to about 9.2 (Wood et al., 1985a). While total abandonment of breastfeeding in this population in the near future seems highly
unlikely, radical changes in the pattern of breastfeeding, with somewhat
less dramatic effect, do not.

It seems apparent from considering household changes associated with
economic development among the Gainj that the European demographic
transition may not be the appropriate model. Fertility change in this population appears to be a much more complex situation than the "development
as contraceptive" slogan would suggest. Looking at only two variables, it
seems obvious that changes in how households recruit their labor force and
how they choose to allocate that labor force can alter the relative impact
of age at marriage and duration of lactational anovulation, and that these
two variables can interact in ways that may produce counteracting effects.
When totally new factors are introduced—such as how households choose
to avail themselves of the educational opportunities that are associated with

modernization, or whether child-caretakers, never very important traditionally, will become another needed labor force as women's uninterrupted labor becomes more valuable—the picture becomes even more complex. Clearly what is needed to understand fertility change as it is affected by household decisions among the Gainj (and I would suggest in other Third World populations), is not an uncritical assumption that it will follow a model derived from Western history, but a much closer focus on the microlevel strategies that determine and are determined by larger societal change.

APPENDIX:
MULTIPLE REGRESSION OF COFFEE GARDENS ON HOUSEHOLD VARIABLES

Dependent Variable

Number of coffee gardens per household: Using the number of coffee gardens producing coffee for a household as a gauge of the household's success in the coffee industry is predicated on the assumption that, since there are not wide disparities in the average number of trees per coffee garden, households selling coffee from a greater number of gardens make more money than those selling from a smaller number of gardens. This is an imperfect indicator, but one that can be measured reliably. For summary of the impossibility of determining actual cash income among the Gainj, see Johnson (1988: 112).

Independent Variables

Migration

The migration variable is a measure of male household head's experience away from the area as a contract laborer. Each migration refers to a 2-year contract. The observed range in the sample is from 0–6 migrations.

Age

The age variable refers to the age of male household head. Since no records are available for Gainj births prior to 1969, the ages used here are estimates based on dental examinations, event calendars, and relative aging, as described in Wood et al., (1985b). Each individual was assigned to a 5 year interval, and the midpoint of the interval was entered as the age of the individual. The observed range in the sample is 32.5–72.5 years. While there is undoubtedly some degree of error involved with these age estimates, they are highly reliable at least as ordinal measures of age.

Wives

The wives variable is a measure of the number of wives resident in a household. The Gainj are a polygynous population. The observed number of wives per household in the sample ranges from 1–3.

Nonwives

The "nonwives" variable is a measure of the number of nonmarried women, aged 20–60, resident in a household. The age range 20–60 was chosen because it encompasses the most fully productive period for Gainj women and includes women who have not yet begun their reproductive careers as well as those who have completed them. The observed number of nonwives per household in the sample ranges from 0–4.

Dependents

The "dependents" variable, the number of dependents per household, is a measure of alternative demands on women's labor. It excludes the women themselves, but includes those bachelors who are fed by households, although not resident. The observed number of dependents in the sample ranges from 1–14.

Both the migration and age variables were included because previous studies in other areas of Papua New Guinea had suggested they affected economic success (see Hayano, 1973; Finney, 1973). The remaining three variables were included because, since women are responsible for both subsistence and coffee gardening as well as for child care, they are indicators of the labor available to a household. For a fuller discussion of women's work, see Johnson (1982).

Data for the same households are available from two rounds of field work, 1978 and 1983. Household variables from 1978, the year in which large-scale involvement in coffee growing began, and from 1983, the year of the most recent field study, were compared to describe the process that took place between 1978–1983. However, one of the variables, resident wives, is so highly autocorrelated across the 2 years ($r = .925$) that only the data for 1983 have been entered. For the same reason, men's age and migration experience have also been limited to 1983 data. Age is perfectly autocorrelated across the two periods, and men's migration experience in 1983 is clearly not independent of prior experience in 1978.

ACKNOWLEDGMENTS

I thank James Wood, Elliot Fratkin, Patricia Draper, and Kenneth Campbell. Supported by a grant from the Wenner-Gren Foundation for Anthropological Research.

REFERENCES

Apter, D., and Vihko, R. (1983). Early menarche, a risk factor for breast cancer, indicates early onset of ovulatory cycles. *Journal of Clinical Endocrinology and Metabolism* 57: 82–86.

Buchbinder, G. (1973). Maring Microadaptation: A Study of Demographic, Nutritional, Genetic and Phenotypic Variation in a Highland New Guinea Population. Ph.D. dissertation, Department of Anthropology, Columbia University, New York.

Buchbinder, G., and Rappaport, R. (1976). Fertility and death among the Maring. In Brown, P., and Buchbinder, G. (eds.), *Man and Woman in the New Guinea Highlands*. American Anthropological Association, Washington, D.C., pp. 13–35.

Campbell, K. L., and Wood, J. W. (1988). Fertility in traditional societies. In Diggory, P., Potts, M., and Teper, S. (eds.), *Natural Human Fertility: Social and Biological Mechanisms*. MacMillan, London, pp. 39–69.

Coale, A. J., and Treadway, R. (1986). A summary of the changing distribution of overall fertility, marital fertility, and the proportion married in the provinces of Europe. In Coale, A. J., and Watkins, S. C. (eds.), *The Decline of Fertility in Europe*. Princeton University Press, Princeton, pp. 31–18.

Finney, B. (1973). *Big-Men and Business: Entrepreneurship and Economic Growth in the New Guinea Highlands*. University Press of Hawaii, Honolulu.

Hayano, D. (1973). Individual correlates of coffee adoption in the New Guinea highlands. *Human Organization* 32: 305–314.

Howell, N. L. (1979). *Demography of the Dobe !Kung*. Academic Press, New York.

Johnson, P. L. (1982). Gainj Kinship and Social Organization. Ph.D. dissertation, Department of Anthropology, University of Michigan, Ann Arbor.

Johnson, P. L. (1988). Women and development: A highland New Guinea example. *Human Ecology* 16: 105–122.

Knodel, J., and van de Walle, E. (1986). Lessons from the past: Policy implications of historical fertility studies. In Coale, A. J., and Watkins, S. C. (eds.), *The Decline of Fertility in Europe*. Princeton University Press, Princeton, pp. 390–419.

MacMahon, B., Trichopoulos, D., Brown, J., Andersen, A., Aoki K., Cole, P., De Waard, F., Kauraniemi, T., Morgan, R., Purde, M., Ravnihar, B., Stormby, N., Westlund, K., and Woo, N.-C. (1982). Age at menarche, probability of ovulation and breast cancer risk. *International Journal of Cancer* 29: 13–16.

Malcolm, L. A. (1970a). *Growth and Development in New Guinea—A study of the Bundi People of the Madang District.* Institute of Human Biology Monograph No. 1. Papua-New Guinea Institute of Human Biology, Madang.

Malcolm, L. A. (1970b). Growth of the Asai child of the Madang District of New Guinea. *Journal of Biosocial Science* 2: 213–226.

McNeilly, A. S. (1988). *Breastfeeding and Fertility.* IUSSP Seminar on Biomedical and Demographic Determinants of Human Reproduction, Baltimore, Maryland, January 4–8, 1988.

Notestein, F. W. (1953). Economic problems of population change. *Proceedings of the Eighth International Conference of Agricultural Economists.* Oxford University Press, London.

Romaniuk, A. (1980). Increase in natural fertility during the early stages of modernization: Evidence from an African case study, Zaire. *Population Studies* 34: 293–310.

Romaniuk, A. (1981). Increase in natural fertility during the early stages of modernization: Canadian Indians case study. *Demography* 18: 157–172.

Watkins. S.C. (1986). Conclusions. In Coale, A. J., and Watkins, S. C. (eds.) *The Decline of Fertility in Europe.* Princeton, University Press, Princeton, pp. 420–449.

Wood, J. W. (1994). Fertility and reproductive biology. In Attenborough, R., and Alpers, M. (eds.), *The Small Cosmos: Studies of Human Biology in Papua New Guinea.* Oxford University Press, Oxford.

Wood, J. W., Lai, D., Johnson, P. L., Campbell, K. L., and Maslar, I. A. (1985a). Lactation and birth spacing in highland New Guinea. *Journal of Biosocial Science* 9: 159–173.

Wood, J. W., Johnson, P. L., and Campbell, K. L. (1985b). Demographic and endocrinological aspects of low natural fertility in highland New Guinea. *Journal of Biosocial Science* 17: 57–79.

10

Variation and Change in Fertility in West Central Nepal

Steven Folmar

As is evident from theory as well as many studies, population growth is a major issue facing many countries as they attempt to raise their living standards—or even maintain them—in the face of environmental problems. Most assumptions regarding population regulation rest on a fairly simple dichotomizing model: There are two fertility regimes, one "natural," one "controlled." In the natural regime, contraception is not consciously practiced and there is concomitantly a high number of births throughout the childbearing years, evident in the so-called "convex" fertility curve, in which age-specific fertility remains high through age 35. Controlled regimes are characterized by conscious choice to use birth control measures, and the consequent reduction in birth rates after age 20 results in a so-called "concave" fertility curve. Folmar demonstrates that in micropopulation studies this simple dichotomy breaks down; people do regulate their family sizes under preindustrial conditions. He shows how in Nepal, high-status, wealthy, high-caste families had high birth rates. They could afford to do so, and children confer social status. Poorer high-caste families have come to adopt fertility-limiting measures because, while children have value in terms of social status, their cost competes with the demands of high-caste life style. Soon low-caste families began to emulate their poor, but high-caste neighbors.

Originally published in *Human Ecology: An Interdisciplinary Journal,* 20(2)(1992): 225–248.

Steven Folmar, Section on Internal Medicine and Gerontology, Bowman Gray School of Medicine, Wake Forest University, Winston-Salem, North Carolina 27157.

Case Studies in Human Ecology, edited by Daniel G. Bates and Susan H. Lees. Plenum Press, New York, 1996.

INTRODUCTION

In this chapter I address the debate over whether "primitive," "traditional," or "preindustrial" people consciously control fertility, a debate which has been resurrected in light of the recent emergence of cultural explanations of fertility decline. The issue of conscious control has theoretical implications for the study of fertility transitions as models of culture change. Understanding the behaviors that determine baseline or pretransitional fertility is critical to revealing how new behaviors, such as use of contraception, emerge and then spread. Attention to the patterns of variation in fertility before major change occurs and analysis of how fertility changes in specific subgroups would improve our understanding of how individuals identify and modify existing adaptive strategies to cope with new social circumstances. This paper presents an illustrative case study from West Central Nepal. It demonstrates that identifiable patterns of intracultural variation in fertility existed prior to the introduction of economic development in the region, and argues that the preexisting patterns of fertility behavior have undergone a fundamental change in structure even though completed family size has changed little thus far.

THE PROBLEM

Until recently there has been a virtual consensus outside anthropology that modern fertility is shaped by rational economic considerations (Becker, 1960), but that high fertility in traditional societies is supported by irrational beliefs and behaviors (Easterlin, 1975; Notestein, 1953) and moving reproduction into the realm of conscious choice is a necessary precondition for fertility decline (Coale, 1974). Evidence for the existence of two fundamentally different fertility regimes, one "natural" the other "controlled" (see Henry, 1961), is said to be reflected in the shapes of their age specific fertility curves, natural having a convex shape and controlled having a concave shape.

Anthropologists have never reached agreement about whether fertility control among so-called primitive people is intentional. Carr-Sanders (1922) was the first of them to argue that primitive fertility is controlled consciously by practices of delayed marriage, abortion, abstinence, and infanticide[1] in deliberate attempts to balance population with available resources. Opposing perspectives imply that control in such societies is

---

[1]Anthropologists often categorize infanticide and even homicide of children as fertility-limiting variables in the same class as abortion. Dickemann (1984), Harris and Ross (1987), and Polgar (1972) present arguments for such a classification.

automatic, and not conscious, as implied by the omission of a homeostatic mechanism in descriptions of how population is controlled (e.g., Cowgill, 1962). Harris and Ross (1987) point out the difficulty of settling the issue of conscious deliberation over fertility among populations long-since dead. However, by consigning the issue to irrelevancy, they obscure one of the most critical and ill-understood issues in cultural adaptation. The issue is that if cultural behaviors respond to physical and social environmental changes, how do individuals recognize these changes, identify possible solutions to them, and implement novel adaptive strategies?

I will attempt to combine data reported in this paper with evidence reported elsewhere (principally Folmar, 1985 and 1992) to demonstrate that the relationship between behavior and motivation is more complex than that. Even in traditional societies, conscious motivations exist for having children and for delaying or discontinuing childbearing. Likewise, some elements of modern fertility are unconscious. Many women in this study began childbearing with little conscious consideration of the benefits or problems of having children and did nothing consciously to influence the probability of conceiving children. The very same women could become quite calculating about fertility later on, some of them contributing to fertility curves that appear to be natural and others to curves that look controlled.

A second shortcoming in our understanding of fertility patterns and motivations is the tendency to dichotomize each of these concepts. Fertility patterns are thought to be either natural or controlled, which people either consciously control or not. I will argue later in this paper that many fertility behaviors fall somewhere between these extremes. In order to disentangle fertility *behavior* from *motivation,* I prefer to describe fertility patterns with more neutral terms such as convex and concave, rather than natural and controlled.

We must also seek a subtler interpretation of motivations than conscious or unconscious ones. The research shows that a myriad of reproductive and contraceptive motivations exist alongside motivations for practices that indirectly affect fertility, such as timing of a daughter's marriage.

More attention to the subtleties of fertility patterns, the intricacies of personal motivation, and how the two relate to each other will facilitate a more realistic treatment of another problem commonly found in the demographic literature, namely, a proclivity for representing whole societies as adhering to one pattern or another. This proclivity persists despite ethnographic and demographic evidence that refutes reproductive homogeneity.

Although it is recognized that fertility regimes are specific to cultural groups and dependent on prevailing local norms (Kreager, 1982) and that they vary over time and space (Warwick, 1988), they are nonetheless generally assumed to be homogeneous at the local level. Such assumptions of intracultural homogeneity overlook a necessary element in the mechanism of change, recognition of which would help complete a cultural theory of fertility, namely the element of patterned microvariation.

Appreciation of microvariation in many groups, for example in Sweden (Low, 1989), and among the caste-Hindus in the Kathmandu area (Ross et al., 1986) has facilitated a more precise understanding of how existing patterns are modified to cope with changing social and economic circumstances.

The formal recognition of variation in fertility behavior is central to understanding fertility change, since variation is the basis for any type of cultural change. Fertility behavior, which is culturally based, is guided by the same principles that shape general cultural evolution (see Hammel and Howell, 1987). Cultural evolution is similar to biological evolution in that variation in cultural elements must exist for a group to adjust to new and stressful circumstances (Bennett, 1976). However, culturally defined behaviors are not the product of random generation of mutations as in the genetic code; rather, they arise from highly patterned cognitive and information processes. For useful variants of cultural behaviors to be recognized and chosen by people in new socioenvironmental circumstances, the variants must exist in patterns that can be recognized, retrieved, evaluated, and applied. If a culture can change its fertility from high levels to lower ones, it is because some identifiable groups have traditionally adhered to a low-fertility schedule (see, for example, Landers, 1990), which other groups can use as a model for changing their own behavior.

This type of transition has, in fact, been the basis of fertility transitions the world over. Recent interpretations of data from historical European populations (Coale and Watkins, 1986) and contemporary non-Western populations (Cleland and Wilson, 1987) suggest that pretransitional societies include small pockets of limited fertility, usually in groups that are bounded by high status, a minority religion, or some other socially significant characteristic (Landers, 1990). It is from these low fertility vanguards that small family ideals diffuse to other groups.

A fully mature cultural theory of fertility decline awaits the examination of a number of hypotheses about the specific mechanisms by which small family norms are transferred among individuals. Several related hypotheses suggest themselves: (1) Since patterned variation based on status may be critical to culture change, the number of children born to women in certain high-status groups would be expected to be fewer than in other groups. (2) These differences need to be apparent before major economic developments apply pressure on the whole of society to have fewer children, and pretransitional fertility curves need to show evidence of fertility limitation in the groups having fewer children. (3) Fertility change at the societal level will be achieved when the behavior of the higher status groups limiting fertility has become emulated by other groups.

RESEARCH SETTING

I studied the relationship among economic factors, culture, and fertility in West Central Nepal for 17 months in 1979–1980, and observed variations in patterns of fertility and associated behaviors among the local population (Folmar, 1985). That experience suggested that some of these data could cast light on questions about the microlevel processes of culture change.

The Kingdom of Nepal, with its range of microenvironmental variation, is especially suited for the study of how local cultures manipulate fertility behavior to match local socioenvironmental constraints. Several studies have documented the fit between local fertility practices and microenvironmental constraints on population growth in Nepal (e.g., Fricke, 1986; Goldstein, 1976; Macfarlane, 1976; Ross, 1984).

Like the rest of the country, the West Central region is geographically diverse. The low-lying plains in the south give way to a series of progressively higher hilly areas and then to the great Himalayas in the north. The hilly region is carved by river systems that result in a tremendous variety of terrain, climate, and vegetation. The valley created by the principal river system, the eastwardly flowing Seti Gandaki, is wide and fertile, and it is the location of the town of Pokhara, a major market and administrative center which is the second largest city in Nepal's hilly regions.

Because Nepal remained closed to foreigners until the middle of the 20th century, the 5400 inhabitants of Pokhara had experienced little contact with the West or with the forces of international development until as late as 1961 (see, e.g., Gurung, 1965).

Starting in the 1960s, however, major social and economic developments began, quickly gathered momentum, and had shown no signs of abating by the time of my fieldwork in 1979–1980. From 1961 on, Pokhara's population increased almost fourfold, to 20,600 by 1971 (Tuladhar et al., 1978), and it more than doubled again to over 46,600 by 1981 (Gurung, 1982). The major cause of Pokhara's population explosion was undoubtedly immigration, principally from the hills, but from other areas as well.

The modern condition of Pokhara reflects its development as a major center for trade, tourism, and administration. Relatively new sections of town include a tourist district along the largest lake in Nepal, Phewa Tal, new administrative and market areas, and new neighborhoods. These developments surround the older areas of town which include the old bazaars and agricultural areas whose residents have long histories in Pokhara.

I collected the data for Pokhara from approximately 750 people in one of the old agricultural neighborhoods. This area, Nadipur, is bounded on three sides by market and business districts and on the fourth by the Seti Gandaki River. It is inhabited mainly by the caste-Hindus, the largest cultural and politically most dominant group in Nepal, who are the subjects of this study.

Contrasting with the rapid development of Pokhara itself was, in 1979–1980, the lack of overt development in the surrounding hills, even in villages just a short distance outside the city. Good examples are the villages of Ghachok (population 2,400) and Kangmang (population 300), a few hours' walk north of Pokhara between the Seti Khola and the Lhosti Khola, two tributaries of the Seti Gandaki. The entire caste-Hindu populations of these two villages were studied in 1979–1980. They contributed an additional rural sample of 1,350 people to the 750 urban inhabitants of Pokhara. About 2,100 caste-Hindus figured into this study.

Because of the rapid modernization of Pokhara, the decision to study Nepali caste-Hindus living in the Pokhara area is particularly appropriate for the investigation of the importance of patterned variation in the process of culture change. Distinct divisions in social status facilitated the search for variation along clearly identifiable lines. These divisions encompass both social dimensions (caste) and economic ones (small vs. large farms), which made possible a comparison of the social and economic forces that lie behind changes in fertility. Furthermore, the contrast in degree of development between Pokhara and the two rural villages enabled me to study the processes of change and the factors responsible for it.

Given the social and economic constraints of caste-Hindu culture, three subgroups are pertinent to my analysis of fertility: (1) the large-farm high castes, (2) the small-farm high castes, and (3) the low castes. The large-farm high castes are the elite status group in caste-Hindu society. They have high social status by virtue of their caste affiliation and high economic status by virtue of their landholdings. The small-farm high castes enjoy social status equal to that of the large-farm high castes, but their economic circumstances seriously limit their pursuit of the good life (see Douglas, 1966). The low castes are at the bottom of the hierarchy, socially and economically.

Caste-Hindus have traditionally occupied the valleys and the lower elevations of the slopes in the Pokhara area. Besides being divided into high and low status, they are also divided socially and economically into numerous castes. These castes migrated from India centuries ago (Fuhrer-Haimendorf, 1960) and have resided in the Pokhara area since before the 17th century (Blaikie et al., 1980). They live side-by-side, speak the same language (Nepali) and are economically interdependent. They share the

Hindu religion, with its prevailing set of ideals, beliefs, and morals. A major feature of Hindu tradition is its reliance on the caste system as a principle for organizing society. Caste traditionally dictated occupation, and today it still constrains occupational choice. Moreover, the caste system has even greater social implications. Each caste represents a tier in a highly and rigidly stratified social hierarchy. A person's social status is largely, though not entirely, ascribed at birth by caste affiliation and a person's primary circle of social intercourse is with members of the same caste. Caste endogamy is the rule.

The most important division in the caste system separates the so-called high castes from the low castes. This distinction, critical to the arguments I present here, rests primarily on ritual purity. The ritually clean castes (high) are the *Brahmins* (traditionally the priestly caste), *Thakuris,* and *Chhetris,* (rulers and warriors), who today are predominately landowners, priests, scholars, and government officials. Low-caste status is accorded to artisans; the *Sarkis* (cobblers), *Damais* (tailors), *Kamis* (smiths), *Gharthis* (house slaves), *Gaines* (musicians), and *Podes* (sweepers). Contact between the high and low castes is potentially dangerous to both parties; it pollutes a high-caste person, who must purify himself or herself as a result, and it may bring serious repercussions, even physical punishment, to a low-caste person.

Caste affiliation is the source of nearly all of a person's ascribed social status, and many of the symbols that locate a person within the boundaries of high or low caste are outward lifestyle ones. A cursory observation of caste-Hindu society clearly reveals that the high castes, almost regardless of economic status, have larger and better constructed houses, better clothing, and more consumer goods than the low castes. Maintaining outward lifestyle symbols is more economically demanding for the high castes than for the low castes.

A second dimension of status stems from a person's freedom to achieve social status through his or her own deeds. Achieved status can cut across caste lines, enabling individuals from lower castes to accrue more respect in specific areas than individuals from high castes. More importantly, achieved status locates people within the social order of the caste itself. An individual's achieved status in caste-Hindu Nepalese society is profoundly affected by the number of living children. This is especially true of women, who are ranked within their castes according to an intricate system of reproductive and childrearing success and also referred to by terms designating their level of achievement (see Stone, 1978).

While the social implications of family size can be viewed as supporting high fertility, the Nepalese are no less practical and rational than other people. The number of children they actually have depends on the intersection of social symbolic needs with economic realities. Therefore, it is not surprising that previous research has shown logical connections between the needs of labor on Nepalese family-owned subsistence farms and large family size (Nag et al., 1978). However, as I show later, not all farms are large; for the high castes owning small farms, economic constraints add to the demands of raising children. Consequently, many people find it difficult to have large families.

The various castes traditionally have made relatively distinct contributions to one overarching economic system based on subsistence farming. Yet while they share one continuous cultural tradition pertaining to childbearing, each caste draws differently upon those traditions. As I have described elsewhere (Folmar, 1992), some fertility motivations in caste-Hindu Nepal enhance fertility while others restrain it. Consistent with its being a high-fertility society, caste-Hindu Nepal emphasizes motivations that enhance fertility. One of these motivations is simply the continuation of the tradition of having children, which can be interpreted as children having an intrinsic value. Children also have, of course, extrinsic values, significant among them the economic, kinship, and religious contributions they make.[2]

Sons are expected to make greater contributions economically to the extended family, and religiously to the patrilineage; their value is much greater than that of daughters.

Nevertheless, having *one* daughter is also seen as necessary. More than one would add to the economic burdens associated with raising them. In addition, their lives in their future husbands' families are expected to be hard. Based on their own experiences, women often note that, "we all know the suffering of a daughter."

While these conscious motivations are expressed similarly by high and low castes, other practices indirectly affecting fertility, especially rules regarding marriage, are differentiated by caste and economic status. The clearest difference between the high and the low castes is in divorce and remarriage. In another paper (Folmar, n.d.), I show that divorce and remarriage are rarely practiced among the high castes, but are more common among the rural low castes (whose rate of divorce and remarriage is over 15%). These differences reflect the amount of control women have over marriage in these two groups. Low-caste women have much more latitude

---

[2]Interestingly, the economic motivations for having children are clearly expressed in the urban area, but not the rural area. This finding was unexpected because it ran contrary to the expectation that economic values of children would be an important pro-fertility motivation among rural farmers, but the economic costs of children in the urban area would be an incentive to have fewer children.

in choosing their own spouses. In traditional contexts, low-caste women exercise choice through divorce and remarriage; in modern areas they make the choice before their first marriage. Rates of love marriage (as opposed to arranged marriage) are higher among urban low castes. Having decision-making power in marriage extends to fertility decision-making; low-caste women exert relatively more authority than high-caste women, although they exercise it in the direction of high fertility.

Differences in economic status serve to divide the high castes into a high-fertility and a low-fertility group, based on farm size. Differences in standard of living are related to differences in how strictly members of higher castes will conform to certain rights and obligations that accrue to the high castes.

For example, high-caste women should, theoretically, observe strict rules of decorum and morality. Those observances that tend to reduce high-caste fertility, such as stricter adherence to post-widowhood celibacy, sanctions against widow remarriage, and a stricter set of sexual mores in general, appear to be more rigidly upheld by high-caste women living on small farms.

Conversely, by virtue of their greater economic status, the large-farm high castes have greater access to resources, and potentially increased fertility. For example, the large-farm high castes can provide more adequate diets for their women and children. Even more important is the effect that wealth has on the ability to absorb new family members. In Nepal, marriage is often followed by a period of up to two years during which the bride lives in her father's home. Available information suggests that this period is shorter among the large-farm high castes because they have more resources to support a new bride and because they need her labor.

Table 1 presents an array of quantitative data illustrating many of the differences among these three groups. Two features of this table are salient. First, the small-farm high castes are demographically distinct from the other two groups. They exhibit the lowest fertility. This is caused by a combination of factors. Women in this group tend to delay their first births, space births farther apart, and terminate reproduction at an earlier age than in the other two groups. Second, the small-farm high castes have more in common economically with the low castes than they do with the large-farm high castes. The explanation for why economic well-being is not more directly related to fertility, which is a major task for the remainder of this paper, is facilitated by reinterpreting fertility patterns and motivations in the manner advocated in the previous section.

Table 1. Fertility and Economic Characteristics of Ever-Married Women by
Caste, Economic Status, and Age Group (15–49 years and 50 years and older)

	Age					
	High caste				Low caste	
	Large-farm		Small-farm			
	15–49	50+	15–49	50+	15–49	50+
Sample size	123	41	110	39	140	47
Mean age	32.5	59.6	31.8	61.4	31.4	56.5
Age at marriage	15.4	15.7	16.2	13.4	16.7	18.7
Age at first birth	19.9	22.7	20.1	23.1	19.4	22.8
Age at last birth	—	37.3	—	34.7	—	38.0
Waiting time[a]	3.7	7.3	3.3	6.6	2.8	4.5
First interval[b]	2.6	3.4	2.8	3.9	2.7	3.0
All intervals[c]	2.8	2.8	3.0	3.2	2.7	3.0
Live births	3.8	6.4	3.1	3.4	3.9	5.6
Survivors[d]	2.9	4.2	2.5	2.1	2.7	3.3
Size of farm[e]	24.6	26.9	5.1	4.1	2.8	4.3

[a] The amount of time from first marriage (or age 14, whichever comes later) until the first live birth.
[b] The amount of time between the first and second live births.
[c] The number of years between the first and last live births divided by the total number of birth intervals.
[d] For women 15–49, the number of children currently alive; for women 50 and over, the number of children alive when the woman reached age 50.
[e] Measured in *ropanis*. There are approximately 18 ropanis per hectare.

METHODS

A primary objective in reducing the data focused on the measurement of social and economic status. Divisions in social status are clear. As noted earlier, self-reported caste identifications are grouped into high and low castes. Economic status poses a more complex problem. The principal economic resource among the caste-Hindus continues to be the land they own, though economic status is also affected by number of livestock, occupation, income from jobs outside agriculture, and home ownership. I use land as the benchmark for economic status.[3] Among the high castes, a farm is considered small if it is equal to, or smaller than, 11 *ropanis* (about 6/10 of a hectare). A large farm has 12 *ropanis* or more. This division represents a

[3] For the purposes of statistical analysis, I attempted to summarize all the economic variables by analyzing them via factor analysis. When factoring their principal components, three statistical "factors" emerged, but the analysis clearly demonstrated that land was the driving force behind economic status. Land was also a better pure predictor of current cumulative fertility than were the three economic factors.

Table 2. Factors Affecting the Total Number of Children Ever Born to Women Aged 50+ in 1979-80, OLS Regression

	B	Beta	Sig T	B	Beta	Sig T
Large-farm high caste	2.306	.281	.002	2.121	.259	.004
Urban	.558	.085	.299	.448	.068	.385
Number children dying	1.109	.707	.000	1.060	.676	.000
Low caste	1.375	.217	.021	1.491	.235	.025
Polygynous marriage				−1.701	−.101	.176
Age at marriage				−0.089	−.187	.023
Widowed				−0.999	−.154	.062
Constant	1.711		.004	3.732		.000
Adjusted R^2			.538			.582
Standard error			2.166			2.061
F		24.626*			17.140*	

*$p < .001$

slight modification from previous analyses, as does the terminology (Folmar, 1985).

ANALYSIS

The first stage of analysis focuses on establishing whether or not membership in the status groups salient to this investigation has measurable effects on fertility, independent of other fertility determinants.

The first three columns of Table 2 present results of the first step of the ordinary least squares (OLS) regression analysis for women aged 50 years and more ($n = 125$). Large-farm high-caste women and low-caste women had significantly more children than small-farm high-caste women. Infant mortality is positively associated with the total number of children and is highly significant statistically. Living in the urban area has only a modest, and not statistically significant, positive effect on fertility.

In the second stage of this analysis, age at marriage (in years) and marital status (either monogamous, polygynous, or widowed) are added to the model, and the more elaborate model is recorded in the second three columns of Table 2. It is important to note that the addition of these marriage variables does not much alter either the degree or the significance of social status on fertility. The marriage variables themselves all have negative effects on fertility, although the coefficient for polygynous unions is not significant. As expected, late age at marriage and widowhood significantly reduce the total number of children ever born.

Table 3. Factors Affecting the Total Number of Children Ever Born to
Women Aged 15–49 in 1979–1980, OLS Regression

	B	Beta	Sig T	B	Beta	Sig T
Large-farm high caste	.509	.084	.055	.371	.061	.128
Age category	.574	.374	.000	.715	.465	.000
Urban	.300	.057	.135	.416	.079	.024
Number children dying	1.029	.553	.000	.943	.507	.000
Low caste	.050	.009	.827	.093	.018	.653
Polygynous marriage				-.776	-.083	.013
Sterilization				.702	.082	.014
Age at marriage				-.111	-.199	.000
Widowed				-1.340	-.148	.000
Constant	.206		.527	1.613		.000
Adjusted R^2		.633			.697	
Standard error		1.586			1.441	
F		75.501*			101.518*	

*$p < .001$

A second two-stage regression model analyzes the role of social and economic status on fertility change after the initiation of modernization, as determined by the total number of children born to women aged 15 to 49 years ($n = 373$) in 1979–1980 (see Table 3). This analysis indicates a change in the influence of social and economic status on fertility: Belonging to low castes no longer sets fertility apart from that of the small-farm high castes, but large-farm high-caste women continue to have higher fertility. The two control variables—age of woman and number of children dying— have significant positive effects on fertility, whereas urban residence adds little to an explanation of variation in fertility.

When marital variables are controlled for, we gain some insight into changes in the patterns of fertility that emerge among the younger women. The second stage of analysis includes use of contraceptive sterilization, if either a vasectomy or tubal ligation is reported. The inclusion of the marriage variables erodes the significance of a woman's belonging to the group of large-farm high castes, presumably because these variables account for some of the variation between these groups. Urban residence now plays a significant, but modest, role in increasing fertility. Low-caste status continues to have no appreciable effect on fertility.

The marital status and age at marriage variables have stronger and more significant effects among these young women than what is found among the older cohort, but they are in the same negative direction. The most interesting effect is the unexpected positive effect of the use of a permanent method of contraception. Since being sterilized cannot cause people to have more children, the explanation for this association is that vasectomies and tubal ligations are sought only by couples who have already had exceptional success in childbearing and childrearing. Sterilization is something of a status symbol, announcing that the couple has enough children to virtually eliminate the risk of losing them all to some disaster.

Next, I examine fertility change over time by plotting age-specific fertility in four different time periods: (1) the pretransitional period, ending about 1950, estimated by the aggregate experience of all ever-married women over the age of 49 in 1980; (2) the onset of modernization, circa 1960, from women aged 40 to 69; (3) the early developmental period, circa 1970, from women aged 30 to 59; and (4) the middle developmental period (the transition was not complete when I left the field), circa 1975, from women aged 25 to 54. The five-year age segments that correspond to these time periods are used to generate the estimates.

In the pretransitional period, depicted in the graph labelled A in Figure 1, three types of convex curves appear. Two of these describe paths toward total fertility rates (TFR) of about six children, the third results in fewer than four children per woman. The first two represent fertility strategies consistent with the pursuit of large families in the large-farm high castes and the low castes. The convex fertility curve for the first group, the large-farm high castes, conforms to the shape of the classic natural fertility population which regulates fertility in a positive direction. This curve begins at a relatively high level in the 20–24-year-old group, gradually decreases through the 35–39-year-old group, and then rapidly decreases. The large-farm high castes have the economic resources to pursue the status of having many children at the same time that they accumulate other status symbols that demand economic expenditures, such as well-constructed houses and good-quality clothing.

The fertility curve of the low caste differs from that of the large-farm high caste in one major respect. The peak period of fertility occurs after the age of 25, a feature that has been found only in Nepal and New Guinea (Wood, 1990) and which may be due to late sexual maturation (Knodel, 1983). The findings presented here suggest that this phenomenon may be confined to the low castes and may be more related to marriage and cohabitation practices characteristic of that group. The important point here is that the low-caste fertility curve suggests that the low castes also do not intentionally limit births. This strategy is consistent with the poorer circumstances of the low castes whose objective of large families does not compete with their pursuit of other outward status symbols.

However, strategies of unlimited childbearing are not consistent with membership in the small-farm high castes who have high social status but are economically constrained. Apparently, they have regulated their fertility downward in an attempt to balance the social pressures for large families with pressures to maintain other status symbols. Evidence that they limit fertility is not reflected by the shape of their fertility curve, which when standardized is nearly indistinguishable from the curve of their large-farm counterparts. Rather, it is from the height of the curve that we are able to isolate the small-farm high castes and conclude that they limited their fertility.

Changes in these fertility curves over time show temporary (birth cohort) and permanent effects of social change on the fertility of these three groups. At the onset of modernization (the time period represented in graph B in Figure 1), fertility increased markedly among young women in all three groups, and this birth cohort of women continued to have higher fertility through their later reproductive years (graph C in Figure 1). More importantly, a fundamental change emerged in the fertility pattern of the small-farm high castes. The shape of the fertility curve changes steadily over time, from a convex shape to one that becomes increasingly concave. There is a clear "scooping out" in the middle of the curve, indicating changes in the timing of births, if not the total number. Over the same period, there is evidence of low-caste fertility's beginning to change in character from convex to linear, a change that has followed the small-farm high-caste change in fertility. No change in the shape of the large-farm high-caste fertility curve is apparent by the last time-period observed (Graph D of Figure 1).

CONCLUSIONS

The patterns of variation in the pretransitional fertility regime of caste-Hindus in West Central Nepal were based on social and economic boundaries. As status-seeking individuals, these Nepalis rely on their social and economic positions to provide them with their ranking. There is no mechanism by which individuals or families can transcend the ascribed status of caste affiliation. However, individual status *within* these bounds *is achieved,* not ascribed, and is very much dependent on individual success in several arenas. Two of these are childbearing and outward lifestyle. Furthermore, within each major caste division, achieved status is attained by deeds and symbolized by reproductive and economic success. While related to each other, these two types of success should not be confused. Nepalis do not choose between children and "consumer durables" with the same alacrity

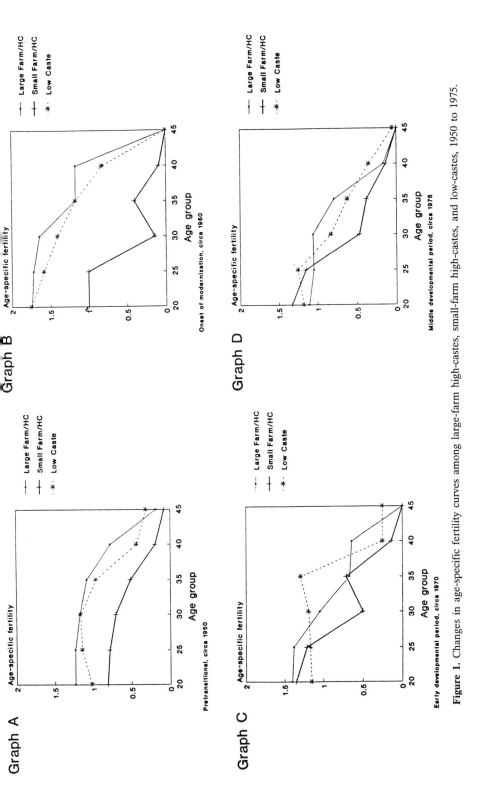

Figure 1. Changes in age-specific fertility curves among large-farm high-castes, small-farm high-castes, and low-castes, 1950 to 1975.

that some societies seem to do. This is because they do not arrange children and consumer goods hierarchically on one standard scale.

Among other values children have to their families, they also serve as status symbols. So far, the large family as a status symbol has endured. Even though there is evidence of reduced fertility among large-farm high-caste women aged 20–29, these reductions do not necessarily signal a change toward lower completed family size in this group. Completed family size will also depend on infant mortality, which is falling in the Pokhara area. Furthermore, the large family continues to retain its value as a status symbol despite the possibility that family size is decreasing, but it will become more difficult to achieve the status of having a large family as more resources (land and income) are needed to accomplish that end.

The effect of economic status on fertility, however, is clear only when appreciated alongside the even greater effect of social status. In the low castes, economic variation, as measured by land, is unrelated to individual fertility (economic considerations, other than land, probably influence their ability to raise large families). The lack of a strong relationship between economic status and fertility among the low castes is partly explained by the fact that outward social markers among the low castes require minimal or no cash outlay. Expenditures on children are relatively small, and the cost of raising them does not interfere very much with social ranking.

The situation is quite different among high-caste people, who are expected to observe lifestyles that put more strain on economic resources. When resources are relatively limited, both the demands of lifestyle and of a large family cannot be supported. Therefore, the small-farm high castes are distinctly different from the large-farm high castes. Even before the forces of socioeconomic development gathered momentum in the Pokhara area, the fertility of the small-farm high castes was highly regulated by practices that delayed first births, slightly increased birth intervals, and terminated childbearing relatively early. The changes that have taken place in their fertility pattern reflect that they continue to limit the number of children they bear, having changed only the methods and timing.

The finding of pretransitional heterogeneity in fertility is consistent with cultural evolutionary models that are based on variability of behavioral characteristics upon which changes in social environment operate. The pace and timing of changes in the age-specific fertility curves suggest that the stresses accompanying major economic development of the region have led the small-farm high castes increasingly to employ modern contraceptives to maintain their relatively low levels of fertility. A similar change is beginning to occur among the low castes.

In conclusion, cultural change toward conscious limitation of family size probably occurs first among groups that traditionally limited family size through less reliable means. Sectors of society that traditionally limited family size may turn to contraception because the traditional practices of contraception may no longer be as reliable. For example, earlier cohabitation by young couples has been made possible by more profitable small farms, effectively lengthening the reproductive lives of married women. The motivation to have fewer children already exists in some groups, such as those that must seek high status but do not have the means to achieve it on all levels. Two types of status symbols are particularly important. One is the number of children people have, which is a major means of achieving status, especially among women. The other is outward lifestyle, which is important in setting the high castes apart from the low castes. The large-farm high castes are not much hampered by competition between these two types of status for they have the economic means to pursue both. Competing status considerations are also not so important among the low castes who need not make major economic concessions to lifestyle and can therefore have many children on the basis of few resources. However, among the small-farm high castes there is an effort to balance these considerations. It is important to have large families, but only if the more economically demanding lifestyle of the high castes can be maintained.

The socioeconomic developmental changes in caste-Hindu society in West Central Nepal have not yet resulted in decreases in completed family size. Modest decreases in fertility have been offset by decreased infant and child mortality. Nonetheless, fundamental changes in fertility are underway. One change is that fertility limitation increasingly depends on the superior reliability of modern technology. Related to such changes is a shift toward deliberate family limitation among the low castes, who are following a course similar to that of the small-farm high castes. Owing to the high social status of the high castes, and the traditional competence of those with small-farms to limit family size, conscious family limitation becomes a behavioral pattern that lower status groups can emulate. Ironically, the elite status of the large-farm high castes may have prevented them from serving as a model of controlled fertility that other groups might copy. It is the ability of the high castes to have large families and to maintain the proper lifestyle that makes them elite, but because of their elite status they are expected to uphold standards that other groups cannot achieve. Because the small-farm high castes are not elite, yet face many of the problems that the low castes do, the small-farm high castes have provided a model of fertility behavior for the low castes.

We should realize that changes in patterns of childbearing and the use of modern contraceptive technology say nothing about consciousness or rationality. As I have shown elsewhere (Folmar, 1992), rationality among the Nepalese is similar to rationality among any social group. Some people are more rational than others, just as some individuals are more rational at some times than they are at others. A point that must not be missed is that their rationality is not determined solely, or even primarily, by economic considerations. Other forces are also powerful, including social concerns, kinship, and religion.

ACKNOWLEDGMENTS

I am grateful for the generous support of the Carolina Population Center, University of North Carolina–Chapel Hill, J. Richard Udry, Director. Other sources of support for the research and writing of this paper were provided by grants from the Case Western Reserve University Alumni Association and the Mellon Foundation. John Gulick, Ben Campbell, Lynn Igoe, Harihar Bhattarai, Anna Richardson, and three anonymous reviewers made many helpful comments on earlier drafts of this paper. Their observations improved the paper considerably and I thank them.

REFERENCES

Becker, G. S. (1960). An economic analysis of fertility. In *Demographic and Economic Change in Developing Countries.* Universities-National Bureau Conference Series, No. 11. Princeton University Press, Princeton, pp. 209–231.

Bennett, J. W. (1976). Anticipation, adaptation, and the concept of culture in anthropology. *Science* 192 (4242): 847–853.

Bennett, L. (1983). *Dangerous Wives and Sacred Sisters: Social and Symbolic Roles of High-Caste Women in Nepal.* Columbia University Press, New York.

Blaikie, P., Cameron, J., and Seddon, D. (1980). *Nepal in Crisis: Growth and Stagnation at the Periphery.* Oxford University Press, Delhi.

Carr-Sanders, A. M. (1922). *The Population Problem: A Study in Human Evolution.* Clarendon Press, Oxford.

Cleland, J. and Wilson, C. (1987). Demand theories of the fertility transition: An iconoclastic view. *Population Studies* 41(1): 5–30.

Coale, A. J. (1974). The demographic transition. In *International Population Conference, Liege, 1973, Vol. 1.* International Union for the Scientific Study of Population, Liege, pp. 53–72.

Coale, A. J. and Watkins, S. C. (1986). *The Decline of Fertility in Europe.* Princeton University Press, Princeton.

Cowgill, D. O. (1962). Transition theory as general population theory. *Social Forces* 41(3): 270–274.

Dickemann, E. (1984). Concepts and classification in the study of human infanticide. In Hausfater, G. and Hrdy, S. (eds.), *Infanticide: Comparative and Evolutionary Perspectives.* Aldine, New York, pp. 427–437.

Douglas, M. (1966). Population control in primitive groups. *British Journal of Sociology* 17: 263–273.

Easterlin, R. A. (1975). An economic framework for fertility analysis. *Studies in Family Planning* 6(3): 54–63.

Folmar, S. J. (1985). Fertility and the Economic Value of Children in Pokhara Valley, Nepal. Unpublished Ph.D. dissertation in Anthropology, Case Western Reserve University, Cleveland.

Folmar, S. (1992). Wive's roles in fertility decision-making among Nepalese caste-Hindus. *Central Issues in Anthropology* 10: 39–50.

Folmar, S. (n.d.). Marital instability and female empowerment in Nepal. Manuscript.

Fricke, T. E. (1986). *Himalayan Households: Tamang Demography and Domestic Processes.* Studies in Cultural Anthropology No. 11. Iowa State University Press, Ames.

Fuhrer-Haimendorf, C. von (1960). Caste in the multi-ethnic society of Nepal. *Contributions to Indian Sociology.* 4(1): 12–32.

Goldstein, M. C. (1976). Fraternal polyandry and fertility in a high Himalayan valley in northwest Nepal. *Human Ecology* 4(3): 223–233.

Gurung, H. B. (1965). Pokhara Valley, Nepal Himalayas: A Field Study in Regional Geography. Unpublished Ph.D. dissertation in Geography, University of Edinburgh, Edinburgh.

Gurung, H. B. (1982). Population increase in Nepal: 1971–1981. *Himalayan Review* 13(1): 1–22.

Hammel, E. A. and Howell, N. (1987). Research in population and culture: An evolutionary framework. *Current Anthropology* 28(2): 141–160.

Harris, M. and Ross, E. (1987). *Death, Sex, and Fertility: Population Regulation in Preindustrial and Developing Societies.* Columbia University Press, New York.

Henry, L. (1961). Some data on natural fertility. *Eugenics Quarterly* 8(1): 81–91.

Knodel, J. (1983). Natural fertility: Age patterns, level, and trends. In Bulatao, R. and Lee, R. (eds.), *Determinants of Fertility in Developing Countries, Vol. 1.* Academic Press, New York, pp. 61–102.

Kreager, P. (1982). Demography *in situ. Population and Development Review* 8(2): 237–266.

Landers, J. (1990). Fertility decline and birth spacing among London Quakers. In Landers, J. and Reynolds, V. (eds.), *Fertility and Resources: 31st Symposium Volume of the Society for the Study of Human Biology.* Cambridge University Press, Cambridge, pp. 92–117.

Low, B. S. (1989). Occupational status and reproductive behavior in nineteenth century Sweden: Locknevi Parish. *Social Biology* 36(1–2): 82–101.

Macfarlane, A. (1976). *Resources and Population: A Study of the Gurungs of Nepal.* Cambridge University Press, Cambridge.

Nag, M., White, B. N. F., and Peet, R. C. (1978). An anthropological approach to the study of the economic value of children in Java and Nepal. *Current Anthropology* 19(2): 293–306.

Notestein, F. (1953). Economic problems of population change. In *Proceedings of the Eighth International Conference of Agricultural Economists, 1953.* Oxford University Press, Oxford, pp. 13–31.

Polgar, S. (1972). Population history and population policies from an anthropological perspective. *Current Anthropology* 13(2): 203–211.

Ross, J. L. (1984). Culture and fertility in the Nepal Himalaya: A test of a hypothesis. *Human Ecology* 12(2): 163–181.

Ross, J. L., Blangero, J., Goldstein, M. C., and Schuler, S. (1986). Proximate determinants of fertility in the Kathmandu Valley, Nepal: An anthropological case study. *Journal of Biosocial Science* 18: 179–196.

Stone, L. (1978). Cultural repercussions of childlessness and low fertility in Nepal. *Contributions to Nepalese Studies* 5(2): 7–36.

Tuladhar, J. M., Gughaju, B. B., and Stoeckel, J. (1978). *Population and Family Planning in Nepal.* Ratna Pustak Bhandar, Kathmandu.

Warwick, W. P. (1988). Culture and the management of family planning programs. *Studies in Family Planning* 19(1): 1–18.

Wood, J. W. (1990). Fertility in anthropological populations. *Annual Review of Anthropology* 19: 211–242.

11

Land Use, Soil Loss, and Sustainable Agriculture in Rwanda

Daniel C. Clay and Laurence A. Lewis

Rwanda has one of the highest population densities of any African country, together with steep slopes and high rainfall. Conservation, then, is not an abstraction; it is central to continued farming. If land use is not compatible with erosion control and soil maintenance, Rwanda will not support itself. Thus, the problems addressed by Clay and Lewis have to do with long-term viability of agricultural systems throughout the Third World, especially where resources are scarce and population densities high. Rwanda's population (at least before the recent war) continues to grow at the rate of 3.7% a year—an extremely high rate that will double the country's population within 30 years. Population pressure continues to push agriculture onto marginal lands and is causing a rapid increase in slope and soil degradation. What are the Rwandan farmers doing about this problem? The quick answer is not enough. From a nationwide sample of 2100 farm households, it emerges that, even though farmers are cognizant of the problem, the selective placement of crops, woodlots, and pastures for the purposes of controlling soil loss is uncommon. The problem is that each family has to sustain itself on the land available. As farmers cultivate marginal areas and increasingly small plots, they cannot afford the luxury of woody crops and crops that serve to stabilize soils; to feed their families they have to maximize their yields within any given growing season,

Originally published in *Human Ecology: An Interdisciplinary Journal,* 18(2)(1990): 147–161.

Daniel C. Clay, Department of Sociology, Michigan State University, East Lansing, Michigan 48824.   **Laurence A. Lewis,** Graduate School of Geography, Clark University, Worcester, Massachusetts 01610.

Case Studies in Human Ecology, edited by Daniel G. Bates and Susan H. Lees. Plenum Press, New York, 1996.

which is incompatible with long-term stability. The issue facing ecologists such as Clay and Lewis is how to promote cropping strategies that work for conservation while still acceptable to local people.

INTRODUCTION

Soil loss is a serious threat to the long-term viability of agricultural systems throughout the Third World. Particularly on fragile lands in regions where land resources are scarce and population growth continues to surge, declining productivity due to soil degradation can have crushing long-term effects on human health and nutrition. Awareness of this truism is no greater among members of the scientific community than it is among members of affected peasant villages.

The farmers of Rwanda are especially mindful of the need to conserve their land resources. Rwanda is among the poorest and most densely populated nations in Africa, with an annual population growth rate of 3.7%. Steep slopes, common throughout the nation, coupled with heavy seasonal rains make the task of erosion control essential to the future of Rwandan agriculture. The efforts of individual farmers, working with extension agents and government officials, have emphasized land management engineering as the dominant approach to controlling soil loss and degradation. Terraces and drainage ditches have been constructed in many parts of the country. Engineering strategies, while potentially very useful, have numerous disadvantages. First, they make hill slopes inherently less stable (Chorley et al., 1984) and as such, continuous maintenance of engineering works is invariably required. Second, they are generally expensive to construct, either in terms of labor or capital, or both. Third, in the Rwandan setting, due to both the steepness of the slopes and the heavy volume of surface water runoff, unlined drainage ditches can eventually lead to gully formation. And finally, in most parts of northwestern Rwanda, topsoils are relatively thin and are underlaid with a very acidic B horizon (the stratum of soil that lies immediately beneath the topsoil layer).

Recently, biological approaches such as planting grass strips and hedgerows have been introduced as complementary methods of reducing soil loss. Yet, because grass strips and hedgerows often remove sizable segments of land from crop production, they can push farmers to cultivate additional, often marginal, lands and thereby increase the potential area undergoing accelerated agricultural erosion.

Another biological approach, one that has received relatively little attention from agricultural extension leaders in Rwanda, is the integration of erosional controls into farmers' cropping and land use systems. Crops and other forms of vegetation vary considerably in their ability to protect the soil from the erosive effects of rainfall and runoff. Differences in the rates of maturity, extent of leaf cover, root systems, and crop-specific farming practices are some of the more important factors that determine the relative effectiveness of various forms of agricultural land use in controlling soil loss. These factors can also affect the overall performance of land engineering strategies. By selectively adapting land use and cropping patterns so that parcels of land particularly susceptible to erosion are covered with vegetation, offering effective protection at critical periods during the agricultural cycle, the loss of soil can be minimized. Furthermore, when both environmental and cultural factors figure into the farmer's crop-selection/field-location decision-making, not only can soil erosion be reduced, but soil improvement may actually result.

This paper demonstrates that there is relatively little association between field slope and crop cover in Rwanda, and examines the question of how this could be so in this highland African nation, where land is a scarce resource and over 90% of all households draw their livelihood from agriculture. It is argued that the reason why farmers do not make more effective use of cropping and land use to control soil loss is not because they are unaware of the soil loss problem. Rather, the traditional settlement pattern and the organization of farming, coupled with more recent demographic pressure, have impeded the development of a cropping system that effectively contributes to the conservation of precious land resources.

LAND USE, SLOPE, AND SOIL LOSS

The degradation of Africa's land resources has often been ignored or gone unnoticed unless it has resulted in spectacular or obvious destruction, such as gully erosion (de Vos, 1975). While there is recent recognition of the soil degradation problem throughout Africa, aggressive and concerted efforts to deal with the situation have emerged almost exclusively in the semi-arid areas, where agricultural and pastoral systems have experienced catastrophic declines (United Nations, 1977). In Rwanda and other humid areas of the continent where the potential for agricultural production is relatively high, the effects of soil loss have been less visible and consequently not perceived to be as damaging as in the drier areas (Lewis and Berry, 1988). Today, however, the problem of land degradation in the humid areas is rapidly gaining recognition (El-Swaify et al., 1985).

Population pressure in Rwanda has pushed farmers onto increasingly fragile lands. Without proper attention, the downward spiral of environmental deterioration in affected areas will be inevitable. In the northwestern region, where the potential for agricultural productivity is high, the expansion of agriculture onto marginal lands is already resulting in serious slope failures (slumps and landslides) (Nyamulinda, 1988). The increase in degradation processes acting on hill slopes will eventually lead to excessive deposition in the valley bottoms—conditions which, over time, can precipitate flood damage and the destruction of lowland crops. In fact, if left untreated, environmental decline will generally accelerate because the various stages of deterioration tend to reinforce one another. Decreasing soil fertility, for example, reduces vegetation cover which, in turn, increases the potential for soil loss and even lower fertility.

The role of plant cover, including both crops and mulches, in controlling soil loss is well established (Wischmeier and Smith, 1978). Vegetation that protects the soil from the direct impact of raindrops are associated with low soil losses. Likewise the application of mulches has consistently proven to be effective in reducing erosion (Soil Conservation Society of America, 1979; Wischmeier and Smith, 1978). Furthermore, in highland settings such as in Rwanda, mulches add important nutrients and increase the soil moisture utilization potential, both of which can increase potential yields. In Kenya, for example, thick mulching of coffee crops on slopes in excess of 15 degrees has resulted in soil losses of less than 3 tons per hectare per year (Lewis, 1985). Mulching of coffee is almost a universal practice in Rwanda, and prior research has shown that soil losses on such fields appear minimal (Lewis, 1988) even though the primary purpose of the mulch is to improve the soil moisture, not erosion control. Other recent research has begun to emphasize the importance of continuous crop cover and minimal ground disturbance in reducing soil loss in Rwanda (Lewis et al., 1988).

DATA AND METHOD

Data for this paper are derived from a nationwide stratified random sample of 2,100 farm households, and were collected as part of the 1983–1984 National Agricultural Survey in Rwanda (Dejaegher et al., 1988). The survey was sponsored jointly by the Ministry of Agriculture, Livestock and Forests, and the U.S. Agency for International Development. Fielded over a 12 month period, the survey was designed to collect information on agricultural systems in Rwanda from a variety of perspectives.

Table 1. Crop Cover Value (C-value) for Selected Crops in Pure Stands and in Association

Crop	C-value	Crop	C-value
Coffee	.02	Beans/sweet potato	.20
Banana	.04	Peanut/beans	.21
Banana/beans	.10	Manioc/beans	.22
Manioc/banana	.10	Potato	.22
Fallow	.10	Sweet potato	.23
Pasture	.10	Eleusine	.25
Woodlot	.10	Manioc	.26
Beans/banana	.12	Maize/beans	.30
Banana/sorghum	.14	Sorghum/manioc	.31
Peas	.15	Cocoyam	.33
Sorghum/banana	.18	Maize	.35
Beans	.19	Sorghum	.40
Beans/potato	.20	Tobacco	.45

Topics addressed in the field-level questionnaires included: crops and crop rotations, land tenure, steepness of slope, location of fields on the slope, soil conservation methods, fertilizer use, distance from the household residence, and perceived productivity of the soil. Of particular importance to the present study is the degree to which various combinations of crops and other types of land use help protect the soil from rainfall and runoff. A well-know measure that reflects this protective quality of crops is the C-value.

The C-value is defined as "the ratio of soil loss from an area with a specific cover and tillage practice to that from an identical area in tilled continuous fallow" (Wischmeier & Smith, 1978). For any given field, the crop cover, canopy, and tillage practices can vary throughout the year. The C-value represents the average soil loss ratio resulting from these factors over the growing season. In the present study, the C-values used (see Table 1 for an illustrative listing) were based on field work undertaken in the Kiambu and Murang'a districts of the Kenya highland (Lewis, 1985) and a pilot study of soil loss in Rwanda (Lewis, 1988).

FINDINGS AND DISCUSSION

The selective placement of crops, woodlots, and pastures for the purpose of controlling soil loss does not appear to be a common practice among Rwanda's 1.2 million farm households. If it were, then one might expect to find that crops and other forms of land use with low C-values

Table 2. Mean Crop Cover Value
(C-Value) by Steepness of Slope
(in degrees) of Fields in Rwanda

Slope	Mean C-value	(N)
0–5 degrees	.17	(1135)
6–9 degrees	.18	(785)
10–14 degrees	.17	(998)
15–20 degrees	.16	(967)
21+ degrees	.16	(931)
Total	.17	(4817)

Eta = –.07; Sig. = <.001.

(i.e., those with dense leaf cover and other protective attributes) would be located disproportionately in fields that were particularly susceptible to erosion (notably those with steep slopes). But this is not the case. Table 2 reports the mean C-value for crops and other vegetation grown in fields of varying degrees of steepness. Though there is a slight negative association (eta = –.07), we must conclude that C-values do not seem to vary much as a function of field slope. This conclusion is consistent with findings reported earlier on the relationship between slope and crop cover in Rwanda's western provinces along Lake Kivu (Lewis and Nyamulinda, 1989).

The intriguing question unearthed by this initial finding asks why, in this country of steep slopes and heavy seasonal rainfall, farmers are not actively pursuing every possible means of protecting their scarce land resources from the damaging erosive effects of the natural environment. Could it be that farmers are simply unaware of the erosion problem or the factors that cause it? Or, might there be other dimensions of their cultural tradition and farming systems that effectively discourage a pattern of land use that will help minimize soil degradation?

Farmer Perceptions and Land Degradation

The proposition that farmers may not be cognizant of the hazards of uncontrolled soil erosion seems implausible for at least two reasons. First, the Government of Rwanda has repeatedly cautioned farmers on the need for proper land management, and has initiated nationwide campaigns to encourage farmers to counter soil erosion through conservation investments and reforestation. Data from a recent study of conservation investments in

Table 3. Decline in Productivity of Cropped Fields by Steepness of Field Slope (in degrees)

| Decline in productivity | Steepness of Field Slope | | | | | Total % |
	% 0–5 degrees	% 6–9 degrees	% 10–14 degrees	% 15–20 degrees	% 21+ degrees	
No decline	53.3	53.8	47.7	49.9	44.3	50.0
Small decline	36.9	39.3	41.5	34.3	39.2	38.2
Large decline	9.8	6.9	10.8	15.8	16.5	11.8
Total	100.0	100.0	100.0	100.0	100.0	100.0
(N)	(1041)	(740)	(907)	(837)	(755)	(4279)

Gamma = .10; Sig < .001.

Rwanda show that 76.2% of farm holdings have received investments in the form of radical terraces, hedgerows, grass strips, or anti-erosion ditches, and that such investments are concentrated on the steeper slopes (Clay and Reardon, 1994).

Second, farmers themselves say that the productivity of their land is declining and that often this is due to soil erosion. The marginal frequencies in Table 3 confirm that farmers have observed a decline over time in the productivity of a full 50% of all of their holdings. In most cases the drop has been small, but farmers report that the decline in productivity has been substantial in nearly one field in eight (11.8%). In either case, the finding that the productivity of half the country's farmland has declined to any appreciable degree at all is disturbing news. Table 3 also confirms that fields experiencing the most serious decline tend to be those on slopes of 15 degrees or greater.

The perceptions of farmers about the reasons for the declining productivity of their fields focus on two causes: Overcultivation and soil erosion (Table 4). Nearly half (48.7%) of the fields identified as declining in productivity are believed by their operators to be overcultivated—undoubtedly a manifestation of the subdivision of farms from one generation to the next and, concomitantly, to the gradually disappearing use of fallow periods in the crop rotation cycle. Second only to overcultivation as a perceived cause of declining productivity is soil erosion, which again indicates a degree of awareness on the part of Rwandan farmers vis-a-vis the problem of soil erosion.

Though overcultivation and soil loss can be closely related, they are often found apart. Overcultivation tends to occur on relatively gentle slopes (Table 4, since these are the fields that farmers most often cultivate. By

Table 4. Primary Reason for Decline in Productivity of Cropped Fields by
Steepness of Field Slope (in degrees)

	Steepness of field slope					
Reason for decline in productivity	% 0–5 degrees	% 6–9 degrees	% 10–14 degrees	% 15–20 degrees	% 21+ degrees	Total %
Soil erosion	3.8	5.3	11.2	18.1	38.1	15.2
Over-cultivated	58.6	60.7	50.4	40.4	33.8	48.7
Disease	3.7	5.3	4.1	3.3	4.3	4.1
Other	25.4	24.9	27.1	33.3	18.1	25.8
Don'tknow	8.5	3.8	7.1	4.9	5.7	6.2
Total	100.0	100.0	100.0	100.0	100.0	100.0
(N)	486	342	475	419	420	2142

Gamma = −.19; Sig < .001.

contrast, fields suffering from soil erosion problems tend to be those situated on steep slopes. However, a focused look at fields on the steepest slopes (15 degrees or more), shows that both erosion and overcultivation are commonly identified, indicating that on such fields the two problems may be interrelated. It is probable that declining soil fertility due to erosion may cause fields on steep slopes to be "mined" more rapidly and to regenerate more slowly.

In the light of these findings we reiterate our initial point—the reason cropping and land use patterns are not effectively used to minimize soil loss in Rwanda is not because farmers are unaware of the soil erosion problem and its related causes. By all counts they are aware and, as the specialists on indigenous knowledge tell us, peasant farmers generally have a very informed and sensible approach to the management of their natural resources.

Soil Loss and the Organization of Farming

Alternatively, we look toward the organization of agriculture and the sociocultural context in which it has evolved for answers to the question of why Rwandan farmers have not developed more effective land use and cropping patterns in their fight against soil erosion. We begin with an examination of some of the spatial aspects of traditional farm settlement in Rwanda.

Through the 1940s the only regions of the country that were extensively inhabited and farmed were those of the western highlands, where abundant rainfall and fertile soils were especially conducive to agriculture (Gourou, 1953). Farmers in these areas initially settled along the upper ridges of their hillsides, where soils were more fertile and cultivation was a simpler task than it was farther down, on the steeper slopes and in the marshy valleys. In many parts of Africa, populations have settled in villages. By contrast, Rwandan farmers have dispersed across the tops of their hillsides, with each family constructing a residence compound (*urugo*) near the center of its property.

Immediately surrounding the *urugo,* farmers have traditionally planted groves of bananas. Bananas have special significance in Rwandan culture because they are used for making a unique home-brewed beer that is served at virtually all formal and informal social gatherings. Though essential for sociocultural reasons, bananas and banana beer have become a mainstay of the local cash economy as well. Banana beer is now marketed heavily among households and through small neighborhood taverns, and has consequently become the primary source of cash income for 40% of Rwandan households (Rwanda, 1988). Other essential crops, notably beans, are typically planted in association with bananas in these nearby fields (Rwanda, 1984, p. 43).

Another reason why bananas and other important crops are most often planted near the family compound is because Rwandan farmers have limited access to organic fertilizers, derived principally from both animal and human waste, and such fertilizers are rarely transported to their more distant fields. Table 5 reports that while 37.5% of nearby fields (within a 5 minute walk) receive organic fertilizer, either alone or with mulch, only 5.0%–12.7% of fields in more distant locations are treated with fertilizer.

Table 5. Use of Organic Fertilizer and Mulch by Distance (in minutes) of Field from the Household Residence

Use of org. fertilizer and/or mulch	Distance from residence (in minutes)					
	0–5	5–15	16–30	31–45	> 45	Total
None	50.8	79.6	89.0	82.8	89.7	60.9
Fertilizer only	33.9	11.6	4.8	5.8	5.0	26.1
Mulch only	11.6	7.6	5.7	9.1	5.3	10.2
Fertilizer and mulch	3.6	1.1	0.5	2.3	0.0	2.8
Total	100.0	100.0	100.0	100.0	100.0	100.0
(N)	(2920)	(874)	(309)	(83)	(92)	(4279)[a]

[a] No information on use of manure and mulch on fields in pasture or woodlot.

Beyond the inner ring of bananas, a series of outer rings can be identified that farmers have traditionally used to meet the needs of their households (Nwafor, 1979, p. 59). The first such ring is farmed intensively with annual crops for both home consumption and sale. Next, and a bit farther down the hillside, coffee is grown. Coffee is the country's principal export crop and as such is vigorously promoted by the government of Rwanda. Beyond the coffee plots, the slope of the hillside is often at its steepest. Consequently, these areas have traditionally been reserved for pasture and woodlots, however, many of the less important crops also are grown here and frequent fallow periods are commonly required. At the very outer rings, toward the base of the slope and in the swampy valleys, cropping is done on ridges that are built up to ensure proper water drainage. Sweet potatoes and other vegetables are grown in these more distant plots to ensure a continuous food supply between harvest seasons.

This traditional system of land use has always been subject to wide variation from one farm to the next, and only on occasion can it be found in its "pure" form today. On average, however, its effectiveness in controlling soil loss has been mixed. On one hand, earlier conditions of plentiful land resources allowed farm households to cultivate only the gentler slopes and maintain woodlots and pastures, which provide excellent erosion protection, on the steeper slopes. On the other hand, bananas also provide dense crop cover but tended to be planted on the relatively flat areas around the family compound, while secondary crops such as maize and manioc were planted on steep slopes, despite their poor soil conservation qualities.

Though still apparent today, increasing land scarcity due to population growth has obliged many farmers in recent decades to depart from this traditional system. As the preferred lands along the hilltops became occupied, young farmers were faced with the decision to either cultivate smaller and less fertile plots farther down the hillside or to migrate elsewhere in search of sufficient land resources. As early as the mid 1950s a mass exodus from the western provinces was under way (Olson, 1989), which later culminated in a government-sponsored resettlement program (*paysannat*) of grand proportion during the 1960s and 1970s. In all, this program displaced over 80,000 farmers and their families into previously unoccupied areas of the country (Clay et al., 1989a; Rwanda, 1985).

As the non-farm sector in Rwanda is still in its infancy, accounting for only 8.6 of all rural employment (Clay et al., 1989c), most young people are obliged to remain in farming. Consequently, farms have become badly fragmented and marginal lands on even the steepest slopes have been brought into production. This is particularly evident in some of the western regions where population densities now exceed 375 persons per km^2

Table 6. Land Use by Steepness of Field Slope

	Steepness of field slope					
Land use	% 0–5 degrees	% 6–9 degrees	% 10–14 degrees	% 15–20 degrees	% 21+ degrees	Total %
Bananas	11.6	11.6	12.9	9.9	7.7	10.8
Beans	17.5	20.2	20.9	16.9	11.3	17.3
Sorghum	10.2	10.8	9.6	7.1	4.2	8.8
Sweet potatoes	12.4	8.5	7.1	9.3	9.9	9.5
Coffee	4.3	4.6	5.7	6.6	5.5	5.3
Maize	1.7	1.4	2.1	2.7	3.4	2.3
Manioc	4.0	9.2	8.3	7.4	10.5	7.7
Fallow	8.7	6.9	8.9	9.7	14.0	9.7
Woodlot	3.1	1.3	3.0	6.6	10.9	5.0
Pasture	4.0	2.4	3.9	4.2	5.3	4.0
Other	22.4	23.0	17.7	19.6	17.5	20.0
Total	100.0	100.0	100.0	100.0	100.0	100.0
(N)	(1135)	(785)	(998)	(967)	(931)	(4817)

(Delepierre, 1980). Data from the current study suggest, indirectly, that even today the household residence tends to be located toward the top of the slope, as 77.6% of fields on the top of the slope are less than a 5-minute walk from the *urugo* as compared to 45.2% of those located farther down in the valleys. Given the continued social and economic importance of bananas in Rwanda, their location on the preferred upper slopes near the family residence seems entirely reasonable (Table 6). Beans and sorghum are two other crops that are favored by farm households and for this reason are less likely to be found on the steeper slopes. The data also indicate that while beans are often located on the gentler slopes surrounding the family compound, sorghum is commonly located on the low slopes at the base of the hillside and in the valley. By contrast, crops that tend to be grown on the steeper slopes are manioc and maize, both of which (but particularly maize) are relatively ineffective in helping to control soil loss. By and large, the traditional practice of relegating non-cropping forms of land use to steep slopes has been maintained. This is especially true for woodlots, but fields on the very steepest slopes (21 degrees or more) are also very likely to be left fallow.

Though woodlots, fallow, and pasture all provide effective protection from erosion, recent findings from the Rwanda Non-farm Strategies Survey (Rwanda, 1988) demonstrate that land in fallow and pasture have been

Table 7. Change in Fallow, Pasture, and Woodlot over the Past Two Years as Reported by Heads of Households

Land use	Change over past two years			
	More	Less	Same	(N)
Fallow	15.8	28.0	56.2	(1015)
Pasture	2.4	13.1	84.5	(1015)
Woodlot	21.7	6.3	72.0	(1015)

declining in recent years because of the need to increase food production (Table 7). Only woodlots seem not to have suffered over the past few years, thanks to a strong government campaign aimed at replanting and maintaining them at both the household and communal levels. Though some of the lost fallow and pasture may be land that is being converted into woodlots, other findings point to the fact that households with insufficient landholdings are being forced to plant ever-increasing proportions of their holdings with manioc and other tubers (Clay and Magnani, 1987; Loveridge et al., 1988). These tubers have a higher calorific value than do other crops, and tend to grow relatively well in poorer soils (Gleave and White, 1969), such as those commonly found on steeper slopes, but with C-values in the .22–.26 range, they do not compare with the traditional uses of these slopes, i.e., woodlots and pasture, in controlling soil loss. In fact, they are clearly associated with accelerated soil loss (Ashby, 1985), and their increasing cultivation on steep slopes could be a major factor contributing to increasing sedimentation along the valley bottoms. Sedimentation often increases flooding and can lower the productivity of these bottom lands. Though we have no data to test the hypothesis, we surmise that the increase in food production resulting from the cultivation of these steep slopes is being offset to some degree by the declining production on the valley floors.

CONCLUSIONS

The conservation of scarce land resources is essential to the long-term viability of agriculture in Rwanda. High population density, steep slopes, and abundant rainfall prevail in the highland portions of this African country, making the task of erosion control uncommonly difficult for the peasant farmer. The specific use to which land is put, e.g., cultivation, fallow, pasture, woodlots, and, if it is cultivated, the particular combination of crops grown, can be seen as contributing to both the cause and the solution of the land degradation problem. Based on data from a nationwide survey of over 4,800 agricultural fields in Rwanda, this study has reviewed the extent to which the land use and cropping patterns employed by farmers are appropriately suited, in terms of erosion control, to the topographical and environmental characteristics of their landholdings.

The selective placement of crops, woodlots, and pastures for the purpose of controlling soil loss does not appear to be a common practice among Rwanda's 1.2 million farm households. C-values appear to vary only slightly as a function of field slope. Crops that tend to be grown on steep slopes are manioc, maize, and other crops that do not provide the kind of cover necessary to protect these fragile lands. Population pressure has forced farmers to cultivate their land more intensively so that even pasture and fallow land, which were traditionally found in the steepest slopes, are disappearing.

With Rwanda's continuing population growth and the heavy reliance on the agricultural sector, the need for maintaining the resource base is of paramount importance to the national government. The long-term future of its economic development depends on not just maintaining, but actually improving, its resource base, and on ensuring that food production will continue to increase. Yet, individual farmers, with limited landholdings (less than 1.2 hectares on average) and capital, are compelled to find ways to maximize their agricultural outputs within each growing season. Often these short-term strategies run counter to the longer-range need for environmental stability. Thus there is a need to develop policies that merge the long-term national needs (environmental maintenance and improvement) with the farmers' short-term needs to maximize calorific outputs from their fields. Similarly, there is an immediate need for Rwanda's agricultural research and extension programs to focus on the changing use of these steep and fragile slopes and to experiment with practices that will improve the sustainability of the country's agricultural systems.

In Rwanda today, following recommendations made by the World Bank (Jones and Egli, 1984), farmers in certain regions are being encouraged to thin their banana fields in order to increase the yields of associated crops grown under the banana canopy. This is not a favorable strategy from the farmers' perspective given the important role of bananas, both socially and economically. Likewise, it contributes little toward improving the resource base in the long-term since steep fields still remain in production with crops that do not minimize soil loss. But if farmers were presented with the option of planting their bananas more densely on relatively steeper fields, or thinning them when planted on gentler slopes, it is possible that the current campaign's acceptability would grow in the eyes of farmers, while simultaneously improving the longer-term viability of the steeper slopes.

Another strategy that would help farmers to incorporate, to a greater degree, physical environmental factors into their agricultural system would be to encourage them to plant other protective crops, such as coffee or peas, on their steeper lands. Likewise, the use of mulches and fertilizers, which are generally concentrated on the fields with lower erosional risks, needs to be extended to fields on steeper slopes. Additionally, new crops must be introduced into the traditional crop mix that can meet both the short-term requirements of the farmers, as well as the long-term needs for environmental conservation. Recent research indicates that the introduction of shrub crops (e.g., Sesbania), in the form of alleycropping, is one such possibility (Eylands and Yamoah, 1989). Clearly, reorienting the spatial arrangement of crops to correspond with variations in topography will create more work for members of affected households, and will undoubtedly run against the grain of certain well-established cultural traditions. However, if the current pattern of crop distribution remains unchanged, the Rwandan landscape will continue to degrade, *ceteris paribus,* both to the detriment of individual farmers and to the country as a whole.

ACKNOWLEDGMENTS

Partial funding for this research has been provided by the U.S. Agency for International Development and the Rwanda Ministry of Agriculture, Livestock and Forests, under the Agricultural Surveys and Policy Analysis Project (ASPAP), USAID contract No. 696-0126, and the Food Security II Cooperative Agreement (AEP-5459-A-00-2041-00) Add-on for Rwanda (FS-II/Rwanda). The authors wish to acknowledge the helpful comments and suggestions made by James Bingen, Serge Rwamasirabo, and Harry Schwarzweller on an earlier version of this paper. The ideas and interpretations found in this paper are uniquely those of the authors and are not necessarily shared by the funding agencies.

REFERENCES

Ashby, J. A. (1985). The social ecology of soil erosion in a colombian farming system. *Rural Sociology* 50(3): 337–396.

Chorley, R. J., Schumn, S. S. and Sugden, D. E. (1984). *Geomorphology,* Methuen, London, pp. 230–275.

Clay, D. C. and Reardon, T. (1994). Determinants of Conservation Investments by Rwandan Farm Households. IAAE Occasional Paper No. 7. Contributed Paper for the 22nd Congress of the International Association of Agricultural Economists, August 1994.

One of the darkest hours of human history began the night of April 6, 1994, when Rwanda's president Juvenale Habyarimana was assassinated. During the subsequent months, hundreds of thousands of innocent men, women, and children were brutally murdered in their homes, and in the schools and churches where they sought refuge. In the wake of this ethnic bloodshed, millions more fled the country.

The research described here was conducted prior to this horrifying tragedy. At the time this book went to press, a new government had been installed, and Rwanda had begun the rebuilding process with assistance from the international community. Though many of the refugees had returned to their homes from camps in nearby Zaire and Tanzania and Burundi, some 2.1 million remained. There was still much uncertainty.

Our hope and belief is that, in time, order will be restored, families will be reunited, and that peace will prevail. And when it does, farmers will pick up where they left off. They will face the same challenges and opportunities present before the war. To be sure, issues of land management addressed in this paper, e.g., land use, cropping patterns, and use of fertility-enhancing inputs, may change on the surface. But the underlying parameters such as population growth, resource scarcity, and physical attributes of the land (steep and degraded slopes) will continue to define the problem, and shape the solution, for Rwanda's future.

We are confident that the findings presented in this chapter will help guide Rwandan farm families and their new government in rebuilding programs for agricultural extension and research. A strong agricultural sector will be essential to a strong economy in Rwanda, and to the goal of ethnic harmony.

Clay, D. C. and Magnani, R. J. (1987). The human ecology of farming systems: Toward understanding agricultural development in Rwanda. In Schwarzweller, H. K. (ed.), *Research in Rural Sociology and Development,* Vol. 3, pp. 141–167.

Clay, D. C., Kayitsinga, J., Kampayana, T., Ngenzi, I. and Olson, J. (1989a). Stratégies Non-Agricole au Rwanda: Rapport Préliminaire. SESA Document de Travail, Service des Enquêtes et des Statistiques Agricoles, Rwanda.

Clay, D. C. and Kampayana, T. (1989b). Inequality and the Emergence of Non-farm Employment in Rwanda. Paper presented at the Annual Meetings of the Rural Sociological Society, Seattle, 1989.

Clay, D. C., Kayitsinga, J. and Kampayana, T. (1989c). l'Emploi en Dehors du Ménage au Rwanda. Document de Travail ASPAP/DAI Rapport No. 74. Service des Enquêtes et des Statistiques Agricoles, Rwanda.

Dejaegher, Y., Clay, D. C., Rwamasirabo, S. and Ngirumwami, J.-L. (1988). *Aperçu Historique et Méthodologique: Enquête National Agricole 1984.* Service des Enquêtes et des Statistiques Agricoles, Rwanda.

Delepierre, G. (1974). Note technique No. 13 de l'ISAR, Rubona, Rwanda.

Delepierre, G. (1980). Tables de Répartition et de Densité de la Population Rwandaise par Secteur Communal et par Région Agricole. Ministère de l'Agriculture, de l'Elevage et des Forêts, Rwanda.

Dressler, J. and Neumann, I. (1982). Agriculture de Couverture du Sol (A.C.S.): Un Imperatif pour la Lutte Contre l'Erosion au Rwanda. *Bulletin Agricole au Rwanda* 4: 215–222.

El-Swaify, S. A., Moldenhauer, W. C. and Lo, A. (1985). *Soil Erosion and Conservation.* Soil Conservation Society of America, Ankeny, Iowa.

Eylands, V. J. and Yamoah, C. F. (1989). Sustaining Soil Fertility with Alley Cropping Systems in the Highlands of Rwanda. Paper presented at the 9th Annual Farming Systems Research/Extension Symposium, Fayetteville, Arkansas.

Gleave, M. B. and White, H. P. (1969). Population density and agricultural systems in West Africa. In Thomas, M. F. and Whittington, G. W. (eds.), *Environment and Land Use in Africa.* Methuen, London, pp. 273–300.

Gourou, P. (1953). *La Densité de la Population au Ruanda-Urundi: Esquisse d'une Etude Géographique.* Institut Royal Colonial Belge, Brussels.

Jones, W. I. and Egli, R. (1984). *Farming Systems in Africa: The highlands of Zaire, Rwanda, and Burundi.* World Bank Technical Document No. 27, Washington, D.C.

Lewis, L. A. (1985). Assessing soil loss in Kiambu and Nurang'a districts, Kenya. *Geografiska Annaler* 67(A): 273–84.

Lewis, L. A. (1988). Measurement and assessment of soil loss in Rwanda. *Catena Supplement* 12: 151–65.

Lewis, L. A. and Berry, L. (1988). *African Environments and Resources.* Unwin Hyman, Boston.

Lewis, L. A., Clay, D. and Dejaegher, Y. M. J. (1988). Soil loss, agriculture, and conservation in Rwanda: Toward sound strategies for soil management. *Journal of Water and Soil Conservation,* 43(5): 418–421.

Lewis, L. A. and Nyamulinda, V. (1989). Les relations entre les cultures et les unités topographiques dans les régions agricoles de la bordure du lac Kivu et de l'Impara au Rwanda: Quelques stratégies pour une agriculture soutenue. *Bulletin Agricole Rwanda* July: 143–149.

Loveridge, S., Rwamasirabo, S. and Weber, M. T. (1988). Selected Research Findings from Rwanda that Inform Food Security Policy Themes in Southern Africa. Paper presented at the Food Security in Southern Africa Fourth Annual University of Zimbabwe/Michigan State University Conference, Harare, 1988.

Nwafor, J. C. (1979). Agricultural land use and associated problems in Rwanda. *Journal of Tropical Geography* 58: 58–65.

Nyamulinda, V. (1988). Contribution a l'etude de l'erosion par mouvement de masse dans les milieux aménagés du Rwanda," *Bulletin Agricole Rwanda* 76–87.

Olson, J. (1989). Redistribution of the Population of Rwanda due to Environmental and Demographic Pressures. Paper presented at the Michigan Academy of Arts, Sciences and Letters. Grand Rapids, Michigan.

Rwanda, Ministère de l'Agriculture, de l'Elevage et des Forêts. (1984). *Description Sommaire des Principales Caractéristiques de l'Agriculture au Rwanda.* Service des Enquêtes et des Statistiques Agricoles (SESA). Presses de la Printer Set, Kigali, Rwanda.

Rwanda, Ministère de l'Agriculture, de l'Elevage et des Forêts. (1985). *Rapports Annuels pour les Années 1960–1985.*

Rwanda, Ministère de l'Agriculture, de l'Elevage et des Forêts. (1985). *Résultats de l'Enquête Nationale Agricole, 1984.* 3 Vols. Service des Enquêtes et des Statistiques Agricoles, Presses de la Printer Set, Kigali, Rwanda.

Rwanda, Ministère de l'Agriculture, de l'Elevage et des Forêts. (1988). Unpublished results of the 1988 Enquête sur les Stratégies Non-agricole. Service des Enquêtes et des Statistiques Agricoles, Rwanda.

Soil Conservation Society of America. (1979). *Effects of Tillage and Crop Residue Removal on Erosion, Runoff and Plant Nutrients,* Special Publication No. 25, SCSA, Ankeny, Iowa.
United Nations. (1977) *Livelihood Systems in Dry Areas.* UN Conference on Desertification. Pergamon, New York.
de Vos, A. (1975). *Africa, the Devastated Continent?* Dr. W. Junk bv Publishers, The Hague.
Wischmeier, W. H. and Smith, D. D. (1978). Predicting rainfall erosion losses, a guide to conservation planning. *Agricultural Handbook No. 537.* USDA, Washington, D.C., pp. 1–58.

12

Agricultural Intensification in a Philippine Frontier Community: Impact on Labor Efficiency and Farm Diversity

W. Thomas Conelly

There has been little research directed specifically at the point of transition between extensive and intensive cultivation, whereby farmers decide or are forced to change techniques in order to maximize outputs through greater investment of human labor. Conelly went to the west coast of Palawan Island (the same island where James Eder studied the Batak) to investigate the transition underway from traditional swidden agriculture to irrigated rice production. On the basis of Boserup's widely accepted theory, he assumed that such a change would be resisted because the farmer has to invest much more labor. With permanent irrigated production the soil is no longer left fallow, forcing cultivators to adopt labor-intensive methods of cultivation to maintain yields. Another widely accepted parallel argument is that because extended agriculture involves a very diverse range of crops through interplanting a number of species in each plot, with intensification the quality and reliability of the food supply will decline. What Conelly found was that while the long-term consequences of intensification may conform to these theories, in the short-term, which is what people take most seriously, standards of living improve. The reason for this is that farmers do not make the transition to irrigation directly from long fallow swidden cultivation. Rather, they make the transition from a short-fallow form of horticulture

Originally published in *Human Ecology: An Interdisciplinary Journal*, 20(2)(1992): 203–223.

W. Thomas Conelly, Department of Anthropology, Indiana University of Pennsylvania, Indiana, Pennsylvania 15705.

Case Studies in Human Ecology, edited by Daniel G. Bates and Susan H. Lees. Plenum Press, New York, 1996.

in which fields are allowed only 2–4 years in which to recover their fertility—which they do poorly. Thus, farmers no longer reap the benefits associated with traditional, highly diversified cropping. At this point, irrigation, even with its high labor requirements, looks attractive.

INTRODUCTION

Many farmers in the frontier community of Napsaan, located on the west coast of Palawan Island in the Philippines, are beginning to abandon their traditional practice of swidden agriculture, in which fields are cultivated for only one year after which they are rested for a period of fallow in order to maintain soil fertility. In the place of swidden cultivation, farmers are adopting a more labor intensive system of permanent irrigated rice production. According to a widely held theory of agricultural change proposed by Boserup (1965), the adoption of irrigation should allow Napsaan farmers to support a larger population by increasing the amount of rice they can produce on each hectare of land. This growth in carrying capacity, however, will be achieved at the cost of lower labor efficiency. With permanent irrigated production the soil is no longer rested during periods of fallow, forcing farmers to adopt more labor intensive methods of cultivation such as plowing in order to maintain yields at adequate levels (Boserup, 1965, p. 39). Because of these costs, Boserup's theory predicts that farmers will resist intensification until they are compelled to make the transition by growing population pressure and land scarcity.

Cohen (1989), in his influential analysis of the impact of agriculture on health and nutrition, proposes an argument that parallels Boserup's claim that intensification leads to a decline in standard of living. He suggests that as a population shifts its subsistence focus from hunting and gathering to extensive agriculture, and from there to intensive farming techniques, the reliability and quality of the food supply typically decline (1989, pp. 55–69). In this view he challenges a long standing assumption that "advances" in agricultural technology have led to a steady improvement in food security and health.

When I arrived in Napsaan in 1980 to carry out a study of agricultural practices in the community, I accepted the conventional view that the more "modern" irrigated agriculture would be less efficient (i.e., require more hours of work to produce a given amount of grain) than the traditional swidden practices of the farmers. I also assumed that irrigation would mean less diversity in the types of food available in the diet because it is a type of monoculture in which only a single crop is cultivated. In contrast, though swidden fields focus primarily on rice, many other crops, such as yams, cassava, vegetables, and fruit trees are often planted alongside the rice.

As I began to collect detailed information about the two systems of agriculture, however, I began to have my doubts. Farmers were enthusiastic about the benefits of irrigation and my data suggested that swidden cultivation was perhaps not such an ideal method of agriculture after all. Because this information did not conform to the accepted view of agricultural intensification, I initially wondered if perhaps I was making mistakes in my data collection. When information contradicts your preconceptions it's easy to ignore or explain away the discrepancy. But sometimes, if pursued, such discrepancies can lead to a better understanding how people make decisions and their behavior. As I collected more systematic data, I became convinced that the benefits of adopting permanent irrigated agriculture might outweigh the costs.

The key to understanding the process and impact of agricultural intensification is to observe specific farming systems *at the point of transition* from extensive to more intensive farming techniques (cf. Barlett, 1976, pp. 127–128; Cohen, 1989, p. 57). Many earlier studies comparing swidden and permanent agriculture contrasted *different* systems, often widely separated geographically and in time. Napsaan, a frontier community first settled in the mid 1950s and now experiencing rapid population growth, provided me with an opportunity to observe the process of agricultural change as it took place. Based on my study, I argue that the interpretation of agricultural intensification developed by Boserup and Cohen, while accurately describing long-term processes, overlooks the positive short-term benefits that intensification may provide. These benefits help us to better understand the actual mechanism by which intensification occurs, and explain why some Napsaan farmers have enthusiastically begun to adopt a more labor intensive system of production. Specifically, I contend that the adoption of irrigation by swidden farmers in Napsaan has resulted in an *improved* standard of living—irrigation has resulted in higher labor efficiency while serving to maintain a diverse and reliable farming system.

THE RESEARCH AREA

The long and narrow island of Palawan (11,700 km^2), located just to the northeast of Borneo, is the fifth largest island in the Philippine archipelago. Historically, geographic isolation and mountainous terrain, the presence of endemic malaria, and the threat of slave raiding by Muslim "pirates" from the Sultanate of Sulu to the south, left Palawan outside the mainstream of Philippine political and economic development during most of the colonial period. Since the 1930s, however, with the influx of thousands of lowland Filipino settlers from overpopulated islands in the central Philippines, Palawan has entered a period of rapid population growth, environmental modification, and economic development. In 1975 the population of Palawan Province, including many small outlying islands, was estimated to be 300,000 persons, with a population density of about 20 people/km^2 (National Economic and Development Authority, 1980). By 1990, estimates of the population residing on the main island of Palawan had increased dramatically to about 500,000. Despite these changes, Palawan remains the least developed of the major Philippine islands and is seen by many as the nation's last frontier. The island is still heavily forested, especially in its mountainous interior where logging companies, migrant lowland Filipino settlers, and indigenous peoples compete for its remaining resources (Conelly, 1985; Lopez, 1987; Eder, 1990).

My research on Palawan was conducted over an 18 month period in 1980–1981 on the central west coast of the island. In the Napsaan area, a group of Tagbanua—indigenous swidden cultivators and hunter–gatherers—who have migrated from the east coast of the island live intermingled with a large population of lowland Christian settlers, most of whom have arrived from the Visayan Islands in the central Philippines. Both groups began settling in Napsaan in the mid-1950s, when the area was still largely primary forest. By 1980, farmers had cleared the forest from a strip of land parallel to the coast up to 3 km inland. Much of the community consists of hilly land used for the production of rice, root crops, maize, and vegetables in swiddens. Small orchards of bananas and tree crops such as cashew are also cultivated. In low lying areas, small, irrigated rice fields have recently been developed, and a number of coconut orchards line the coast. Though agricultural production in Napsaan is primarily for subsistence, the marketing of local products such as cashew, bananas, and maize has become more important in recent years.

In addition to these farming activities, Napsaan settlers also have access to a productive inter-tidal zone. A variety of marine resources from the ocean are also exploited. In the still-forested mountain slopes above the community, some Tagbanua continue to hunt animals, especially wild pig, and to collect a variety of forest products for the market, including rattan (primarily *Calamus caesius*) and Manila copal, a resin produced by the tree *Agathis dammara* (Conelly, 1983, 1985).

POPULATION PRESSURE AND INTENSIFICATION
OF SWIDDEN AGRICULTURE

During the 1950s and 1960s, all of the settlers produced their rice, the mainstay of the Philippine diet, in long fallow swidden fields cleared from both primary forest and mature secondary forest regrowth. Population densities were low and forest land was freely available to new settlers as they migrated into the community. By the 1970s, however, the availability of land for swidden farming began to decline at an alarming rate. Early in the decade a logging road was constructed connecting Napsaan with the provincial capital of Puerto Princesa, located about 40 km away on the east coast of the island. Without the barrier of the difficult two-day walk through the forest, a new wave of settlers arrived in Napsaan after 1972. By 1980, there were about 350 people in the community living in 65 households, with a population density of roughly 75 persons/km^2.

Land scarcity began to be a concern by the early 1970s, but the rapidly growing population was initially accommodated by expansion of the community farther upstream along the Napsaan River where many newly arrived settlers claimed uncleared forest land. By the mid-1970s, however, local forestry officials started to effectively enforce Philippine legislation prohibiting the clearing of swiddens on forest land by "squatters" who were seen as illegally destroying government land.[1]

With this development, as predicted by Boserup, acute land pressure began to be felt and fallow periods decreased rapidly as farmers were forced to rotate their fields within the boundaries of land they had already cleared. By 1980 typical fallow periods in Napsaan swiddens had declined from more than ten years to only two to four years. As a consequence, rice yields plummeted and Napsaan settlers began to emphasize alternative means of producing food and securing a living. Some Tagbanua began to intensify their collection of forest products for sale on the market (Conelly, 1985, 1989), while other settlers started to focus more attention on ocean fishing, the production of tree crops such as cashews for the market, permanent rain-fed plow agriculture, or migrant wage employment. Many farmers responded to the scarcity of land by choosing to intensify their farm production through the adoption of irrigated rice cultivation. This

---

[1]Though some illegal forest swiddens were still cultivated on the west coast of Palawan in the early 1980s because of less than complete enforcement of the law, these were relatively rare because of the fear of government penalties. Twice during my stay in Napsaan two large groups of farmers in neighboring communities were arrested and imprisoned in Puerto Princesa City for clearing illegal swiddens in the forest. Events such as these have convinced most Napsaan farmers to refrain from cultivating forest land.

paper explores the impact of the latter decision on labor efficiency and farm diversity.

SHORT FALLOW SWIDDEN PRODUCTION

In 1981, considered a poor year because of a 3-week drought just before the harvest, gross rice yields in Napsaan averaged only 556 kg/ha. The previous year, which enjoyed adequate and well-distributed rain throughout the growing season, farmers reported gross yields averaging 836 kg/ha. However, the 2-year average of just under 700 kg/ha is only 33%–50% of the yields potentially achieved under conditions of long fallow cultivation (Conklin, 1957; Schlegel, 1983), and is one of the lowest yields recorded for any swidden system in Southeast Asia (Conelly, 1983).[2]

Boserup predicts that swidden farmers faced with population pressure and declining yields will *increase* their labor inputs in an attempt to maintain yields at previous levels (1965: 30–31). This, however, does not seem to be the strategy employed by Napsaan settlers, who average only 825 hours of labor/ha in their short fallow swidden production system. Compared to forest fallow swiddening, which requires in the range of 1000–2500 hours of labor/ha (Conelly, 1983), this level of labor expenditure is quite low.

These low labor inputs can be explained by a description of the short fallow swidden cycle. Clearing the vegetation usually requires relatively little effort when bush and low weeds or grasses are being removed rather than large forest trees (as was the case in the past). Likewise, burning the cleared vegetation is less time consuming and planting is easier on the uncluttered surface of fields cleared from short fallow vegetation than in the long fallow fields strewn with the remains of large trees. Since poor burns fail to eliminate the seeds of competing wild vegetation, the major task in short fallow swidden production becomes weeding. Napsaan farmers report

---

[2]Data on swidden and irrigated rice yields are based on farmers' reports of the number of *cavan* of rice they harvested. A *cavan* is equal to 44 kg of unhusked rice. As all households keep careful track of the amount of rice seed they plant and the number of *cavan* they harvest, I believe these data are quite accurate. Of course most swidden systems in Southeast Asia, though dominated by rice, may also produce significant quantities of other cultigens such as root crops, maize, and vegetables. Thus, their total productivity in terms of calories produced per hectare may be different than the figures discussed in the text. I use rice as the measure of productivity because (1) in most swidden systems in the region rice is clearly the dominant crop; (2) it is much more difficult to develop accurate data on the yields of other cultigens, especially root crops (I was unable to collect sufficient data for an accurate estimate); and (3) there are almost no reliable sources of data on the yields of non-rice crops in Southeast Asia that could be used for comparison.

Table 1. Estimated Labor Expenditures for Short Fallow Swidden and Rainy Season Irrigated Rice Production in Napsaan, 1981

Swidden labor[a]	Ave. hrs/Ha	Irrigation labor[a]	Ave. hrs/Ha
Field preparation	150	*Field preparation*	310
Slashing vegetation	140	Clear canals	10
Burning vegetation	10	Harrow/plow	300
Planting	145	*Planting*	410
		Seedbed	10
		Transplanting	400
Field maintenance	390	*Field maintenance*	10
Weeding #1	135	Water management	10
Weeding #2	245		
Guarding	10		
Harvesting	140	*Harvesting*	320
Field harvest	105	Field harvest	250
Carry/thresh/dry	35	Carry/thresh/dry	70
Total	825		1050

[a] See footnote 3 for details of labor data methodology. Walking times to fields not calculated, but typically it is less than 5 minutes.

that they need to complete two tedious weedings of the field during the growing season to achieve the best possible yields.

Guarding the maturing crops from animal pests, reported to be a time consuming activity among some forest fallow cultivators such as the Hanunoo (Conklin, 1957), is not a significant task today in Napsaan. Many fields are now located at a distance from forest boundaries and are less prone to animal predation than in the past. Even fields cleared close to the forest edge, where monkeys and wild pig remain a hazard, are rarely guarded with any diligence, though a few farmers employ "pig bombs" to kill marauding wild pigs. Despite the lack of crop protection practices, farmers reported no significant losses to animal pests during 1980–1981.

Finally, the labor required for the harvesting, threshing, winnowing, drying, and storage of the rice, though it varies from year to year, also declines with short fallow production simply because yields are significantly lower than with long fallow cultivation. Table 1 summarizes the labor requirements of Napsaan short fallow swidden rice production. The data exclude any work carried out solely on nonrice crops (e.g., planting sweet potatoes).[3]

---

[3]Data on the labor costs per hectare for each task in the swidden and irrigation cycle in Table 1 were calculated as follows. The total area covered by a group of workers as they carried out a task was calculated using a tape measure at the end of the day. This area measurement was then divided by the total number of person-hours of labor invested. The average hr/ha was then estimated, based on 5–15 such measurements of each task.

In terms of efficiency, the returns to labor in Napsaan swiddens averaged 0.8 kg of rice/hr over the two-year period. In 1980, a year with good rainfall, returns were 0.93 kg/hr. In the poor rainfall year of 1981, returns fell to only 0.67 kg/hr (Table 2). Though reliable data are difficult to find, these figures for Napsaan rice swiddens are much lower than the very high efficiency believed possible in long fallow production, with estimates as high as 2.25 kg of rice/hr (Bronson, 1972, cited in Cohen, 1989, p. 171).

ADOPTION OF IRRIGATED RICE PRODUCTION

With the decline of swidden yields, some households in Napsaan have responded by developing permanent irrigated rice fields. After a slow expansion in the early 1970s, when only a few farmers had small *basakan* (irrigated fields), the number of irrigated rice fields grew rapidly in the second half of the decade, reaching a total of 13 households (20% of total) by 1980. Five of the *basakan* were operated by Tagbanua families, the remainder by Visayans who had migrated from the central Philippines, where irrigated rice production is widespread.

Reflecting their recent development, all of the irrigated rice fields in Napsaan are relatively small and technologically unsophisticated. During 1980–1981, the largest area planted to wet rice was 1.03 ha. The average field size in the rainy season was only .64 ha. In the dry season, when portions of some *basakan* cannot be irrigated because of lack of water, the average field size fell to .56 ha. This compares to an average swidden size in Napsaan of just over one hectare per household (Table 2).[4]•

All of the fields are irrigated by short, hand-excavated canals connected either to small nearby streams or to ponds that were developed by constructing simple earthen dams. Although small hand-operated tractors are fairly common on more prosperous farms located on the east coast of Palawan, mechanization has yet to reach Napsaan. All land preparation is carried out by human labor and the use of water buffalo. Farmers continue to rely for the most part on locally made tools, though some own a metal shovel, plow, or harrow purchased in the city. Napsaan *basakan* farmers have begun to plant improved "green revolution" varieties of rice, but typically they use early strains that have since been superseded elsewhere in

---

[4]The average size of swidden fields reported in the text and Table 2 was determined by carefully measuring a sample of 15 fields and noting the amount of rice seed planted (in *ganta*, equal to 1.7 kg), a figure that each household carefully measures. Based on these data, the size of fields not physically measured was estimated by collecting data on the number of *ganta* planted in each field. The size of all irrigated fields was directly calculated using a tape measure.

Table 2. Estimated Inputs, Yields, Efficiency, and Cash Returns for Napsaan Swidden vs. Dry and Rainy Season Irrigated Rice

	Swidden			Irrigation		
	1980 (n = 21)	1981 (n = 35)	Ave.	Dry (n = 6)	Rainy (n = 6)	Ave.
Field size (ha)	1.17	1.08	1.12	.56	.64	.60
Labor inputs[a] (hrs/ha)	897	826	862	1274	1050	1162
Gross yield (kg/ha)	836	556	696	1809	1080	1445
Gross labor efficiency (kg/hr)	.93	.67	.81	1.42	1.03	1.24
Net yield[b] (kg/ha)	736	489	613	1263	818	1040
Gross cash returns[c] (pesos/ha)	—	—	605	—	—	1256
Cash costs[d] (pesos/ha)	—	—	90	—	—	290
Net cash returns (pesos/ha)	—	—	515	—	—	966
Net cash labor efficiency (pesos/hr)	—	—	.60	—	—	.83

[a] Labor inputs are total of household labor combined with non-household exchange, share, and wage labor. Measured only for 1981 swidden and 1981 rainy irrigated seasons. Labor for 1980 swidden and 1980–1981 dry season irrigation are estimates based on increased harvest and post-harvest labor required to process larger yield in these two seasons. See Table 1 and footnote 3 for methodology.
[b] Net yield is gross yield minus the proportion of harvest paid to non-household workers, primarily for share labor. See footnote 2 for yield methodology.
[c] Gross cash value is farm gate sale price of the gross yield calculated at local sale price of 50 pesos per cavan of threshed rice (57.5 kg). U.S. $1.00 = 8 pesos.
[d] Cash costs are for wage labor hired plus costs of chemical fertilizer and pesticides for irrigation.

the Philippines by more productive and pest-resistant varieties. The use of chemical fertilizers and pesticides is still limited.[5]

After the water delivery canals have been cleaned of debris and the field prepared for planting by plowing and harrowing, the 3–4-week-old rice seedlings are transplanted into the field from nearby seed beds. During the rainy season (late May to December) field preparation and transplanting are usually accomplished between June and early August, after the swidden rice fields have been planted. After the rice is transplanted, relatively little labor is normally required in the *basakan* because the constant supply of water controls most weed growth. The main tasks are to patch occasional breaks in the bunds at the edge of the fields and repair any damage caused by heavy rains. The irrigated rice harvest normally takes place from mid-November to early December. The rice is then hauled from the field, threshed to remove the grain from the stalk, winnowed to separate the chaff from the grain, dried in the sun, and placed in bags for storage. Table 1 summarizes the total labor costs of *basakan* rice production during the 1981 rainy season, which averaged 1050 hrs/ha (see footnote 3 for methodology).

At the conclusion of the rainy season harvest, most farmers immediately prepare the *basakan* for a second dry season crop. This second crop is ideally planted between mid-December and early January. If planted on time, the second rice crop benefits from another month or so of rain before the dry season starts in earnest in late January or early February. The sequence and timing of dry season labor tasks is basically the same as described for the rainy season.

Based on limited comparative data from Southeast Asia, the labor input of just over 1000 hrs/ha for irrigated rice in Napsaan falls within the mid-range of labor requirements for nonmechanized, transplanted wet rice production involving the use of the plow for land preparation. Moerman (1968: 206) calculated an expenditure of only 99 days of labor per ha in northern Thailand, while Gourou reported as many as 200 days labor in a similar irrigated system in the Red River delta of Vietnam (1940, cited in Moerman 1968: 206). Ruthenberg, citing two case studies from Thailand

[5]The simple technology employed in Napsaan *basakan* and the paucity of chemical inputs indicates that the stimulus of external factors such as government development programs and the technology of the green revolution have been relatively unimportant for understanding the process of agricultural intensification. Likewise, despite the road connection to Puerto Princesa City in the early 1970s, market incentives also do not appear to be important for explaining the adoption of irrigated rice. In 1981, while commodities such as cashew and bananas were increasingly produced for the market, rice was very rarely sold by Napsaan farmers.

and Sri Lanka, reports a labor requirement of between 825 and 1998 hrs/ha for comparable irrigation systems (1976: 190).

Rice yields in Napsaan irrigated fields ranged from an average of 1080 kg/ha in the 1981 rainy season to more than 1800 kg/ha in the 1980 dry season. Thus, irrigated rice production is roughly twice as productive as short fallow rice cultivation in Napsaan.

ADVANTAGES OF IRRIGATED RICE PRODUCTION

Efficiency

The experience of Napsaan farmers as they make the transition from swidden to irrigated rice production helps to clarify the mechanism by which agricultural intensification takes place, as well as its impact on the quality of life. My data indicate that, contrary to Boserup, irrigation is both more productive and more efficient than short fallow swidden cultivation. Gross *basakan* yields are double those typically achieved by swidden rice production, averaging 1445 kg/ha. While the labor efficiency of swidden rice in Napsaan averaged only .81 kg of rice/hr of labor in 1980 and 1981, irrigation during the same period produced returns of 1.24 kg/hr (Table 2).

Labor, of course, is not the only input that must be considered in evaluating the costs and productivity of irrigated rice farming in Napsaan. More so than for swidden cultivation, irrigated rice generally requires a cash investment in the hiring of nonhousehold laborers and, in some cases, the purchase of small quantities of chemical fertilizer and pesticide. Laborers who help in land preparation and transplanting are sometimes paid in cash, but they may also be remunerated with a share of the crop after the harvest is complete.

Even considering the greater cash costs of irrigation, *basakan* rice production remains significantly more efficient than short fallow swidden cultivation in Napsaan. The average cash costs of irrigated production (290 pesos/ha) are more than three times the costs of swidden cultivation (90 pesos/ha). Nonetheless, efficiency calculated in terms of cash returns to labor (the net cash labor efficiency in Table 2, or the cash returns if the crop was sold, after deducting production costs, divided by the total labor inputs) remains almost 40% higher.

I believe irrigation is the more efficient production system for two reasons. First, as indicated earlier, short fallow swidden cultivation in the Napsaan environment has led to precariously low yields, well below the production levels of long fallow cultivation. By comparison, the transition to irrigation permits significant increases in yield. Second, the image of irrigation as a technique that requires endless hours of labor, as popularized in Geertz's (1963) description of the involuted production system of Java and argued by Boserup (1965: 39–40), may be misleading. Small-scale irrigation (the type of system appropriately compared to short fallow swiddening) can produce good yields with relatively low labor requirements. As a result, from the vantage point of farmers calculating costs and benefits at the point of transition, irrigation provides a clearly more efficient and attractive option (cf. Bronson, 1972; Barlett, 1976, 1982).

Reliability and Farm Diversity

Efficiency is not the only factor that motivates Napsaan farmers to adopt irrigation. Irrigation also provides increased reliability compared to swidden farming and maintains a high level of farm diversity as well. One reason that irrigation is more reliable than swidden rice production is that the constant supply of water in irrigated fields provides protection against the effects of drought and controls most weed species. This reduces the year-to-year fluctuations in yield characteristic of rainfed swidden cultivation (Ruthenberg, 1976: 171). Swidden rice fields generally can tolerate no more than 20 days without rain before suffering serious damage (Moormann and Breemen, 1978: 33) while irrigated fields, in contrast, can remain productive even during prolonged periods without precipitation.

Furthermore, as Napsaan farmers are keenly aware, irrigation has the added advantage of permitting the production of two, rather than only one, crop of rice each year. While swidden production of rice is largely confined to the single long rainy season (a few farmers attempt to cultivate small dry season swiddens of maize and root crops), irrigated rice can be produced with confidence during the dry season. This increases the reliability of the household supply of grain, reducing or eliminating altogether the shortages of rice that plague many Napsaan farmers who rely solely on swiddens for their subsistence (Ruthenberg, 1976: 171).[6]

With an average swidden size of 1.1 ha and yields of only 700 kg of rice/ha in 1980–1981, the typical Napsaan swidden produces enough rice to feed a family for only about six months after the harvest. At this point,

---

[6]While this is true for irrigated farming in general, it should be noted that in Napsaan the simple design of the water delivery system sometimes results in crop losses in irrigated fields during extended periods of drought, when portions of some fields dry up entirely. Nonetheless, the damage inflicted on the rice crop by the August 1981 drought appeared to be much less serious in irrigated fields than in rainfed upland fields.

swidden households must buy rice or, if they have inadequate income, borrow it from better-off farmers. In the "hunger" months before the August–September harvest season, women in poor swidden households often spend hours each week visiting relatives and neighbors attempting to borrow rice to feed their families. A common form of loan is the *timpuan,* in which the borrower promises to repay the lender with a portion of the next harvest. Typically, a loan of one sack of rice is repaid with two sacks at harvest time, an interest rate of 100% over a period of 2–6 months.

Reflecting their more secure production system, members of households with irrigation rarely need to borrow or purchase rice. Moreover, irrigation farmers are unlikely to lose a portion of their harvest to debt repayment. I have no record of any rice harvested from an irrigated field being used to repay a *timpuan* debt. Likewise, in a sample of 7 irrigated households only 1 (14%) lost any of its harvest from supplemental swidden fields in 1981 to debt repayment. In contrast, of 26 households depending solely on shifting cultivation for rice production, 11 (42%) reported forfeiting a portion of their swidden harvests to fulfill *timpuan* obligations. These debt payments accounted for 12% of their total harvest.

In addition to its greater reliability, irrigation in Napsaan has also led to greater, not less, farm diversity. Cohen argues that the move from swidden production with extensive intercropping to intensive permanent cultivation, often focusing on a single crop such as irrigated rice, typically results in a loss of diversity and a greater risk of crop failure (1989: 55–67). While the risks of low diversity he describes may indeed be real for long-established, intensive irrigation systems in very populous areas of Southeast Asia, I found the opposite to be the case with the small-scale irrigation system adopted by Napsaan farmers. Farmers using irrigation maintain diversity by concentrating rice production in a small area of the farm, freeing the remainder of the holding for a variety of other uses, including tree crop production and continued shifting cultivation.

Typical farm size is now between 3–7 ha in the community. For many farmers, tree crops such as coconut, banana, and cashew, sources of both food and cash, compete with swidden production for the limited land area. With reliance on swidden rice, farmers must leave much of their land fallow as part of the 2–4 year field rotation. The competing demands of tree orchards and shifting cultivation were apparent during 1981. At least a half dozen swiddens in the community were cleared in still immature orchards of coconut, banana, and cashew because no other suitable land was available to the household. Though tree crops, especially coconut, can sometimes survive swidden fires that do not burn too intensely, at best the fires seriously delay the maturation of the orchards. In other cases, tree crops are simply lost and must be replanted, provided suitable land can be found.

Tree orchards are more compatible with a land-use pattern involving irrigated rice farming. Irrigation focuses the production of rice on low-lying soils, where farmers say fruit trees do not do well anyway. This leaves upland areas free for the production of tree crops. In addition, because irrigated farming is more productive in terms of yield-per-hectare than shifting cultivation, and because it does not require a fallow rotation, less land is needed for rice production and more can be devoted to tree crops. For these reasons, even if their total land holdings are the same size, households with irrigated fields have more land available for tree crop farming than farmers who rely solely on shifting cultivation for the production of rice.

Irrigation in Napsaan also maintains diversity because it is not an exclusive method of rice production. All irrigated households also cultivate swiddens—though typically these are smaller in size than in the past. This permits the production of additional rice during the rainy season, as well as secondary swidden crops such as sweet potato, cassava, and vegetables that are important for the maintenance of a balanced diet. Figure 1 shows the complex and diversified land use of one typical irrigated rice farm household in Napsaan.

The timing of irrigation labor is generally compatible with the swidden labor cycle so that farmers are able to maintain both cropping systems simultaneously without serious scheduling conflicts. While there is some overlap in the timing of labor requirements in the two systems, the periods of *peak* labor demand do not coincide. Land preparation and the transplanting of the rainy season irrigated rice occur after the period of intense labor in early May when swidden fields are planted. The heavy labor demand of the swidden rice harvest occurs from late August to early October when little labor is required to maintain the maturing rice in the irrigated fields. The harvest of the rainy season irrigated crop and the planting of the dry *basakan* take place in November through January, when little swidden labor is required. The harvest of the dry season irrigated fields is normally completed in April, before it is time to begin planting the next year's rice swidden.

WHO ADOPTS IRRIGATION?

The adoption of irrigation in Napsaan has been gradual and not all families have participated in the transition. Barlett's study of the intensification of agriculture in Paso, Costa Rica (1976, 1982) makes the astute observation that the pressure on land resources exerted by growing population density may not be felt equally within the community because of

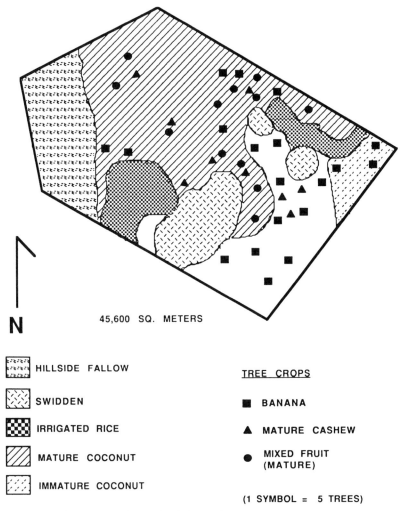

Figure 1. Land use pattern integrating irrigated rice, shifting cultivation, and tree crops.

differences in size of land holding. Rather, she argues, households with small parcels will be the first to experience land scarcity in the form of reduced yields of maize and beans in their overworked and infertile swidden fields. Larger, well-to-do farmers, in contrast, are able to maintain a sufficient fallow period, as well as high levels of productivity and labor efficiency in their swidden system.

As a result of these differences, only households with small land holdings in Paso have been motivated to intensify production by the adoption of permanent terraced fields in which maize and beans are grown in combination with tobacco. For these farmers, as in Napsaan, intensification results in an increase in labor efficiency. Large landowners in Paso, on the other hand, have for the most part not adopted the intensive terraced agriculture because for them it would result in a decline in the efficiency of their labor.

Can we expect this pattern of early innovation by farmers with the smallest land holdings to be a key for understanding the mechanism of agricultural intensification in general? The experience of Napsaan settlers suggests that this is not necessarily the case. In Napsaan, though there is not yet dramatic inequality in the size of land holdings, it has been primarily the households with larger farms (about 5 ha or more) that have made the transition to irrigated rice cultivation.

One reason for this pattern of intensification in Napsaan is that historically the larger farm households have removed a considerable portion of their land from the swidden rotation by planting tree crops such as coconut along the coastline, and cashew and bananas farther inland. As a result, like small farmers, these large-farm holders also often find themselves with insufficient land for swidden rice production, and suffer as well from short fallow periods and low yields. Thus, like the households with little land, they also feel the incentive to intensify rice production.

If all households are experiencing similar difficulties with their short fallow swidden system, why has the adoption of irrigation been undertaken primarily by large farmers in Napsaan? The reason appears to be a factor not emphasized by Barlett in her study of Paso—the establishment costs of developing permanent agriculture. Since irrigation requires access to a water buffalo and control over sufficient labor to transform swidden land into the completely cleared, flat, and bunded fields needed for permanent rice cultivation, these costs may be significant.

It is possible to work an irrigated field with a borrowed or rented water buffalo, but this can be risky if the animal is not available when it is really needed. Purchasing a mature water buffalo is very expensive, costing over P2000 ($250). In fact, most households that own a plow animal did not buy it as an adult. Rather, they typically purchase a much less expensive young buffalo and wait for it to mature. Sometimes they obtain an animal by agreeing to take on the expense and labor of feeding and maintaining a neighbor's buffalo for a year or two in return for the right to one of its future offspring. These alternate methods of obtaining livestock greatly reduce the cost of acquiring a water buffalo for irrigated rice production.[7]

A second difficulty in establishing an irrigated rice field is the time and expense required to clear and level the land, establish the irrigation system, build canals, and construct the berms surrounding each individual portion of the larger field. One young farmer, who kept a written record of the work put into his field, reported spending approximately 400 hours to open up his first *basakan* of only .05 ha in 1981. Except for hiring a neighbor who did the initial plowing of the new field with his buffalo, the field owner and his unmarried adult siblings performed all the necessary work.

Though this newly established *basakan* was exceptionally productive, the high labor costs of establishing the field reduced the gross labor efficiency in the first year of production to only .60 kg of rice/hr. This is less than half the average efficiency for established *basakan* and lower than the typical return of about .81 kg/hr for swidden rice cultivation. Thus, the greater efficiency made possible by the transition to irrigated farming cannot be achieved in the first few years while a field is being developed. The farmer must be able to defer gaining the full benefits of irrigation until the *basakan* is completely established. The intensity of labor required to initially develop an irrigated field helps to explain why many families who own irrigable land have not yet been able to establish a *basakan*.

Because of these establishment costs, unlike in the case of Paso studied by Barlett, irrigation has been adopted first in Napsaan primarily by larger farmers with a greater ability to take on the costs of a water buffalo and command the necessary labor. A socioeconomic survey that measured the quality and size of houses, ownership of household items such as lanterns and radios, and possession of productive equipment (Conelly, 1983), indicates that all *basakan* households are in either the upper (54%) or middle (46%) income categories. In most cases, *basakan* are also owned by more mature households in which grown children are able to contribute a significant amount of the labor needed to open up and maintain the irrigated fields.

---

[7]Boserup also argues that the labor expenditures and cost of fodder to maintain plow animals should be included in calculations of efficiency for permanent agriculture such as irrigation. This is certainly true in many highly intensive systems with severe land scarcity. In Napsaan, however, the maintenance of water buffalo is not a major cost because considerable fallow land and fodder are still freely available. The animals are normally simply tethered near the home either to graze on the scrub vegetation or wallow in ponds or mud holes. The labor requirements for this system of livestock management are not onerous and much of the work such as tethering can be carried out by children. Data from a year-long time allocation survey indicate that adults in households with irrigation spend an average of less than 10 minutes per day caring for animals (Conelly, 1983). Thus, I argue that at the early stages of transition to small-scale irrigation, animal maintenance costs do not significantly alter the overall efficiency of the system.

Security of land tenure is another factor that may influence the adoption of irrigated farming. When the settlers first arrived in Napsaan they were viewed by the government as illegal squatters and thus had no legal title to the parcel of land they were farming. In the 1960s, however, many households in the community began to petition the government for titles of ownership based on the planting of "permanent" tree crops, such as coconut and cashew. By 1981, only seven of the thirteen households with irrigation had successfully obtained a title and were recorded as taxpayers by the Land Assessor's Office in Puerto Princesa City. All of the remaining *basakan* households were still in the process of applying for title to their land. Thus, secure title does not appear to have been a prerequisite for developing a *basakan*. Rather, the opening up of an irrigated field could be viewed as a strategy, like planting permanent tree crops, for eventually securing a legal title to the land and increasing security of tenure.

DISCUSSION AND CONCLUSION

What then does the experience of agricultural intensification by Napsaan farmers say about Boserup's model? I believe that, in the long run, if we compare forest fallow swiddens to permanent irrigated agriculture, there is strong evidence to support Boserup's claim that labor efficiency declines. This long-term view, however, does not help us understand the actual mechanism by which more intensive technology is adopted; nor does it properly characterize the relationship at the point of transition between short fallow swidden production and the early stages of small-scale irrigation (the point at which farmers actually make the calculation concerning the costs and benefits of intensification). From this vantage point, irrigation provides an option that improves, rather than lowers, the efficiency of their labor.

Based on data in Table 2, Figure 2 summarizes the argument. Beginning from a presumed high level of efficiency for long fallow swidden cultivation, Boserup posits a steady decline in returns to labor as the farming system moves to short fallow and then to permanent techniques of cultivation. By contrast, the Napsaan data indicate that land scarcity leads initially to a precipitous decline in yields and efficiency with the forced adoption of short fallow swidden production. As new irrigated fields are opened, farmers suffer a further temporary decline in returns to labor because of the high establishment costs of irrigation. After these establishment costs are absorbed in the first few years, however, *basakan* farmers enjoy clearly improved efficiency compared to short fallow swidden pro-

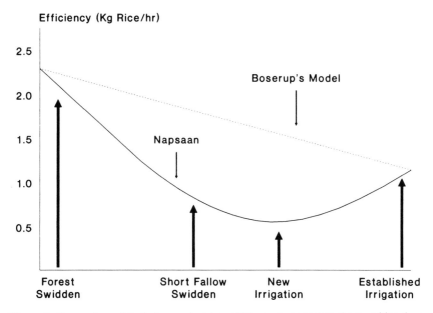

Figure 2. Boserup's model of changes in labor efficiency compared to the transition from swidden agriculture to irrigation in Napsaan.

duction. This helps explain their willingness to adopt irrigation despite its increased labor demands. Nonetheless, the efficiency of irrigated production remains lower than that of traditional *long* fallow swidden production.[8]

A similar argument can be made concerning changes in crop diversity and quality of diet as farmers move from long fallow through short fallow to irrigated production. As argued by Cohen, the initial high diversity and productivity of long fallow swidden production, combined with continued exploitation of wild resources, would typically result in a highly diverse and reliable diet. With short fallow production, as in the case of Napsaan, yields decline, while at the same time diversity may be lost because most land must be held in reserve as fallow for future production. In addition, the

---

[8]I intentionally separate establishment costs in the first years from a discussion of the efficiency of irrigation once the fields are established. It would be possible to average or amortize the establishment costs of irrigation into the overall efficiency of the system over a 10–20 year period. This, however, would not accurately reflect the experience of farmers who must typically absorb the added labor costs of establishment in the first few years of production. Therefore Figure 2, I believe, represents a realistic view of actual changes in labor efficiency, with an initial decline in the first few years because of the establishment costs followed by a significant increase once the *basakan* is fully developed.

availability of wild food resources is reduced because of population increase in the region. With short fallow production, swiddening as a viable subsistence system has collapsed and food scarcity and a decline in the diversity and quality of diet can be expected.

At this point of collapse in the farming system, however, I argue that irrigation, at least in the near term, reverses the trend and provides increased reliability and crop diversity. Irrigation permits the production of a dependable second rice crop each year and improves the security of cultivation by providing an artificial source of water to maintain soil fertility and protect against drought. At the same time, because irrigation concentrates production of the staple rice crop in a small field and eliminates the need to maintain large areas of fallow, it permits a more diverse use of the farm parcel. Irrigation farmers in Napsaan are able to cultivate supplemental swiddens and develop large tree orchards on their non-irrigated land (once needed as part of the fallow rotation). This diverse land use pattern provides the family with both a source of cash income and a balanced, high quality diet.[9]

Initially then, the adoption of small-scale irrigation in Napsaan has been a rational decision for farmers and has led to an improved standard of living, whether measured in terms of labor efficiency or farm diversity. This case study suggests that we need to see agricultural intensification as being more complex than an inevitable process of decline in the quality of life. It also indicates the importance of observing the process of intensification as it occurs in particular farming systems rather than developing models that compare agricultural systems that may be widely separated in time and space.

There is also the risk, however, of focusing analysis too narrowly and failing to see the long-term processes that Boserup and Cohen are ultimately attempting to explain. Based on the experience of irrigated production systems elsewhere in Southeast Asia, it is reasonable to expect that eventually the adoption of irrigation in Napsaan could lead to the negative consequences that they predict. As population densities continue to increase in the community, the growth of irrigation at the expense of other, currently complementary, land uses could indeed lead to a loss of diversity in the diet. In addition, increased reliance on monocropping of rice often

---

[9]These claims about the maintenance of adequate nutrition despite intensification are supported by limited data collected on diet intake and anthropometric measurements of children in Napsaan. Records of household food consumption by a representative sample of households over a 9 month period indicate that families with *basakan* enjoy better than average diets by community standards. Likewise, anthropometric measurements show that preschool age children in irrigated households are less likely to suffer from malnutrition than children from households that rely solely on swiddening for their food production (Conelly, 1983).

results in growing insect pest problems (Litsinger and Moody, 1976; Marten, 1986) that require greater dependence on costly pesticides. Likewise, as irrigated fields are used over long periods of time, fertility typically declines, requiring increased labor expenditures and the cost of chemical fertilizers to maintain yields. When these additional long-term costs that accompany intensive irrigation are calculated, the future efficiency of Napsaan irrigation may fall from its current levels.

In the near-term calculation of farmers concerned with the capacity of the land to support their families, however, irrigation appears to promise a better future. It is from their perspective that we can come to a more complete understanding of the mechanism by which agricultural intensification takes place and its impact on the quality of life.

ACKNOWLEDGMENTS

I am especially grateful to Luis Dulce, Tingting Fulgarines, Galon Gansing, Venancio Israel, and Rudy Sublemente for their assistance in my research on swidden farming and irrigation in Napsaan. I also want to thank Miriam Chaiken, Steve Sanderson, and the several anonymous reviewers who made many helpful suggestions for improving this paper. The research was partially funded by the Institute for Intercultural Study and the University of California, Santa Barbara.

REFERENCES

Anderson, D. M. (1989). Agriculture and irrigation technology at Lake Baringo in the nineteenth century. *Azania* 24: 71–83.
Barlett, P. F. (1976). Labor efficiency and the mechanism of agricultural evolution. *Journal of Anthropological Research* 32: 124–140.
Barlett, P. F. (1982). *Agricultural Choice and Change: Decision Making in a Costa Rican Community.* Rutgers University Press, New Brunswick, New Jersey.
Boserup, E. (1965). *The Conditions of Agricultural Growth: The Economics of Agrarian Change Under Population Pressure.* Aldine Publishing Company, Chicago.
Bronson, B. (1972). Farm labour and the evolution of food production. In Spooner, B. (ed.), *Population Growth: Anthropological Implications.* MIT Press, Cambridge, Massachusetts.
Clarke, W. C. (1966). From extensive to intensive shifting cultivation: A succession from New Guinea. *Ethnology* 5: 347–359.
Cohen, M. N. (1989). *Health and the Rise of Civilization.* Yale University Press, New Haven.
Conelly, W. T. (1983). *Upland Development in the Tropics: Alternative Economic Strategies in a Philippine Frontier Community.* Ph.D Thesis, University of California, Santa Barbara.
Conelly, W. T. (1985). Copal and rattan collecting in the Philippines. *Economic Botany* 39: 39–46.

Conelly, W. T. (1989). Ethnicity, economic choice, and inequality in a Philippine frontier community. In Chaiken, M.S. and Fleuret, A.K. (eds.), *Social Change and Applied Anthropology: Essays in Honor of David W. Brokensha*. Westview Press, Boulder.

Conklin, H. C. (1957). *Hanunoo Agriculture: A Report on an Integral System of Shifting Cultivation in the Philippines*. FAO, Forestry Development Paper #12, Rome.

Eder, J. F. (1977). Agricultural intensification and the returns to labour in the Philippine swidden system. *Pacific Viewpoint* 8: 1–21.

Eder, J. F. (1990). *After Deforestation: Migrant Lowland Farmers in the Philippines*. Paper presented at the Annual Meeting of the American Anthropological Association, New Orleans.

Geertz, C. (1963). *Agricultural Involution: The Processes of Ecological Change in Indonesia*. University of California Press, Berkeley.

Gourou, P. (1945). *L'utilization du Sol en Indochine Francaise*. (Translated by S.H. Guest). Institute of Pacific Relations, New York.

Hakansson, T. (1989). Social and political aspects of intensive agriculture in East Africa: Some models from cultural anthropology. *Azania* 24: 12–20.

Harris, M. (1988). *Culture, People, Nature* (5th ed.). Harper and Row, New York.

Litsinger, J. A. and Moody, K. (1976). Integrated pest management in multiple cropping systems. In *Multiple Cropping*, American Agronomy Society, Special Publication #27.

Lopez, M. E. (1987). The politics of lands at risk in a Philippine frontier. In Little, P. D. and Horowitz, M. M. (eds.), *Lands at Risk in the Third World: Local Level Perspectives*. Westview Press, Boulder, pp. 230–248.

Marten, G. G. (ed.) (1986). *Traditional Agriculture in Southeast Asia: A Human Ecology Perspective*. Westview Press, Boulder.

Moerman, M. (1968). *Agricultural Change and Peasant Choice in a Thai Village*. University of California Press, Berkeley.

Moorman, F. R. and van Breemen, N. (1978). *Rice: Soil, Water, Land*. International Rice Research Institute, Los Banos, Philippines.

National Economic and Development Authority (NEDA) (1980). *Philippine Statistical Yearbook*. Republic of the Philippines, National Economic Development Authority, Manila.

Netting, R. M. (1985). *Population Pressure and Intensification: Some Anthropological Reflections on Malthus, Marx, and Boserup*. Paper Presented at the Annual Meeting of the American Anthropological Association.

Padoch, C. (1985). Labor efficiency and intensity of land use in rice production: An example from Kalimantan. *Human Ecology* 13: 271–289.

Ruthenberg, H. (1976). *Farming Systems in the Tropics*. Clarendon Press, Oxford.

Schlegel, S. A. (1979). *Tiruray Subsistence: From Shifting Cultivation to Plow Agriculture*. Ateneo de Manila Press, Quezon City, Philippines.

Schlegel, S. A. (1983). Tiruray traditional and peasant subsistence: A comparison. In Olofson, H. (ed.), *Adaptive Strategies and Change in Philippine Swidden-Based Societies*. Forest Research Institute College, Laguna, Philippines, pp. 105–116.

Simon, J. (1983). The effects of population on nutrition and economic well-being. In Rotberg, R. I. and Rabb, T. K. (eds.), *Hunger and History: The Impact of Changing Food Production and Consumption Patterns on Society*. Cambridge University Press, Cambridge, pp. 215–239.

Spooner, B. (1972). *Population Growth*. MIT Press, Cambridge, Massachusetts.

Stone, G. D., Netting, R. M. and Stone, M. P. (1990). Seasonality, labor scheduling, and agricultural intensification in the Nigerian savanna. *American Anthropologist* 92: 7–23.

Waddell, E. (1972). *The Mound Builders: Agricultural Practices, Environment, and Society in the Central Highlands of New Guinea*. University of Washington Press, Seattle.

13

Seventeenth-Century Organic Agriculture in China

Wen Dazhong and David Pimentel

The quest for sustainable, high-yield agriculture which is not dependent on costly and polluting artificial inputs has occupied a number of ecologists and agricultural development experts over the past two decades. Wen Dazhong and David Pimentel offer a contribution by looking to China's past using documentation from the seventeenth century relating to Zhejiang province. They examine a number of different techniques, including crop rotation, paddy rice production using either fertilization by compost or green manure, winter crops, mulberry-silkworm production, and livestock. The authors were able to discover documentation providing quantitative figures for a great variety of inputs and yields, and can trace quantitatively the energy flows through the systems described. This study is unusual for the degree of precision in numerical data it is able to provide, offering us a window on the past and an alternative to experimentation for the discovery of

This chapter is a synthesis of two articles that were published in *Human Ecology: An Interdisciplinary Journal* under the titles "Seventeenth-Century Organic Agriculture in China: I. Cropping Systems in Jiaxing Region" (14[1][1986]: 1–14) and "Seventeenth-Century Organic Agriculture in China: II. Energy Flows through and Agroecosystem in Jiaxing Region" (14[1][1986]: 15–18).

Wen Dazhong, Institute of Applied Ecology, Chinese Academy of Sciences, P.O. Box 416, Shenyang, China.   **David Pimentel,** New York State College of Agriculture and Life Sciences, Cornell University, Ithaca, New York 14853.

Case Studies in Human Ecology, edited by Daniel G. Bates and Susan H. Lees. Plenum Press, New York, 1996.

beneficial techniques of agriculture. With this information at hand, farmers in the region have a better basis to decide whether to attempt to apply techniques that were useful in the past, knowing the requirements, and the outcome.

INTRODUCTION

China has a long history of agriculture, starting about 6000–7000 years ago. Over this period the Chinese people have evolved various agricultural techniques, many of which have led to a stable, productive agriculture. Fortunately, several scholars investigated and recorded the early history of Chinese agriculture. *Shen's Agricultural Book (Shenshi Nongshu),* also called *Supplementary Agricultural Book (Bu Nongshu),* in particular, provides a careful assessment of agricultural practices in the Jiaxing region of Zhejiang province from the end of the Ming dynasty to the beginning of the Qing Dynasty (1640–1660) (Chen Hengli, 1958). No precise data were given for the seventeenth-century agricultural practices in the Jiaxing region; however, some valuable information was presented in *Shen's Agricultural Book* and other references. Also, based on facts presented in some of the reference material, we were able to make some numerical estimations for this early agriculture.

Because of the growing need to make agriculture more sustainable, a careful assessment is made here of the seventeenth-century agricultural practices in Zhejiang province in order to study various techniques that might be of contemporary use. In addition to examining the sustainability of agricultural and resource management, energy flows in the agroecosystem have been analyzed.

China has long been noted for its successful organic agriculture. Since early times Chinese peasants established efficient, high-yielding agroecosystems. These systems relied on managing local natural renewable resources to produce food, fuel, and clothing for human needs. The agroecosystem in the Jiaxing region, Zhejiang province of eastern China during the seventeenth century is an outstanding example of an organic agricultural system. Crop rotations and certain cropping patterns were fundamental to productive agriculture in the Jiaxing region. In order to understand the dynamic relationship that existed among all of the components in the agroecosystem and how these systems functioned, we analyzed the interaction of the various factors that made up this agroecosystem.

POPULATION

Records were available upon which to estimate human population numbers in this region for the seventeenth century, but the census data for that period were reported to be underestimated because many people did not register in order to avoid taxation (Chen Hengli, 1958). However, figures for 1765 taken in a census of Tongxiang county in the Jiaxing region (the birthplace of Zhang Luxiang, one of the authors of *Shen's Agricultural Book*) appear reliable (Chen Hengli, 1958). That county, with 32,603 ha of farmland, had a human population of 253,348 (Yan Chen, 1887), equalling 7.8 people per hectare of farmland. Today in the same region there are 21 people per ha.

LAND USE

At that time, the farmland in Jiaxing region was divided into two parts: *Tian,* the area for growing paddy rice and dryland crops, and *Di,* the area for mulberry plantations (Zhang Luxiang, 1956). In general, the higher land was used for *Di,* and further land was artificially raised by adding soil from pond bottoms. Fish ponds, *Chi,* were made to rear fish and for irrigation. In 1581, the total farmland in Jiaxing region was 287,418 ha. Of this, 256,907 ha was used for *Tian,* about 90% of the total farmland. The remaining 30,511 ha was used for *Di* (Xu Yaoguang, 1879; Chen Hengli, 1958). Clearly, the paddy rice-dryland cropping pattern was the major component in the agroecosystem. No information exists on how large an area was occupied by *Chi,* but it might have been about 30,000 ha, or similar to the *Di* area.

CROP ROTATION

Following the harvest of paddy rice in September and early October, two-thirds of *Tian* area was planted with winter crops like wheat, barley, rape, and beans, while the other third was planted with a green manure crop, Chinese milk vetch (*Astragalus sinious*). The best seeds were saved from each successive harvest of the grain for planting the next crop. The organic fertilizers came from the agroecosystem itself and included human and animal manure and green manure, which was the major nutrient source. In the Jiaxing region there were also a few other cropping systems,

Table 1. Labor Inputs in Compost-Fertilized and Green
Manure-Fertilized Rice Production

	Compost fertilized (hrs/ha)	Green manure fertilized (hrs/ha)
Producing organic fertilizer	760	80
Collecting and applying organic matter and silt from fish ponds	80	80
Tilling	490	490
Applying organic fertilizer and weeding	100	100
Transplanting seedlings	320	320
Weeding; top-dressing	50	50
Irrigation	130	130
Harvesting	400	400
Total	2330	1650

such as the compost-fertilized paddy rice-dryland crop rotation system and the paddy rice-fallow field system. Unfortunately, information on these systems is incomplete, making any analysis of them impossible.

PADDY RICE PRODUCTION

In the seventeenth century in Jiaxing region, rice accounted for nearly 60% of the early grains produced (Zhang Luxiang, 1956). Although rice continues to be an important food today in China today, it accounts for only about 40% of the total nation's grain resources.

While some draft animal power was employed in Chinese agriculture as early as 2000 years ago, rice production in Jiaxing region depended mostly on human labor (Zhang Luxiang, 1956; Chen Hengli, 1958). Farming operations included tilling the soil, spreading manure compost or green manure, seeding and transplanting, weeding, intertilling, top dressing with manure, irrigating, and harvesting, as well as collecting and composting livestock, human, and green manure.

For this analysis, seventeenth-century rice production is divided into two production systems: Compost-fertilized rice and green manure-fertilized rice. According to some information we estimated that the compost-fertilized rice production required 2,330 hours of labor per hectare during the growing season (Table 1). Nearly 760 hours/ha were required just for collecting, processing, and transporting livestock and human manure for use as compost fertilizer. In addition, organic matter and silt containing nutrients were dredged from ponds and streams and added to the paddy field.

In contrast, the green manure-fertilized rice required 1650 hours/ha or 30% less labor than compost-fertilized rice (Table 1). Only 80 hours were required to produce and apply green manure to a hectare of rice. Although green manure significantly reduced the labor inputs per hectare of rice production, an additional 1/3 of a hectare of land was needed to produce the green manure. Usually, the green manure was grown during the winter months. The major green manure crop used in the system was Chinese milk vetch. Milk vetch seeds were broadcast into the paddy just before rice harvest in September, but the seedlings did not develop until after the rice harvest in October. By the following April, the vetch had grown and the plants were turned under in the paddy. Vetch is an excellent green manure; the fresh above-ground vegetation contains 0.33% nitrogen (N), 0.08% phosphorus (P), and 0.23% potassium (K). Milk vetch will produce an average of 22.5 tons per hectare of fresh aboveground vegetation. Generally about 1/3 ha was planted to vetch, and this was sufficient to fertilize the entire hectare with 25 kg of nitrogen.

The labor inputs for the specific tasks involved in producing paddy rice are summarized as follows. First, about 490 hr/ha of labor were employed in tilling and mixing the paddy soil. An iron rake-like tool was used to mix the soils from a depth of 23–27 cm. This depth is more than twice the 10 cm tillage depth achieved using a water buffalo-drawn plow (Chen Hengli, 1958).

After the paddy soil was tilled, 10,000 kg/ha of compost (80% water) or 7,500 kg/ha of fresh Chinese milk vetch (about 70% water) were added to fertilize the crop, and any weeds were pulled and buried in the mud between the rice rows. The application of organic fertilizers and weeding totaled an average of 100 hr/ha of labor. Immediately after weeding, seedling rice plants were transplanted into the paddies. This required 320 hours of labor. Another 50 hr/ha of labor was required to weed again after the plants were well established and growing, and to apply a top-dressing of bean cake and/or rape cake, byproducts of vegetable oil extraction.

The paddy rice was irrigated using a foot water wheel pump. According to one estimate, a pump must be operated by three men for 4 days to irrigate 0.91 hectare of paddy each growing season (Chen Hengli, 1958). This means about 130 hr/ha of labor were devoted to irrigation each season. Harvesting also required a significant labor input, averaging about 400 hr/ha.

Effective weed control plus large inputs of compost or green manure nutrients and ample irrigation resulted in exceptionally high rice yields. According to the seventeenth-century records, average rice yields were about

3900 kg/ha with the highest rice yields ranging between 6700–8400 kg/ha. At present in the Jiaxing region, the average yield of early season rice is 5700 kg/ha, and the average yield of late season rice is 6500 kg/ha, giving a total rice yield per hectare of paddy during the year of 12,200 kg/ha. The 17th-century rice yields also compare favorably with modern rice production technology in Dawa county, in northeastern China, which averages 8100 kg/ha. The highest seventeenth-century yields are also greater than present rice yields in California, which are reported to be about 6500 kg/ha.

Clearly, high rice yields in the Jiaxing region have been maintained for a long time. This suggests that both land and water resources have been managed carefully to maintain the productivity of the land. As described, great care was taken to maintain the soil nutrients as well as the organic matter in the soil by adding either 10,000 kg/ha of composted manure or 7500 kg/ha of green manure each cropping season. In addition, bean or rape cake and pond mud were added to the paddy to augment nutrients and organic matter. The free-living, nitrogen-fixing microorganisms (blue/green algae) grown in the paddies added more nutrients to the soil. However, over the years, valuable nutrients were lost from the agroecosystem in various ways. The harvest of rice and straw from the paddy accounted for a major loss. Denitrification and leaching also caused additional nitrogen loss. An estimate of the soil nutrient budget suggests that the compost system maintained a balance of nutrient inputs and outputs, while the green manure system appeared to have some deficiencies in terms of P and K. However, these deficiencies may have been offset by the slow upward movement of P and K from the deep soil layer.

WINTER CROPS

In the seventeenth century as today in the Jiaxing region, winter crops (called *Chunhua* or "spring flowers") like wheat, barley, rape, and broadbean were planted after the rice harvest and harvested in the early spring. Local maxims at the time stated that "*chunhua* harvests are enough for a half year's food" (Xu Yaoguang, 1879) and "half of the total income in a year is from paddy rice harvests and the other half comes from *chunhua* and silkworms" (Zhang Luxiang, 1956).

Like rice, wheat, one of the major winter crops of the seventeenth century, was also produced entirely by hand. This included tilling, ditching, sowing, fertilizing, weeding, hilling, and harvesting. Based on the wheat yield of 1300 kg/ha, we estimate that about 28 kg/ha of nitrogen were applied with the manure. This would mean that about 9 metric tons of manure (85% moisture) was applied per hectare. However, records show the manure was further diluted with water to ensure it was well distributed when applied to the fields, bringing the moisture content up to approximately 94%. Because the diluting procedure needed the additional labor input, even though the amount of manure used for fertilizing wheat was slightly less than that for fertilizing rice in Jiaxing region, the labor input for collecting and making the diluted manure in wheat production was the same as that for making compost in rice production, i.e., 760 hr/ha.

MULBERRY-SILKWORM SYSTEM

China has more than a 5000-year history of planting mulberry trees and rearing silkworms (sericulture). During the period of the Tang Dynasty and Five Dynasties (from the seventh to the tenth century), sericulture developed rapidly in the Jiaxing region. During the seventeenth century, Jiaxing became a major sericultural area producing high value silk, and today this region remains one of China's most important sericulture areas.

In 1581, about 10% of the total farm land in the Jiaxing region was used to plant mulberry trees (Xu Yaoguang, 1879; Chen Hengli, 1958). Mulberry is a perennial with a life span of 15–30 years. Mulberry tree cultivation includes planting the trees and then providing limited annual maintenance. In the Jiaxing region in the seventeenth century, planting mulberry trees included hilling and planting the seedlings. After three years of growth, the mulberry leaves could be collected from the tree to feed silkworms. The routine maintenance of the trees each year included cultivating the soil in winter and spring, hoeing out weeds, pruning branches, rebuilding drainage systems, fertilizing soils, and controlling pests. All of these tasks were carried out by hand (Zhang Luxiang, 1956).

Unfortunately, there is no recorded information on how many manhours were needed for these individual mulberry tree operations. *Shen's Agricultural Book,* however, did report that each year a full-time peasant could manage 0.5 ha of *Tian* plus 0.25 ha of *Di* or 0.625 ha of *Tian* alone. This suggests that about twice as much labor was needed per hectare of crops compared with mulberry trees, which would thus have required about 1450 hours of labor per hectare per year.

Organic fertilizer inputs in mulberry production included 27,000 kg/ha of composed farmyard refuse as fertilizer plus 30,000 kg/ha of wet manure as top dressing (Zhang Luxiang, 1956). Assuming that 20% of the farmyard refuse was crop residues, the remains of the composted farmyard refuse were water and soil, and wet manure contained 90% water, then the organic fertilizer inputs in mulberry production were equivalent to 5400 kg/ha of crop residues (dry) plus 3000 kg/ha of dry manure each year. In addition, large amounts of silt from ponds and canals were collected and applied to the mulberry plantations each year. Much of this silt originally came from the eroded plantation soil, and so this helped offset the erosion from the plantation.

According to Shen, fresh mulberry leaf yield ranged from 7500–9400 kg/ha, while Zhang Luxiang estimated that mulberry leaf yield was about 10000 kg/ha (Zhang Luxiang, 1956). The average of the two estimates is 9200 kg/ha, which was similar to the yield of 9500 obtained in the region during the 1970s. The leaves were fed to silkworms, and, during the autumn, to sheep. We estimate that the autumn leaf yield was 4600 kg/ha of fresh leaves (1400 kg/ha of dry leaves).

In the seventeenth century, rearing silkworms was done almost entirely by women. On average, 300 hours per woman were required to manage ten *Kuang* (large baskets) of silkworms. It took 1000 kg of mulberry leaves to produce 63 kg of cocoons, which produced 5 kg of silk (Zhang Luxiang, 1956; Chen Hengli, 1958). Thus, each year, each hectare produced 9200 kg of mulberry leaves and about 600 kg of cocoons. This is only 20% below the current cocoon production for this region. During the autumn, one ha of mulberry trees produced 4600 kg of fresh leaves, which is sufficient to feed two sheep.

In addition to the silk output, silkworms eating 9200 kg of mulberry leaves produce about 6000 kg of excrement (70% water) (Zhong Gongfu, 1982).

LIVESTOCK

The livestock system—pigs, sheep, and poultry—was an important component of the Jiaxing agroecosystem because it produced meat for the people and manure needed for crop production. Because all agricultural operations in the seventeenth century were carried out by humans without animal power, it was not necessary to maintain draft animals. The animals were reared by individual peasant families.

With intensive rearing, a pig fed 180 kg of bean or rape cake, or 250 kg of barley, produced about 50 kg of pork during a six-month period (Zhang Luxiang, 1956; Chen Hengli, 1958). Thus, the feed to pork ratio was 5 kcal : 1 kcal. Most pigs were fed several kinds of feed, including chaff and other by-products of grain processing. In addition, the pigs were often fed distillers' grain that was produced as a by-product of an alcoholic drink. Based on the historical reports, we estimate that perhaps a third of the grain harvested was used to make alcohol (Zhang Luxiang, 1956; Chen Hengli and Wang Da, 1983).

Shen's Agricultural Book states that each sheep needed about 800 kg of dry mulberry leaves and hay per year, and produced 1.6 kg of wool plus manure. Assuming the life span of a sheep was 5 years and the mature weight was 40 kg, of which 45% was dressed carcass, then each sheep produced about 3.6 kg of meat each year.

During the seventeenth century, rearing poultry seems to have been done on a small scale, with each peasant family having a few ducks, hens, or geese (Zhang Luxiang, 1956). Because the numbers were so small, the costs and outputs of this endeavor were omitted from this analysis.

Although information sources about seventeenth-century agriculture during this time do not comment on the amount of human labor expended in rearing animals, it is known that women usually cared for the farm animals. We estimated that about 180 hours of labor were expended each year per pig or sheep.

ENERGY FLOWS THROUGH THE AGROECOSYSTEM

In this study, *Shen's Agricultural Handbook* (Zhang Luxiang, 1956) and some local historical chronicles were used to obtain the basic information on the agroecosystem. Before 1840, the economy of the Jiaxing region was self-sustainable, and most people were involved in agriculture (Xu Heyong et al., 1982). We considered the whole region as one agroecosystem and analyzed the following agricultural components: Paddy rice-dryland crop and green manure rotation system, the mulberry-silkworm system, and the animal husbandry system. The energy inputs and outputs in these various systems were investigated, and the relationship between the agroecosystem and the human population of this region was examined.

To illustrate the energy flows through the simplified Jiaxing agroecosystem, data on the outputs/inputs of the various systems previously described are scaled to a hectare unit. Based on the known distribution that 90% of the farmland was *tian* and 10% was *di,* a unit is comprised of 0.9 ha of paddy rice-wheat and green manure and 0.1 ha of mulberry. Other components such as silkworm production, animal husbandry, and human population were also scaled per hectare.

The interrelationship among the components in the agroecosystem are listed in the energy flow chart (Figure 1 and Table 2). Animal manure was the major fertilizer for both crop and mulberry production, and the yield from both areas depended on the organic fertilizers available each growing season. An important purpose of rearing pigs appeared to be to produce manure. In fact, it appears that the farmers did not get much monetary return from rearing pigs (Chen Hengli, 1958). The combined need of the

Table 2. Estimated Energy flows through the Typical Agroecosystem Until in the Jiaxing Region in the Seventeenth Century[a]

Item	Quantity	Energy (kcal)	Numbers shown in Fig. 1
Total photosynthetic active solar radiation[b]	8,000,000,000 kcal	8,000,000,000	
Tian[c]	7,200,000,000 kcal	7,200,000,000	1
Di	800,000,000 kcal	800,000,000	2
Total fossil fuel (tools) input	1.9 kg	39,353	
Tian[c]	1.8 kg	37,282	3
Di[d]	0.1 kg	2,071	4
Total human labor needed	3,756 hr	676,080	5
Tian[c]	2,618 hr	471,420	6
Di[d]	145 hr	26,100	7
Rearing silkworms[e]	290 hr	52,200	8
Rearing pigs[f]	666 hr	119,880	9
Rearing sheep[f]	36 hr	6,480	10
Total human and animal manure	930 kg	4,185,000	11
Tian[c]	630 kg	2,835,000	12
Di[d]	300 kg	1,350,000	13
Local residents[g]	312 kg	1,404,000	14
Sheep[h]	30 kg	135,000	15
Silkworm[e]	180 kg	810,000	16
Pigs[i]	408 kg	1,836,000	17
Total harvested photosynthetic biomass	9,384 kg	33,733,680	
Tian[c]	8,970 kg	31,917,600	18
Crop products[c]	4,290 kg	15,315,300	
Alcoholic drinks and pig fodder[j]	1,430 kg	5,105,100	19
Outside the agroecosystem[k]	83 kg	296,310	20
Seeds[c]	119 kg	424,830	21
Bean cake and rape seed cake used as fertilizers[c]	306 kg	1,092,420	21
Use as food for local residents[l]	2,352 kg	8,396,640	22
Harvested crop residues[c]	4,680 kg	16,602,300	23

Organic fertilizer			
Tian[c]	1,168 kg	4,143,480	24
Di[d]	540 kg	1,915,650	25
Fuel for household[m]	2,972 kg	10,543,170	26
Di	414 kg	1,816,080	27
Mulberry leaves fed			
Silkworms[d]	276 kg	1,210,720	28
Sheep[d]	138 kg	605,360	29
Total animal products	223 kg	765,367	30
Silk cocoon[e]	60 kg	109,440	31
Pork[n]	162 kg	652,537	32
Mutton[o]	0.7 kg	1,950	33
Wool[p]	0.3 kg	1,440	31
Fish products[q]	Unknown	Unknown	34–37

[a] On the basis of 1 ha farmland including 0.9 ha of crops and 0.1 ha of mulberry (see Fig. 1).

[b] The photosynthetic active solar radiation in the Jiaxing region in 8000 Mkcal/ha for the growing season (IGCAS, 1980).

[c] Based on Table I.

[d] Based on Table II.

[e] Based on Table III.

[f] It is estimated that 180 hours of human labor each year were needed for rearing a pig or a sheep in Chinese traditional methods (Wen Dazhong and Pimentel, 1984b).

[g] The population density was 7.8 people per hectare farmland (Yan Chen, 1887). Each person produces 60 kg (dry) manure each year (Beijingshi Nonglinju, 1980).

[h] 0.1 ha mulberry leaves could feed 0.2 sheep (see section on the Mulberry-Silkworm System). Each sheep produces 150 kg of manure (dry) each year (Beijingshi Nonglinju, 1980).

[i] It is estimated that 3.6 pigs were kept in the system (see section on Energy Flows through the Agroecosystem). Each pig produced 113 kg of manure (dry) each year (Beijingshi Nonglinju, 1980).

[j] About one-third of crop products was used to make an alcoholic drink and the distillers' grains was then fed to pigs (Zhang luxiang, 1956; Chen Hengli and Wang Da, 1983).

[k] Based on Yan Chen (1887).

[l] Total crop products minus fodder for pigs, seeds, bean cakes for fertilizers and outside the system were assumed to be food for residents.

[m] Total harvested crop residues minus the residues returned to Tian and Di.

[n] It is assumed that 15% of pigs were female for reproduction and 85% male for producing pork. The feed to pork ratio was 5:1 (see section on Livestock).

[o] Based on Livestock section of this paper.

[p] Eleven sheep produced 17.9 kg of wool each year (Zhang luxiang, 1956).

[q] Insufficient information available to calculate these energy flows (hence, the dotted lines in Fig. 1).

322   Wen Dazhong and David Pimentel

Energy Flows in Jiaxing Region

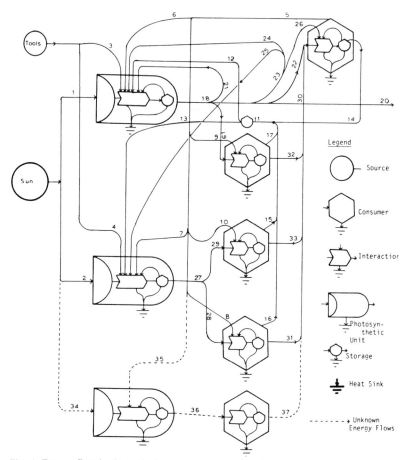

Fig. 1. Energy flow in the typical agroecosystem unit in Jiaxing region in the seventeenth century (10^3 kcal per hectare farmland including 0.9 ha cropland and 0.1 ha mulburry plantation). Energy flow symbols from Odum (1972).

0.9 ha rice-wheat and green manure rotation system and 0.1 ha mulberry plantation was 4.2 Mkcal of manure energy for fertilizer. The humans, sheep, and silkworms in the system supplied 2.4 Mkcal of manure. The remaining 1.8 Mkcal of manure was produced by pigs. This suggests that the farmers needed 3.6 pigs per hectare to meet these organic fertilizer needs.

The yearly total of human and animal manure produced per hectare in this system was about 930 kg (dry), including 312 kg of human manure,

180 kg of silkworm excrement, and 438 kg of pig and sheep manure. About 68% of the total manure was used in the crop system and 32% in the mulberry plantation (Table 2).

The total harvested biomass from the photosynthetic systems (the cropping system and mulberry system) was about 9384 kg or 33.7 Mkcal. This included 8970 kg or 31.9 Mkcal from crops, and 414 kg or 1.8 Mkcal from the mulberry system (see Table 2). Thus, crops provided 95% of the yield.

The harvest of crop biomass was 4290 kg (15.3 Mkcal) of grains and 4680 kg (16.6 Mkcal) of crop residues. Approximately 55% of the grain was directly consumed by local residents, and about 33% of the grain was used to make alcohol and the distillers' grains fed to pigs. About 10% was used for top dressing organic fertilizers (bean cake or rape cake) and returned to the field, while only 2% of the grains were exported outside of the agroecosystem (see Table 2). Almost 66% of the harvested residues was used as household fuel, while the remainder was returned to the field as organic fertilizers.

The yearly production of animal products/ha was about 223 kg or 0.77 Mkcal. Pork accounted for about 85% of the total animal product energy and silk cocoons accounted for 14% (see Table 2). Many ponds were built in this region when the mulberry plantations were established. These were used to rear fish and to accumulate water for irrigation. However, *Shen's Agricultural Handbook* says little about the fish production system.

Solar energy was the basic energy source for the seventeenth-century agroecosystems. The annual average solar incident radiant energy in the Jiaxing region was about 120 kcal/cm^2 and the photosynthetic active solar radiation was about 80 kcal/cm^2. Thus, an agroecosystem unit of one ha would receive about 8000 Mkcal of photosynthetic active solar radiation during the growing season. With a total biomass harvest of 33.7 Mkcal/ha (Table 2), therefore, only 0.4% of the photosynthetic solar energy was harvested. Relative to total solar energy, only 0.3% was harvested. This agrees favorably with current harvests.

The energy input for hand tools, the only fossil energy input in the entire system, was only about 0.039 Mkcal (0.037 Mkcal in the crop system and 0.002 Mkcal in the mulberry plantation; see Table 2). The other energy used in the agroecosystem unit was renewable bioenergy produced within the agroecosystem. Human labor provided all the power. The yearly labor input per hectare was 3756 hours or 6.7 Mkcal, including 2619 hours expended in the crop system, 145 hours in the mulberry plantation, 290 hours rearing silkworms, and 702 hours for rearing pigs and sheep (see Table 2). Thus, a major share or 70% of the total labor was expended in the cropping system.

CONCLUSION

From the seventeenth century to the present, organic agriculture has flourished in China. By the seventeenth century and perhaps before, organic agriculture was well-established. Farmers carefully recycled all wastes, including human, livestock, and crop, back to the land by composting these resources. This has helped maintain the level of soil nutrients high enough to sustain high crop productivity. In addition, the farmers planted green manure crops, like vetch, to add more nitrogen for the soil. The early Chinese farmers appear to have been masters at managing land, water, biological, and other natural resources for optimal crop production. Their crops of rice, barley, wheat, soybean, and vetch, and vegetables like radish and spinach were carefully selected and planted in planned rotations to make full use of the favorable climate and other natural resources. Multiple cropping technology in China has been practiced since the first century AD; and since the third century, people in the southern provinces grew green manure crops in the multiple cropping systems. Year after year, these farmers raised two crops of food per year on the same land.

The seventeenth-century farmers and their families devoted themselves mainly to food production. About 2000 hours of labor were involved in producing a hectare of rice and similar food crops per growing season. At eight hr/day, this is nearly the equivalent of a full-time laborer for one year (40 hr/wk × 52 wk). This is about 200 times the labor input for most mechanized grain production today.

Understanding the organic agricultural techniques of the 17th century suggests methods and modifications that might be employed in agriculture today. Of special value were the techniques that allowed the farmers to manage land, water, and biological resources in a sound manner for a sustained agriculture without the use of commercial fertilizers from fossil fuels.

Of major importance in maintaining the relatively high yields was maintaining both the nutrient level and high organic matter content of the soil. Soil nutrients were conserved by minimizing erosion and recycling crop residues into the soil. Agricultural soils in this region of China were treated as a valuable resource that should be protected and maintained in a high state of productivity.

The success of the organic agricultural system in the Jiaxing region of China during the seventeenth century suggests that this system was generally sustainable. The prime deficiency in the system was a lack of wood or similar fuel to replace the need to burn crop residues. Almost 2/3 of the residues were being removed for household fuel. Burning crop residues removed nutrients from the soils as well as reducing the organic matter content of the soil. Both are essential for a productive agriculture. Removal of crop residues also increased the susceptibility of the cropland to erosion. Had the farmers planted some fuel wood trees, they might have been able to improve the sustainability of the system. This could have been accomplished by reducing the number of pigs produced and by consuming more grain directly instead of feeding the grain to pigs. The land freed by this means could have produced ample fuel wood while improving the nutrient cycling in the system. Overall, the sustainability of the system might have been improved by reducing the number of pigs.

Another means of improving nutrient cycling would have been storing any manure and other wastes in a pond instead of composting. Composting is extremely wasteful of nitrogen (and perhaps other nutrients) because it is lost to the atmosphere and some, by leaching.

The human population appeared to be near the maximum carrying capacity of the natural resources of the region. More flexibility in using resources and a better diet would have been possible with fewer humans per hectare. Nevertheless, this early agricultural system, despite some of its deficiencies, appeared to do an excellent job of managing land and water resources.

REFERENCES

Chen Hengli (1958). *The Study of "Supplementary Agricultural Handbook" (Bu Nongshu Yanjou).* Zhonghua Shunjue, Beijing.

Chen Hengli and Wang Da (1983). *Collation and Explanation of Supplementary Agricultural Handbook (Bu Nongshu Jiaoshi).* Agricultural Press, Beijing.

Odum, H. T. (1972). An energy circuit language for ecological systems. In Pattern, B. C. (ed.), *Systems Analysis and Simulation in Ecology* (Vol. II). Academic Press, New York, pp. 140–211.

Xu Heyong, Zheng Yunshan, and Zhao Shanpai (1982). *Modern History of Zhejiang (Zhejiang Jindaishi).* People's Press of Zhejiang, Hangzho.

Xu Yaoguang (Ed.) (1879). *The Annals of Jiaxing Prefecture (Jiaxing Fuzhi)* (Chap. 22). *China's Annals Series No. 53.* Cheng Wen Co., Chewenpb, Taipei.

Yan Chen (1887). *The Annals of Tongxiang County of Zhejiang Province (Zhejiangsheng Tongxiang Xianzhi). China's Annals Series No. 17.* Chengwen Co., Chewenpb, Taipei.

Zhang Luxiang (1956). *Shen's Agricultural Handbook (Shenshi Nongshu).* Zhonghua Shunjue, Beijing (originally published in 1658).

Zhong Gongfu (1982). Some aspects about the mulberry-dyke-fish pond ecosystem on the Zhujiang (Pearl River) Delta (Zhujiang Sanjiazhou Shangjiyutang Shengtaishitong Ruoganwenti Yanjiu). *Ecology (Shengtaixue Zazhi)* 1: 10–13.

14

Kofyar Cash-Cropping: Choice and Change in Indigenous Agricultural Development

Robert McC. Netting, M. Priscilla Stone,
and Glenn Davis Stone

*Amidst failures in planned development by government and international
agencies, Netting, Stone, and Stone examine what appears to be a highly
successful process of "spontaneous" economic development in Nigeria
over a period of thirty years. The Kofyar of Plateau State have been
gradually migrating from their homeland in the Jos Plateau to take up
cash cropping. They have been obliged to change the social organization
of labor as they have changed from shifting to intensive agriculture, and
have become increasingly dependent upon market interactions to satisfy
what have become basic needs. Among their accommodations to the
requirements of the new system of production include cooperative and
exchange labor groups, though labor is mostly organized on a household
basis, as households have grown larger and more complex. Kofyar
colonization of the fertile valley region for the purpose of cash cropping
resulted from the individual decisions of thousands of farmers that
independent subsistence agriculture was less attractive than the benefits
of having a cash income, and all that cash could buy, even at the cost
of harder work and dependence upon others. They made the transition
on their own, first using indigenous tools and techniques, then learning*

Originally published in *Human Ecology: An Interdisciplinary Journal,* 17(3)(1989): 299–319.

Robert McC. Netting, Late of the Department of Anthropology, University of Arizona,
Tucson, Arizona 85721.   **M. Priscilla Stone and Glenn Davis Stone,** Department of
Anthropology, Washington University, St. Louis, Missouri 63130.

Case Studies in Human Ecology, edited by Daniel G. Bates and Susan H. Lees. Plenum Press,
New York, 1996.

new practices through their own experience of what worked and what did not. The authors attribute the success of this colonization in large part to the absence of government interference.

INTRODUCTION

According to all accounts Nigeria in the 1970s went through an agricultural change of alarming proportions with dizzying speed. Exports of palm products, cocoa, groundnuts, rubber, and cotton declined both relatively and absolutely, while domestic food supplies failed to keep pace with demand, resulting in spiraling imports and inflation (Watts, 1984; Berry, 1984; Iyegha, 1988). The oil boom fueled explosive urban growth and rural exodus without a sign of Green Revolution crops or technology changes on the farm, and with a marked deterioration in rural terms of trade and even nutrition (Matlon, 1981; Rimmer, 1981). It was conclusively demonstrated that major agricultural development projects had disastrous cost/benefit ratios (Andrae and Beckman, 1985; Mortimore, 1987). Total production of food crops and total land under cultivation in Nigeria was said to be going down (Iyegha, 1988, pp. 42–50). Cheap food supplies that the national government regarded as necessary for industrialization (Bates, 1983) and the indirect support of a burgeoning governmental and commercial urban elite (Lipton, 1976) were not forthcoming. There appeared to be little surplus to be captured from the peasantry (Hyden, 1980). Vast arable areas remained underutilized while the population ballooned.

Nigeria, it would seem, was ripe for the opening of agrarian frontiers—the adoption of new crops and more productive techniques—and for a more inclusive movement from subsistence to market-oriented agriculture. Nationally, there was no evidence of this happening, and indeed no one seems to have imagined that increased food production could possibly take place without capital-intensive mechanization and applied science, without decreasing labor and increasing farm size, and without the planned provision of seeds, fertilizers, extension services, and rural credit. The dominance of a Western model of agriculture was unquestioned, and "indigenous agricultural revolution" (Richards, 1985) was a contradiction in terms.[1]

---

[1]Though rapid population growth, declining agricultural exports, and higher food prices are all obvious, the indices of sharply declining production in Nigeria are open to question, and charges of "mass starvation and malnutrition" (Iyegha, 1988, p. 51) have not been substantiated. Though there may have been regional African crop declines, subsistence food production estimates are often little more than wild guesses (Berry, 1984). "While the evidence is weak that food production per capita has declined, it is non-existent that food consumption per capita has fallen." (Caldwell and Caldwell, 1987; but see Cohen, 1989, p. 29).

For these reasons, the experience of the Kofyar (Netting, 1968) in Plateau State is instructive. In a little over 30 years, thousands of farm households have migrated voluntarily from the southern edge of the Jos Plateau to largely vacant bushlands of the Benue valley, and they have begun producing yams on a vast scale for the Nigerian internal market. They have continued to provide their own subsistence crops with traditional hoe techniques while implementing new systems of land use. In addition, they have mobilized substantially increased labor supplies by existing social means, and they have used their cash earnings enthusiastically to purchase a variety of manufactured goods and modern educational, medical, and transportation services.[2] Though a new all-weather road and artificially low gasoline prices facilitated this process, there was almost no direct governmental intervention to establish extension services, to provide agricultural inputs or subsides, or to influence prices, wages, or market arrangements. Because agricultural expansion is taking place without sophisticated technology or bureaucratic planning and control, it is officially unobserved and its existence may even be denied. The Kofyar story may be unrepresentative (though there must certainly be other unheralded farmers increasing their food supplies to a national population estimated at 88.5 million in 1991) and their present trajectory of growing prosperity may yet encounter declining economic returns and ecological deterioration, but a case study of uncoerced, self-generated development may still illuminate significant variables in a particular historic process of genuine change.

SPONTANEOUS MIGRATION AND PIONEER SETTLEMENT

Kofyar movement from their traditional village areas of Kwalla, Doemak, and Merniang (Kwa, Kwang) at the base of the Jos Plateau southern escarpment and the hills above did not become important until the 1950s. Following British conquest in 1909 and the establishment of colonial rule, there had been some occupation of Guinea savanna lands adjacent to Kwalla and Doemak for shifting cultivation of outfield plots, but this

[2]The re-study of the Kofyar including 15 months of field research in Nigeria by Priscilla and Glenn Stone and 6 months by Robert Netting was supported by grants from the National Science Foundation (BNS-8318569 and 8308323) and the Wenner-Gren Foundation for Anthropological Research. Computer analysis of the data directed by Glenn Stone was aided by additional funding from the University of Arizona Social and Behavioral Sciences Research Institute and the Department of Anthropology. Fellowships from the Ford Foundation Foreign Area Studies Program and the Social Science Research Council underwrote Netting's studies of the Kofyar in the 1960s.

reflected little more than a minor expansion of subsistence by local populations with densities often exceeding 300 persons per square mile. Several walled, nucleated communities to the south, like Namu (linked ethnically to the Kofyar), Kurgwi with its Hausa traders, and Kwande, a Goemai settlement, maintained a desultory trade in salt and farmed adjacent bits of the forested plain by slash-and-burn techniques. Seasonal rainfall of 1143–1270 mm is generally adequate to sustain both tubers and grains. A few Kofyar had begun to head-load food crops from this area to sell in the tin mining areas of the high Plateau. A 1946 government report mentions farms of Kofyar, Tiv, and other tribes east of the Shemankar and in the southern Goemai bush (Rowling, 1946). Permanent colonization began in 1951 when around 30 Doemak households established farms in Mangkogam south of Kwande. In 1953, the Chief of Kwa opened a farm south of Namu and encouraged his people to follow him, growing extra food for subsistence and perhaps for trade and tax payments. Kofyar from the most crowded home areas with the lowest per capita crop and livestock production (Stone et al., 1984) were the first to begin seasonal treks to the area, killing the trees with fire in the dry season and planting sesame, followed by yams, and then staple grains, sorghum and millet. They continued to maintain their permanent, intensively-tilled and fertilized homestead fields in the old villages, moving household members back and forth to the bush farms as their labor was needed.

Migration increased rapidly in the 1960s, going from 22.4% of 655 households surveyed in 1961 to 45.5% of 677 households in 1966 (Stone et al., 1984, pp. 95–96). With limited swidden lands available in Kwa where population densities exceeded 200 per km^2, 76% of the households had established migrant bush farms in the Namu area by 1966. The hill village of Bong that had depended solely on its homesteads and local shifting cultivation in 1961 had 26.5% of its households going to distant plains farms by 1966 (Stone et al., 1984, p. 96). Over the next 18 years, the movement increased, and growing numbers of people settled permanently on the bush cash-crop farms. A 1984 survey of 979 households showed that 74% had migrated and 518, over half the sample, had transferred their sole residence to the bushlands. The original homesteads of these migrants were abandoned and rapidly disintegrated. Their homestead fields were untilled or taken over by neighbors for growing groundnuts or grazing. A hill hamlet of Bong village was almost deserted, with only 2 of the original 17 homesteads still occupied. At the same time, the cash-crop farms changed from small collections of makeshift sleeping huts and crop-drying racks to permanent residences with a number of round huts or rectangular, metal-roofed houses plus kitchens, brewing huts, yam barns, pigsties, goat shelters, and granaries. Remaining homesteads in the traditional villages often housed elderly or retired people as well as children who had temporarily left the cash-crop farms in order to attend primary and secondary schools.

The magnitude of population migration to the frontier and demographic growth in place can only be estimated because of the absence since 1963 of an officially accepted national census in Nigeria. Within a mapped 36.22 km² sector of bush farms south of Namu, the 138 homesteads visible in 1963 aerial photograph increased to 546 in 1984. Using an average household size of 6.58 based on our 1984 survey, population in this area rose from 902 to 3593. This represents an almost 300% increase in density from 24.9 to 99.2 per km² (Stone, 1988). A biennial registration of population compiled for tax purposes in Namu District shows the numbers of rural Kofyar rising from 7050 in 1972 to 12,602 in 1984 with increments of about 1000 per year until 1978. A declining rate of growth, 500 a year (1978–1980) and 150 a year (1980–1984), may represent the filling-in of frontier lands and the beginnings of significant out migration to more distant bushlands. The size of Kofyar population in Namu town has increased rapidly, up 24% to 1661 between 1980–1984 alone. Adjoining Namu District is Kwande District where 11,364 Kofyar, mostly originally from Kwalla, were settled by 1984. It appears probable that a minimum of 25,000–30,000 Kofyar now occupy the Benue Valley lowlands south of their original homeland, and that their migration has taken place within the last 40 years. The entire Kofyar population was calculated in 1952 at 55,174 people (Netting, 1968, p. 111).

The timing and extent of involvement in migratory bush farming was always a matter of individual decision-making. Some families never participated. People from the same village who began making the thirty-mile trip to Namu at the same time might live temporarily with the Chief of Kwa or form a large temporary compound for a few years. But households quickly dispersed along the paths, building huts on their fields that straddled a ridge and often reached down to a shallow stream valley (Stone, 1991). There was little sign of patrilineal lineages forming residential units, and neighborhoods could incorporate members of several Kofyar home villages and even an occasional family of the Angas or Mwahavul (Sura) ethnic groups.[3] Younger men might work for kin or friends until they had accumulated some seed yams, and then select a vacant spot with good soil

---

[3]Though the neighborhoods integrated households from diverse origins in new cooperative labor groups and religious congregations (Roman Catholic chapels have been built by the residents in most neighborhoods, but there are also Protestants, Moslems, and traditional adherents), economic choices do not appear to be constrained by "communalist relations" or the "economy of affection" (Hyden, 1986). Even in the home communities, where lineage and clan descent groups were significant socially and politically, extra-household kinship played little role in organizing production (cf. Lewis, 1981).

and easy access to drinking water. As yields from shifting cultivation declined and grass fallows became harder to work, households would seek new field sites in the bush.

The gradual extension of settlement and commuting between home and bush farms contrasted with an earlier attempt at forced relocation of Kofyar. Following the killing of a British district officer in Latok in 1930, seven villages and some 3000 hill Kofyar had been rounded up and evacuated to the plain (Netting, 1987). Only after annual military patrols had removed people and livestock and repeatedly burned huts for some 9 years were the Kofyar allowed to return to the hills. Despite the availability of unoccupied plains land, the attempt at permanent resettlement failed, and all the Kofyar returned to their ancestral homesteads.

The more recent movement of Kofyar into migratory, and then permanent, cultivation has converted the frontier from a patchwork of fields with dead trees and partially burned trunks, bush and grass fallows, and undisturbed forest into a relatively continuously cultivated, open farmland with perhaps 20% short fallow (1–3 years) land. Hardwoods such as mahogany and iroko in the better watered valleys were cut in the late 1960s, and the less valuable species (silk cotton, copaiba) are now being harvested by timber contractors who use chain saws to reduce the trees to 4 × 6 inch, 12-foot beams for further processing into planks by sawmills in the towns. Only locust bean (*Parkia clappertoniana*), sheanut (*Butyrospernum paradoxum*), and other economically useful trees remain in the fields. Our earliest aerial photographs from 1963 show about 20% of the frontier land in use, but by 1978, 65% was under cultivation with another 11% in fallow. The original plots, typically 4–6 ha in size were laid out along watersheds on well-drained, nonlateritic soils. As the landscape was filled in, more recent arrivals or new households fissioning from those of original settlers took up less desirable plots that were farther from water (Stone, 1986). A number of farmers tried low-lying areas in Danka (the name itself means "heavy clay") but found after a few years that the fields became waterlogged and there were few house sites not subject to swampy conditions. Often they returned to lands that had been farmed and vacated. By 1984, farms in the areas of early settlement were being fragmented, with smaller portions being inherited, given to kin and friends, or in some cases sold.

A rather typical case is that of Datoegoem of Ungwa Kofyar who moved to the frontier in 1963. Datoegoem's original 14 ha farm was more than his household needed, and he gave a 5 ha section to his friend Doewat in the early 1970s. When Datoegoem's eldest son Christopher began to acquire wives, Datoegoem moved to a new compound across the road, leaving almost 4 ha of land to the son. The son's household had grown (he took his fourth wife in 1984), and he has received another parcel from his father as well as gaining control over part of the farm given to Doewat, whose own household has shrunk. Another friend has farmed the parcel that had been Doewat's, but has not been allowed to build a compound there.

Other Kofyar had sought virgin bushlands up to 80 km from the homeland at Kuka not far from Ibi on the Benue River and in Lafia division south of Assaikio. Everywhere the phase of frontier shifting cultivation appears to be transitory, with a tendency to bring fields into permanent production by crop rotation, frequent weeding, intercropping, manuring, and chemical fertilization (Netting et al., 1993). Unlike the Tiv who migrated from the south into the same area and maintained large areas for bush fallow rotations around their compounds, Kofyar intensified their agriculture as bush population density increased and farm size declined.

MOBILIZING LABOR

Pioneer occupation of a large forested frontier zone, followed by permanent settlement and intensifying farming, required increased application of labor. The opening of these extensive tracts of land for shifting cultivation meant that increases in production came directly from more workers and additional hours in the fields. Neither Kofyar migration nor greater output was contingent on the adoption of a new technology. The broad-bladed Sudanic hoe remained the principal tool, and the traditional farming system based on interplanted millet, sorghum, and cowpeas was not discarded, but rather modified to include a yam rotation or relay cropping (Stone et al., 1990). Kofyar households usually function as independent economic units, and they quickly reproduced their traditional dispersed settlement pattern, with each of the new homesteads occupying its own cultivated land and fallow.

The bulk of labor in both the home and migrant communities was, in the 1960s, and continues to be drawn from, the household labor force. In a sample of 15 households for which daily labor records of all adults were kept in 1984, household labor applied to household fields constitutes 62.8% of all hours devoted to farming and remains particularly important for the cultivation of the traditional cereal crops of millet and sorghum (Stone et al., 1990). Of all the hours devoted to cereals, 75.8% is contributed by the household to the household fields. Relatively more of the labor time on the cash crops of rice and yams comes from interhousehold cooperative work or from individuals cultivating their independent plots, but 49.9% of all hours spent on rice farming and 59.7% on yams are performed by the household itself.

To meet the increasing needs for labor, households grew in size. Large households could both concentrate labor power to meet the seasonal demands of cash-cropping and also divide their forces to maintain the old homestead farm that provided a secure subsistence. Whereas non-migrant Kofyar households had averaged 4.54 (1961) and 4.17 (1966) members, those with migrant bush farms averaged 6.44 in the 1960s (Stone et al., 1984, p. 99). By 1984, the average household size in the Namu area was 8.38 people. Growth in household size has continued progressively with number of years spent in bush farming, peaking at a mean of 9.26 for those households 16–20 years into their developmental cycles. Larger size reflects, in part, increasing frequency of polygyny and multiple family formation (Netting, 1965, 1968). Cash income from the sale of yams, millet, and rice could be used for bride wealth and additional wives, increasing the number of adult workers immediately and providing children as a future source of labor. Keeping married sons on their fathers' farms also enlarged the household work force.

Although polygynous households and the extension of a residential family to include two or more married couples (multiple family households) had always existed as culturally acceptable options, they were less frequently realized in the home communities where farm sizes were constrained by population pressure and larger labor groups were unnecessary for most tasks. The proportion of polygynous family households among non-migrant Kofyar was 32.3% in 1966 (Stone et al., 1984, p. 99) and had climbed to 51.5% among 1984 bush farmers. The corresponding proportions of multiple family households had risen from 7.3–17.0%.

With the filling of the frontier and the increasing abandonment of hill farms, the utility of large extended and multiple households may be reduced. Cash-cropping households formed in the last 5 years have tended to be less complex and smaller, averaging only 5.70 members. Of these predominantly younger families who have moved permanently to the cash-crop farms, 41% are polygynous and 10% are multiple. Households with a longer history of migration and a continued maintenance of both home and bush farm residences tend to be complex, with 69% having at least one polygynous marriage and 26% being multiple. Three hundred households that are either extended polygynous or multiple polygynous families have an average membership of 12.09. There are also growing numbers of children per household. The proportion of the population in the 0–15 age range has grown from 37% in 1966 to 47% 18 years later. But for the present, increasing household size and labor potential is regularly associated with higher grain and yam production, more use of consumer goods, and higher household incomes.

While the resident family household remains the fundamental labor and consumption unit, households also depend on agricultural work performed by cooperative groups of friends and neighbors. Though Kofyar have always exchanged some assistance in such tasks as field ridging, harvesting, and thatching, we had predicted that the major emphasis on cash-cropping and the end of the free land for frontier expansion would lead to more wage labor and less interhousehold collaboration. Indeed, agricultural monetization in Africa is often seen to involve the replacement of allegedly expensive, inefficient traditional exchange labor with the hiring of local or seasonally migrating workers (Saul, 1983). This wage labor is seen to be drawn from the impoverishment of rural smallholders and the landless (Hill, 1980; Watts, 1983a) with increasing land consolidation and economic inequality (Reyna, 1987). Hiring of labor does indeed exist among the Kofyar, but its contribution to total work inputs has remained relatively minor.

Cooperative work groups, in contrast, may have increased in their incidence and variety. One form is a 30–80 person voluntary group composed of neighbors from the same-named neighborhood (*ungwa*) of 20–50 households. These *mar muos* (farming for beer) parties assemble to accomplish one farming task and are entertained by their host with millet beer at the end of the day. Such festive labor (Erasmus, 1956; Moore, 1975) is scheduled well in advance and may last a few hours or half a day, with some groups absorbing a full day's work. Men and women work side by side at ridging, making yam heaps, and storing millet after the early August harvest, but men do somewhat more of the heavy hoeing while women grind and cook the millet beer. It is not unusual for 400 pounds of millet to be prepared, so that each participant will have about two gallons of the nutritious brew to drink (Netting, 1964). Some beer may be brought to the field, and the work is spurred by young men who set a fast pace and drummers who accompany the hoeing.

Smaller groups (called *wuk*) bring together 8–20 people that regularly exchange work, and women and adult sons have organized groups of their own to work on their individual fields (Stone, 1988a). No cash or beer accompanies the labor, although close track is kept of reciprocity. New forms of collective labor have also emerged in the plains, including church and school groups and social clubs who farm collectively for their members and to generate group funds.

In our labor records, 21.4% of all agricultural work is some form of extrahousehold exchange. The festive labor groups account for 8.2%. Of the remaining work groups, the largest part is accounted for by cooperative beer brewing (7.6%).

Almost as significant, in terms of hours, is the time spent on cultivating personal fields. Individuals may grow yams, rice, peanuts, and minor
crops for sale. Women derive a significant independent cash income from
such activities (Stone, 1988b). Overall, 19% of agricultural hours are devoted to personal fields within the household. When combined with festive
labor groups and exchange labor applied to personal fields in other households, work devoted to individual production reaches 22.4% of all agricultural labor.

The use of beer party labor has not been supplanted by wage labor.
In our larger survey of 799 cash-cropping households, two-thirds of them
had used beer party labor on at least one occasion in the last year. The
average number of these events was 0.9, with a median size of 50 workers.
In comparison, 37% employed hired labor, and these households use a median of 20 person days annually at a median cost of ₦90. In general, household size and use of paid labor went up together, suggesting that these two
modes of labor mobilization were not alternatives but were complementary.

While many studies have shown that rural wage labor in Africa is actually cheaper than cooperative labor (Latour Dejean, 1975; Charsley, 1976;
Saul, 1983), the stated preference of Kofyar household heads is for beer
party or exchange labor as opposed to wage workers. They contend that
(1) costs of agricultural labor including food are high in comparison to the
cost of buying millet and making beer for a cooperative work party, (2)
hired workers are demanding, undependable, and less careful in agricultural operations than neighbors, and (3) there are not enough hands available at bottleneck periods when 40–100 workers can complete a crucial
task in 1 day. Most hired workers are young men coming down in groups
of two or three from the Angas and Mwahavul (Sura) ethnic areas on the
high plateau. They may hill up yam heaps for ₦5 per 100 (about 1 day's
work), and they are also entitled to board and lodging. Kofyar claim that
some workers ask for oil and meat, threatening to leave before the task is
completed if these are not forthcoming. Mean costs of a workday are approximately ₦5.41 plus food, while comparable effort from a Kofyar would
be recompensed with ₦1–1.30 for brewing grain. Two bags or 400 lbs of
millet costing about ₦100 are considered adequate for approximately 80
workers. The malted millet is ground and cooked by perhaps 20 women
who exchange labor and receive a portion of the beer. Firewood and water
must also be fetched. Even when the time of these women, as well as the
loose obligation of reciprocal work on the fields of others, is considered,
the Kofyar feel it is cheaper (and certainly less requiring of immediate cash)
to sponsor beer parties than to pay workers. In fact, the time women spend
brewing for work parties is only about 15% of the total labor hours invested
in this type of group labor.

As intensification increases, the *quality* of work and the lack of a need for close supervision also become important factors.[4] The prevalence of interplanting means that there may be millet, sorghum, cowpeas, and groundnuts at different stages of growth in the same field. Weeding and ridging operations must be discriminating as well as fast. Heaps for next year's yams are made among stalks of maturing sorghum in the same field where millet has just been harvested. Kofyar rely on the skill and experience of their neighbors, who will expect similar attention when they in turn receive help.

In savanna cultivation, a long dry season (November–March) and often inconsistent rains set universal planting periods and create successive bottlenecks for cultivation, weeding, and harvesting. Kofyar work parties both mass labor in order to finish a task near the optimum time and supply incentives of social competition, emulation, and rewards (beer and the relaxation of drinking in a group are highly valued) for increasing the vigor and amount of labor applied. Any slacking or failure of a household to send a worker is publicly noted and ultimately penalized. Though households and individuals continue to work on their own fields during other parts of the day, Kofyar regard their cooperative work as both effective and pleasurable. If hoeing a single field is stretched out over weeks, it cannot be planted at one time, or planting is seriously delayed. The crop may not ripen all at once. Growing weeks may also drastically lower yields in part of a big field not reached promptly by a small household labor group. During the agricultural season, Kofyar labor input is so steady that there are practically no breaks in the tight schedule, and a longer time spent on one crop will interfere with necessary tasks for other cultigens.

Only those who have not been able to schedule a festive labor party, who are attempting to increase their cultivated area, or who pursue other occupations in town are likely to hire labor. Though new farms are becoming smaller and harder to establish, most Kofyar can still acquire some land. They are not pressed by lack of resources to do wage work, and there is not yet a landless proletariat with no choice but to accept depressed pay scales. At crucial times in the agricultural year the demand for labor far outstrips supply. For a few specialized dry season tasks such as well digging

---

[4]Saul (1983) argues to the contrary that the big expensive volunteer parties among the Bisa of Burkina Faso are inefficient, careless, cannot be pushed, and try to combine work with diversion. Only the poor integration of the labor market with few workers available during the bottleneck weeding and harvesting periods prevented more frequent hiring of wage workers. His discussion, however, refers to large, bush-fallow fields at some distance from the village and with relatively free usufruct land rights. A more extensive system of this kind with less intercropping and an absence of fine-comb techniques does not require the careful attention that Kofyar groups regularly provide their hosts.

and cereal threshing, crews of Hausa long-distance seasonal migrants from the Kano area are now beginning to appear. Just how soon Kofyar economic inequality will force some individuals into the labor market on a permanent basis is unclear. As long as population density on the frontier remains below the level at which small holdings are economically viable, intensification maintains adequate returns on labor, and out-migration reduces pressure on land, the role of wage labor may not appreciably increase. Intensive, careful techniques also put a premium on the skills and unsupervised responsible efforts of household members and neighbors with common understandings and shared economic interests.

CASH-CROPPING AND DEPENDENCE

Selling agricultural products in Africa is often seen as being synonymous with incorporation into a market economy, capitalist penetration, and the capture of a peasantry by urban, commercial, and bureaucratic sectors of the economy (Hyden, 1980; Shenton, 1986). A postulated earlier "Golden Age" of economic self-sufficiency, political independence, and communal equality inevitably falls victim to forces from the city, the nation, and the world system that systematically exploit the countryside.[5] • Though the Kofyar are subject to the same local government, taxation, terms of trade, and mercantile institutions as other Nigerian farmers, they appear to have voluntarily embraced a growing degree of market involvement and to behave in a manner that furthers their economic goals. In so doing, they have not sacrificed their own ability to provision themselves, maintain their nutritional status, and preserve their household autonomy. They have not become dependent on wages, indebted, or subject to administrative control. They appear to have chosen to migrate, to work longer and harder than they did in the past, to sell crops on the market, and to buy new goods and services. The economic situation is assuredly still in flux and its positive aspects may be transitory, but the Kofyar do not react to either the state or the market in terms of loss of control, insecurity, or powerlessness. Their conditions arise from an environment and a recent economic and political history in which constraints, choice, and chance all play their parts.

The characteristics of the Benue valley are undeniably relevant. A well-watered area of reasonably fertile soils was (1) almost devoid of settlement, and (2) near enough to the Kofyar Jos Plateau homeland to be reached and cultivated without pulling up stakes and moving from still-productive

---

[5]Hill (1986, p. 70) points out that this sentimental, largely unconscious "Golden Age fallacy" is shared by Marxists and non-Marxists alike.

traditional village homesteads. The Guinea savanna climatic and edaphic conditions would support both the staple crops familiar to the Kofyar, and the yam, a valued food for the increasingly urbanized Ibo and Yoruba peoples from southern Nigeria. There was also a market for millet and sorghum grain that could absorb any surplus the Kofyar produced (Little and Horowitz, 1987). The geographic centrality of the Nigerian Middle Belt that includes the Benue and Niger river valleys, and the dry season that made possible the evacuation of produce along rudimentary bush roads meant that transport costs for bulky food crops were economically feasible. The Kofyar had comparatively easy access to land and markets.[6]

The fact that the Kofyar area lay between the core regions that supported Nigeria's great colonial export crops—cocoa, palm oil, and groundnuts—meant that they came later to cash production, but possibly more propitiously. The Kofyar were never encouraged to concentrate on a crop monopolized by state marketing boards, so they were not subject to fluctuating world prices or the irresistible temptation for national governments to depress producer prices and skim profits for public projects or private speculation (Hart, 1982, pp. 92–93; Bates, 1983, p. 131). Kofyar yams and cereals are bought for cash by entrepreneurs who bring lorries to the farm gate, or the products are carried by bike, motorcycle, pick-up, or taxi to local periodic markets where middlemen bulk and ship to cities. There is competition among buyers and prices that appear to respond to seasonal, regional, and local changes in supply and demand.[7] This indigenous system of food supply was certainly affected by national events including: The Biafran war effort of the late 1960s that impeded transport and drained wealth, vaulting urban demand powered by the oil boom of the 1970s (Watts, 1984), and the cheap imports of flour (Andrae and Beckman, 1985) and rice that the government encouraged to feed (and quiet) the cities. Raising the price of bread by restricting wheat imports, as the present Nigerian military government has proposed, may increase demand for internally produced yams and millet, for which there is no direct equivalent in international trade, but we cannot estimate what this will mean to the Plateau State farmer. We lack the daily market reports or the price series that would measure

---

[6]The provision of roads has been perhaps the most important contribution of government to the advance of the frontier of settlement onto the Middle Belt plains and the accompanying expansion of cash-cropping (Gleave, 1966).

[7]A study of marketing margins among Hausa farmers in rural Zaria during 1971–1972 showed that the producer received an average of 68% of the final retail price of millet and almost 70% of that for sorghum (Norman et al., 1982, p. 85). Though up to seven intermediaries such as traders, transporters, and retailers claim part of the profit on grain transactions, it does not appear that their incomes are excessive, considering services provided, and rural–urban marketing functions reasonably efficiently (Norman et al., 1982, pp. 87–90).

changes in supply and demand for Kofyar crops. Nor can we follow the distribution links, though the completion in 1982 of an all-weather east–west road connecting Namu with Shendam and Lafia, along with an explosive increase of motor vehicles powered by plentiful, inexpensive petrol, enabled the routine shipping of crops and livestock as far as Port Harcourt or Kano. We can say that thousands of Kofyar farmers are finding prices in active national markets sufficiently attractive that they now devote up to half of their labor time to producing food for sale.

Neither migration to the plains nor entry into the market was hasty or particularly risky for the Kofyar. As we have mentioned, they gradually increased their time and effort on Namu bush farms while maintaining the homestead as a secure source of food. Burning trees and advancing the farm boundary took place over a number of years. Any produce that was not sold could potentially be eaten, and a bad harvest meant less money income rather than severe local food shortages.[8] Moreover, individual farmers had the leeway to experiment with crops, learn the characteristics of the soil catena on their farms, and try out new variants on intercropping and rotations (Richards, 1986). Because farmers were self-selected and self-supported, they could make individual decisions on how to use resources, when and what to sell, and how to organize their labor. Payment of bridewealth, keeping a son in the household by helping him to buy a motorcycle, giving a sister's son a field, and retiring to the hill homestead were all personal choices that directly affected the agricultural enterprise.

Because no one told the Kofyar what to do or when to do it, they have made mistakes, but both successes and failures have been their own and they have had the opportunity, with time and experience, to learn from them. The original yam variety grown (*akuki*) has been replaced with one (*danganitcha*) from Iboland that may have smaller tubers but that is of better quality and stores without shrinkage into the wet season. Almost every Kofyar farmer now raises pigs, which were entirely unknown as recently as 1960. A few innovators are now growing cassava or bananas for the market. Commercial fertilizer has been widely adopted since 1979, but, lacking extension advice, dosages may be too little or too much. Kofyar sorghum yields are being threatened by parasitic *striga,* for which they have no effective remedy. Purchased seed dressings are frequently used. The Kofyar are, we believe, willing to accept further cost-effective inputs and scientific advice, but these must be geared to their particular needs and

---

[8]The generally favorable Kofyar environment meant that they have been spared the serious, recurrent famine conditions of the Sahel to the north (Franke and Chasin, 1980; Mortimore, 1987), and their recent entry into the mercantile economy has rendered them less vulnerable to state capitalism (Watts, 1983a).

aimed at improving their existing farming system rather than replacing it with a "package" of expensive inputs and technology.

It is clear that the major incentive for innovation as it was for the original migration to the frontier is the cash to be gained by marketing food crops. High value yams were, from the beginning, cultivated for sale, and to this day Kofyar prefer to subsist on grain rather than eating the crop. By 1965, truck-loading records indicate that 514,000 yams were being exported from the Kwande hinterland. In 1983, a dry year with a distinctly depressed production, the average Kofyar farming household had a total of 3189 yam heaps, while rich farmers put in 8000–10,000. Our censused population of 729 reporting households sold an average of 561 yams, 3.57 bags of millet, 0.63 bags of sorghum, 0.4 bags of rice, and smaller quantities of groundnuts, locust beans, cowpeas, and vegetables. Yams alone generated ₦438,925, an average of ₦615 per household, and total mean annual income as ₦1160. Almost all Kofyar smallholder households produce for the market, and income is not concentrated in a small group of big farmers with wage labor (Cohen, 1989, p. 23). (Incomplete evidence for the 1984 agricultural year of good rains suggests that farm income more than doubled.) Of total farm income, approximately one-fourth was made up of individual, as opposed to household, income, and most of the individual returns were from individual yam and peanut production by women.

Cash crops in the aggregate not only represent large quantities grown and major money earnings, but they also absorb a significant proportion of labor time. Daily records of hourly labor expenditure by the adult members of 15 households over 50 weeks show that more than 36% of all work in the fields is devoted to yams, with·rice, that is also sold, accounting for an additional 6.9% (Stone et al., 1990). Since neither of these crops was grown traditionally, and considering that the cash-crop farms are at least eight times the size of the original homesteads (Netting, 1968, p. 200), it is apparent that both total labor (estimated at 1600 hours per adult annually) and work specifically directed to marketable surpluses have been greatly increased. Because 40 percent of the millet harvest may also be sold, along with other crops and occasional goats, sheep, pigs, and chickens, it is possible that as much as 50 percent of all Kofyar farming effort is now committed to production for the market.

The money income of the Kofyar goes in part for bridewealth, taxes, and cloth as it did in the past, but expenditures for manufactured goods and services are impressive. Every household now buys soap, kerosene for lamps, flashlight batteries, and Maggi bouillion cubes. Round huts have locked metal doors with carpentered frames, and 16% of all compounds have at least one galvanized metal roof. A bicycle was one of the first big purchases of a migrant, and now each household is likely to have several.

Official records show that between 1980–1983, the Kofyar purchased almost 6000 motor vehicles, predominantly light motorcycles, but including taxis, pick-up trucks, cars, and mini-buses. School fees, especially board and books at distant secondary schools, are a charge that many families meet. There has been a quite extraordinary surge of interest in medical care, requiring payment for clinic visits, medicines, hospital maintenance (even when health care is provided free by the state), and transportation to health facilities. A survey of 136 households indicated that in the preceding month, 81, or 60% of these households had at least one member seeking medical attention. One hundred and twenty-nine individuals were treated at a cost of ₦2595, with the highest total of ₦204 for four people in one household. Mean monthly cost was over ₦32 for each household seeking health care.

A variety of agricultural inputs must now be purchased. More than half of all farmers buy chemical fertilizer and seed dressings. Some people buy the millet for festive labor beer parties rather than using their own stocks. Instead of selling produce to middlemen at the farm gate or carrying their own goods to market, over 50% of farmers pay transport costs for the hauling of their grain and yams. A smaller but still significant proportion, 28%, are purchasing grain to supplement food supplies, to brew, or for resale.[9] It is becoming increasingly difficult to cash-crop without monetary investments and costs.

INDIGENOUS DEVELOPMENT: SIGNIFICANT CONDITIONS

Case studies of change are always open to the charge that they reflect unique historical circumstances and that their complex multiple variables resist generalization. The simpler models from environmental and technological determinism to the capitalist world system seldom seem adequate to capture essential regularities in a complex process. Furthermore, our studies are often *post hoc* reconstructions of what went wrong in a specific project of planned development, and the incongruous appearance of rapid, seemingly nontraumatic indigenous economic change is regarded as a fluke, a sport of nature.

The Kofyar indeed enjoyed some fortunate conditions for their agricultural transformation in space, time, and the market. Necessary as it was

---

[9]There is as yet no parallel among the Kofyar for the practice of poorer Hausa farmers who must habitually sell cash crops and buy staple food grains on the market, nor do Kofyar in general have dry season craft, trade, or wage employments (Matlon, 1981). Indeed, Kofyar teachers and low-ranking government employees compare their wages unfavorably with the incomes of full-time farmers.

to have a frontier of near-vacant, easily-worked, well-drained lands in the Benue trough at their doorstep, open tracts of land are not in themselves sufficient to draw large numbers of permanent settlers. It is possible to have so much land that shifting cultivators can utilize it in extensive fashion, keeping well apart from neighbors and harvesting a leisurely subsistence, as did many Tiv pioneers. Kofyar fields grew gradually and by accretion rather than being marked out, assigned, and regulated by some external authority.[10] The Kofyar came from the Jos Plateau where space was scarce. Though they sometimes migrated from their initial bush farms to others, they had a repertoire of techniques, intensive ridging and weeding, inter-cropping, rotation, and manuring for establishing permanent farms and in-creasing production per unit area.[11] They could cope with the constraint of constricting land resources. The closeness of the new lands to the home-land meant that they could commute to the bush farms on foot or, more rapidly, by bicycle. Attempts to clear big new fields did not mean leaving the security of their old small homesteads and dependable sources of food.

Time was also on the side of the Kofyar. In gradual explorations and exploitations of the forest, farmers could choose their own times to begin and, finally, to migrate permanently. They could take their time in experi-menting with crops, soils, and water. They could devise new schedules of, for instance, making yam heaps in a field of growing sorghum after the millet harvest, thus combining weeding and shoring up the sorghum with providing heaps for the next year's yam rotation. This used slack time in the grain cultivation calendar, avoided working the hard soils of the dry season, and saved time in the planting bottleneck after the rains. With care-ful interdigitation of cropping cycles for millet, sorghum, yams, cowpeas, peanuts, and rice, along with sequential harvesting and processing and con-tinuous livestock care, Kofyar adults work through the entire year, averag-ing less than 4 hours per day of agricultural work in only 16 weeks, with

---

[10]Agricultural development projects too often begin with a set of requirements, including areas to be cultivated, crops and amounts to be grown, inputs and techniques to be used, and types of labor organization. The characteristics, previous agricultural experience, and motivations of the farmers are disregarded. An early, ill-fated colonial project in Nigeria, the Mokwa Scheme, asked local shifting cultivators in an area of abundant land to undertake the hand weeding of machine-plowed 24 acre parcels (Baldwin, 1957, p. 4). The settlers could not accommodate this use of land to their existing labor supplies nor their customary farming calendar, and the need to give two-thirds of their production to the company was a major disincentive to work hard.

[11]Unlike the less successful migrants to the Brazilian Amazon, the Kofyar had an excellent working knowledge of the local environment and an effective technology. They also had low capital requirements, were not involved in land speculation, and did not find off-farm em-ployment more lucrative. In these respects, they differed from most frontier populations (Moran, 1988).

men averaging 1729 hours per year and women averaging 1473 (Stone et al., 1990).[12] The outside observer can only conclude that Kofyar willingly use time in farm labor because (1) they know how from previous experience in intensive agriculture, (2) they are not coerced to undertake this extra toil, and (3) they receive reasonable prices for their produce. As independent smallholders coping with problems of weather, plant growth, and mobilizing human muscle power *on their own,* they decide how to allocate labor time. Their efficiency is achieved without time clocks, hourly wages, alarm bells, or any of the temporal trappings of externally regimented time.

The conscious decision of thousands of Kofyar farmers to produce for the market entailed clear and growing costs in agricultural labor, migration, and the sacrifice of leisure time. It is evident that many who came to the frontier could have continued to provide an adequate subsistence for themselves from their homestead farms. Rather than continue at a subsistence level, both men and women opted for new sources of cash, and they produced food, sold it in large and growing quantities, and readily bought manufactured goods, medical services, and education.[13] Without the incentive of what they considered an adequate return on their efforts and a market that provided them with motorcycles, house-building materials, iron bedsteads, flashlights, and medicines, it is doubtful if such wholesale changes would have taken place. The rapid expansion of a national market, new roads and motor vehicles, and a burgeoning urban population, all resulting in part from international oil revenues, made cash-cropping profitable, and a flourishing, competitive entrepreneurial sector contributed to a reasonably responsive pricing mechanism. Kofyar individuals, while avoiding full dependency on the market, reached similar positive conclusions on the costs and benefits of market participation in an area where genuine market places had only been in existence since the 1930s.

Regardless of how much their economic ends may be congruent with national goals, the government did nothing directly to foster or to impede Kofyar agricultural development. In fact, the means used by the Kofyar— hand tools, traditional cultigens, a farming system that they themselves evolved and adapted, and the organization of labor by households, local

---

[12]The high and remarkably sustained labor input surpasses that of Hausa on-farm adult male employment of 609 hours (709 with travel time included), and an additional 453 hours in off-farm occupations (Norman, 1969). Hausa women provide only 9% of total farm labor.
[13]It is not far-fetched to see many of the Kofyar hill households of the 1960s as self-sufficient and self-contained units characterized by the production of use values in a generally noncapitalist social formation. These same social groupings and individuals have become petty commodity producers, but unlike historic peasantries, there is no sign that "commoditization is or has been resisted by the reproduction of institutional and social relations limiting the mobility of land and labor" (Watts, 1983a, p. 20).

exchange, and festive groups—were radically inconsistent with the model of planned, technologically modern, capital-intensive development that government and outside donors have usually advocated. The mistakes made in the course of innovation were made by individuals who had the time, the advice of the community, and their own growing experience to correct them. Government rigidity in providing "scientific" packages of seeds, machines, fertilizers, and schedules without considering local needs and achievements or utilizing local experience and expertise was thereby avoided. Tractor plowing services and irrigation at government installations west, south, and north of the Namu area have not been extended to, or adopted by, the Kofyar, presumably because cost/benefit ratios were unfavorable and because the innovations were not compatible with the growing agricultural intensification and independent flexibility of Kofyar farmers. Contract tractor plowing has been employed sparingly to break lands on old volcanic flows that resist hand tools, but the Kofyar contend that even ox plows are poorly adapted to their methods of dense intercropping and yam mounding. As examples of populist, indigenous development (Richards, 1985; but see Watts, 1983b), the Kofyar may have succeeded in part because outsiders were largely unaware of their existence, and government agencies never tried to "improve" their cultivation or control their economy.

Good, free, accessible land, the time to adapt to new conditions without risking a secure subsistence base, and attractive producer prices in an expanding national economy are all important considerations in Kofyar voluntary, spontaneous change, but there may be further cultural and normative elements that distinguish Kofyar from other ethnic populations (Burnham, 1980, p. 278) that have not taken such dramatic advantage of similar conditions. We may speculate that habits of hard, disciplined work, individual initiative, and household economic autonomy that characterize sedentary intensive cultivators in land-short areas of high population density would dovetail neatly with the requirements of transforming bushlands into high-yielding, permanent smallholdings and producing a surplus for the market.[14] Certainly, the traditional background promoting a degree of

[14]Others have speculated that the best settlers for new lands are not the local extensive cultivators but rather farmers from overpopulated areas where they have only been making a precarious livelihood (Baldwin, 1957, p. 187). The colonial government-sponsored Shendam Resettlement Scheme, not far southeast of the Kofyar, encountered difficulties with establishing ex-soldiers on cleared plots with two years' subsistence, tools, seed, and cattle, but uneducated Hill Yergam settlers from an area of high population pressure on the Jos Plateau made a successful adaptation to the frontier, even though only minimal subsidies were provided for them (Meek, 1957, pp. 283–291). This does not mean, as Hart (1982) contends, that only historically deprived or exploited peasants could meet the labor demands of such intensive production as that of irrigated we rice. "Has the [West African] work force been

labor input that other groups might regard as unrelieved drudgery, mobilizing men and women as equal contributors to production, and making the family household a self-reliant and largely self-determining economic entity was in some sense a preadaptation to an individualistic, competitive economy. Kofyar options had not been limited in the past by either hierarchical lineage relationships or an autocratic traditional state, and their own society had not been significantly disrupted by the colonial government. It may be romantic exaggeration to seek some "ethic of intensification" among a group of terrace farmers whose transition from subsistence to cash-cropping on a bush frontier has been relatively rapid and, in the short term, effective and rewarding. But well-socialized habits of work and cultural templates of achievement (Ottenberg, 1959; LeVine, 1966) are neither irrelevant nor epiphenomenal to that distinctive material concatenation of environment, economics, and politics from which agricultural change emerges.

REFERENCES

Andrae, G., and Beckman, B. (1985). *The Wheat Trap: Bread and Underdevelopment in Nigeria*. Zed Books, London.
Baldwin, K. D. S. (1957). *The Niger Agricultural Project*. Basil Blackwell, Oxford.
Bates, R. (1983). *Essays on the Political Economy of Rural Africa*. Cambridge University Press, Cambridge.
Berry, S. S. (1984). *Farmers Work for their Sons: Accumulation, Mobility, and Class Formation in an Extended Yoruba Community*. University of California Press, Berkeley.
Burnham, P. (1980). *Opportunity and Constraint in a Savanna Society*. Academic, New York.
Caldwell, J. and Caldwell, P. (1987). Famine in Africa. Unpublished paper for the Seminar on Mortality and Society in Sub-Saharan Africa, IFORD, Yaoundé.
Charsley, S. R. (1976). The Silika: A cooperative labor institution. *Africa* 46: 34–47.
Cohen, R. (1989). The unimodal model: Solution or cul de sac for rural development? In Gladwin, C., and Truman, K. (eds.), *Food and Farm: Current Debates and Policies. Monographs in Economic Anthropology, No. 7.* University Press of America, Lanham, Maryland pp. 7–33.
Erasmus, C. (1956). Culture, structure, and process: The occurrence and disappearance of reciprocal farm labor. *Southwestern Journal of Anthropology* 12: 444–469.
Franke, R. W., and Chasin, B. H. (1980). *Seeds of Famine: Ecological Destruction and the Development Dilemma in the West African Sahel*. Allanheld, Osmun, Montclair.
Cleave, M. B. (1966). The changing frontiers of settlement in the uplands of northern Nigeria. *Journal of the Geographical Association of Nigeria* 8: 127–141.

---

sufficiently prepared by famine, impoverishment, and proletarianization to constitute a reliable, hard-working, paddy-field peasantry? Our assessment is that it has not. Agricultural intensification means getting people to work harder, and that undertaking usually requires coercion. The compulsion would have to be especially severe in the forest areas, where labor-efficient techniques of production yield up the population's food need with comparatively little effort (hence the popularity of manioc)" (Hart, 1982, p. 48).

Hart, K. (1982). *The Political Economy of West African Agriculture.* Cambridge University Press, Cambridge.

Hill, P. (1980). *Population, Prosperity, and Poverty: Rural Kano 1900 and 1970.* Cambridge University Press, Cambridge.

Hill, P. (1986). *Development Economics on Trial: The Anthropological Case for the Prosecution.* Cambridge University Press, Cambridge.

Hyden, G. (1980). *Beyond Ujamaa in Tanzania: Underdevelopment and an Uncaptured Peasantry.* Heinemann, London.

Hyden, G. (1986). The invisible economy of smallholder agriculture in Africa. In Moock, J. L. (ed.), *Understanding Africa's Rural Households and Farming Systems.* Westview, Boulder, pp. 11–35.

Iyegha, D. A. (1988). *Agricultural Crisis in Africa: The Nigerian Experience.* University Press of America, Lanham, Maryland.

Latour Dejean, E. de (1975). Transformation du Regime Foncier: Appropriation des Terres et Formation de la Classe Dirigeante en Pays Mawri (Niger). In Amin, S. (ed.), *L'Agriculture Africaine et le Capitalisme.* Editions Anthropos, Paris.

LeVine, R. (1966). *Dreams and Deeds: Achievement Motivation in Nigeria.* University of Chicago Press, Chicago.

Lewis, J. Van D. (1981). Domestic labor intensity and the incorporation of Malian peasant farmers into localized descent groups. *American Ethnologist* 8: 53–73.

Lipton, M. (1976). *Why Poor People Stay Poor: Urban Bias in World Development.* Harvard University Press, Cambridge.

Little, P. D., and Horowitz, M. M. (1987). Subsistence crops are cash crops: Some comments with reference to eastern Africa. *Human Organization* 46: 254–258.

Matlon, P. (1981). The structure of production and rural incomes in northern Nigeria: Results of three village case studies. In Bienen, H., and Diejomaon, V. P. (eds.), *The Political Economy of Income Distribution in Nigeria.* Holmes and Meier, New York, pp. 323–372.

Meek, C. K. (1957). *Land Tenure and Land Administration in Nigeria and the Cameroons. Colonial Research Studies No. 22.* Her Majesty's Stationery Office, London.

Moore, M. P. (1975). Cooperative labor in peasant agriculture. *The Journal of Peasant Studies* 2: 270–291.

Moran, E. F. (1988). Social reproduction in agricultural frontiers. In Bennett, J. W. and Bowen, J. R. (eds.), *Production and Autonomy: Anthropological Studies and Critiques of Development.* University Press of America, Lanham, Maryland.

Mortimore, M. (1987). Shifting sands and human sorrow: Social response to drought and desertification. *Desertification Control Bulletin* 14: 1–14.

Netting, R. McC. (1964). Beer as a locus of value among the West African Kofyar. *American Anthropologist* 66: 375–384.

Netting, R. McC. (1965). Household organization and intensive agriculture: The Kofyar case. *Africa* 35: 422–429.

Netting, R. McC. (1968). *Hill Farmers of Nigeria: Cultural Ecology of the Kofyar of the Jos Plateau.* Seattle, University of Washington Press.

Netting, R. McC. (1987). Clashing cultures, clashing symbols: Histories and meanings of the Latok War. *Ethnohistory* 34: 352–380.

Netting, R. McC., Stone, G. D., and Stone, M. P. (1993). Agricultural expansion, intensification, and market participation among the Kofyar, Jos Plateau, Nigeria. In Turner, B. L., II, Hyden, G., and Kates, R. W. (eds), *Population Growth and Agricultural Change in Africa.* University Press of Florida, Gainesville, pp. 206–249.

Norman, D. W. (1969). Labor inputs of farmers: A case study of the Zaria Province of the North Central State of Nigeria. *Nigerian Journal of Economic and Social Studies* 11: 3–14.

Norman, D. W., Simmons, E. B., and Hays, H. M. (1982). *Farming Systems in the Nigerian Savanna*. Westview, Boulder.

Ottenberg, S. (1959). Ibo receptivity to change. In Bascom, W. R., and Herskovits, M. J. (eds.), *Continuity and Change in African Cultures*. University of Chicago Press, Chicago, pp. 130–143.

Reyna, S. P. (1987). The emergence of land concentration in the West African Savanna. *American Ethnologist* 14: 523–541.

Richards, P. (1985). *Indigenous Agricultural Revolution: Ecology and Food Production in West Africa*. Hutchinson, London.

Richards, P. (1986). *Coping with Hunger: Hazard and Experiment in an African Rice-Farming System*. Allen and Unwin, London.

Rimmer, D. (1981). Development in Nigeria: An overview. In Bienen, H., and Diejomaon, V. (eds.), *The Political Economy of Income Distribution in Nigeria*. Holmes and Meier, New York, pp. 29–87.

Rowling, C. W. (1946). *Report on Land Tenure in Plateau Province*. National Archives, Jos Provincial Files 2/27 3324, Kaduna.

Saul, M. (1983). Work parties, wages and accumulation in a Voltaic village. *American Ethnologist* 10: 77–96.

Shenton, R. W. (1986). *The Development of Capitalism in Northern Nigeria*. James Currey, London.

Stone, G. D. (1986). The Cultural Ecology of Frontier Settlement. Paper presented at the Meeting of the Society of American Archeology, April, 1986.

Stone, G. D. (1988). Agrarian Ecology and Settlement Patterns: An Ethnoarchaeological Case Study. Ph.D. dissertation, Department of Anthropology, University of Arizona, University Microfilms, Ann Arbor.

Stone, G. D. (1991). Settlement ethnoarchaeology: Changing patterns among the Kofyar. *Expedition* 33: 16–23.

Stone, G. D. (1992). Social distance, spatial relations, and agricultural production among the Kofyar of Namu District, Plateau State, Nigeria. *Journal of Anthropological Archaeology* 11: 152–172.

Stone, G. D., Johnson-Stone, M. P., and Netting, R. M. (1984). Household variability and inequality in Kofyar subsistence and cash-cropping economies. *Journal of Anthropological Research* 40: 90–108.

Stone, G. D., Netting, R. McC., and Stone, M. P. (1990). Seasonality, labor scheduling, and agricultural intensification in the West African savanna. *American Anthropologist.* 92: 7–23.

Stone, M. P. (1988a). Women doing well: A restudy of the Nigerian Kofyar. *Research in Economic Anthropology* 10: 287–306.

Stone, M. P. (1988b). Women, Work and Marriage: A Restudy of the Nigerian Kofyar. Ph.D. dissertation, Department of Anthropology, University of Arizona, University Microfilms, Ann Arbor.

Watts, M. (1983a). *Silent Violence: Food, Famine, and Peasantry in Northern Nigeria*. University of California Press, Berkeley.

Watts, M. (1983b). Good try Mr. Paul: Populism and the politics of African land use. *African Studies Review* 26: 73–83.

Watts, M. (1984). State, oil, and accumulation: From boom to crisis. *Environment and Planning D: Society and Space* 2: 403–428.

15

Time, Space, and Transnational Flows: Critical Historical Conjunctures and Explaining Change in Northern Nigerian Agriculture

Louise D. Lennihan

In this chapter Lennihan presents us with an approach to the understanding of historical change that centers on the examination of the intersection of social and environmental events. In this example, she accounts for the progressive adoption of wage labor among the rural Hausa of Northern Nigeria in the first part of the twentieth century. The puzzle presented to historians by this case is that wage labor was established even though the rural population was not deprived of its land, and continues to this day to maintain widespread individual land ownership. Nevertheless, landowners found themselves obliged to obtain wage labor through cash payment. Lennihan traces the progressive development of dependence upon cash itself in what was formerly an economy and society where labor, to a large extent, was provided by the household, sometimes including slaves, and neighbors. This arose through a series of political, economic, and environmental crises that are directly related to the region's interactions with distant regions through colonialism and trade. Initially, local farmers are obliged to grow export commodities such as cotton in order to pay taxes imposed

This paper was originally presented at a seminar at Hunter College, New York, New York, March 13, 1982, and was originally published in *Human Ecology: An Interdisciplinary Journal,* 12(4)(1984): 465–480.

Louise D. Lennihan, Department of Anthropology, Hunter College, City University of New York, New York, New York 10021.

Case Studies in Human Ecology, edited by Daniel G. Bates and Susan H. Lees. Plenum Press, New York, 1996.

by British colonial authorities; the values of their crops vary with international trade conditions, which themselves reflect a variety of local situations elsewhere. At the same time, their own local conditions vary with the weather. When two or more such shifts—such as a drop in the price of cotton and several successive years of drought—occur together, farmers are forced to adopt wage labor even though they own land. Lennihan refers to such intersections of social, political, economic, and environmental events as "critical historical conjunctures" that should provide useful keys to historical investigation.

INTRODUCTION

The following is primarily a methodological note that bears on the study of human–environment interaction. Its point of departure is the reality of intensified transnational flows of capital, information, and people during the colonial and postcolonial periods, and the need this poses for an analysis that tacks back and forth between the global and the local. As such it contributes to the new anthropology of modernity, a field being defined by cultural anthropologists and human geographers (see Comaroff and Comaroff, 1993; Pred and Watts, 1992; Watts, 1992; Gupta and Ferguson, 1992; Harvey, 1989; Appadurai, 1988; Lennihan, in press). In addition to addressing the issue of space, which is a central focus of the anthropology of modernity, it raises the issue of time. Obviously, both time and space are critical in how one delineates one's unit of analysis. Unfortunately, in much of the literature that constitutes the anthropology of modernity the need to theorize space has taken place at the expense of consideration of time. A partial explanation may be found in Soja's (1989) interesting observation that the history of the social sciences contains a radical marginalization of the geographical imagination and, conversely, a powerful historicism according pride of place to history. What is ignored in often ahistorical treatments of the postcolonial, post-Fordist, or postmodern period is Soja's view that places indeed *do* have "distinctive historical geographies, [their] own time-place structuration" (Soja, 1989:158 cited in Pred and Watts, 1992:14). Beyond repeating the call for historically informed analyses (see Pred and Watts, 1992; Comaroff and Comaroff, 1993), my purpose here is to suggest a method for selecting points of entry, a way into the stream of history at moments that have the potential to result in transformation.

This methodological note derives from the task of documenting the emergence of agricultural wage labor in Northern Nigeria.[1] The basic question has been one of explaining how the expanded production of agricultural commodities for market has affected the manner in which labor itself has become a commodity. In approaching this question, I have found that formulating an answer has depended on determining the dynamics of what I call critical historical conjunctures. I see such conjunctures as being constituted of historical moments in which a local ecological calamity converges with a crisis in the political economy, the latter usually being transnational in character. The result of this convergence multiplies the ramifications of each of these two crises simultaneously.

If one considers, for example, the fifty years from the onset of colonial rule in Northern Nigeria until the end of World War II, it is possible to identify a series of such conjunctures, historical benchmarks that can be shown to have fundamentally altered the conditions of production and exchange in Hausa society. The drought-related famine of 1913 and the outbreak of World War I in 1914, when the closing of shipping lanes to Europe caused the collapse of export crop prices, is one such conjuncture. Another occurred in 1919, when epidemics of influenza, cerebral-spino meningitis, and rinderpest coincided with the post-World War I European trade depression and a second collapse in the export market. In 1926–1927 and in 1930–1931, first drought, then locust-related famines again coincided with European trade depressions.

While the following analysis is highly specific to the Northern Nigerian case, it is of broader relevance for two reasons. First, the political–economic crises involved are international crises. As such, they constitute logical points of entry for understanding the essential dynamics of local–international interaction not only in Northern Nigeria, but in many other regions which have confronted the transnational movement of capital. Second, its method addresses a number of issues central to human ecological study today. In summary, the issues at hand are those of boundary definition, scale, and time depth in human ecological study. At a deeper level, given the field's characteristic ahistoricism as well as its inability to relate adaptive behavior to wider socioeconomic contexts, there is the question of epistemology (see Watts, 1983a). It is in this context that the following analysis is offered.

---

[1]This is not to be confused with the long-standing practice of migrant dry season labor described by Prothero (1957) and others.

AGRICULTURAL WAGE LABOR IN NORTHERN NIGERIA

Let us begin by considering literature on rural production in Northern Nigeria. At the empirical level, the discussion of agricultural change rests on a number of facts and assumptions concerning labor in relation to land, technology and capital. In Northern Nigeria, rural producers in general have not been separated from the land.[2] A landless proletariat laboring for a landed rich has not emerged (Hill, 1972; Norman, 1972; Williams, 1976, 1979; Williams and Beer, 1976). Agricultural wage labor is recognized to have taken place as far back as the pre-colonial period (Usman, 1972; Lovejoy and Hogendorn, 1993). It is, however, considered insignificant both in terms of frequency of occurrence as well as a principle of labor organization when compared with servile labor in the pre-colonial period or with labor organized along the lines of kinship since then. The household is, as it has been for centuries, the primary unit of the domestic economy (Smith, 1955, p. 22; Fika, 1978, p. 42).

When it comes to technology, while tractors are seen in the country-side, the fact that they are often broken down and/or belong to a ministry of agriculture scheme means that, with the exception of the small number of World Bank-targeted progressive farmers, virtually all rural producers use the hand plow and hoe. Added to these features of land, labor, and technology is the nature of capital. With a few notable recent exceptions, industrial capital is not present in the rural areas and has not undertaken to alter directly the social relations of production by establishing agricultural estates.

In view of these facts and assumptions, analysts operating in both the neoclassical and the more radical socialist traditions have reached the same conclusion when it comes to the question of agricultural wage labor and the accompanying process of rural differentiation.

The neoclassical treatment of these issues in the Northern Nigerian case is as follows. First, the existence of peasants in the face of capitalist development poses no contradiction, for in reality, peasants are small capitalists (Hill, 1972; Norman, 1972). Second, while empirically inequalities exist, the absence of land scarcity and the fact that what wage labor there is "is seldom undertaken at the expense of one's own farming" (Hill, 1972, p. 106) is seen to have precluded the emergence of opposing classes of capitalist farmers and agricultural wage workers. Third, there is a view that, because the distribution of inequalities does not remain stable either within

---

[2]This is not true in densely settled areas surrounding large cities like Kano, Sokoto, and so forth (see Hill, 1977).

individual lifetimes or inter-generationally, they do not amount to "class stratification" (Hill, 1972, p. 176). This leaves accounting for why the rich are rich and the poor are poor. When it is discovered that rich and poor cannot be distinguished by characteristics such as number of adult sons, nature of start in life, amount of land inherited, etc., in the last analysis, luck and innate farming aptitude are presented as the underlying basis of rural wealth (Hill, 1972, pp. 172–173, 188).

The radical interpretation turns on the following points. First, it rejects the neoclassical tenet that peasants are small capitalists (Williams, 1976; Williams and Beer, 1976). It does, however, join the neoclassical position that inequalities do not amount to opposing rural classes. When it comes to explaining why the rich are rich and the poor are poor, great difficulty is experienced. As for poverty, Chayanov's explanations of illness, natural disaster, and lack of family labor are cited (Williams, 1976, pp. 147–148). In addition, it is stated that peasants are exploited by urban-based merchants, state-buying monopolies, and European trading firms (Williams and Beer, 1976: pp. 138–139). But how? Here, the notion of unequal exchange is cited, that is, buying a product below and/or selling it above its value. The problem with this is that, while no one disagrees that merchants accrue profits through unequal exchange, this transaction neither directly transforms the conditions of production nor provides an explanation for the appropriation of surplus value. In plain English, merchants by definition make profits by controlling markets, not by revolutionizing production. In conclusion, by offering unequal exchange as an explanation of rural poverty, the radical position tells us nothing about either capital accumulation or dissipation in the countryside, or about the transformation of agriculture.

HOW DID WAGE LABOR ARISE?

That, then, is the empirical and theoretical context in which I undertook my research. My field site was a small town that at the turn of the century had been a small walled village. With the building of a railroad through the area in 1912, the village became a railhead on the line. As a result, it both increased in size and took on more market functions vís a vís other settlements with which it had interacted. A hub for brokerage activities, a bulking center where export crop buying stations and European canteens sprang up, it became increasingly important in relation to other population centers, especially when a cotton ginnery opened in the town in the 1920s.

Ultimately, the town proved an appropriate choice in light of my desire to work in an area where I would be able to document in the archives the increased production of crops for market. There were annual railway statistics documenting outward railings of produce, records from the cotton ginnery showing fluctuations in the price and purchases of cotton, and so forth. What I had not anticipated, however, given the existing literature, was the high incidence of agricultural wage labor in the town. One-third of the town's households were unable to get through an annual agricultural cycle without selling their labor and/or mortgaging unharvested crops at 100% interest. Inundated with stories of woe from both the buyers and sellers of labor, it was clear that production relations were undergoing dramatic alteration. The important question became explaining how the expanded production of agricultural commodities for market had affected the manner in which labor itself has become a commodity.

In addressing this question, I became aware of the importance of identifying those historical moments that can be seen to constitute critical conjunctures in the nascent transformation of agrarian society in Northern Nigeria. Let me offer a more detailed example of this approach in an analysis of three such conjunctures, the famines and trade depressions of 1913–1914, 1926–1927, and 1930–1931. My concern is to illuminate both the causes and consequences of famine in Northern Nigeria by showing its relation to transnational trade depressions that resulted from, first, the closing of shipping lanes to Europe during World War I; second, the British General Strike of 1926; and, third, the crash of 1929. My description will be limited to one of the northern provinces, that of Zaria.

THE ADVENT OF EUROPEAN MERCHANT CAPITAL, ZARIA PROVINCE, 1902–1914

In seeking to understand the conditions leading up to the crisis of 1913–1914, a good starting place is the remarks made by the Provincial Resident in 1904, two years after the British conquest of Zaria Emirate. In his view, what was most needed was "an *incentive to the people to grow surplus produce,* over and above what they require for their own food . . ." (ZarProf 2551 Annual Report for Zaria Province, 1904, his emphasis).[3] According to him, this could be achieved best "by setting up stores at large centres like Zaria, where the people could purchase such things as cloth, agricultural and culinary implements, *Birmingham goods* of all sorts, soap, oil, sugar, European provisions, etc." (ZarProf 2551 Zaria Province Annual Report, 1904). A common enough strategy, the remark was odd only in juxtaposition to the fact that Zaria was at that moment experiencing

[3]All archival references are from the National Archives, Kaduna, Nigeria.

famine. As the Resident noted, 1904 had been "marred by such scarcity of corn, owing to the blight which affected the preceding harvest, that in some districts there was a regular famine and actual hunger" (Ibid).

The following year, the first merchant firm arrived in Zaria. It was noted, however, that it did "not give much promise for trading operations in the future" (ZarProf 2552 Zaria Province Annual Report, 1905). Nevertheless, numerous other companies followed.

By 1911, the Niger Company had four branches in Zaria Province, their purchases for that year totaling 10,263.14.0 (SNP 7 975/1912 Zaria Province Annual Report #50, 1911, p. 29). In 1913, the Resident had cause to write that "[t]rade has gone ahead by leaps and bounds . . ." (SNP 10 58p/1914 Zaria Province Report, December 1913). Cash sales totaled £8000 per month and rivalry between firms was "very active." The first quarter of 1914 recorded cash trade double that for the corresponding period of 1913. In only nine years, the pessimistic projections of the Resident of Zaria in 1904 had been proved wrong.

There was, however, one complication. In 1913, it was noted once again that Zaria had "scarcely any corn reserve" (SNP 10 738p/1913 Zaria Province Report, September Quarter 1913). There were several causes. One was that taxation during the previous year had increased by almost 300%, forcing farmers to sell grain (Arnett, 1920: 21). Another was that the 1912 planting season had been marked by "a very serious period of drought" (SNP 10 178p/1913 Zaria Province Annual Report, 1912). To make matters worse, in 1913 rainfall in Zaria was well below average. Similarly, scarce rain and poor crops struck Kano, Bornu, and Sokoto, provinces to the north of Zaria.[4] Fears of wholesale "drainage of supplies by agents or by caravans" from these provinces led the Emir of Zaria to warn farmers against the temptation of high prices "lest famine overtake them [the people of Zaria] later on" (SNP 10 58p/1914 Zaria Province Report, December 1913).

But by 1914, the same report that had heralded the expansion of the export trade stated:

> . . . scarcity of corn has been severely felt in the Northern portion of the Province . . . Guinea corn [sorghum] is now sold in the Zaria market at 1d per *mudu* (about 1/2 lb.) and I anticipate in a few weeks time there will be no food left; and, unless native traders import from other provinces, for a few weeks before the *gero* [millet] crop is reaped the people of Zaria will be in a bad way. (SNP 10 410p/1914 Zaria Province Report, June Quarter 1914)

---

[4]See Watts (1979: 279–290) for a grisly description of what was a far more severe famine in the more northern provinces (also see Watts, 1983b).

As it turned out, the drought and food scarcity of 1912–1913 were only the first problems in what later years would show to be an established round of difficulties. As a result of the increased cereal cultivation that occurred the following year, the 1914 harvest brought overproduction and a corresponding drop in the price of grain.

But that was not all. The year 1914 also brought the outbreak of World War I, a transnational crisis with dire local ramifications in Zaria Province. For a time, "trade almost ceased" (SNP 10 197p/1915 Zaria Province Annual Report No.65, 1914). A general trade depression in the purchase of all export crops followed. While sales for the first half of 1914 had doubled those for the first half of 1913, during the last half of 1914 they dropped by 35%.

In summary, 1905–1914 were roller-coaster years of boom and bust. Exports steadily grew as food crops were increasingly neglected. The boom year of 1913 coincided with drought and serious food shortages. The year 1914 brought the cycle of trade full circle. Local overproduction and the collapse of grain prices coincided with World War I and an international depression in export crop prices.

Such was the first conjuncture of ecological and trade crises in Northern Nigeria. In 1926–1927 and in 1930–1931, similar conjunctures would occur, as first drought, then locust-related famines in Zaria Province coincided with European trade depressions. Let us consider the events of these two periods. In doing so, analysis will focus on one crop—cotton, and one merchant firm—the British Cotton Growers' Association (BCGA).

THE BRITISH COTTON GROWERS' ASSOCIATION AND THE CASE OF COTTON[5]

In 1902, the BCGA had arrived in Northern Nigeria to develop a cotton export industry. Its goal was to offset irregularities of supply from the United States that had plagued the health of the British textile industry since the 1860s. Most effective of its numerous tactics was the development of a buying system designed to guarantee that cotton growers would not only sell to the BCGA, but at practically any price.

For some time, merchants who bought on commission for the BCGA under its buying monopoly, and who were therefore bound to pay the BCGA's fixed price, competed with one another over the volume of their purchases by issuing their buying agents quantities of salt and cloth. An

[5]The following is drawn from Shenton and Lennihan (1981) and Lennihan (1983, Ch. 3) which contain fuller documentation.

agent, in turn, would offer these as gifts to the cotton producer if he promised to sell to him at harvest. The eager acceptance of such advances was not hard to explain. Each year, rural producers found themselves requiring larger and larger sums of ready cash. Part of this need related to taxation, the incidence of which not only climbed, but the collection of which was deliberately carried out before the cotton harvest. Furthermore, with the arrival of foreign firms, there took place in the sphere of necessary consumption a substitution of European goods for goods previously produced locally. Thus, for example, a young man seeking a wife did not get very far with a few carved calabashes and shea nut oil, now having to compete with men offering enamel pots and umbrellas as part of the bridal payment. Similarly, European tea and sugar became a socially defined necessity for breaking the fast at Ramadan. The ease with which such luxuries became established as necessities probably related to the fact that, in the first 5 years of the colonial period, producer prices were relatively high, and the amount of labor required to obtain these items was not exorbitant.

The years 1915–1924 saw the realization of merchants' hopes as sales climbed each year (see Table 1). But this was not surprising, given a steady rise in price.[6] In 1924, the situation changed when the BCGA gave up its buying monopoly. Given the figures of the preceding years, it felt that cotton export was entrenched firmly enough to do away with a fixed price, not to mention buying commissions, and to throw the market open to competition.

In the 1924–1925 buying season, the first year of open competition, the price of cotton dropped by 25%, but purchases did not drop correspondingly. Sales along the Bauchi Light Line remained constant, and sales for Zaria Province as a whole actually increased by 26%. Obviously, the local market did not offer serious competition. During the following buying season, 19251926, prices dropped by another 25%. In this period, Bauchi Light Line sales increased by 23%, and Zaria Province sales rose by 11%. Producers' willingness to increase production in the face of lower prices can be understood to have been other than perverse when it is realized that falling prices were experienced as deterioration in the terms of exchange of the commodities the household sold relative to those it bought. This meant a reduction in levels of consumption and/or an expansion of commodity production.

Such was the background leading up to the events of 1926–1927. While cotton prices continued to plummet, the situation changed. This time, sales were halved. Labor unrest in Britain had created great uncertainty in the home market. As the Resident of Zaria reported:

[6]One exception was the price decline of the 1921–1922 buying season (see Lennihan 1983: 138).

Table 1. Total Purchases of Cotton in 400 lbs Bales New Weight[a]

Buying season	Northern provinces	Zaria Province	Bauchi Light Line	Price (1 lb.)[b]
1915–1916	121	nd	nd	1 3/4d
1916–1917	433	nd	nd	1 3/4d
1917–1918	855	nd	nd	2 1/2d
1918–1919	2,248	nd	nd	2 3/4d
1919–1920	3,568	nd	nd	3 3/4d
1920–1921	5,403	3,854	nd	4 1/2d
1921–1922	9,883	6,639	nd	2d
1922–1923	11,224	6,230	nd	2 1/2d
1923–1924	15,683	7,892	4,193	4–3d
1924–1925	27,996	9,961	4,433	3d
1925–1926	37,556	11,074	5,456	2 1/2d
1926–1927	16,659	5,244	2,504	1 1/8–1 3/4d
1927–1928	16,316	3,549	1,578	2 3/8–2 1/8d
1928–1929	24,686	4,880	2,786	2 1/4–2 1/8d
1929–1930	34,389	5,631	3,630	1.6–1.2d
1930–1931	13,849	1,667	1,124	0.8–0.5d
1931–1932	4,811	676	383	0.6–0.8d
1932–1933	22,228	4,191	2,629	0.8–0.9d
1933–1934	23,013	5,520	3,197	0.9–1.2d
1934–1935	50,022	11,473	6,259	1.1–1.5d
1935–1936	49,795	8,650	5,070	1.1–1.6–1.1d
1936–1937	49,196	9,740	5,617	0.9–1.3d
1937–1938	23,174	8,062	4,580	0.6–0.8d
1938–1939	19,588	5,058	2,829	0.7–0.6d
1939–1940	50,000[c]	8,648	4,215	1.4–1.2d

[a] Compiled from NAK SNP 17 10199 Vol. I Agriculture Department Reports on Cotton Growing Industry in Nigeria 1923–1929. Report on the Cotton Export Industry for the Half-Year, March 31, 1927, and NAK MINAGRIC 20121 Crop Marketing and Cotton Export Tax. Unfortunately, comparable data for grains do not exist.
[b] Multiple prices indicate price fluctuations through the buying season.
[c] Approximate.

Trade conditions were promising at the beginning of the year, but the General Strike and Prolonged Coal Strike in England have had a depressing effect, and conditions at the end of the year can only be described as bad. (SNP 17 K111 Vol.III Zaria Province Annual Report, 1926: 26)

To make matters worse, a huge American cotton crop reduced the world price of cotton, leaving Nigerian cotton uncompetitive. As a result, firms stopped buying, leaving the BCGA the sole purchaser. In the absence of competition, no advances were offered, and many farmers had to sell grain to find cash for tax payments (SNP 17 10199 Vol.I Agricultural Department

Reports on Cotton Growing Industry in Nigeria; Half-Yearly Cotton Report, March 31, 1927: 1).

There was another reason for reduction in cotton sales, however. Poor rains had yielded a very small crop. Even more important for the rural producer was the drought's effect on his food crops. Famine conditions prevailed by April 1927 (SNP 17 10199 Vol. I Agricultural Department Reports on Cotton Growing Industry in Nigeria; Half-Yearly Cotton Report, Sept.30, 1927).

If 1927–1928 saw farmers suffering from famine, this period also brought stability back to the British home market. European merchants quickly reentered the Northern Nigeria market with renewed vigor. But given the food shortages and the lack of advances the previous year, it was food, not cotton, that had been planted. The severity of the situation was illustrated starkly when in many instances the cotton seed eagerly distributed by the BCGA was eaten by the starving rural population (SNP 17 10199 Vol.I Agricultural Department Reports on Cotton Growing in Nigeria 1923-1929, Half-Yearly Cotton Report, Sept. 30, 1927). Nevertheless, an expanding and highly competitive merchant sector was keen to buy. Given the rural producers' need to purchase food, the fierce competition among an inordinate number of firms over a very small crop, the advance system flourished as never before.

It is fair to conclude that this influx of cash into the rural areas on the heels of a severe food shortage had an uneven effect on the population. Prior to the arrival of European merchant capital, indigenous merchants had been neither able nor likely to infuse huge masses of capital into rural circulation in order to capitalize on the producers' predicament. In this new circumstance, the more prosperous farmers who had weathered both the bad harvest and the necessity to sell grain to pay their taxes with food reserves still intact could turn their cash advances into productive capital by hiring wage laborers, increasing the size of the following year's crop and, consequently, of the next year's advance. Such investments were facilitated by an abnormally swollen labor pool consisting of numerous small local farmers. With grain reserves depleted by both the bad harvest and the need to sell grain to pay taxes, small farmers found themselves forced to labor on the farms of their more fortunate neighbors in order to purchase food.

In this way, the operation of the advance system in the context of a severe food shortage had two effects. First, it made producers increasingly dependent on expanding commodity production in order to get access to much needed cash. Second, it allowed for the creation of a local market for food and labor in the rural economy on a scale previously unknown. Hence, it is significant that the advance system, a feature of the political economy of trade, working in a particular ecological context (in this case reduced rainfall) was drastically altering the conditions of production both within and between households.

A second crisis soon followed, and like the first it was heralded by 3 years of low prices (see Table 1). In the 1929–1930 buying season prices dropped by 50%. But once again, cotton planting strategies had been based on the previous year's price, so sales did not reflect this decline. Not until the following year would the full effect of the Crash of 1929 and the World Depression be felt. In the 1930–1931 buying season, cotton prices dropped by another 50%. As the Resident commented, the prices offered would "hardly repay the native for this labour" (SNP 17 14830 Zaria Province Annual Report, 1930: 4). Cotton sales dropped by 79% as farmers withheld their crop from market in hopes of an eventual price rise.

But, as had been the case in 1926, factors other than low price affected cotton sales in Zaria. Severe locust invasions had caused farmers to focus attention on food crops. In these same months, "reports were received, especially from the Southern Districts, of wholesale destruction by locusts" and the possibilities of a famine in Southern Zaria became a certainty (Ibid, p. 41).

Despite numerous replanting efforts, the 1930–1931 harvest brought famine. A more devastating conjuncture of disasters could hardly be imagined: Pestilence, famine, and a worldwide depression leading to the collapse of export prices. As the Resident reported, "The year 1931 was a black one for Zaria" (SNP 17 16678 Vol.I Zaria Annual Report, 1931, p. 16).

In the following buying season of 1932–1933, cotton prices remained at the previous year's dismal low. Nevertheless, cotton sales increased by 519% for Zaria Province as a whole, and by 586% along the Bauchi Light Line.

The severity of the producer's worsening situation during the interwar crisis of capitalism was underlined by a report on taxation and the colonial economy. It stated that, taking 1926 as the base year, export prices had fallen from 107 in 1928 to 37 in 1933. In one year alone, 1932–1933, they had fallen from 64 to 37, or 40%. Taxation, however, did not reflect this fall. Data provided by the Department of Agriculture showed the incidence of rural taxation at 38–40% *of total income* (Jacobs, 1934: 37).

By the late 1930s, the situation had so deteriorated that the colonial administration commissioned a major study of indebtedness in the cotton growing area along the Bauchi Light Line, including my field locale. This report went far in documenting how the changing nature of rural production was generating changes in the reproduction of the rural household itself. It reported that between 30–42% of all rural producers could not get through an annual agricultural cycle without borrowing (ZarProf 1486A

Report on Cooperation in Zaria). Inquiries as to why people borrowed showed the three most frequent causes to be food shortage, marriage expenses, and tax payment. With evidence revealing over a third of society to be indebted, information on the sources of loans and interest rates indicated a mechanism which perpetuated even greater inequality and differentiation in the countryside.

The two most important ways to obtain a loan were, first, through the mortgaging of unharvested crops to local rich farmer/traders for a quantity of grain (or sometimes its cash equivalent in order to circumvent Koranic prohibitions against usury), and second, taking a cash advance from a produce buyer against an unharvested export crop. In the first case, a needy man borrowed a given quantity of grain in return for twice that amount at harvest. Given this rate of repayment, from the time of harvest, the borrower faced the next agricultural cycle with an already depleted grain store. As a result, it was likely that he would run short of grain again and have to resort to borrowing. Like laboring on another man's farm, mortgaging food crops established a vicious cycle of exploitation and poverty for the borrower, while for the lender it constituted a cycle of enrichment and capital accumulation. In the second case, that of taking an advance from a produce buyer, the cost of borrowing was more difficult to calculate, as theoretically, an advance was interest-free. In reality, it carried its own hidden costs. For example, a producer already mortgaged to a buyer had little recourse should the lender try to short-weight him or offer an uncompetitive price at harvest.

CONCLUSION

Operating at the methodological level, what I have tried to show is that to understand the changing nature of rural production, and in particular to understand so-called ecological disasters, as analysts, we must be prepared to move up and down and across two axes, a vertical one that carries us from the macro to the micro level, from Lancashire to the countryside of Northern Nigeria, if you will, and a horizontal one that moves us back and forth between the domains of ecology and political economy, from drought and pestilence to World War I, the General Strike, the depressions of 1919 and the 1930s, and so forth. In my own work, I have come to see such historical conjunctures as representing the intersection of these two axes. If one is interested in the transformation of agrarian societies and their experiences of modernity in a transnational context, identifying such conjunctures is a useful method for entering the stream of history at moments that have the potential to result in transformation.

REFERENCES

Appadurai, A. (1988). Putting hierarchy in its place. *Cultural Anthropology* 3, 1: 36–49.

Arnett, E. J. (1920). *Gazetteer of Zaria Province.* Waterlow and Sons, London.

Banaji, J. (1976). Summary of selected parts of Kautsky's "The Agrarian Question." *Economy and Society* 5(1): 1–49.

Bartlett, P. (1980). Adaptive strategies in peasant agricultural production. *Annual Review of Anthropology* 9: 545–573.

Bates, D. G. and Lees, S. H. (1979). The myth of population regulation. In Chagnon, N. and Irons, W. (eds.), *Evolutionary Biology and Human Social Behavior: An Anthropological Perspective.* Duxbury, North Scituate, MA.

Bernstein, H. (1977). Notes on capital and the peasantry. *Review of African Political Economy* 10: 60–73.

Brookfield, H. and Kirkby, A. (1974). On man, environment and change. Working notes, IGU Workshop on Man-Environment Relations.

Chayanov, A. V. (1966). In Kerblay, B., Thorner, D. and Smith, R. E. F. (eds.), *The Theory of Peasant Economy* (translation). R. W. Irwin, Homewood, IL.

Clarke, W. G. (1977). The structure of permanence; The relevance of self-subsistence communities for world ecosystem management. In Bayliss-Smith, T. P. and Feacheam, R. G. A. (eds.), *Subsistence and Survival: Rural Ecology in the Pacific.* Academic Press, New York.

Comaroff, J. (1993). Ethnicity, nationalism, and the politics of difference in the age of revolution. Paper presented at the City University of New York, Ph. D. Program in Anthropology Colloquium, November 5.

Comaroff, J. L. and Comaroff, J. (eds.) (1993). *Modernity and its Malcontents.* University of Chicago Press, Chicago.

de Crisenoy, C. (1978). *Lenine Face aux Moujiks.* Editions du Seuil, Paris.

de Crisenoy, C. (1979). Capitalism and agriculture. *Economy and Society* 9(1): 9–25.

Evans, L. and Block, R. (1976). *Leon Trotsky on China.* Monad Press, New York.

Fika, A. (1978). *The Kano Civil War and British Over-Rule 1882–1940.* Oxford University Press, Ibadan.

Gramsci, A. (1975). *Selections from the Prison Notebooks.* International Publishers, New York.

Gupta, A. and Ferguson, J. (1992). Beyond "culture": Space, identity and the politics of difference. *Cultural Anthropology* 7, 1: 6–23.

Harvey, D. (1989). *The Condition of Postmodernity.* Blackwell, Cambridge, MA.

Hewitt, K. (ed.) (1983). *Interpretations of Calamity.* Allen and Unwin, Boston.

Hill, P. (1972). *Rural Hausa.* Cambridge University Press, Cambridge.

Hill, P. (1977). *Population, Prosperity and Poverty.* Cambridge University Press, Cambridge.

Hogendorn, J. (1978). *Nigerian Groundnut Exports.* Ahmadu Bello University and Oxford University Press Nigeria, Zaria and Ibadan, Nigeria.

Lenin, V. I. (1969). *The Development of Capitalism in Russia.* Beekman, New York.

Lennihan, L. (1983). The origins and development of agricultural wage labor in Northern Nigeria 1886–1980. Unpublished doctoral dissertation in anthropology, Columbia University, New York.

Lennihan, L. (in press). The anthropology of modernity and the postmodern anthropology of "development" discourse. *Reviews in Anthropology.*

Lovejoy, P. and Hogendorn, J. (1993). *Slow Death for Slavery: The Course of Abolition in Northern Nigeria, 1897–1936.* Cambridge University Press, New York.

Marx, K. and Engels, F. (1979). *Pre-Capitalist Socioeconomic Formations*. Progress Publishers, Moscow.

McCay, B. (1978). Systems ecology, people ecology, and the anthropology of fishing communities. *Human Ecology* 6(4): 397–422.

McGovern, T. (1980). Cows, harp seals, and church bells. *Human Ecology* 8(1): 247–275.

Moran, E. (ed.) (1984). *The Ecosystem Concept in Anthropology*. Westview Press AAAS Selected Symposia Series, Boulder, CO.

Morren, G. (1980). The rural ecology of British drought 1975–1976. *Human Ecology* 8(3): 33–63.

National Archives, Kaduna, Nigeria. ZarProf 2551, Annual Report for Zaria Province, 1904.

National Archives, Kaduna, Nigeria. ZarProf 2552, Zaria Province Annual Report for 1905.

National Archives, Kaduna, Nigeria. SNP 7 975/1912, Zaria Annual Report No. 50 for 1911.

National Archives, Kaduna, Nigeria. SNP 10 58p/1914, Zaria Province Report for December 1913.

National Archives, Kaduna, Nigeria. SNP 10 175p/1915, Zaria Province Annual Report No. 65 for 1914.

National Archives, Kaduna, Nigeria. SNP 10 738p/1913, Zaria Province Report for September Quarter, 1913.

National Archives, Kaduna, Nigeria. SNP 10 178p/1913, Zaria Province Annual Report for 1912.

National Archives, Kaduna, Nigeria. SNP 10 410p/1914, Zaria Province June Quarter 1914.

National Archives, Kaduna, Nigeria. SNP 10 197p/1915, Zaria Province Annual Report No. 65 for 1914.

National Archives, Kaduna, Nigeria. SNP 17 10199 Vol. 1, Agricultural Department Reports on Cotton Growing Industry in Nigeria 1923–1929. Report on the Cotton Export Industry for the Half-Year Ending March 31, 1927. Half-Yearly Cotton Report for the Period Ending September 30, 1927. Half-Annual Cotton Report for the Six-Months Ending 31st March, 1931.

National Archives, Kaduna, Nigeria. MINAGRIC 20121, Crop Marketing and Cotton Export Tax.

National Archives, Kaduna, Nigeria. SNP 17 KIII Vol. III, Zaria Province Annual Report 1926.

National Archives, Kaduna, Nigeria. SNP 17 14830, Zaria Province Annual Report, 1930.

National Archives, Kaduna, Nigeria. SNP 17 16678 Vol. 1, Zaria Annual Report, 1931.

National Archives, Kaduna, Nigeria. SNP 17 22185 Vol. III, Regulations in Regard to Purchase, Sale, Inspection and Grading of Cotton.

National Archives, Kaduna, Nigeria. ZarProf 14864, Report on Cooperation in Zaria.

Nietschmann, B. (1972). Hunting and fishing focus among the Miskito Indians, eastern Nicaragua. *Human Ecology* 1(1): 41–67.

Norman, D. (1972). *An Economic Survey of Three Villages in Zaria Province*. Institute of Agricultural Research, Samaru Miscellaneous Papers, 37, 38, and 39, Samaru, Nigeria.

Orlove, B. (1980). Ecological anthropology. *Annual Review of Anthropology* 9: 235–273.

Pred, A. and Watts, M. J. (1992). *Reworking Modernity: Capitalism and Symbolic Discontent*. Rutgers University Press, New Brunswick, NJ.

Prothero, R. M. (1957). Migrant labor in Northeastern Nigeria. *Africa* 27: 251–262.

Shea, P. J. (1975). The development of an export-oriented dyed cloth industry in Kano Emirate in the nineteenth century. Unpublished doctoral dissertation in history, University of Wisconsin, Madison.

Shenton, R. W. and Lennihan, L. (1981). Capital and class: Peasant differentiation in Northern Nigeria. *Journal of Peasant Studies* 9(1): 47–70.

Smith, M. G. (1955). *The Economies of Hausa Communities in Zaria.* HMSO, London.

Soja, E. (1989). *Postmodern Geographies: The Reassertion of Space in Critical Social Theory.* Verso Press, London.

Usman, Y. B. (1972). Some aspects of the external relations of Katsina before 1804. *Savanna* 1(1): 175–198.

Vayda, A. P. (1980). Buginese colonization of Sumatra's coastal swamp lands and its significance for development planning. In Bird, C. F. and Soegiarto, A. (eds.), *Proceedings of the Jakarta Workshop on Coastal Resource Management.* United Nations University, Tokyo, pp. 80–87.

Vayda, A. P. (1983). Progressive contextualization: Methods for research in human ecology. *Human Ecology* 11(3): 265–281.

Vayda, A. P. and McCay, B. (1975). New directions in ecology and ecological anthropology. *Annual Review of Anthropology* 4: 293–306.

Vayda, A. P. and McCay, B. (1977). Problems in the identification of environmental problems. In Bayliss-Smith, T. P. and Feacheam, R. G. A. (eds.), *Subsistence and Survival: Rural Ecology in the Pacific.* Academic Press, New York.

Vayda, A. P., Lolfer, C., Pierce, J. and Brotokusumo, M. (1980). Interactions between people and forest in East Kalimantan. (UNESCO) *Impact of Science on Society* 30(3): 179–190.

Watts, M. J. (1979). A silent revolution: The nature of famine and the changing character of food production in the Nigerian Hausaland. Unpublished Ph.D. dissertation in geography, University of Michigan, Ann Arbor.

Watts, M. J. (1983a). On the poverty of theory. In Hewitt, K. (ed.), *Interpretations of Calamity.* Allen and Unwin, Boston.

Watts, M. J. (1983b). *Silent Violence: Food, Famine, and Peasantry in Northern Nigeria.* University of California Press, Berkeley.

Watts, M. J. (1992). Space for everything. *Cultural Anthropology* 7(1): 115–129.

Williams, G. (1976). Taking the part of the peasants in Nigeria and Tanzania. In Gutkind, P. C. W. and Wallerstein, I. (eds.), *The Political Economy of Contemporary Africa.* Sage, London.

Williams, G. (1979). *Nigeria: Economy and Society.* Rex Collins, London.

Williams, G. and Beer, C. E. F. (1976). The politics of the Ibadan peasantry. In Williams, G. (ed.), *Nigeria: Economy and Society.* Rex Collins, London.

16

Ecology and Mormon Settlement in Northeastern Arizona

William S. Abruzzi

The process of colonization has been important in the ecological understanding of evolution since Darwin's observation of the radiation of finch species as they colonized new island habitats. Human colonization processes, however, though historically documented, have rarely been interpreted using ecological concepts and models. Abruzzi provides a start in filling this gap with a reinterpretation of the history of Mormon colonization of northeastern Arizona in the last quarter of the nineteenth century. Like other modern human ecologists, he takes great care to delineate details of local differences in environment and economy among the different settlements. In this arid region, perhaps the most critical variable is water availability, through rainfall as well as surface and groundwater, which are partially dependent on rainfall and also affected by geological features such as landform and soil characteristics. While drought was a periodic problem, flooding, which caused dam failures, was a significant problem that varied among communities. The physical environment, while directly affecting the potential and the limitations of human settlement, provides only part of its context here. The other significant factor is the social environment, both locally and at a distance. The relationship between the colonists and their home base in Salt Lake City is significant both in that the Mormon Church provided subsidies for the colonies and in that it laid

Originally published in *Human Ecology: A Multidisciplinary Journal,* 15(3)(1987): 317–338.

William S. Abruzzi, Department of Anthropology, Pennsylvania State University, Ogontz Campus, Abingdon, Pennsylvania 19002.

Case Studies in Human Ecology, edited by Daniel G. Bates and Susan H. Lees. Plenum Press, New York, 1996.

down directives for local community interaction and interdependence. When individual communities suffered from crop failure or the destruction of a dam, they could acquire resources from their neighboring communities, which had been obliged by the church to set aside part of their production for tithes, and to share with their needy brethren. This interdependence provided for viability of vulnerable local communities over the long run. Other cooperative enterprises were also established among the settlements, though each eventually failed after initially prospering, perhaps because, unlike tithing, they did not incorporate all the settlements and hence were too small and too subject to local environmental problems. Eventually, other social and environmental conditions altered the context of Mormon colonization, as non-Mormons migrated into the area in numbers.

During the second half of the nineteenth century, the Mormon Church in Salt Lake City undertook an extensive colonization program designed to safeguard Mormon autonomy in the face of increasing non-Mormon immigration into the American West (see Stegner, 1942, 1964; Arrington, 1958). Between 1847 and 1900, over 500 Mormon agricultural settlements were established in arable valleys from Canada to northern Mexico in an effort to limit non-Mormon settlement throughout this vast region (see Arrington, 1958: 88). Several Mormon farming settlements were founded in the Little Colorado River Basin of northeastern Arizona as part of this larger effort. The colonization of this basin proceeded under close Church supervision; not only was settlement initiated by the church, but church leaders remained actively involved in the temporal affairs of these communities into the early years of the twentieth century (see Peterson, 1973; Leone, 1979; Abruzzi, 1993a).

Mormon colonization of the Little Colorado River Basin was largely a success. By the close of the nineteenth century, nearly twenty Mormon farming communities existed throughout this 5000 square mile region. The overall success of Mormon settlement in the basin was due in large part to the development of a system of tithing redistribution which offset the destabilizing consequences of local environmental variability (see Abruzzi, 1989). Tithing, most of which was paid in kind, was collected and stored in local church warehouses and redistributed to those in need. Through tithing redistribution, communities which experienced poor harvests or dam failures gained access to surplus resources produced elsewhere in the basin.

However, despite active church involvement, the redistribution of resources, and extensive intercommunity cooperation, significant local developmental differences quickly emerged. Some towns grew to several hundred persons by the end of the century, while others contained barely more than a few families. Several settlements were even abandoned within a few years of their founding. Agricultural production also varied sharply among these towns, as did the complexity of the economic, social, and political organization achieved by each community. By most measures of community development, some settlements were clearly more successful than others.

In the following paper, I present an ecological explanation of Mormon colonization of the region. In offering an ecological explanation of this settlement process, however, I do not simply show that physical environmental factors influenced community development in this region. I also propose that several developments accompanying the settlement process conform to expectations derived from general ecological theory. Specifically, I suggest that both local differences in community development and the role of tithing redistribution in successful Mormon colonization can be accounted for by an ecological model of the evolution of complex communities.

MORMON SETTLEMENT IN THE LITTLE COLORADO RIVER BASIN

Mormon colonization of the Little Colorado River Basin began in 1873 when a well-equipped company of over 100 men, women, and children was sent to the region by church leaders in Salt Lake City (Tanner and Richards, 1977: 12). This initial effort failed, however, and a second attempt was made in 1876. This time, 500 pioneers were organized into four companies to maximize the success of the mission, and four settlements—Sunset, Brigham City, Obed and St. Joseph—were established along the lower valley of the Little Colorado River (see Figure 1). These settlements quickly served as bases for the founding of additional colonies throughout the river basin, including Woodruff, Snowflake, Taylor, and Showlow along Silver Creek, and St. Johns, Eagar, and Alpine along the upper reaches of the Little Colorado River. While most Little Colorado Mormon towns had been founded by 1880, immigration continued throughout the nineteenth century. A continuous supply of manpower was needed to secure smaller outlying valleys and to reinforce existing settlements. Because colonization proved difficult and emigration remained high, church leaders were repeatedly forced to dispatch new settlers to the region in order to replace those who left.

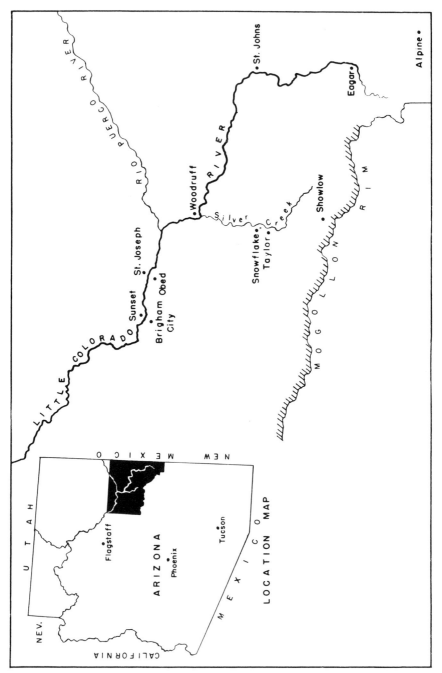

Figure 1

Although political conflict with non-Mormon interests provided a significant drain on local Mormon resources during the early years of colonization (see Peterson, 1973: 217–241; Abruzzi, 1993a: 175–180), the greatest enduring hardship was imposed by vagaries of the natural environment. Crop losses from droughts and floods were a common occurrence, with additional damage inflicted by insects, hailstorms, high winds, and early frosts. So variable were local environmental conditions that individual settlements frequently lost crops to several causes during a single year (cf. Abruzzi, 1993a: 23–25). Consequently, agricultural productivity remained limited and highly variable throughout the settlement period. While farmers at Sunset produced nearly 7000 bushels of wheat and corn in 1879 (Peterson, 1973: 19), that year's harvest exceeded the total crop raised there during the previous 3 years combined. Sunset was eventually abandoned in 1883 following several years of poor harvests. Brigham City also suffered repeated crop failures prior to its dissolution in 1881, while St. Joseph experienced near-total crop failure during three of the seven years between 1876–1882.

Agricultural productivity was equally variable throughout the remaining years of the nineteenth century. More than half the years between 1880 and 1900 witnessed either poor harvests or general crop failures throughout the basin, while two devastating droughts caused the additional loss of thousands of head of cattle during the 1890s (see Abruzzi, 1994). So variable was agricultural productivity and so high was the cost of maintaining agricultural settlements in this climatically unstable region that many more towns would have disappeared had it not been for the judicious application of church resources and for the strategic availability of non-agricultural employment.[1] • Although some settlements depended upon such subsidies more than others, no town was completely independent of extra-regional resources for its survival.

[1]Church subsidies were critical to the survival of most settlements in the region (see Abruzzi, 1993a: 180–181, *passim*). Among other things, the church furnished material support for the rebuilding of dams; it redirected tithing revenues to offset poor harvests; it subsidized land purchases; it negotiated grading contracts with the Atlantic and Pacific Railroad to provide needed employment; and it repeatedly provided manpower through its "calls" for pioneers to settle in the basin. Externally-generated employment was also important. A railroad grading contract negotiated by the church enabled many settlers to replace their dangerously depleted food stocks following the severe winter of 1879 and the general failure of the 1880 harvest. Freighting, particularly to Fort Apache to the south, was also of considerable economic importance to early settlements. Freighting contracts provided an important income for the Arizona Cooperative Mercantile Institution (ACMI), the church-related mercantile establishment in the region (see Peterson, 1973: 136–153; Leone, 1979: 79–82). This institution provided temporary employment for many early settlers. It was, for example, an important source of income for settlers at Woodruff following each of several dam failures.

Table 1. Population, Productivity, Stability, and Functional Diversity among Little Colorado Mormon Settlements, 1887–1905

Town	Total tithing (1887–1900)		Per capita tithing (1887–1900)		Population size (1807–1905)		Number of occupations (1900)	Number of businesses (1905)	Number of business categories (1905)
	X^*	V	X	V	X	V			
St. Johns	3561	.239	7.09	.179	506	.201	22	34	22
Snowflake	3025	.195	7.58	.203	404	.148	16	24	20
Eagar	1810	.180	5.15	.157	310	.231	8	20	14
Taylor	1463	.217	4.75	.169	308	.111	8	3	3
St. Joseph	1124	.435	8.49	.349	118	.269	5	3	3
Woodruff	915	.389	5.44	.358	153	.265	12	8	6
Alpine	449	.327	4.54	.419	105	.302	3	2	2
Showlow	431	.335	2.40	.323	182	.261	7	6	6

$^*X$ = mean (in dollar values), and V = coefficient of variation.
Source: Abruzzi (1987:322).

Due to their limited and variable agricultural productivity, most Mormon settlements remained economically marginal throughout the nineteenth century. However, as already indicated, significant local developmental differences occurred. Tithing records show that annual agricultural productivity varied substantially among individual settlements and within the same settlement during different years (see Table 1).[2] Agricultural productivity at Snowflake and St. Johns, as represented by the mean annual tithing collected at each of these towns, was six times greater and only half as variable as that at either Showlow or Alpine. Tithing by field crops, a particularly revealing indice of agricultural productivity, shows even greater local differences (see Abruzzi, 1993a: 38). Population size and stability varied substantially among these settlements as well (see Table 1).

In terms of agricultural productivity, four towns—Snowflake, St. Johns, Taylor, and Eagar—were the most productive and least variable Mormon settlements in the region. They also contained the largest and most stable populations and achieved the greatest occupational and business diversity (see Table 1). Two of these four towns—Snowflake and St. Johns—ranked highest overall. By 1900, they were the most productive agricultural communities in the entire basin and had evolved a greater occupational and business diversity than any other Mormon settlements in the region. They had also developed the most complex church organizations and had achieved their respective organizations within the shortest period of time (see Abruzzi, 1993a: 43).[3]

---

[2]Cash was a scarce commodity in this frontier region. Consequently, nearly all tithing received in the Little Colorado Settlements during the nineteenth and early twentieth centuries was paid in kind. Items were tithed as they became available, and tithing stocks were generally most abundant during the fall, following the harvest. Tithing data, therefore, provide reliable indices of community productivity.

[3]The Mormon Church is divided administratively into stakes and wards, which may be compared to diocese and parishes respectively in the Roman Catholic Church. Each of these administrative levels is composed of different organizations performing distinct functions. During the nineteenth century, each settlement contained one ward, and by the close of the century two stakes had been established in the region, one at Snowflake and the other at St. Johns.

Differences in local church organization are important for understanding the evolution of community complexity among these early settlements. The local church organization provided the near-exclusive governmental apparatus through which the temporal affairs of these communities were administered. Local church leaders presided over such matters as land distribution, dam construction and maintenance, property disputes, distribution of tithing, and punishment for such local offenses as theft and adultery. The full complement of ward and stake organizations were not established simultaneously. Rather, specific organizations were formed as resources, most notably manpower, were available to perform their specific functions. Differences in the complexity of church organization, thus, reflect local differences in the availability of administrative resources.

In order to understand the differences in community development that occurred during Mormon colonization of this region, as well as the role that tithing redistribution played in that colonization effort, it is necessary to examine the conditions to which these early pioneers had to adapt. Inasmuch as the physical environment imposed the greatest enduring stress on these towns, it is necessary to understand the nature of that environment, in particular its spatial and temporal variation.

The Little Colorado River Basin

The Little Colorado River Basin forms an undulating plain sloping to the north and northeast. Elevation rises from 5000 feet near St. Joseph to about 8500 feet along the Mogollon Rim, a steep escarpment 75 miles to the south. The southeastern portion of the basin contains several peaks exceeding 10,000 feet, including Mount Baldy, the second highest peak in Arizona, which reaches an elevation of 11,403 feet.

Climate throughout the region is arid to semi-arid, with annual precipitation ranging from 9 inches near St. Joseph to over 25 inches in parts of the southern highlands. Precipitation occurs primarily from December through March and from July through September, with little or no moisture received at most locations during the remaining months. Winter precipitation is of greater importance for local agriculture, because it is released gradually as runoff, and because it is more evenly distributed geographically. In contrast, summer precipitation occurs mostly as torrential storms that deposit large amounts of water for brief periods of time within highly restricted areas. Most summer precipitation surges down well-worn arroyos and is not available to local farmers. Furthermore, because of their intensity, summer storms are highly erosive; they remove large amounts of soil particles and increase the sediment load in streams at lower elevations.

In contrast to precipitation, length of the growing season varies inversely with elevation. The mean number of frost-free days ranges from 87 at Alpine to 179 near St. Joseph, and growing season variability increases as the mean decreases. Consequently, both the length and reliability of the growing season vary inversely in relation to average annual precipitation. This inverse relationship has made dry farming a marginal adaptive strategy locally (see Harrell and Eckel, 1939: 32) and has effectively limited successful agricultural settlements to river valleys below 6000 feet where adequate growing seasons exist and where suitable surface water sources could be exploited.

The direct relationship between elevation and precipitation is reflected in a more or less clear plant community gradient throughout the region.

Northern desert vegetation predominates in the lower valley of the Little Colorado River near St. Joseph and is succeeded southwards at increasingly higher elevations by grassland, juniper–piñon woodland and montane forest communities. Grasslands constitute the largest single vegetative community, comprising 40% of the total land area, followed by juniper–piñon woodland at 38% (Abruzzi, 1993a: 88). Bare soil accounts for 55–65% of total surface cover in the grassland community (Dames and Moore, 1973; [Section 4]: 201), a condition which contributes significantly to the high sediment content of streams at lower elevations. Due to increasing moisture at higher elevations, tree size, and density increase southward within the juniper–piñon woodland community, and both juniper and piñon are replaced by forests of ponderosa pine at 6000 feet. Ponderosa pine is, in turn, succeeded by aspen and Englemann spruce at 8000 feet, while lush alpine meadows occur widely throughout the basin above 9000 feet.

Sub-Regions in the Basin

Based largely on climate and precipitation, the Little Colorado River Basin may be divided from north to south into three broad subregions: (1) the lower valley of the Little Colorado River, (2) intermediate elevations, and (3) the southern highlands. Locations within the lower valley receive about 9 inches of annual precipitation and have an average growing season of about 180 days. St. Joseph and Woodruff are both situated within the lower valley. St. Joseph is located within the northern desert plant community, while Woodruff is situated within a small valley along the northern margin of the grassland community.

The growing season at intermediate elevations ranges from 130 to 160 days, with precipitation averaging between 12 and 13 inches. Mormon settlements at intermediate elevations include Snowflake, St. Johns, Taylor, and Eagar. Snowflake and Taylor are located in adjoining valleys within the juniper–piñon woodland community, while St. Johns is situated within the grassland community. Eagar is located in a valley at the foothills of the southern mountains where the ascending vegetation succeeds rapidly from grassland through woodland to montane forest communities. While Eagar's elevation is higher than that of all other intermediate settlements, it is climatically in the shadow of nearby mountains. Consequently, Eagar experiences climatic conditions similar to those of settlements at intermediate elevations.

Alpine and Showlow are both located in the southern highlands and are situated within the montane forest community. Precipitation averages 18 inches at Showlow and about 25 inches at Alpine, the highest settlement.

While the growing season at Showlow averages about 120 days, as previously indicated it is only 87 days at Alpine.

Soils

Although soils throughout the basin are generally thin and loamy, local soil characteristics and quality vary sharply (see Kester et al., 1964; Miller and Larsen, 1975). Soils in the lower valley, particularly at St. Joseph, are generally of low fertility, being low in organic matter and deficient in both nitrogen and phosphorus. Soils in this sub-region possess low permeability and are, therefore, highly susceptible to flooding, especially during the heavy summer rains. They are also relatively high in sodium, a problem that has been seriously aggravated by irrigation (see Abruzzi, 1985).

Soils at intermediate elevations are superior to those in the lower valley, with Snowflake and Taylor possessing among the best soils in the entire basin (see Kester et al., 1964: 11). Soil permeability is moderate among all intermediate settlements except Eagar, where a temporary water table occurs in some irrigated areas during the growing season. Alkalinity is moderate in the soils at St. Johns and Eagar, while soils at Snowflake and Taylor are generally free from harmful accumulations of soluble salts, even after a century of continuous irrigation (Bureau of Reclamation, 1947, p. 42; Salt River Project, 1974 [Section 3]: 78).

Due to the greater precipitation and denser vegetation which prevails at higher elevations, soils in the southern highlands resemble those in the northeastern United States more than they do neighboring soils at lower elevations. Of particular significance is their high organic content and water-holding capacity. Unlike the soils near Showlow, however, those at Alpine are poorly drained and susceptible to flooding. They are also slightly acidic.

Water

The single most important physical factor influencing community development in this arid river basin has been the availability of suitable water for irrigation (see Abruzzi, 1985). Early settlements had access to water in only two forms: precipitation and surface flow. As already indicated, precipitation is highly variable, inversely related to length of the growing season, and generally inadequate to support farming. The regional precipitation cycle is also incompatible with local agricultural requirements. As much as 45% of annual irrigation needs must be applied to fields during the dry months of April, May, and June when there is generally little or no rain (see Bureau of Reclamation, 1947: 72; U.S. Geological Survey, 1975: 40–43).

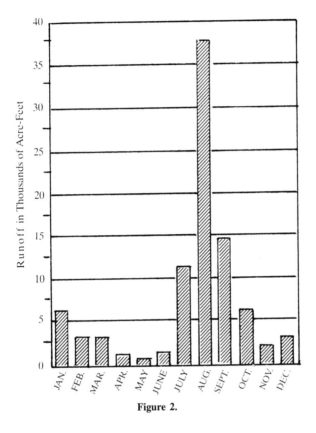

Figure 2.

The vagaries of precipitation made all early farming settlements in the region necessarily dependent on surface water for irrigation. However, since streams throughout the region flow largely in direct response to precipitation, surface water availability follows an annual cycle closely linked to that of precipitation (see Figure 2). Runoff is generally moderate between January and March due to the melting of snowpacks at higher elevations. As snowpacks disappear, runoff declines, and by June most streambeds in the region are dry, save those at higher elevations. With the onset of intense summer storms in July, streamflow volume and velocity increase sharply. As the summer storms pass, surface flow subsides until snow reaccumulates at higher elevations.

Pronounced short-term fluctuations in surface flow also occur, and it is not uncommon for dry streambeds to be transformed within hours into dangerously swollen rivers destroying all manmade obstacles in their path.

This is particularly true of the Little Colorado River at lower elevations, where flooding remains a serious problem for towns situated along its route. For early Mormon settlements, the risk of flooding was especially high during spring runoff and following intense summer storms (see Abruzzi, 1993a: 121–142).

Although stream-flow variability was widespread, it was greatest in the lower valley of the Little Colorado River where the largest surface area is drained. However, because no suitable reservoir sites exist at lower elevations, lower valley settlements could only construct diversion dams. These towns, therefore, remained completely vulnerable to the highest level of stream-flow variability in the basin. As a result, agricultural productivity throughout the lower valley remained among the most variable in the region.

Stream-flow variability also yielded a significantly higher incidence of flooding and dam failures among the lower valley settlements. St. Joseph and Woodruff suffered 13 and 10 dam failures respectively between 1876 and 1900, compared with two at St. Johns, three at Snowflake and Taylor, one at Showlow, and none at Eagar and Alpine. The greater vulnerability of irrigation systems in the lower valley was due to the inherent weakness of dams in this subregion. Owing to the deep alluvial composition of the lower Little Colorado River bed, lower valley settlements were unable to build their dams upon firm foundations (see Abruzzi, 1993a, pp. 123–131). In addition, when sharp increases in stream-flow caused the collapse of dams at higher elevations, chain reactions generally resulted in dam failures downstream as well.

The direct costs imposed by flooding and dam failures included not only the time, materials, and manpower required to rebuild the dams themselves, but also those needed to repair ditches and replant fields. The indirect costs of dam failures included the labor that could not be invested in other productive activities, as well as the deleterious effect that repeated flooding had upon soil fertility. The fact that only two of the six towns established in the lower valley survived strongly suggests that the cost of farming was highest in this subregion of the basin. No other portion of the basin lost as many settlements. Furthermore, the history of dam failures at St. Joseph and Woodruff clearly demonstrates that these two settlements would likely have become extinct as well had it not been for the repeated subsidies of cash, materials, produce, and labor they received from other Mormon towns within and outside the basin (see Abruzzi, 1989, 1993a, pp. 123–131).

Stream-flow variability added a further burden to farming in the lower valley. Because settlements in this subregion had to rely upon surface water as it became available, which was primarily during periods of greatest flow, they had to use this water precisely when it contained the highest sediment concentrations. Without reservoirs, farmers in the lower valley could not store surface water and allow its sediment to subside. Because the sediment load in streams at lower elevations approaches 20% of stream flow (Bureau of Reclamation, 1950: 3), continued irrigation there caused a decline in agricultural productivity by reducing soil aeration and permeability.

Only two streams of consequence exist in the region: The Little Colorado River and its principal tributary, Silver Creek. Most agricultural settlements were located along these two streams, whose specific characteristics contributed significantly to local differences in agricultural productivity during the settlement period. The Little Colorado River originates as snowmelt from Mount Baldy and descends quickly in a narrow stream bed. It is perennial south of St. Johns due to seeps from underground springs. However, below St. Johns, the river opens into a flat, sandy bed and the gradient declines to only 10 feet per mile (Harrell and Eckel, 1939: 29). Surface flow is intermittent below St. Johns and is confined exclusively to subsurface channels during late spring and early summer. Water quality in the Little Colorado deteriorates rapidly downstream from St. Johns as the river flows through salt-bearing formations and receives increasing amounts of water from tributaries originating in these strata. As the Little Colorado flows through the lower valley, concentrations of sodium and other solids accumulate steadily and render its water increasingly unacceptable for domestic, agricultural, or industrial use (see Abruzzi, 1985, 1993a: 101–103).

Silver Creek contrasts sharply with the Little Colorado River. Originating from a series of springs known collectively as Silver Creek Spring about ten miles southeast of Snowflake and Taylor, it is the only fully perennial stream in the entire river basin. The most significant feature of Silver Creek Spring is the abundance, reliability, and quality of the water it discharges. Several documents reveal that this spring has never failed to flow, not even during the most protracted drought in the region (see Harrell and Eckel, 1939: 30; Bureau of Reclamation, 1947, p. 50). In addition, as already indicated, the quality of water in Silver Creek near Snowflake and Taylor exceeds that of all other water sources in the basin, save those at the highest elevations. However, as with the Little Colorado, water quality in Silver Creek deteriorates at lower elevations, and stream-flow variability increases.

Human Impact

Human resource exploitation in the Little Colorado River Basin exacerbated local environmental differences. The two most prominent factors that intensified local differences in agricultural productivity were overgrazing and irrigation, both of which affected the availability of suitable quality irrigation water. The effects of overgrazing and irrigation were felt shortly after settlement had begun, and both appreciably increased the relative stress imposed upon lower valley settlements.

Overgrazing began in the 1880s when the Aztec Land and Cattle Company, a consortium of Texas ranchers and eastern businessmen, imported over 40,000 cattle into the basin (see Kennedy, 1968; Abruzzi, 1993a: 171–175, 1994). Overgrazing resulted in a sharp decline in vegetation throughout the grassland community which, in turn, increased soil erosion and the sediment content of streams at lower elevations. Much of this sediment accumulated behind the dams and upon the fields established by the lower valley settlements. While the most destructive consequences of overgrazing followed the devastating droughts of the 1890s, negative results appeared shortly after the Aztec Company arrived in the region (see Abruzzi, 1994).

Irrigation also increased the cost of agriculture in the lower valley. As already indicated, the continuous application of silt-laden water exacerbated the inherent low productivity of the poorly drained, alkaline soils of this sub-region. Besides producing a layer of fine silt that reduced soil permeability and aeration, irrigation also raised to the surface sodium particles located deep within the soil structure. Furthermore, as the settlements founded upstream from Woodruff and St. Joseph grew and diverted larger amounts of water from the Little Colorado River and Silver Creek, farmers in the lower valley were left dependent upon a river which became increasingly composed of water discharged by the Rio Puerco and other more northern tributaries. This northern water is of substantially lower quality than that originating to the south (see Abruzzi, 1985, 1993a: 99). Thus, while storage reservoirs constructed at Snowflake, Taylor, St. Johns, and other settlements upstream enabled these towns to diminish the impact that stream- flow variability had on their agricultural productivity, these same reservoirs reduced the quantity, stability, and quality of irrigation water available to farmers in the lower valley.

The Physical Environment and Community Development

In summarizing the role that the physical environment played in local community development, it may be stated that individual settlements evolved complex community organizations to the degree to which they were able to overcome critical limiting factors in their local environments. Settlements at the highest elevations were severely constrained by a growing season that was generally too short and too variable to allow consistently adequate harvests. Because an inadequate growing season imposed a limiting factor beyond effective human control, towns at the highest elevations remained the smallest, least productive, and least complex of all Mormon settlements in the region.

While lower valley settlements did not have to contend with inadequate growing seasons, they consistently endured high summer temperatures, dust storms, and an annual spring dry season which limited agricultural productivity throughout this subregion. In addition, they had to irrigate relatively infertile soils with the poorest quality, least reliable surface water in the entire region. Lacking suitable reservoir sites, lower valley settlements were also unable to overcome the increasing instability and decreasing quality of their water supply caused by activities upstream. The growth of these towns was further limited by recurring dam failures. Each dam failure produced a decline in population which, in turn, undermined the maintenance and repair of irrigation systems and the planting and care of crops. Thus, while the lower valley settlements achieved a higher average annual agricultural productivity than those in the southern highlands, their greater productivity was largely offset by its variability and by the substantial costs required to achieve it.

In contrast to all other settlements in the basin, those at intermediate elevations suffered neither inadequate growing seasons nor unreliable water supplies. All four towns at intermediate elevations enjoyed an average growing season in excess of 120 days, while proximity to perennial streams and suitable reservoir sites spared these towns the degree of surface water variability that plagued settlements in the lower valley. The four intermediate settlements were also situated in the largest and most fertile valleys and were able to irrigate those valleys with relatively abundant, reliable, and silt-free water. While not without problems, irrigation systems at intermediate settlements suffered significantly less destruction than those at lower elevations. Furthermore, when damage to irrigation systems did occur, these settlements contained the largest populations among which to distribute the costs of repair. Released from having to expend excessive amounts of time and energy just to maintain their infrastructure and their existing levels of productivity, farmers at intermediate settlements could channel surplus resources into those activities that improved and expanded irrigation systems, increased agricultural production, and promoted population growth. Together, these activities provided the material basis from which more complex communities evolved. Of all the Mormon towns in the basin, it was primarily the intermediate settlements—in particular Snowflake and St. Johns—that most closely approached the nineteenth century Mormon ideal of stable, diversified agricultural villages independent of surrounding non-Mormon communities and containing the full complement of church institutions.

Tithing Redistribution

Local environmental variability clearly imposed a considerable stress on these early pioneers. It resulted in highly variable harvests, frequent crop failures, and devastating dam losses. Indeed, the consequences of this variability caused the extinction of four out of the six settlements established in the lower valley and repeatedly threatened the entire colonization effort. However, through the collection, storage, and redistribution of tithing resources, the Little Colorado Mormon settlements were able to substantially offset the negative consequences of local environmental variability. As a result of tithing redistribution, individual towns facing a crop failure and/or a dam loss could acquire the resources they needed to survive until the following year's harvest.

The effectiveness of tithing redistribution was based in large part on the fact that it used the region's spatial diversity to offset its temporal variability. The various Mormon towns were situated in widely scattered river valleys, which generally experienced distinct schedules of variability. Thus, due to local differences in elevation, precipitation, temperature, growing season, soil quality, and surface water availability, droughts, floods, and other catastrophes occurred at diverse locations during various years. As a result, no clear correlation existed in the annual pattern of agricultural productivity achieved among the various towns in the region (see Lightfoot, 1980: 206–208).

For example, when warm years occurred throughout the region, they generally increased the length of the growing season at higher elevations and raised the probability of a successful harvest at towns such as Showlow and Alpine. However, these same higher temperatures increased the likelihood of crop failures at St. Joseph, Woodruff, and other towns through the heat stress and higher evapotranspiration rates they imposed on crops at lower elevations. Similarly, while cooler temperatures reduced heat stress on crops at lower elevations and raised the prospects of a good harvest in the lower valley, they increased the likelihood of destructive early frosts in the southern highlands. Likewise, while abundant rainfall generally increased agricultural productivity at lower elevations where permanent surface water sources were unavailable, it also resulted in flooding and crop damage at higher elevations, where soil permeability is low, and increased the risk of dam washouts along the lower valley of the Little Colorado River where the alluvial streambed inhibited the construction of dams able to withstand sharp increases in streamflow. In 1890, for example, most towns within the region experienced increased harvests due to an unusually wet agricultural season. However, during that same year crops rotted in the fields at Alpine and dams washed out at Snowflake, Taylor, Woodruff, and St. Joseph as a result of the flooding that occurred.

Significantly, tithing redistribution was not the only system of resource redistribution developed by the Little Colorado Mormon pioneers. Previously, the lower valley settlements jointly operated a series of productive enterprises in the southern highlands, including a sawmill, a dairy, a grist mill, and a tannery. These enterprises provided the lower valley settlements with cheese, butter, meat, lumber, and other products that could not be produced locally and that supplemented the wheat, corn, barley, sorghum, and garden vegetables they raised by irrigated farming along the Little Colorado (see Abruzzi, 1989). However, while these *conjoint enterprises* prospered initially, they all eventually failed and, unlike tithing redistribution, never served as an effective system of resource redistribution counteracting local environmental variability.

The failure of the conjoint enterprises was primarily due to the fact that they were supplementary operations that were ultimately dependent upon prevailing environmental conditions in the lower valley. Since all four enterprises were primarily summer operations, they necessarily competed for labor with farming in the lower valley. They, therefore, could only be developed to the extent that surplus labor was available among the lower valley towns during this time of the year. However, the lower valley settlements were all situated at neighboring locations within the same subregion and experienced nearly identical schedules of environmental variation. Most importantly, they generally experienced simultaneous dam failures and the intense demand for labor that subsequent dam reconstructions imposed. Thus, as St. Joseph, Woodruff, and the other lower valley towns continuously struggled with floods, poor harvests, and recurring dam failures, their populations dwindled and their ability to provide the additional manpower needed to operate the various conjoint enterprises declined. With the dissolution of Sunset, Brigham City, and Obed and the decline of population throughout the lower valley, the conjoint operations could no longer be maintained and were eventually abandoned.

The system of tithing redistribution, thus, succeeded for the very reasons the conjoint enterprises failed. First, tithing redistribution included every town in the basin and was, therefore, not limited by the environmental conditions that prevailed in just one portion of the basin. Furthermore, the productivity upon which tithing redistribution depended was based on the *total labor* of over 2000 individuals inhabiting some two dozen separate communities situated in numerous, diverse, and functionally independent local environments which were influenced by quite different schedules of variability. The conjoint enterprises, on the other hand, depended on the *surplus labor* of some 200 persons inhabiting a handful of towns in nearly identical neighboring environments experiencing nearly identical schedules of variability in the most unstable portion of the basin. Finally, unlike the conjoint enterprises, the relative effectiveness of tithing redistribution was enhanced by the fact that (1) it operated through a centrally administered religious organization that encompassed every town in the region, and (2) the local institutions through which it operated were affiliated with encompassing parent organizations outside the region that were independent of local environmental conditions (see Abruzzi, 1989).

It has thus far been shown that local differences in community development among pioneer Mormon settlements in the Little Colorado River Basin were largely consequences of divergent environmental conditions. It has also been shown that tithing redistribution: (1) was critical to the success of this colonization effort because it effectively offset the destabilizing consequences of local environmental variability for community development; and (2) was more effective in counteracting environmental variation than the previous system of conjoint enterprises because it linked some two dozen communities located in diverse habitats widely scattered throughout the basin and was not limited, as was the system of conjoint enterprises, to the surplus productivity of a few towns that were situated in neighboring locations within a single highly variable subregion. However, it still remains to be seen that all of these developments can be explained by general ecological theory.

The Evolution of Ecological Communities

Ecological communities, be they single or multi-species communities, evolve to the extent that the individual organisms and populations within them are able to exploit an increasingly narrow range of resources and, thus, occupy more specialized niches. Since competition promotes adaptive specialization and niche differentiation (see Levins, 1968: 10–38; Vandermeer, 1972: 114–116), natural selection produces the greatest functional diversity possible within a community.[4] Community evolution, thus, repre-

---

[4]Ecological theory regarding community evolution has been developed largely in relation to multispecies communities. Consequently, species number and variety have been used to determine the functional diversity of these communities (cf. Margalef, 1968; Brookhaven National Laboratories, 1969; Whittaker, 1975; Cody and Diamond, 1976). However, studies of functional diversity have also focused on single-species communities including, examining such topics as caste diversity among social insects (Wilson, 1968) and the organizational complexity of nonhuman primates (cf. Kummer, 1971). In the meantime, occupational categories and such functional units as farms, churches, businesses, lineages, or military societies have been used in a variety of disciplines to define the functional complexity of human societies

sents an incessant developmental process climaxing in the most diverse community structure that can be supported by available resources. Consequently, in order to explain the evolution of complex ecological communities, it is necessary to understand those factors that enhance or constrain adaptive specialization and niche differentiation within ecological systems. *Maintenance costs* pose the principal constraint upon specialization and community evolution. Ecological communities exist because abundant supplies of potential energy occur in their environments, and their complexity increases to the extent that this potential energy is converted into community productivity, biomass (population), and functional diversity. However, those activities that are needed to maintain organisms and populations within a community consume energy and are lost to the system. That is, they cause energy to flow *out of* the community rather than *through* it. For example, the cost of maintaining organisms at one trophic level within multi-species communities reduces the amount of net productivity that can be transferred to all subsequent trophic levels. Maintenance costs, thus, limit both the number and the diversity of species that can be maintained within a community. A decrease in maintenance costs increases community diversity by increasing the net productivity of a community, or the total amount of energy that flows through the community. As net productivity increases, the adaptive advantage of specialization increases, which leads to greater community diversity. An increase in maintenance costs has just the opposite effect. As maintenance costs increase, the total flow of energy through a community declines. As a result, the adaptive advantage of specialization is reduced, and community diversity decreases.

Complex ecological communities evolve, then, as a result of the selective advantage gained by organisms exploiting an increasingly narrow range of resource and from the interdependent network of energy flows that such increasing specialization creates (see E. Odum, 1971: 37–85; H. Odum, 1971: 58–103; Whittaker, 1975). The conditions that enhance community diversity are, therefore, those which increase the amount and reliability of energy flowing through the community and reduce community maintenance costs. All external factors influencing the flow of energy through ecological communities may, therefore, be classified according to the effect they have upon maintenance costs and community evolution. Those factors that reduce maintenance costs and increase community diversity are defined as

---

(cf. Naroll, 1956; Thomas, 1960; Carneiro, 1962, 1967, 1968; Clark et al., 1964; Gibson and Reeves, 1970). In each of the above situations, the analytical unit employed delineates the organization of productive functions within the respective community studied and varies in its dimensions in response to conditions of resource availability. Each can, therefore, be equally considered an Operational Taxonomic Unit (OTU) within niche theory (see Vandermeer, 1972).

energy subsidies, while those which increase maintenance costs and reduce community diversity are classified as energy drains (see E. Odum, 1971: 43–53; Abruzzi, 1993: 58–59, 68). Although numerous specific environmental conditions act as either subsidies to, or drains upon, community evolution, research has shown that certain general considerations prevail. *The most complex ecological communities evolve in environments that are both productive and stable* (cf. MacArthur and MacArthur, 1961; Pianka, 1966; Margalef, 1968; Rosenzweig, 1968; Sanders, 1968; Slobodkin and Sanders, 1969; May, 1973; Whittaker, 1975; Cody and Diamond, 1975; Abruzzi, 1987, 1993: 55–78).

Environmental productivity is positively associated with community diversity because greater productivity increases the likelihood that resources which might otherwise be insufficient to support a particular adaptive specialization will be sufficient for its maintenance. Conversely, those factors which decrease productivity reduce the adaptive advantage of specialization. As a result, organisms that inhabit unproductive environments must generally exploit a broader range of resources than those in more productive ecosystems (cf. Terborgh, 1971).

However, while environmental productivity has traditionally been considered the *a priori* condition needed for the evolution of complex ecological communities, research has demonstrated that the developmental benefits of high productivity can be compromised and even negated by environmental instability (see Sanders, 1968; Holling, 1973; May, 1973; Leigh, 1976). Since a high degree of adaptive specialization can only evolve where the availability of required resources is reliable, the same selective factors that limit functional diversification in unproductive environments restrict its development in unstable ones as well. Consequently, complex ecological communities evolve only in highly predictable environments with low variability. The greater diversity of tropical multispecies communities, for example, derives less from abundant productivity than from environmental stability (cf. Sanders, 1968).

For several years, ecologists have debated the precise relationship between diversity and stability in ecological systems. While the thesis outlined above, that stability enhances diversity in ecological communities, has received widespread empirical support (cf. Sanders, 1968; May, 1973; Pielou, 1975; Cody and Diamond, 1976), considerable research also exists supporting the alternate thesis that complexity promotes stability (cf. McArthur, 1955; McArthur and Connell, 1966; Margalef, 1968; Brookhaven National Laboratory, 1969; Rogers and Hubbard, 1974). The controversy surrounding the causal priority of diversity versus stability in ecological communities likely reflects processes operating at distinct levels in hierarchically organized ecological systems (see Leigh, 1977; Alexander and Borgia, 1978;

Abruzzi, 1982: 28–31; Ricklefs, 1987). The enhanced community stability that results from community diversity derives ultimately from the productivity and stability of the encompassing ecosystems within which ecological communities exist (see Abruzzi, 1987).

However, functional diversity promotes stability in ecological communities under very specific conditions based on the degree to which redundancy exists in the flow of energy/resources through a community. Sufficient redundancy can only exist when the various energy/resource flows of a community originate in numerous functionally independent channels. Only then can the destabilizing effects of environmental perturbations be offset by a complex network of overlapping energy/resource flows. Where sufficient redundancy does not exist, the negative consequences of environmental variability are more likely to ramify throughout a community and reduce its stability, even within relatively diverse communities (May, 1973; Holling, 1973; Leigh, 1976; Abruzzi, 1993a: 62–64).

If the above ecological considerations are to prove applicable to the Little Colorado Mormon settlements, then the most functionally diverse of these towns should have evolved in the most productive and stable environments and should have been characterized by the largest and most stable populations and agricultural productivities. Conversely, the least diverse communities should have been situated in the least productive and stable environments and should have been characterized by small, unstable populations and by limited and variable agricultural productivities. Furthermore, the contribution of tithing redistribution to the colonization effort should have derived from the fact that it provided sufficient redundancy in the flow of resources to offset the impact of local environmental variability on community survival. Moreover, the degree of redundancy provided by tithing redistribution in the flow of energy/resources among local communities should have substantially exceeded that provided by the unsuccessful system of conjoint enterprises. A brief reconsideration of the material presented above will show that the developments that occurred during Mormon colonization in the Little Colorado River Basin conform to ecological expectations.

Ecological Theory and the Little Colorado Mormon Communities

Mountain valley settlements were located within small, narrow valleys at elevations that offered generally inadequate and highly variable growing seasons. Low environmental productivity and stability prevailed under such conditions and resulted in both limited and highly variable community productivity among settlements in this subregion. As predicted by ecological theory, mountain valley settlements were the smallest and least functionally diverse communities in the region. Additional problems existed at Alpine, due to its higher elevation, which made it the least diverse even of the mountain communities (see Abruzzi, 1993a: 119).

St. Joseph and Woodruff are situated within larger valleys than either Alpine or Showlow, offering them the potential for greater aggregate community productivity. However, poor soils, high evapotranspiration, and inferior quality irrigation water limited the natural productivity of these valleys. In addition, sharp fluctuations in the water supply restricted each community's productivity and contributed to its substantial variability. Climatic instability also caused frequent dam losses, which imposed high maintenance costs upon these two settlements and exacerbated their highly variable populations and agricultural productivities. St. Joseph, Woodruff, and the other lower valley settlements also endured the greatest negative consequences of human environmental activities elsewhere in the basin, which consistently reduced the already low environmental productivity and stability of this sub-region. Although lower valley settlements achieved slightly higher levels of community productivity than did those at the highest elevations, the positive developmental effect of these higher levels was negated by both intense environmental instability and oppressive maintenance costs. Consequently, this subregion witnessed the greatest number of failed settlements, and the functional diversity attained at St. Joseph and Woodruff by the close of the nineteenth century was not substantially greater than that achieved by the mountain valley settlements.

As already indicated, all of the most successful settlements in the region were situated at intermediate elevations. In each instance, large valleys, sufficient growing seasons, good soils and abundant, superior quality irrigation water yielded high environmental productivity. Environmental stability resulted from perennial surface water sources, and was enhanced through the construction of storage reservoirs. Maintenance costs were also the lowest in the region. With high environmental productivity and stability yielding large populations subject to relatively low maintenance costs, intermediate settlements generated the highest and most stable levels of net productivity of any settlements in the region. As predicted by ecological theory, they also achieved the greatest functional diversity.

The same ecological considerations used to explain sub-regional variations in community development may also be applied to account for individual differences in community development as well. Table 2 ranks and compares individual settlements according to composite indices of population, productivity, and stability on the one hand and functional diversity

Table 2. Rank-Order of Mormon Settlements (1887–1905)[a,b]

Settlement	Composite population, productivity, and stability rank-order	Composite diversity rank-order
Intermediate settlements		
Snowflake/Taylor	1	1
St. Johns	2	2
Eagar	3	3
Lower valley settlements		
St. Joseph	4	6
Woodruff	5.5	4
Mountain settlements		
Showlow	5.5	5
Alpine	7	7

[a] Source: Abruzzi (1981, 269).
[b] $r_s = .884$, $p < .01$.

on the other. In the first column, each settlement's composite population-productivity-stability ranking is achieved by averaging its separate individual rankings for mean (X) and coefficient of variation (V) of annual tithing and population size. Column two presents each settlement's composite functional diversity ranking by averaging its individual ranking for number of occupations, businesses, and business categories. Snowflake and Taylor are treated as a single community in the calculations performed.[5] As predicted by ecological theory, a strong positive rank-order correlation is achieved.

Finally, ecological theory accounts for the role that tithing redistribution played in successful colonization. Through tithing redistribution, local church leaders were able to channel considerable resources into local projects that enhanced community productivity and stability and that, therefore, advanced the colonization effort. Since the system of tithing redistribution encompassed every town, it integrated the productivity and labor originating in every occupied habitat throughout the region. Redundancy clearly existed in this system of resource redistribution, as it was based on the exploitation of diverse habitats by permanent and independent populations not simultaneously affected by the same environmental pertur-

[5] Due to their close proximity and functional interdependence, Snowflake and Taylor must be considered a single community in the analysis of community development in this region. Located in adjoining valleys less than three miles apart and sharing Silver Creek's water, Snowflake and Taylor quickly established a unified irrigation system. Close proximity led to the integration of most other community functions as well.

bations. It, therefore, contained numerous, overlapping resource flows that originated from independent sources whose productivities displayed distinct schedules of variation. In addition, this system's link with comparable systems outside the basin augmented its inherent redundancy by connecting it to resource flows that were completely independent of environmental conditions within the basin. From the perspective of ecological theory, tithing redistribution stood in sharp contrast to the earlier system of conjoint enterprises. The latter system contained little redundancy because it was ultimately dependent upon environmental conditions that prevailed within the highly variable lower valley. Consequently, whereas tithing redistribution effectively offset the destabilizing consequences of local environmental instability, the system of conjoint enterprises succumbed to it.

CONCLUSION

The above discussion of Mormon colonization in the Little Colorado River Basin has shown that physical environmental differences underlay variations in community development in the region. The dominant role of the natural environment is strongly suggested both by the similar pattern of development displayed by settlements in the same sub-region and by the regional pre-eminence achieved exclusively by towns located at intermediate elevations. More importantly, however, the present investigation shows that local differences in community development can be systematically explained through the application of general ecological theory. Specifically, ecological theory explains (1) individual differences in community development, (2) subregional variation in community development, (3) the greater complexity of intermediate settlements, (4) the regional preeminence of Snowflake and St. Johns, (5) the contribution of tithing redistribution to successful colonization, and (6) the greater success of tithing redistribution compared to the conjoint enterprises as a mechanism for counteracting the negative consequences of environmental variability.

Ecological theory, therefore, provides a precise and parsimonious explanation of Mormon colonization in the Little Colorado River Basin that concurs with explanations for the evolution of non-human ecological communities. By demonstrating that specific developments associated with Mormon settlement in this region conform to general ecological expectations, the present analysis suggests that it may be possible to develop a single theoretical framework to explain the evolution of human and non-human communities alike (see Abruzzi, 1993a: 55–78).

REFERENCES

Abruzzi, W. S. (1982). Ecological theory and ethnic differentiation among human populations. *Current Anthropology* 23: 13–35.

Abruzzi, W. S. (1985). Water and community development in the little Colorado River Basin. *Human Ecology* 13: 241–269.

Abruzzi, W. S. (1987). Ecological stability and community diversity during Mormon colonization of the Little Colorado River Basin. *Human Ecology* 15: 317–338.

Abruzzi, W. S. (1989). Ecology, resource redistribution and Mormon Settlement in Northeastern Arizona. *American Anthropologist* 91: 642–655.

Abruzzi, W. S. (1993a). *Dam That River! Ecology and Mormon Colonization of the Little Colorado River Basin.* University Press of America, Landam, MD.

Abruzzi, W. S. (1993b). Ecological Concepts in Anthropological Human Ecology: Illustrations from Mormon Settlement in Northeastern Arizona. In Wright, S. (ed.), *Crossing Boundaries: Advances in Human Ecology.* Society for Human Ecology. College Park, MD, pp. 255–271.

Abruzzi, W. S. (1995). The Social and Ecological Consequences of Early Cattle Ranching in Northeastern Arizona. *Human Ecology* 23: 75–98.

Alexander, R. D. and Borgia, G. (1978). Group selection, altruism and the levels of organization of life. *Annual Review of Ecology and Systematics* 9: 449–474.

Arrington, L. J. (1958). *Great Basin Kingdom: Economic History of the Latter-Day Saints, 1830–1900.* University of Nebraska Press, Lincoln.

Brookhaven National Laboratory. (1969). *Diversity and Stability in Ecological Systems.* Brookhaven Symposia in Biology No. 22. U.S. Department of Commerce, Springfield.

Bureau of Reclamation. (1947). *Snowflake Project Arizona.* Project Planning Report 3-8b. 2-0. U.S. Department of the Interior, Washington, D.C.

Bureau of Reclamation. (1950). *Report on Joseph City Unit, Holbrook Project, Arizona.* Project Planning Report 3-8b. 6-1. U.S. Department of the Interior, Washington, D.C.

Carneiro, R. L. (1962). Scale analysis as an instrument for the study of cultural evolution. *Southwestern Journal of Anthropology* 18: 149–169.

Carneiro, R. L. (1967). On the relation between size of population and complexity of social organization. *Southwestern Journal of Anthropology* 23: 234–243.

Carneiro, R. L. (1968). Ascertaining, testing and interpreting sequences of cultural development. *Southwestern Journal of Anthropology* 24: 354–374.

Clark, P. J., Eckstrom, P. T., and Linden, L. D. (1964). On the number of individuals per occupation in a human society. *Ecology* 45: 367–372.

Cody, M. L. and Diamond, J. M. (eds.) (1975). *Ecology and Evolution of Communities.* Belknap Press, Cambridge.

Dames and Moore, Inc. (1973). *Environmental Report, Cholla Power Project, Joseph City, Arizona.* Arizona Public Service Company, Phoenix.

Gibson, L. J. and Reeves, R. W. (1970). Functional bases of small towns: A study of Arizona settlements. *Arizona Review* 19: 19–26.

Harrell, M. A. and Eckel, E. B. (1939). *Ground-Water Resources of the Holbrook Region, Arizona.* U.S. Geological Survey Water-Supply Paper 836-B. U.S. Government Printing Office, Washington, D.C.

Holling, C. S. (1973). Resilience and stability of ecological systems. *Annual Review of Ecology and Systematics* 4: 1–23.

Kennedy, S. A. (1968). A General History of the Hashknife Range under the Aztec Land and Cattle Company, Limited. Unpublished manuscript, Arizona Collection, Arizona State University Library.

Kester, G. (1964). *Soil Survey: Holbrook-Showlow Area, Arizona.* U.S. Department of Agriculture, Soil Conservation Service. U.S. Government Printing Office, Washington, D.C.

Leigh, E. G. (1976). Population Fluctuations, Community Stability and Environmental Variability. In Cody, M. L. and Diamond, L. M. (eds.), *Ecology and Evolution of Communities,* Belknap Press, Cambridge, pp. 51–73.

Leigh, E. G. (1977). How does selection reconcile individual advantage with the good of the group? *Proceedings of the National Academy of Sciences* 74: 4542–4546.

Leone, M. P. (1979). *The Roots of Modern Mormonism.* Harvard University Press, Cambridge.

Levins, R. (1968). *Evolution in Changing Environments.* Princeton University Press, Princeton.

Lightfoot, K. (1980). Mormon sociopolitical development in Northern Arizona, 1876–1906: Implications for a model of prehistoric social change. *Ethnohistory* 27: 197–223.

MacArthur, R. H. (1955). Fluctuations in animal populations and a measure of community stability. *Ecology* 36: 533–537.

MacArthur, R. H. and MacArthur, J. (1961). On bird species diversity. *Ecology* 42: 594–598.

MacArthur, R. H. and Connell, J. H. (1966). *The Biology of Populations.* Wiley, New York.

Margalef, R. (1968). *Perspectives in Ecological Theory.* University of Chicago Press, Chicago.

May, R. M. (1973). *Stability and Complexity in Model Ecosystems.* Princeton University Press, Princeton.

Miller, M. L. and Larsen, K. (1975). *Soil Survey of Apache County, Arizona: Central Part.* U.S. Department of Agriculture, Soil Conservation Service. U.S. Government Printing Office, Washington, D.C.

Naroll, R. (1956). A preliminary index of social development. *American Anthropologist* 58: 687–715.

Odum, E. P. (1971). *Fundamentals of Ecology, Third Edition.* Saunders, Philadelphia.

Odum, H. T. (1971). *Environment, Power, and Society.* Wiley, New York.

Peterson, C. S. (1973). *Take Up Your Mission: Mormon Colonizing Along the Little Colorado River 1870–1900.* University of Arizona Press, Tucson.

Pianka, E. R. (1966). Latitudinal gradients in species diversity: A review of concepts. *The American Naturalist* 100: 33–46.

Pielou, E. C. (1975). *Ecological Diversity.* Wiley, New York.

Ricklefs, R. E. (1987). Community diversity: Relative roles of local and regional processes. *Science* 235: 167–171.

Rogers, D. and Hubbard, S. (1974). How the Behavior of Parasites and Predators Promotes Population Stability. In Usher, M. B. and Williamson, M. H. (eds.), *Ecological Stability,* Chapman and Hall, London, pp. 99–119.

Rosenzweig, M. L. (1968). Net primary productivity of terrestrial communities: Predictions from climatological data. *American Naturalist* 102: 67–74.

Salt River Project. (1974). *Environmental Report, Arizona Station Project: Snoeflake and St. Johns Generating Station Sites.* Salt River Project, Phoenix.

Sanders, H. L. (1968). Marine benthic diversity: A comparative study. *The American Naturalist* 102: 243–282.

Slobodkin, L. B. and Sanders, H. L. (1969). On the Contribution of Environmental Predictability to Species Diversity. *Diversity and Stability in Ecological Systems.* Brookhaven Symposia in Biology 22: 82–95.

Stegner, W. (1942). *Mormon Country.* Hawthorne Books, New York.

Stegner, W. (1964). *The Gathering of Zion: The Story of the Mormon Trail.* McGraw-Hill, New York.

Tanner, G. M. and Richards, J. M. (1977). *Colonization on the Little Colorado: The Joseph City Region.* Northland Press, Flagstaff, Arizona.

Terborgh, J. (1971). Distribution of environmental gradients: Theory and a preliminary interpretation of distributional patterns in the avifauna of the Cordillera Vilcabamba, Peru. *Ecology* 52: 23–40.

Thomas, E. N. (1960). Some comments on the functional bases for small Iowa towns. *Iowa Business Digest* 31: 10–16.

United States Geological Survey. (1975). *Surface Water Supply of the United States, 1966–1970. Part 9, Volume 3: Lower Colorado River Basin.* Water-Supply Paper 2126. U.S. Government Printing Office, Washington, D.C.

Vandermeer, J. H. (1972). Niche theory. *Annual Review of Ecology and Systematics* 3: 107–132.

Whittaker, R. H. (1975). *Communities and Ecosystems, Second Edition.* Macmillan, New York.

Wilson, E. O. (1968). The ergonomics of caste in social insects. *American Naturalist* 102: 41–66.

Index

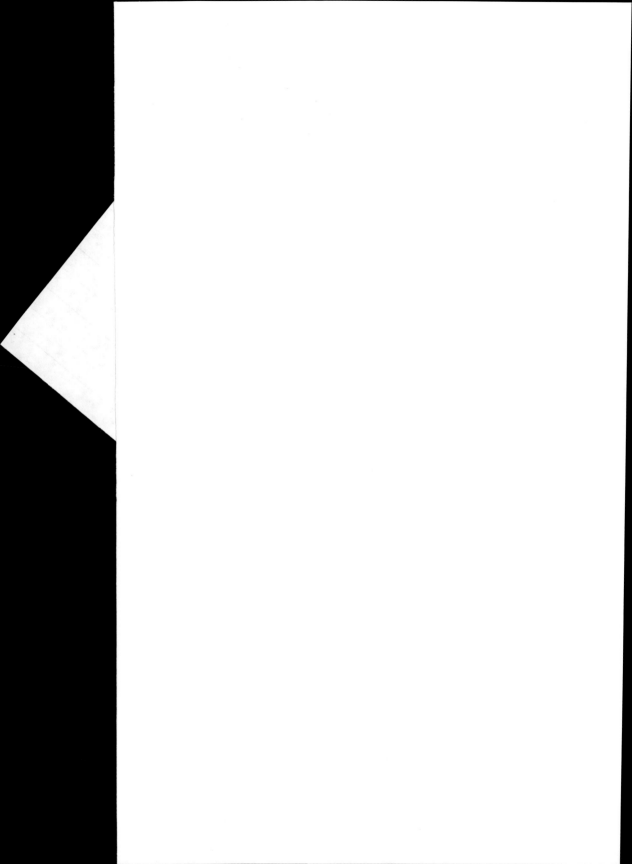

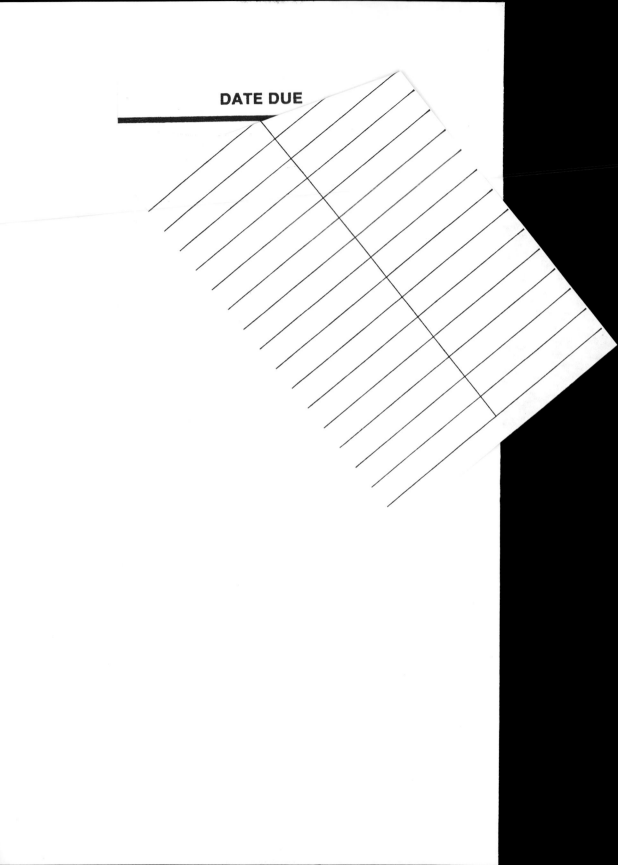

DATE DUE